Arctic Mirage

Arctic Mirage

The 1913–1920 Expedition in Search of Crocker Land

Winton U. Solberg

McFarland & Company, Inc., Publishers
Jefferson, North Carolina

LIBRARY OF CONGRESS CATALOGUING-IN-PUBLICATION DATA

Names: Solberg, Winton U., 1922– author.
Title: Arctic mirage : the 1913–1920 expedition in search of Crocker Land / Winton U. Solberg.
Description: Jefferson, North Carolina : McFarland & Company, Inc., Publishers, 2019. | Includes bibliographical references and index.
Identifiers: LCCN 2019029650 | ISBN 9781476679952 (paperback) ∞
ISBN 9781476638096 (ebook)
Subjects: LCSH: Crocker Land Expedition (1913–1917) | Arctic regions—Discovery and exploration—American.
Classification: LCC G670 1913 .S44 2019 | DDC 910.9163/27—dc23
LC record available at https://lccn.loc.gov/2019029650

BRITISH LIBRARY CATALOGUING DATA ARE AVAILABLE

ISBN (print) 978-1-4766-7995-2
ISBN (ebook) 978-1-4766-3809-6

© 2019 The estate of Winton U. Solberg. All rights reserved

No part of this book may be reproduced or transmitted in any form or by any means, electronic or mechanical, including photocopying or recording, or by any information storage and retrieval system, without permission in writing from the publisher.

Front cover: *top left*, Borup Lodge, Crocker Land trip departure (photograph by Donald Baxter MacMillan, courtesy of the Peary-MacMillan Arctic Museum, Bowdoin College); *top right*, Fitzhugh Green at Peary's Cairn, Cape Thomas Hubbard, Axel Heiberg Island, Canada, May 2014 (American Museum of Natural History Library); *background*, Arctic landscape (© 2019 Shutterstock/Incredible Arctic)

Printed in the United States of America

McFarland & Company, Inc., Publishers
  Box 611, Jefferson, North Carolina 28640
     www.mcfarlandpub.com

To Gail E. Solberg,
Andrew W. Solberg,
Kristin R. Solberg

Acknowledgments

This book is based primarily on documents in various archives. They include the American Museum of Natural History and the American Geographical Society, both in New York City, the Booth Family Center for Special Collections at Georgetown University in Washington, D.C., and the University of Illinois in Urbana, Illinois. The American Geographical Society Archives are at the University of Wisconsin–Milwaukee. I am grateful to Susan M. Peschel for making this collection available. The Fitzhugh Green, Sr., Papers are in the Booth Family Center for Special Collections at Georgetown. Elizabeth Wilkinson, curator of manuscripts, and Scott S. Taylor, manuscripts archivist, were most helpful during my visit there and by correspondence. At the University of Illinois William J. Maher, the archivist, and Linda S. Stahnke, archival reference specialist, earned my gratitude by their efforts on my behalf. I am pleased to thank Valerie Hotchkiss, director of the Rare Book and Manuscript Library at the University of Illinois, for assistance that expedited the completion of this book. I express my gratitude to Lillian Helms, Rhonda Jurinak, John Paul Goguen, and Helen Zhou of the IT Help Center at the University of Illinois for assisting me in vaulting many hurdles.
—Winton U. Solberg

This book was published posthumously. The author's granddaughter, Giulia Nicita, handled the page proofs, proofreading, and indexing. We extend thanks to her.—Gail, Andrew and Kristin Solberg

Table of Contents

Acknowledgments   vi
Prologue   1

Part I. The Expedition in the Polar North

1. In the Beginning   13
2. "Hail, the Conquering Hero Comes"   27
3. Searching for Crocker Land   40
4. The Murder of Peeahwahto   55

Part II. The Expedition and Scientific Research

5. The Expedition Party in the Arctic   71
6. More Research, More Adventures   98
7. MacMillan's Arctic Research   119
8. Returning Home   129
9. MacMillan's Geographical Report   151
10. Full Circle   168
11. Fitzhugh Green: After Crocker Land   183

Epilogue   210
Chapter Notes   213
Bibliography   230
Index   239

Prologue

In early modern times the Arctic, the Northwest Passage, and the North Pole excited the public imagination and adventurers began sailing to the fabled North. Vikings had been there earlier. They were followed by the Englishmen John Cabot and his son Sebastian Cabot, Sir Martin Frobisher, John Davis, Henry Hudson, and William Baffin, all of whom left their mark on the search for new lands and riches.

In the early nineteenth century the quest to explore the Arctic intensified. In 1818 Sir John Ross, an experienced naval officer, sailed in both the *Isabella* and the *Alexander* in an attempt to make the Northwest Passage through Davis Strait. His nephew, James Clark Ross, sailed with him. John Ross rediscovered Baffin Bay and parts of the coastlines of Ellesmere Island and Devon Island. In 1819–20 Sir James Clark Ross undertook similar scientific work in the *Hecla* under William Edward Parry, who named Cape James Ross on Melville Island after Ross. Sir James found what is now known as Parry Channel, which forms a component of four Northwest Passages. In 1827 James Clark Ross joined his uncle John's expedition in the *Victory* to search for the Northwest Passage. In a series of sledging journeys Sir James proved that Boothia was a peninsula, not an island as Sir John had hoped. On 1 June 1831 James Clark Ross raised the British flag at the north magnetic pole.

Not least, in 1845 Sir John Franklin undertook his fourth voyage into the Arctic in search of the Northwest Passage. His ships, the *Erebus* and the *Terror*, with a crew of 129 men including Franklin, were provisioned for three years. When this interval passed without word of the navigator, Lady Franklin encouraged the Admiralty to send out search expeditions for the lost party. She funded some searches and enlisted American aid in the effort to find Franklin. In 1847 Sir John Ross urged on the Admiralty the advisability of dispatching an expedition for the relief of Sir John Franklin, as he had promised Franklin he would do.

With English explorers having pioneered, American participation in the

Arctic began in 1850–51 when Henry Grinnell, a New York shipping magnate, sent out the *Advance* and the *Rescue* to find the missing Franklin party. Elisha Kent Kane, the senior medical officer on this first American Arctic venture, published a book about it, *Access to an Open Polar Sea in Connection with the Search after Sir John Franklin and His Companions* (1853). The fleet failed to locate the missing Franklin expedition, but on Beechey Island it found the campsite where Franklin had spent his first winter. Evidence indicated that Franklin and his crew had abandoned ship and ultimately had died there. More than a century later, in September 2014, searchers from the Canadian national parks agency found the wreckage of one of the abandoned ships near King William Island, the place where the Inuit had long said that the Franklin ships were crushed by sea ice.

Kane organized and led the Second Grinnell Expedition, which set out on 31 May 1853, presumably to search for Sir John Franklin. Traveling northward along the west coast of Greenland in the *Advance,* Kane charted the coasts of Smith Sound and discovered Kane Basin, which forms the beginning of a passage later called the American route to the North Pole. Kane penetrated farther north than any predecessor. He believed in the existence of an open polar sea. Heavy ice trapped Kane and his men in the Arctic for the winter, and the summer thaw failed to release his ship from the ice. Led by Isaac Israel Hayes, the ship's surgeon, twelve of Kane's men rebelled, demanding to go south to the Greenland settlements. Kane and his remaining men spent another winter in the Arctic doing scientific work. The rebels, finding bleak prospects, returned to the camp. During the 1855 summer Kane led his men in three open boats south to the Greenland settlements. Although Kane's second expedition was unsuitably equipped, inadequately supplied, and manned by inexperienced volunteers, he became America's first Arctic hero. His book, *Arctic Explorations: The Second Grinnell Expedition in Search of Sir John Franklin, 1853, '54, '55* (1856) was an instant success.

The pace of Arctic exploration then quickened. In 1853 Hayes, the surgeon on Kane's expedition, sailed from New York in the *Advance*. During the following winter, when the vessel was beset in the Kane basin northwest of Greenland, Hayes engaged in several expeditions on Ellesmere Island. On 28 May 1854 he discovered Grinnell Land. The ship was forced to spend a second winter in the ice, whereupon Hayes with nine men attempted to reach Upernavik on the west coast of Greenland. When the attempt failed, the party turned back and reached the *Advance* in December 1854. The following summer the entire crew reached Upernavik in August. In October they went on to New York. Hayes left an account of this experience in *An Arctic Boat Journey in the Autumn of 1854* (1860).

Hayes believed that there must be an open sea near the North Pole and that he could discover it. In July 1860, sailing from Boston in command of a schooner, he wintered south of the point at which the *Advance* had been frozen in, and in the spring of 1861 he proceeded northwest by sledge, reaching a point only slightly north of 80° N. In July he sailed for Boston, arriving in October. A careful scientific observer, Hayes made valuable contributions in natural history, meteorology, glaciology, and hydrology. He recounted his Arctic experience in *The Open Polar Sea: A Narrative of a Voyage of Discovery towards the North Pole, in the Schooner United States* (1867) and in *The Land of Desolation: Being a Personal Narrative of Adventure in Greenland* (1871).

Another Arctic explorer, Charles Francis Hall, was a family man and a Cincinnati newspaper publisher when he became obsessed with an ambition to reach the Pole. In May 1860, having won the support of Henry Grinnell, he sailed from New London, Connecticut, on a whaler bound for Greenland. When he saw snow, ice, icebergs, the long day and the Arctic night, his soul communicated with God in silent and reverential awe. He went ashore at Baffin Island, where he spent much of the next two years in search of Sir John Franklin.

Returning to America, Hall published *Arctic Researches, and Life Among the Esquimaux: Being the Narrative of an Expedition in Search of Sir John Franklin* (1865). Hailed as a hero, he received $50,000 from the U.S. government for future explorations. On his second Arctic expedition, sailing from New London in July 1871 on the *Polaris*, he attained 82° 11' N, the farthest north of an Arctic explorer. However, Hall's crew believed that his zeal to reach the Pole endangered their lives. In a dispute with a sailor, Hall shot the man, who died two weeks later. The party was wracked with dissension. When Hall suddenly became sick and died, he believed that he had been poisoned. Hall left a *Narrative of the Second Arctic Expedition Made by Charles F. Hall ... and Residence Among the Eskimos During the Years 1864-'69* (1879).

Despite these vicissitudes, Hayes and Hall revived belief in an open Polar Sea. They suggested that land extended to the north and west of Robeson Channel. Thus the Smith Sound route seemed the best line of advance to the Pole. The Arctic expedition led by Sir George S. Nares in the *Alert* and the *Discovery* sailed in May 1875 and reached winter quarters on the coast of Ellesmere Island. With the *Alert*, Nares reached a latitude of 82° 27' N, which surpassed the previous record. The following spring sledge parties sent out by Nares attained Cape Columbia at 83° 20' N on the northern coast of Ellesmere Island.

In June 1879 Lt. George Washington DeLong, a U.S. Naval Academy graduate, persuaded James Gordon Bennett, the owner of the *New York Herald*, to back his scheme to find a Northwest Passage and to attain the Pole. DeLong purchased the *Pandora*, renamed it the *Jeannette*, and gathered a crew. When engineers doubted that the ship could make a long polar voyage, they informed DeLong, who ignored the warning. Bickering among expedition men broke out while the *Jeannette* was still in the navy yard. In July, the ship sailed from San Francisco. It called at St. Michael, Alaska, and then headed for Wrangel Island by way of Bering Strait. Somehow it went off course and drifted more westerly than northerly. By the end of the first year of the voyage the ship was frozen in the ice about 180 miles northeast of New Siberia Islands. The ice pack proved impenetrable. Trapped, the ship drifted slowly to the west and withstood the stress for two winters.

In June 1881 the *Jeannette* broke apart and sank off of the coast of Siberia. Abandoning ship, the crew marched south toward the New Siberian Islands. They suffered from frostbite, and the drift of ice dictated their pace. When they set foot on land, it was an island unmarked on DeLong's charts, so he took possession of it in the name of God and the United States and named it Bennett Island. The men then navigated their three boats toward the Siberian coast, which Chief Engineer George Melville's boat reached. He guided it up the Lena River delta. There, Siberian natives and Russian exiles succored them. Melville directed a vigorous search for DeLong and his party. He finally found the bodies of men who had succumbed to starvation and scurvy. The third boat had apparently been lost at sea. Melville made his way back to America by way of St. Petersburg, Russia, where Czar Alexander III received him. Of the original thirty-two men, only thirteen survived the ineptly planned and poorly directed expedition. Years later debris from the sunken vessel was found on the coast of south Greenland. *The Voyage of the Jeannette: The Ship and Ice Journals of George W. DeLong*, edited by Emma Delong, was published in two volumes (1883–84).

The Arctic experience of Adolphus W. Greely was both harrowing and tragic. Born in Newburyport, Massachusetts, in 1844, Greely enlisted as a volunteer in the Federal army and fought throughout the Civil War, rising from private to brevet major. After the war he joined the regular army. In 1882–83 the U.S. government sent the *Proteus* commanded by Greely to establish one of a global chain of circumpolar stations at Lady Franklin Bay on Grinnell Land, the most northerly station for collecting the desired data. This venture was the product of an international agreement by which the participating nations were to establish stations beyond the Arctic Circle to undertake a systematic collection of meteorological and magnetic data. Greely's party of twenty-five encamped at Fort Conger on Discovery Harbor, from which Greely sent out exploratory parties. Sergeant David Brainard and Lt. James B. Lockwood mapped the area to the northwest, gathered scientific information, took weather readings, and made important discoveries, including Lake Hazen, a body of fresh water fifty miles long and averaging six miles wide, located seventy-five miles southwest of Cape Sheridan. In May 1882, Lockwood reached 83° 24'8" N, bettering the British record by four miles. Sledging parties explored the interior of Ellesmere Island, including Lake

Hazen, and reached the west coast at Greely Fiord. Greely sighted a mountain range in the interior of Ellesmere Island that he named the Conger Mountains.

When supply parties failed to reach the men in 1882 and 1883, Greely decided to abandon Fort Conger. The party retreated to Cape Sabine, some three hundred miles to the south, where they were forced to winter, almost without clothing, light, heat, or food, and yet never without courage, faith, and hope. At last the struggle for life became each man for himself. Seventeen men died from cold and starvation, others were charged with cannibalism, and Greely shot and killed one man for stealing food. Public interest in the fate of the expedition was aroused, whereupon Congress authorized a rescue operation. In June 1884 Commander Winfield Scott Schley of the U.S. Navy arrived with a relief expedition. He found evidence of squalid misery in the hut in which the occupants had lived.

In 1888, after the search for the Northwest Passage and the North Pole had become more cosmopolitan, Fridtjof Nansen, a Norwegian, sought to attain the North Pole by approaching it from the east, using the natural drift of the polar ice to reach the prize. In 1894 he approached the Pole 314 miles closer than any predecessor. The following March the Norwegian and one companion left the *Fram* and went north. In twenty-three days they covered one-third of the distance to the pole, reaching 86° 12' N. To go farther meant death, so they turned back. In late August they reached Franz Joseph Land.

In 1898, Otto Sverdrup, also a Norwegian, explored Baffin Bay. He was forced to overwinter on Ellesmere Island. Between 1898 and 1902, Sverdrup overwintered three more times with the *Fram*. Sverdrup continued to explore and map Ellesmere Island. He discovered the islands west of Ellesmere Island—Axel Heibserg, Amund Ringnes, and Ellef Ringnes. They were collectively known as the Sverdrup Islands.

In 1901 Luigi Amedeo, the Duke of the Abruzzi, a member of the Italian royal family, made a dash to the Pole on the *Polar Star*. The expedition set out in 1899 from Oslo with Umberto Cagni and others in the *Stella Polaris*. The party established a camp on Rudolf Island, from which it planned to reach the North Pole by dogsled. On 11 March 1900 Cagni made a dash to the Pole. He reached 86° 24' N, a record for farthest north, but fell short of his goal.

Roald Amundsen, also a Norwegian, completed the first navigation of the Northwest Passage in 1906 after having spent the three preceding winters at Gjoa Haven on southeast King William Island. He succeeded where countless predecessors had failed by turning south along the west coast of Boothia Felix to the southernmost point of King William Island and then proceeding westward, closely following the coast.[1]

America was a comparatively young nation when Robert Peary, a former civilian employee of the U.S. Navy, became known for his zeal to attain the North Pole. In the 1890s he explored the possibility of advancing to the coveted goal from the coast of northern Greenland. When he realized the futility of that approach, he transferred his base to northern Ellesmere Island, from which he made assaults on the North Pole in both 1906 and 1909. He claimed to have seized his goal in 1909, but his joy was diluted by Dr. Frederick Cook's announcement that he had attained the prize in 1908. In the dispute between Cook and Peary that followed, bankers, congressmen, and government scientists among others supported Peary. He and his friends persuaded Congress to retire him as a navy admiral with a pension.[2]

In 1906, on his penultimate attempt to attain the North Pole, Peary said that in looking northwest from a point on Axel Heiberg Land he saw a vast archipelago. He named it Crocker Land in honor of George Crocker, a wealthy benefactor who gave Peary $50,000 to fund his expedition.[3] If it existed, Crocker Land would be important. Did it exist?

The American Museum of Natural History was eager to find out. The museum owed its origins mainly to Albert S. Bickmore, who specialized in chemistry, geology, and mineralogy at Dartmouth, from which he graduated in 1860. He went on to study natural history under Louis Agassiz in the Museum of Natural History at Harvard. While a professor of zoology and geology at what became Colgate University, Bickmore interested a group of prominent New Yorkers in founding a museum of natural history in New York City, which trailed Cambridge, New Haven, and Philadelphia in this respect. In 1869, the Comptroller of Central Park granted a number of gentlemen their desire to establish a great museum of natural history in Central Park. On 9 April 1869, the State of New York chartered the American Museum of Natural History and the founders launched a fund drive.

In 1881 Morris K. Jesup, one of the founders, became the third president of the board of trustees of the American Museum. He put the museum on its feet and served as its president for twenty-seven years. Born in Connecticut of pious New England stock, Jesup and his seven siblings were brought up in New York City by their widowed mother. At twelve he quit school and went to work as an errand boy for a firm that manufactured locomotives and cotton-mill machinery. At twenty-four he resigned and went into business with a friend, selling railroad supplies on commission. In 1868, when he joined the museum's incorporators, he was a multimillionaire and a fine product of the New England Puritanism that had shaped American thought and culture from colonial times to the twentieth century. Jesup retired from business in 1884 to devote himself to religious, philanthropic, educational, and civic activities. In 1899 he gave $30,000 to the museum. Giving, he believed, should be as much of a habit with Christians as praying or eating. Accordingly, he gave millions to the museum. To Jesup, science was a sealed book, but he had faith in its results. He oversaw the museum's expansion and much of its golden age of exploration and collection until his death in 1908.

Henry Fairfield Osborn followed Jesup as the president of the American Museum. At Princeton, from which he graduated in 1877, President James McCosh had turned his thoughts to science. The summer after graduating Osborn did research in southwest Wyoming for a monograph on vertebrate paleontology that he published in two volumes fifty-one years later. Osborn was on the faculty of both Princeton and Columbia before becoming president of the board of trustees of the museum. He published *From the Greeks to Darwin* (1913) and *The Origin and Evolution of Life* (1917). His Uncle Pierpont was the banker J. Pierpont Morgan. Osborn was on familiar terms with many wealthy men. He consolidated the museum's expansion and developed it into one of the world's foremost natural history museums.[4]

The American Geographical Society was also eager to find out if Crocker Land existed. The society had been founded in 1851 in New York City by philanthropists, historians, publishers, and editors interested in polar exploration. They organized the society upon the request of Lady Franklin to search for her husband, Sir John Franklin, who had been lost on an expedition to the Far North. In 1854 the State of New York chartered the society, which was especially interested in the Arctic, the Antarctic, and Latin America.

After Peary claimed to have reached the Pole, the American Museum and the Geographical Society prepared to send a party to search for Crocker Land. Both Donald B. MacMillan[5] and George Borup had been with Peary on his 1908–09 expedition. The museum wanted Borup as expedition leader, but it was decided that Borup and MacMillan would be co-leaders. In April 1912, however, Borup drowned in a boating accident off Long Island. The following October museum officials named MacMillan to lead the expedition. The museum and the geographical society needed another participant in the enterprise to help pay the expenses of a search. So President Osborn invited the University of Illinois to sponsor the expedition. Why Illinois? Most probably the answer is that President Edmund J. James was eager to vault Illinois into the front rank of American universities and Osborn acted accordingly.

Although the expedition party planned on being in the Arctic two years, it became locked into place and had to stay longer. During their "imprisonment" the men engaged in valuable scientific research. By the end of four years all members of the expedition party had returned home.

The Crocker Land Expedition is important in the history of the Arctic. Since early modern times explorers had sought to find the Northwest Passage and to reach the North Pole. The pioneers gathered valuable geographical and scientific data, often as a by-product of their main purpose. The Crocker Land Expedition was different. It went out to find out if Crocker Land existed and to pursue scientific research. On finding that Crocker Land did not exist,

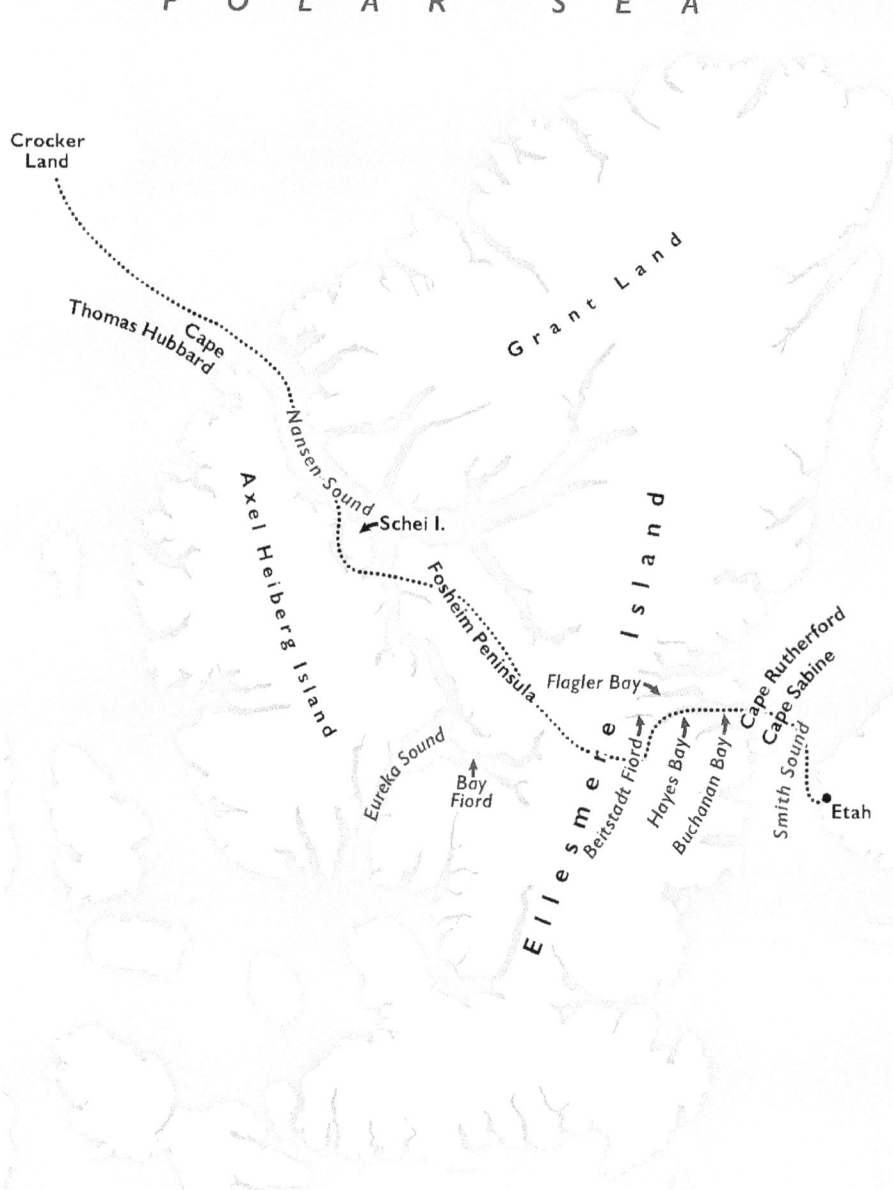

The proposed route of the Crocker Land Expedition. Although the explorers intended to return in 1915, they became stranded and did not return home until 1917.

the explorers conducted research and made valuable contributions to knowledge of the Arctic.

The natives who inhabited the Arctic were known as Eskimo (singular) and Eskimos (plural), words from an Algonquian language meaning eaters of raw flesh. An Eskimo was a member of one of the most widely spread people inhabiting the Arctic from Eastern Siberia to Greenland. This book deals with the natives who inhabited the area where the Crocker Land Expedition made its base. They referred to themselves as Inuk (both singular and plural), and that usage is followed in the text.

PART I

The Expedition in the Polar North

1

In the Beginning

In 1912 the American Museum of Natural History and the American Geographical Society prepared to support an expedition to look for a large body of land in the Polar Sea about one hundred and thirty miles northwest of Cape Thomas Hubbard. Robert Peary believed that he had seen this landmass in 1906. He named it Crocker Land in honor of George Crocker, who gave Peary $50,000 to pursue the search.

The American Museum prepared to dispatch an expedition to investigate the matter. Its leaders were to be George Borup (AB, Yale 1907), an assistant curator in geology and invertebrate paleontology in the museum, and Donald B. MacMillan (AB, Bowdoin, 1908). They were well known to the public through their work under Peary on his previous polar expedition (1908–09), through Borup's book, *A Tenderfoot with Peary* (1911), and through MacMillan's lectures around the country. During the previous two years Borup had devoted himself to studies in the field and at Yale to fit himself for exploration, while MacMillan had studied ethnology and practical astronomy at Harvard. In the summer of 1910 MacMillan had been a member of a party that crossed central Labrador, and in the summer of 1911 he had studied the Inuit in Labrador.

The museum and the geographical society had agreed to support the two men in an expedition to map Crocker Land. En route, they were to make all the geological, geographical, and other scientific studies circumstances would permit.[1] Both men were well known to the general public and the scientific public as members of Peary's last polar expedition, through Borup's book, and MacMillan's lectures. Both had received Peary's endorsement. They would serve without salary. Not less than $50,000 was required for the expedition.

In 1911, MacMillan decided to return to the Arctic to explore Crocker Land. Friends offered to contribute funds to support his plans, and Borup asked him to postpone his departure a year so that they could go as joint leaders of an expedition with the patronage of the American Museum.

MacMillan was outfitting the expedition when Borup drowned on 28 April 1912 near Crescent Beach, Connecticut, while trying to save the life of a companion. In May the executive committee of the museum's board of trustees decided to postpone the venture for a year and undertake it as a memorial to George Borup.[2]

Thus it became necessary to reorganize the Crocker Land Expedition. The task fell to Edmund O. Hovey, curator of geology at the American Museum and chairman of the museum's Committee in Charge of the Crocker Land Expedition. Professor Joseph Barrell of Yale University recommended W. Elmer Ekblaw to take the place left vacant by Borup's death. Ekblaw had an AB (1910) and an AM (1912) from the University of Illinois, where he was an assistant in geology. Ekblaw and Borup had become well acquainted when they took the Yale Summer School course in field geology in 1911, Professor Barrell wrote. "So far as I know everyone who has come in contact with him [Ekblaw] likes him well personally and has faith in him. He was the best man from the scholastic point in that class of about twenty men.... I do not know of anyone who taking him altogether I would recommend as high as Ekblaw."[3]

Professor W.S. Bayley, head of the geology department at Illinois, wrote that "Ekblaw is exactly the man you need. He knows far more geology than did Borup and has a far better conception of the science. He also knows how to take observations for use later, is an excellent writer of English and is an all-around athlete. His disposition is excellent. He is companionable and determined. He is a leader of men."[4]

By early November Hovey had made several appointments, though he did not wish to announce them yet. MacMillan was to be the leader. Ekblaw was the geologist and zoologist. Lincoln Ellsworth, another appointee, was described as a civil engineer who specialized in cartography, topography, and terrestrial magnetism. Fitzhugh Green, a 1909 graduate of the U.S. Naval Academy, had requested to join the expedition, and the navy had detailed him to the appointment. At the time he was on shore duty as a graduate student at the George Washington University. Green was to be a specialist in map work, navigation, sounding, tidal observations, and other marine work. Later, Hovey engaged Jonathan C. (Jot) Small as cook, mechanic, and handyman. MacMillan had known Jot Small for years and had recommended him. He was illiterate. The navy named Jerome Allen as the radioman with the expedition. The surgeon had not yet been selected. The museum hoped to secure one from the army or the navy. He would be expected to carry on microscopic and megascopic biological work.[5]

As soon as all preliminary arrangements had been made, the museum and the geographical society would announce the personnel and the revised expedition plans.[6] The organizing institutions wished to keep two appointments out of the papers at present. Fitzhugh Green was one. But why? Hovey may have thought that he should defer to the navy in announcing Green's appointment. Lincoln Ellsworth was another. He was born in Chicago in 1880, the son of a wealthy coal man. He lived in Hudson, Ohio, as a child and later attended Western Reserve Academy. We do not know why Ellsworth was not accepted. He later gained fame as an Arctic and Antarctic explorer.[7]

Soon after constructing the semblance of a party, the museum invited the University of Illinois to join with it and the geographical society in an expedition to find Crocker Land and to do scientific research in the Arctic. The University was a product of the Morrill Land-Grant Act. Chartered in 1867, it opened in 1868 on the Midwestern prairie and developed largely as an engineering school until the early twentieth century. In 1904 Edmund J. James, a political economist with a German PhD, became the president. He was determined to transform the school into a first-class university.[8] President Henry Fairfield Osborn had probably discerned this. He turned to the University for a collaborator, and James gladly accepted the invitation.

The relation between the sponsor and the expedition was a concern. "It makes a big difference," Hovey wrote, "whether the organizing institutions

Henry Fairfield Osborn (far right), with expedition members (from left) Elmer Ekblaw, Maurice Tanquary, Harrison Hunt, Donald MacMillan and Fitzhugh Green, beside the S.S. *Diana,* New York City, July 2, 1913 (American Museum of Natural History Library).

are putting a man into the expedition and getting from his labors all that he learns and collects or somebody else is putting him in and taking the results of labors. If we are going to give up the publication of the results obtained by any member of the party, the institution that sends that man—if we accept him—will have to pay a good deal more than the actual additional cost of his going." Hovey had put in too much work on this expedition to be willing that any of the credit that properly belonged to the American Museum should go to any other institution.[9]

Two places on the scientific staff remained to be filled. The *Army and Navy Register* announced that a volunteer from the Army Medical Corps was desired for the expedition. More than a dozen men applied for the position. Hovey met with some of these men. The Surgeon General of the Army suggested Dr. J.W. Goodsell, who had applied to the Secretary of War for the position. MacMillan, who had been with Goodsell on the last Peary expedition, was entirely opposed to the appointment.[10]

Meanwhile, Hovey was seeking funds for the expedition. In January 1913 President Henry Fairfield Osborn noted that about $15,000 was required to complete the equipment and bring the expedition home. He was delighted to hear of contributions that had been made, but he warned Hovey not to count on the museum to make up any deficit. He had promised the trustees that the appropriation made would cover all demands upon their funds.

A meeting of the scientific staff of the Crocker Land Expedition was planned along with dinner at the home of President Osborn at 850 Madison Avenue in New York on Saturday, 4 January 1913. In addition to MacMillan, Ekblaw, and Green, those present included Thomas H. Hubbard, Dr. Walter B. James, and Chandler Robbins, members of the American Museum's Honorary Committee on the Crocker Land Expedition; Herbert L. Bridgman and Edmund O. Hovey of the museum's Committee in Charge of the expedition; and Henry D. Borup, a retired army lieutenant colonel and the father of George Borup. After dinner, those present studied the maps and route of the planned expedition. According to Hovey, "the young men made a most excellent impression as to their personal character and their attitude toward everything connected with the expedition."[11]

Meanwhile, in mid–December Hovey had contacted President Edmund J. James of the University of Illinois about the expedition. The staff was partially assembled, but the securing of funds remained urgent. The museum had about $40,000 in hand or in sight when Borup drowned; it needed about $15,000 to proceed. The high value of the expedition's task could hardly be questioned. After exploring Crocker Land the party would divide, one part going southwestward from Cape Thomas Hubbard to explore the region north of the Parry Islands and connect on Prince Patrick's Land with the second Stefansson Arctic Expedition; the other part, after completing the coast line work from the northern extremity of Axel Heiberg Land eastward along the northwestern coast of Grant Land, would return to Flagler Bay and make a journey from Inglefield Gulf to the summit of the Greenland ice cap in its widest part.[12]

In January, Ekblaw informed President James that the museum would be glad to give the University Arctic specimens for its museum if the University subscribed some considerable amount to the expedition. Ekblaw thought that the opportunity should not be lost.[13] Days later, William S. Bayley urged President James to provide financial support for the Crocker Land Expedition because of the intense interest being taken by scientific men in its plans. The selection of Ekblaw to take charge of the expedition's scientific work was regarded as a warrant that this branch of the work would be better handled than had usually been the case on Arctic expeditions. In view of the scientific benefits of the enterprise and of the excellent advertisement for the scientific branch of the University, Bayley suggested that the University "ask to be permitted to help finance the expedition to the extent of $10,000 payable in three installments of $3,333[,] ⅓ each, in 1913, 1914, and 1915." In return, it would be understood that a practically "complete suite of specimens of Arctic animals and plants be furnished the Museum of the University, especially of those animals that are now nearly extinct; that due credit for support be given to the University in official documents of the Expedition; and that a member be appointed on the advisory committee of the Expedition to represent the University."[14]

Writing on 24 January, Bayley informed Hovey that the University of Illinois was about to ask to be allowed to contribute to the Crocker Land Expedition to the extent of $10,000. If this sum was accepted by Hovey's committee, it would be expected that a representative of the University be placed on one of the committees in charge of the expedition and that the name of the University appear on the letterheads and other printed matter pertaining to the expedition. These arrangements were absolutely necessary in order that University authorities might explain to the state legislature the cause for the expenditure of money. "This is the first time … that the State's money has ever been used for scientific work that is not directly related to some problem of practical importance to the people of the State. The only condition that the University will make is that a portion of the fund be spent in securing and maintaining an assistant to Mr. Ekblaw, who shall help in the scientific work."[15]

President Osborn was inclined to believe that the Honorary Committee and the Committee in Charge would gladly welcome the proposition made by the University of Illinois. Osborn would bring the matter to the attention of both committees so that he would be in a position to answer the formal letter to which Bayley referred.[16]

With preparations made, Osborn invited the University of Illinois to join the American Museum and the American Geographical Society in an expedition to the Polar North. The University welcomed an opportunity to participate in such a splendid enterprise.

In February 1913, Dean David Kinley discussed the University's participation with Hovey in New York. Separately, they described the terms of their agreement. The American Museum assumed entire control of the expedition and of its results. All material obtained by the party was under the control of the museum for disposal. The museum would endeavor to satisfy the institutions and the U.S. government agencies that were cooperating and contributing to the enterprise. No promises had been made to any institution. The University of Illinois might reasonably expect some good specimens of walrus hide and skeleton, musk oxen, caribou, seal, and "esquimau ethnological material." The museum was to retain primary control and conservation of the diaries, scientific notes, and negatives obtained by the party. Hovey agreed that the museum literature should bear the name of President James as a member of the honorary committee, but he did not agree that the name of William S. Bayley be listed on such literature as a member of the committee in charge. In sum, the American Museum was organizing the expedition and would welcome cooperation but could not give up the control of the arrangements or make specific promises about the distribution of the specimens obtained. The question was whether the University had sufficient confidence in the museum authorities to contribute $10,000 on the terms described. Kinley believed that the University would be justified in doing so.[17]

On 5 March 1913 James presented to his Board of Trustees an invitation to contribute to the expenses of the Crocker Land Expedition under the auspices of the museum and the society. The purposes of the expedition were purely scientific. Harvard, Yale, some smaller colleges, some scientific societies, and U.S. government agencies intended to participate. The University was asked to contribute $10,000 in three installments. The American Museum had entire charge of the expedition; it would have the complete ownership and title to all the scientific results of the expedition. After the expedition returned, the museum proposed to distribute the material collected among the contributing institutions. The Board of Trustees discussed the proposal but took no action.[18]

A week later Ekblaw gave the trustees an account of the proposed undertaking, after which President James described the terms of the agreement made by Kinley and Hovey. He informed the trustees that the expedition was organized for purely scientific purposes and was going out with every prospect of success. The University could reasonably count upon such an accession to its mineralogical, geological, and natural history collection as would justify the proposed expenditure of money. James thought it perfectly legitimate for the trustees to make the $10,000 subscription. A trustee so moved, provided that the executive faculty of the Graduate School agreed with the action and that President James approved of the guarantees concerning the distribution of the scientific material. All ten trustees present voted aye.[19] At that time, James's salary as president of the University was $12,000 per annum. Translated into modern equivalents, the University was contributing some $500,000 or $600,000 to the Crocker Land Expedition.

In mid–March, Hovey interviewed members of the natural science faculty in Urbana. Days later James stated the terms of the agreement in a letter to Hovey. They provided that the University would receive equal recognition with the museum and the society on the expedition's letterheads and in all publications related to the project, that the name of the president of the University of Illinois would be added to the Honorary Committee, and that W.S. Bayley would be made a member of the Committee in Charge of the Expedition. The material collected by the expedition would be distributed among the contributing institutions. Also, Maurice C. Tanquary was to be appointed as a specialist in zoology. An entomologist with a 1912 doctorate from the University of Illinois, Tanquary was then on the faculty of Kansas State College. James wanted no announcement of these arrangements other than for practical reasons until he was ready to make it.[20]

On 22 March President Osborn expressed his gratitude and that of the Honorary Committee of the Crocker Land Expedition with Hovey's report and congratulated President James upon having two such "well-equipped" science graduates as Ekblaw and Tanquary. "We are sure that you will not fail to receive much scientific credit abroad as well as at home, and much valuable material for your exhibition and study collections from participation in this enterprise." The cooperation of Illinois in the Crocker Land Expedition "makes the enterprise of national interest—a feature that is particularly pleasing to the organizing institutions and valuable to American science in general."[21] In April, both Hovey and Osborn assured President James that the University's action emphasized the national character of the Crocker Land Expedition. The University's contribution, Osborn added, made the amount subscribed sufficient for the equipment and dispatch of the expedition.[22]

In mid–April, Fitzhugh Green, who was in Washington, drafted a document, "Some of the Scientific Results Expected of the Crocker Land Expedition." He sent it to New York by special delivery. Bursting with knowledge and energy, Green outlined what might be done in several areas—Geophysical, Meteorological, Geographic, Magnetic, Seismographic, Chemical, and Electrical. The great results anticipated would far more than justify the tremendous expenditure of time and money necessary to prepare and dispatch such an expedition.[23]

On 28 May the search for an expedition surgeon ended with the appointment of Harrison J. (Hal) Hunt. The lure of adventure with a purpose attracted him. He signed up, leaving behind a wife and young daughter. Later, he regretted his decision.[24]

In late May, Urbana enthusiasts formed the Illinois Arctic Club as a tribute to their explorers and to provide them such personal equipment as they might need. Nearly one hundred people became members and paid dues. "The Crocker Land Expedition," President James declared, "is one of the most noteworthy Arctic expeditions ever sent out. Its object is entirely scientific research and exploration; the element of adventure had been reduced to a minimum." Tanquary contributed an article to *Illinois Magazine* that cited examples of how such enterprises had advanced geographical knowledge and made scientific contributions. Ekblaw declared in the same place that the eyes of the scientific world were on the expedition in the hope of solving many problems and collecting valuable material and data. He closed by quoting Rudyard Kipling:

> None but the Master shall praise us, and none but the Master shall blame;
> And no one shall work for money, and no one shall work for fame,
> But each for the joy of the working, and each in his separate sphere,
> Shall do the Thing as he sees It for the God of Things as They are![25]

Thus, with the best wishes of President James and President Osborn, all was in order.

On 30 June 1913, two days before the expedition was due to sail, the American Museum asked the men involved to sign the contract. Hovey gave them no time to read it. Ekblaw, however, had read it and had not liked it. Why, we do not know. He requested changes, which Hovey promised to make. Dr. Hunt signed because he had no real choice, believing that the museum was square and that the changes would be made. A few days earlier Dr. Hunt had asked Peary if he was certain that he had seen Crocker Land and not a mirage. Peary replied as if no one had a right to question him, which led Dr. Hunt to guess that the purposes of the museum might be subordinated by certain individuals to their own glory or gain. The members of the expedition were not given copies of the contract.[26]

According to the contract, the American Museum of Natural History, Donald B. MacMillan, Jerome L. Allen, W. Elmer Ekblaw, Fitzhugh Green, Harrison J. Hunt, and Jonathan Small, with the aid of the American Geographical Society, the University of Illinois, and sundry others had organized an expedition to the North Polar regions, which was to sail from New York in the S.S. *Diana* in July 1913, for an absence of two or more years of exploratory scientific work. The expedition was to be known as "The Crocker Land Expedition under the auspices of the American Museum of Natural History and the American Geographical Society with the cooperation of the

1. In the Beginning

University of Illinois." The objects of the expedition were scientific in character and were summarized as follows: the visiting, reconnoitering and mapping of the "Crocker Land"; the scientific exploration of the region between Flagler Bay and Cape Thomas Hubbard; the scientific exploration and mapping of the region across the border of the Polar Sea northeastward and southwestward from Cape Thomas Hubbard at the north end of Axel Heiberg Island; the attainment of the summit of the Greenland Ice Cap east of Cape York; and the collecting of data and specimens along all scientific lines as far as may be practicable.

The parties to the contract mutually covenanted and agreed on the following:

1. The American Museum would provide an ample equipment of food, clothing, scientific apparatus, and other necessary articles required for carrying out the purposes of the expedition.
2. The American Museum agreed to provide for the return to New York of the expedition members, together with their collections, in the summer of 1915 or 1916.
3. The expedition members agreed to serve the American Museum faithfully in respect to the interests and objects of the Crocker Land Expedition as set forth in the agreement, and to make every effort to attain these objects. The pecuniary remuneration of the expedition members had been determined by individual agreement with E.O. Hovey as chairman of the Committee in Charge.
4. In case any expedition member failed to reach Crocker Land or in case he returned to civilization or to means of communication with the civilized world ahead of the party, he was not to reveal any of the results of the expedition in advance of the return of the other expedition members or afterward without the written permission of the American Museum.
5. Expedition members individually assumed all the personal risks pertaining to the expedition, and they relieved the American Museum from any and all claims for damages, for loss of life or limb, or for illness due to any cause, whether accidental or otherwise. The surgeon on the expedition staff would render all possible medical and surgical treatment in case of need.
6. All payment of salary to one of the parties of the expedition or his assigns would cease immediately upon his death or complete disability.
7. The American Museum assumed no responsibility as to the positions or means of livelihood of the expedition members after the return of the expedition to New York.

8. The positions and special fields of work of the expedition members were as follows: Donald B. MacMillan: leader, ethnology, practical astronomy, ornithology. W. Elmer Ekblaw: geology, botany, ornithology. Fitzhugh Green: cartography, seismology, terrestrial magnetism, wireless telegraphy. Maurice C. Tanquary: zoology in all its branches. Harrison J. Hunt: surgery and medicine, bacteriology. Jerome L. Allen: electricity, wireless telegraphy. Jonathan C. Small: mechanic and cook. It was understood and agreed upon by all expedition members that MacMillan was the sole leader of the expedition; he was responsible for its success from the time it left New York until it returned there; his authority was to be recognized at all times; insubordination, disobedience or incompetence might be punished by suspension or expulsion from the staff, and the salary of the man affected being withheld by the American Museum during the period designated by the leader of the expedition; that the men in the expedition party agreed to and abided by the order of precedence of rank embodied in a letter of sealed instructions given by the American Museum to Donald B. MacMillan.

9. All material of every kind, including all photographic negatives, notebooks, journals and scientific data obtained by the parties of the second part through collecting, purchase, exchange or otherwise while on this expedition shall be the exclusive property of the party of the first part. The disposition of this material and the publication of the scientific results obtained shall rest primarily and exclusively with the party of the first part, it being the intention of the party of the first part to favor the members of the expedition in the assignment of the preparation of material and notes for study and publication and to push such preparation and publication as rapidly as possible.

10. Donald B. MacMillan shall have the exclusive right to prepare and deliver, or publish, such popular accounts, whether in lectures, book form or in magazines, as he chooses, after the first declaration of scientific and other results through the party of the first part. This right or privilege carries with it the use of copies or reproductions of the photographs. The American Museum assumes no responsibility regarding such popular use of the results of the expedition and claims no part of the pecuniary return therefrom, except as provided in article 12 of this agreement.

11. In the event of the death of Donald B. MacMillan before the return of the expedition and before he has had reasonable opportunity to take advantage of the rights and privileges mentioned in article 10

of this agreement, all such popular rights as to lectures, books, magazines and photographs revert to and vest in the party of the first part, to be disposed of for the benefit of the estate of Donald B. MacMillan.
12. The American Museum reserves the right to dispose of the "newspaper rights" pertaining to the experience and results of the expedition for the benefit of the enterprise and expedition members are to refrain from sending any communication to any newspaper except through the American Museum.
13. Expedition members, for value received, hereby give permission to the American Museum to use their photographic portraits in any manner desired for all illustrative purposes.

On 30 June 1913, Henry F. Osborn signed the contract for the American Museum, and D.B. MacMillan, W. Elmer Ekblaw, Fitzhugh Green, Maurice C. Tanquary, Harrison J. Hunt, Jonathan C. Small, and Jerome Lee Allen signed as members of the party of the second part. E.O. Hovey and Chester A. Reeds, members of the Committee in Charge of the Expedition, signed as witnesses of seven of these signatures. MacMillan signed as witness of Small's signature.[27]

Meanwhile, the resources needed to support the Crocker Land Expedition were assembled and made a public record. The George Borup Guarantee listed $13,379, including $1,000 from Yale University, $15 from Franklin D. Roosevelt, and $10 from Theodore Roosevelt. The D.B. MacMillan Guarantee stood at $8,214, including $2.00 from a Sunday school class. Cash Contributions Not Designated as to Guarantee contained $23,150, including the American Museum of Natural History, $4,750; the American Geological Society, $9,000; the University of Illinois, $5,000; Colgate University, $1,000; Henry Fairfield Osborn, $1,000; the Peary Arctic Club, $500; and Robert E. Peary, $500. Assistance in Other Ways Than Through Gifts of Money included the following:

> (1) Federal Departments: the U.S. Navy detailed two men to detached duty on the venture, provided dockage for the *Diana*, and loaned instruments. The U.S. Hydrographic Office loaned a full survey outfit. The Weather Bureau of the U.S. Department of Agriculture loaned a full weather bureau outfit together with kite equipment. (2) Institutions: The Carnegie Institution loaned equipment for the study of terrestrial magnetism, and Georgetown University loaned a Wiechert seismograph. The Harvard Division of Anthropology loaned measuring instruments. (3) The Canadian Government offered free transmission through government wireless stations of daily weather reports and all scientific messages. (4) Firms and Individuals: sixty-four named persons. Several firms gave special discounts on orders "in consideration of the peculiar character of the Expedition." (5) Contributors of Books to the Expedition: fifty-two persons.[28]

The Expedition Members

Donald B. MacMillan was born in 1874 in Provincetown, Massachusetts, the son of a sea captain who had perished at sea. At fifteen, with both parents dead, the impoverished youth went to live with his sister at Freeport, Maine. He prepared at the local high school and entered Bowdoin College in Brunswick, Maine, where he was an excellent student and an excellent athlete. He graduated AB (1898) and then taught in the high school in North Gorham, Maine, in preparatory schools in Swarthmore, Pennsylvania, and in Worcester, Massachusetts. When Peary learned of the nautical camp that MacMillan and a fellow teacher operated on Bustin's Island in Casco Bay, he offered MacMillan an opportunity to go north. A member of Peary's Polar Expedition in 1908–1909, MacMillan had earned a Harvard MA in 1910, and in 1911–12 he did ethnological work among the Labrador Inuit.

Walter Elmer Ekblaw, the son of Swedish immigrants, was born on 10 March 1882 near Rantoul, Illinois. He was christened in the Swedish Lutheran Church at Paxton, Illinois. On the Illinois prairie he developed a lively curiosity regarding the natural world. After a brief secondary schooling he passed the County examination and taught briefly in rural elementary schools. With money saved, he attended the Y.M.C.A. night school in Chicago and later Austin College in Effingham, Illinois. In 1907 he entered the University of Illinois, some twenty miles from Rantoul, and enrolled in chemical engineering. He graduated in 1910 with a BA in general science and then became a graduate student and assistant in the geology department. Ekblaw had been closely associated with Borup during a field course in geology which they had taken in Virginia. In 1912 Ekblaw received an AM from Illinois with a thesis on the "Stratigraphy and Paleontology of the Devonian System in Rock Island, Illinois," and he published a paper titled "Correlation of the Devonian System of the Rock Island Region."[29] Ekblaw was a prominent student in the University. He was a member of a national social fraternity and was active in a senior honorary society, a writers' group, and a graduate scientific fraternity. He was a member of the Y.M.C.A. cabinet and at one time the editor of the campus newspaper. Ekblaw was the founder of the first college "homecoming" in America, a festival quickly adopted by other colleges and universities.

Maurice C. Tanquary was born on 26 November 1881. Reared on a farm near Lawrenceville, in Lawrence County, Illinois, he attended the local high school, taught public school to earn his way through college, attended Vincennes University, Indiana, from 1899 to 1903, and then entered the University of Illinois. He received a BA in general science (1907), was an assistant in the entomology department, and earned an AM (1908). He studied at Harvard during the summer of 1910, and in 1912 he received a PhD from Illinois and

Members of the expedition assembled near the American Museum of Natural History shortly before their departure for Crocker Land. From left, Jerome Allen, Jonathan (Jot) Small, Elmer Ekblaw, Harrison Hunt, Fitzhugh Green and Maurice Tanquary (American Museum of Natural History Library).

became an instructor in entomology and zoology at Kansas State Agricultural College in Manhattan.

Fitzhugh Green was born in St. Joseph, Missouri, on 16 August 1888. He received his early education in the local public schools and in 1905 he was appointed a midshipman at the U.S. Naval Academy. Graduating in 1909, he did sea duty on both the U.S.S. Idaho and the U.S.S. Michigan. In 1911 he became an ensign. A year later he was detailed to the U.S.S. Iowa, and then to the Bureau of Ordnance for temporary duty in ordnance instruction. Later that year he was assigned to duty for graduate work at George Washington University in Washington, D.C., from which he received an MS in 1913. On 23 May 1913 the navy detailed him for detached duty on the Crocker Land Expedition.

MacMillan wanted a strong, fearless, enthusiastic surgeon, and no quitter for the expedition. Dr. E.A. Vickery, a surgeon in the Naval Hospital at the Brooklyn Naval Yard was chosen. His application to the Navy Department for a leave of absence had been favorably acted on when his mother persuaded him to abandon his plans in view of her advanced years and his anticipated long absence. Harrison J. Hunt of Bangor, Maine, was chosen sometime after 17 May. He was a graduate of Bowdoin College (1902), where he was an athlete, active in outdoor sports, and had known MacMillan. He graduated from the Bowdoin Medical College (1905) and was practicing medicine in Bangor when the lure of adventure (with a purpose), led him to sell his property, go against his father's wishes, and leave a wife and a young daughter to join the expedition.

The scientific staff was young: MacMillan, thirty-nine; Hunt, thirty-six; Tanquary, thirty-two; Ekblaw, thirty-one, and Green, not yet twenty-five. The support staff included Jerome Lee Allen, the chief electrician, wireless operator, and gas engine expert, and Jonathan (Jot) C. Small, from Provincetown, Massachusetts, the cook and handy-man.[30]

The payment of the men of the expedition varied. MacMillan agreed to have no salary in return for sole permission to market publications on his Arctic experience after he returned to America. Dr. Hunt was to be paid $75 a month, which was about the same as the $900 a year paid the office assistant in the Household Science department at the University. Green was to be paid $150 a month by the navy. Allen also was to be paid by the navy; the amount is not recorded. Ekblaw, Tanquary, and Jot Small were each to be paid $50 a month.[31] This was less than an assistant in soil fertility at the University, who was paid $840 for twelve months, and less than an assistant in the Illinois mathematics department, who was paid $60 a month on ten-month contract.

With these arrangements completed, all was ready for the Crocker Land Expedition to sail for the Arctic. What future did the expedition hold for the men who were about to depart? And in what way might the expedition contribute to man's knowledge of the universe? The following chapters answer these questions and more.

2

"Hail, the Conquering Hero Comes"

In late June, with all preparations made, the sealing steamer S.S. *Diana* was brought to the Brooklyn Navy Yard, the expedition party assembled, and loading commenced. The ship was to sail on 2 July, but the weather was oppressive and almost nothing had gone aboard. So the men hired a dozen stevedores to lend a hand, and by six o'clock they had finished the job.[1]

On 2 July the Navy Yard pier hummed with preparations for departure and the farewells of those who had come to wish the party off. That evening the American Museum and the American Geographical society tendered a "Godspeed Dinner" to the Crocker Land Expedition members at the University Club. The hosts were Henry Fairfield Osborn, the president of the American Museum; Archer M. Huntington, stepson of the railroad magnate and industrialist Collis P. Huntington, the president of the Geographical Society; Dr. Walter B. James, the vice-president of the Geographical Society; Edmund J. James, the president of the University of Illinois; Arthur T. Hadley, the president of Yale; and William DeWitt Hyde, the president of Bowdoin College. The forty invited guests included wealthy museum benefactors; museum trustees and officials (including Madison Grant); Josephus Daniels, the Secretary of the Navy; Robert E. Peary; and Theodore Roosevelt. Also present were William S. Bayley of the University of Illinois and Edmund O. Hovey of the American Museum. Ekblaw sat next to Rear Admiral Peary, who declared that MacMillan would find Crocker Land. Peary gave the closing speech.[2]

When the *Diana* left the Navy Yard and passed under the stern of the U.S.S. *Hancock*, its band struck up, "Hail, the Conquering Hero Comes." The *Diana* went on to Boston, where Henry B. Ward, a University of Illinois professor, and W.L. Pillsbury, the former University registrar, came to see off Ekblaw and Tanquary. Ward "set up the Illinois crowd" for dinner.

A little after midnight two weeks out, the ship vibrated and ended on the rocks forty miles west of Battle Harbor. All hands shoveled the deck load of coal overboard and unloaded the cargo into fishing boats and then on shore. At daylight everything had been restored in the hold and about the decks. The *Diana* went on to Battle Harbor. From there MacMillan sent a wire urging the museum to charter a larger and better ship to complete the trip. On 5 August the expedition sailed north in the *Erik*.[3]

On 15 August the *Erik* arrived at Cape York. Inuit in kayaks came out to greet them, whereupon Green's idea of the natives changed. "He does not smell offensively. Only a slight musty odor arises from his skin clothing. He is jolly and better mannered than most men I know."[4]

On 18 August at 11 p.m. the *Erik* arrived at Etah. The party hoped to cross over Smith Sound the next day to the site selected for winter quarters at the mouth of Flagler Bay, but the ship's captain absolutely refused to buck the ice in Smith Sound. So MacMillan ordered everything landed at Etah, eighty miles from his objective. The resident Inuit allegedly viewed the place as the most disagreeable site along the whole coastline,[5] but the expedition party chose to put a settlement there.

Despite the handicap of open water and rough ice between them and their objective point some six hundred miles to the northwest, the enforced selection of Etah had many advantages. There was an abundance of meat, which meant that they need not fear scurvy, and ready communication was possible with the Smith Sound tribe, from which they could select the best hunters and dog drivers for their trips.

Etah was on Foulke Fiord on the western shore of Northern Greenland, the largest island in the world, a pear-shaped land mass 1,500 miles long and something like 900 miles wide with an ice cap in the middle that reached over 9,000 feet high. On the narrow coast skirting the ice dome the Inuit dwelled in scattered parties. In A.D. 981 Eric the Red, exiled from Iceland for five years for a murder, had gone to this barren waste, named it Greenland and described it glowingly, inducing friends to join him. His son, Leif Ericson, later sailed from Greenland to America. The Norse colonies in Greenland maintained connection with Denmark, and for centuries the Danish king enjoyed exclusive rights to the land. Years later the Inuit, whose ancestors may have crossed a land bridge from northeast Asia to what is now Alaska, invaded the island, and in 1346 they destroyed the two earlier settlements. When the explorer John Davis reached Greenland in 1585, he found that the Inuit had taken possession of the whole coast. The Danish possession of Greenland dated from 1721, when Hans Egede, a trader and missionary, fitted out a combined trading, whaling, and missionary expedition to Greenland, believing that Norsemen were to be found there. He spread the Gospel and founded a colony in the name of the Danish king, who claimed exclusive right to the colony. Under the authority of the Royal Greenland Trading Company, Greenland became one of the most closed countries in the world. The company tried to maintain and protect the native way of life while importing Danish and Norwegian workmen and sailors to work in the colonies and at the whaling stations. The distinction between native and European was long maintained. Many of the Europeans took Inuit wives. Most of the small settlements were on the southwestern coast below Melville Bay. Here Denmark was sovereign, with Godthaab the seat of authority. Danish missionaries carried the Gospel to the people in the settlements.

Far north of the Greenland settlements under Danish authority was Umanak. In 1910, Knud Rasmussen established a trading post there in which he swapped guns, ammunition, needles, and knives to the Inuit for fox furs. Born in Greenland in 1879, Knud's father was a Danish missionary and his mother was an Inuit. Growing up with the Inuit, he knew and understood them and cared deeply about their welfare. Peter Freuchen had joined Rasmussen in operating the trading station. A former medical student at Copenhagen University, Freuchen was a socialist who believed in free love, was a voluble if not always credible talker, and a good but not always dependable companion. The men named their trading post Thule, or Ultima Thule, because it was north of everywhere.[6]

Etah, some 150 miles north of Thule at 78° 20' N, was the home of the Smith Sound Inuit (often known as the Polar Eskimos), a small tribe of less than three hundred. The Inuit village consisted of five permanent huts of sod and stone built up against the hillside and nineteen men, women, and children. MacMillan brought with him from Cape York three Inuit families and their dogs. South of Etah a line of settlements with some 260 Inuit stretched all the way to Cape York at the northern end of Melville Bay. Danish authority did not reach to Etah. It did reach south of Melville Bay on the Greenland coast. The Danish government administered this area from Upernavik, where a number of missionaries were located.

The *Erik* put the expedition party ashore at Reindeer or Provision Point, where they anchored the ship while unloading their lumber and provisions. At the head of the harbor was a strip of land about 200 yards wide, then a little lake, and beyond that Brother John's Glacier, which came down from the ice cap. The men considered the place on account of the excellent landing facilities, a 700-foot cliff suitable for the wireless aerial, and apparently giving a fair shelter for the house. They pitched their tents and began building a house at Etah.

They leveled the foundations with dynamite and with Inuit helpers excavated two large rooms. Ekblaw built an eight-foot shed to encircle the house and a snow house or igloo. The house, thirty-five feet square, had double walls, floors, ceiling, and windows, and was covered with Cabot quilting. The ground floor had eight rooms. Four bedrooms off the living room also served

The *Erik* at Provision Point, where it landed and the men of the expedition began their adventure (American Museum of Natural History Library).

as workrooms. Coal for heating was carried up from the beach, where it had been landed in bags before the ship sailed south.

The men installed a workshop, electrical room, and photographic dark room. A dynamo generated the current for the electric lights with which the house was fitted. On either side of a square central room were two bedrooms. The double windows were stuffed with oakum, and about six inches of rock salt was between the windows to take up the moisture. The house was warm; even on the coldest days the windows did not frost over.[7]

The builders named the place Borup Lodge. By October they were pretty well settled. The men took turn standing the three night watches. Only two regular meals were served, but they also had two "mug-ups." They exercised one hour a day. The three Inuit families and their dogs brought from Cape York lived in tents while they built rock igloos. Forty Inuit crowded into the house, while two hundred loose dogs prowled about outside. Each white man formed particular friendships among the natives in order to assimilate the habits and tricks of Inuit life. This involved a deliberate descent to primitive existence for the purpose of mastering such arts as dog driving and building snow houses. Sipsoo, who took Green's fancy, taught Green how to build a snow house, start a native lamp with moss and blubber, and care for his feet. "Each white man took his course," Green wrote. "It was not easy; rotten meat

Borup Lodge: Members of the expedition built this house at Etah and hoisted the American flag (American Museum of Natural History Library).

and vermin could not go easily with ten centuries of culture. We stuck it out, though, and thereby bought our lives, as later experience showed us."[8]

Allen wired the house, stringing incandescent lamps, leading the Inuit to think the sun had returned when the switch was thrown.[9] From late September to mid–October Green labored to install various measuring devices. Later, all hands helped get the big wire for the aerial up the hill. Despite hours of "listening in" they heard nothing. Green also set up the "magnetic tent" in the ruins of an unused igloo and a mark on the Point and took a series of observations for declination in order to have some approximate results for possible use later.[10]

The long winter night began in mid–October. The Inuit were free to call on the explorers at any time up to ten o'clock. Perhaps a dozen or so did. Ekblaw amused them with games of all sorts, Tanquary sang to them, and Small caused laughter by waving his arms. On a late October night the men had a game of poker, but the arguments over rules were so violent that the party was not a success.

One night the men had a session with Etookashoo and Ahpellah, Sverdrup's map, and *My Attainment of the Pole* (1911), the book in which Frederick A. Cook claimed to have reached the Pole before Peary did. The two Inuit, who had been with Cook on his "North Pole" trip, agreed as to the course they took and insisted that they were never out of sight of land. At different times each Inuit traced the same course on the map without knowing the other had done so. Separately, they declared that they had four cartridges left when they arrived back in Greenland, whereas Cook declared they had none. They had no hardship whatever until nearly home. The picture that Cook claimed was taken at the North Pole they located on the map near Ellesmere Island, some 400 miles from the Pole. "The frank, open-faced manner with which these men answered our questions convinced us all of the truth of their story," Dr. Hunt wrote. "We tried in vain to break down their testimony, but could not budge them."[11]

On 19 October Tanquary and Ahnowka returned to the lodge about dinner time from an overnight camping trip during which they had a fourteen hours' sleep in an igloo and each had shot one rabbit. The day being Sunday as near as Hunt could figure, dinner consisted of a caribou roast with potatoes, cranberry sauce, and a gelatin pudding. One of the Inuit boys played the Victrola during the dinner. Days later Dr. Hunt took the blood pressure of each member of the party. All were in fine trim physically and were eating well.

By late October the men had enough caribou skins to make each man a sleeping bag. They nailed the fresh skins to the ceiling to dry, three at a time. The skins were needed for cold-weather pants. Dr. Hunt placed pictures of his wife and daughter over his bunk so that he could see them on awakening. "Oftentimes I wonder whatever I could have been thinking of when I left them for such a long time," he confided to his diary. "I guess we are all thinking of home more than any of us tell."[12]

The expedition party exhibited the Puritan influence on American culture by redeeming the time one day a week when possible. "We observe Sunday by stopping all work and playing no games," Green wrote on 2 November 1913. "We usually go for a long tramp on this day." A week later three men took their regular Sunday afternoon walk, going around Sunrise Point in a smother of drifting snow. On Sunday, 16 November, Green recorded, "we played all of our hymns on the phonograph after breakfast. Then Tank[,] Allen, and I sang all the songs we knew. They have good voices and I string along with a tenor to fill out Tank's bully baritone." Sabbath observance, part of the culture that nurtured the explorers, did not last long in the Arctic.

Meanwhile, on 25 October MacMillan had witnessed a case of "pibloktoq" (Arctic hysteria), a catch-all term which explorers used to describe various Inuit anxiety reactions, symptoms of physical illness and perhaps feigned illness, expressions of resistance to patriarchy or sexual coercion, and shamanistic practice. Many of these behaviors were apparently induced by the stresses of early contact between Euro-Americans and Inuit between 1890 and 1920. The affliction was widespread among the Inuit of northwest Greenland. Peary had been first to characterize it as hysteria. A pibloktoq attack, said MacMillan, who had sailed with Peary, was a childish cry by women for attention. MacMillan offered a report that provided the basis of a scientific discourse on pibloktoq as the physical and psychological effects of the long, dark, dreary Arctic night that often drove Inuit women mad.[13]

Fitzhugh Green reported a case of Arctic hysteria which he saw firsthand. According to Green, 13 November was "a bully day," but that night "Alnea went, or became, Piblokto." This affliction, common among Inuit women, was a form of hysteria that sprang from diverse emotions, especially the general gloom and depression that peaked in the fall. It manifested itself with a low, crooning note accompanied by a swaying of the body, a beating of the hands, an abandoned yell, and a dash for the rough ice, ripping off clothes and spitting, clawing, and biting. Dr. Goodsell, the surgeon on the 1908–09 Peary expedition, had reported a case of an Inuit woman who stripped to the waist and, singing, started seaward across the floes. The Inuit finally tied her arms and legs, but she continued to flop around the deck, so they wrapped her in canvas and tied her up by the shoulders and feet to a spar over the main deck where she hung until the attack subsided.[14] In her previous fit, Green noted, Alnea had been a walrus. He wondered what she was imitating this time. She was crazy to have children. Her trouble, Green thought, was the outcome of abuse. When Green arrived at her igloo, the wild-looking woman was struggling, swearing, and spitting. When he turned to go, she grabbed a pot and would have thrown it had not her husband deflected her aim.[15]

On Thanksgiving Day, the party enjoyed a traditional dinner, except for caribou in place of turkey, served by an Inuit boy in spotless white. After the feast, Jot Small fed thirty-seven Inuit bellies until they were stuffed like balloons. The after-dinner event, a "mumukto," was a tribal rite for which the lights were put out for a program of chanting, of which there were a dozen variations. According to Green, two men went through "the list" standing in the center of the crowd, which joined in, humming the air at all times. The leader beat time with a stick and a pan, while the other man sang loudly. When the time came to cease, the second man held a small white stick before the leader. Instantly the tune stopped with a laugh and everyone seemed to feel that the song had been a success.

According to Dr. Hunt, when the Inuit gave the Americans such a concert on 2 November, two men sang at a time, one beating time with a stick on a tin plate, all the while swinging the body from side to side. Many natives were experienced in the state of trance. MacMillan, once hearing singing in the igloo of the Smith Sound people, had crawled into its semi-darkened interior. The singing stopped. He took a seat and waited. An old woman and two teen-age girls began again. "Slowly, faintly, the crooning started, a mystic chant, accompanied by the swaying of the body and beating hands, the guttural note of age blending with the treble of youth, the old teaching the young what was undoubtedly some of the most ancient music on earth." The girls became frenzied under the hypnotic influence.[16]

The description of these tribal rites suggests that they were a variant of shamanism. Shamanism has been variously defined, but it may be described as hysteria with masochistic elements. A shaman was one who held himself half-hidden or hidden. Shamans alone were able to command helping spirits. Their séances depended on religious uses of hypnotic trances. Different depths of trance were specific to different goals and activities, such as summoning helping or hostile spirits and journeying as free-souls. Having learned to be active rather than passive when ecstatic, the Inuit turned to self-hypnotic trances in which he acquired helping spirits and practiced séance techniques.[17] The "mumukto" seems to be a variant of shamanism.

On 1 December, Minnik, an Inuit in his early twenties, arrived in Etah and asked to stay. MacMillan, thinking that he would be of assistance as an interpreter, accepted him. Born in the Arctic in 1890 or 1891, Minnik was the only survivor of the six Inuit whom Peary had taken with him to New York City in 1897 for anthropological research. Both of his parents had worked for Peary. In 1897, Qisuk, his father, had helped Peary get the huge meteorite near Cape York aboard the ship to take to America. While that operation was taking place, Minnik had climbed a cliff, killed a gyrfalcon and an owl, and received a reward. Peary persuaded Qisuk, Minnik, and four other Smith Sound Inuit to go with him to America.[18]

The *Hope* bearing the meteorite and the Inuit arrived in the Brooklyn Navy Yard in late September 1897. Peary assumed that the natives would go to the American Museum of Natural History, although no arrangements had been made for their reception. A day or two later they were taken there.[19] Peary probably thought that an anthropological study of the Inuit would be a credit to the museum and would appeal to Morris Jesup, his wealthy benefactor. Franz Boas, an anthropologist at Columbia University and a member of the museum staff, had made an ethnological study of the Inuit on Baffin Island. He asked Peary to bring him one Inuit so he could obtain ethnological information of scientific importance. Peary brought not one but six. "There is no doubt," Kenn Harper wrote, "that he brought them to secure publicity, official notice, and the goodwill of the officials of the American Museum of Natural History."[20]

The natives were put in the care of William Wallace, the superintendent of the museum, who had an apartment there. They developed tuberculosis,

2. "Hail, the Conquering Hero Comes"   35

and in early November all six were taken to Bellevue Hospital. In February Qisuk died; the others were moved to a cottage on Wallace's property in New York City. Three others soon died, one returned to Greenland, and Mene, as Minnik was known, was the sole survivor of the six Inuit Peary brought to America.[21]

When Qisuk died, museum and hospital officials agreed to allow Bellevue to make such use of his body as possible in the dissecting-room and to allow the museum to mount and preserve the skeleton.[22] So at this point the museum needed to stage a fake burial. The question was, how? Alfred Kroeber, an anthropologist who had studied the Smith Sound Inuit, described an authentic Polar Inuit funeral. With this prompting, the museum decided to duplicate a primitive funeral on museum grounds. Staff members got an old log about the length of a human corpse, wrapped it in cloth, attached a mask to one end, placed it on the ground, and piled a mound of stones on top of it. At dusk they took Mene out to the imitation body. The ruse worked. Mene told others that he had seen his father buried.[23]

Morris Jesup encouraged William Wallace to take Mene into his family, agreeing to pay for the boy's financial support. He also urged Wallace to give the boy a name; thus the young Inuit became Mene Wallace. William Wallace and his wife, Rheeta, who had a son about Mene's age, cared deeply for the Inuit. He became part of their family while Jesup absolved himself of all responsibility. This arrangement was brief. In January 1901, museum officials discovered that William Wallace had mismanaged the museum's financial affairs and had taken kickbacks from contractors and suppliers. Under pressure he resigned from the museum.

Nevertheless, he continued to take an interest in Mene. For a time the youth was a good student at a public school in the Bronx, but often he ran away from school and home and was increasingly at risk in the unwholesome atmosphere of the city slums. Chester Beecroft, a publicist associated with the Hotel Astor, who had met Mene before Rhetta's death, asserted that the museum neglected Mene because of its unfortunate relations with William Wallace. Beecroft and Wallace were interested in securing financial support for Mene and providing for his education before he returned to the Arctic. But Mene had left the Wallace home, believing that he was responsible for that family's problems. For a time he lived with Beecroft at the Hotel Astor. Later, he took a room at a boarding house on Forty-fourth Street.[24]

When Mene discovered that his father had not been buried but had been made a museum exhibit, he asked for the return of Qisuk's bones. The museum director put him off. Years later, when Mene demanded the return of his father's body, the director admitted that Qisuk's skeleton was now a museum exhibit. Mene tried to get his father's bones, but to no avail.[25]

In April 1909 Mene suddenly left New York. A friend reported that Mene was broken-hearted over his treatment in America, did not have much love for Peary, and had "some scheme in mind to try and defeat Perry in his hunt for the north pole." So far as the friend knew, Mene had only five dollars when he left New York.[26]

In early August, Mene was on the schooner *Jeannie* under Captain Bob Bartlett going north to Etah. When the ship stopped in Labrador, Mene exchanged everything he owned in return for liquor. He arrived at North Star Bay without a penny.[27] Freuchen and Rasmussen took him in at Thule, their trading post. They tried to help him, but found him utterly unreliable, hysterical, and lazy. Viewing him as a born good-for-nothing, they finally threw him out.[28]

So Mene went to Etah and MacMillan took him in. Now in his early twenties, he knew English but had forgotten the Inuit language. On 6 December, after MacMillan had given Dr. Hunt leave to go see a sick child at Umanak, Hunt left with Mene and Ootah. They stopped for the night at Nerky and went on the next morning for the island of Keato, where Dr. Hunt found a man with both legs partially useless for two years. Dr. Hunt told him to come to Etah and he would do what he could for him. Proceeding to Umanak, Dr. Hunt found Ooblooya still in bed after two months with rheumatism and a girl of about twelve who seemed to have had typhoid fever. She had been sick about a month, was sometimes out of her head, and had become very thin. At Umanak on 10 December, Dr. Hunt moved into the house of the missionaries, South Greenland Inuit who had gone to Upernavik for the winter. The next day a man came as expected and Dr. Hunt, with Mene's assistance with the ether, amputated one finger from each hand. The stiff and useless fingers had been shattered some months earlier by an exploding rifle cartridge. Dr. Hunt arrived back at Etah on 19 December. The following day the man with the paralyzed legs arrived. Dr. Hunt fitted a pair of crutches for him. Eight sledge loads of visitors now left for their homes. They had crowded their hosts, who had given them tea and crackers twice daily.

In late December MacMillan told Ekblaw to prepare to go to examine Rasmussen's meteorite on the shores of Melville Bay. Ekblaw had seen the great meteorites in the American Museum of Natural History brought home by Peary, and he was ready to start on a 250-mile sledge journey to Cape Melville, where there was another "great meteorite" to examine.[29]

Dramatic meteorite falls had long taken place in the Arctic. In 1818 Captain John Ross of the Royal Navy had come across natives on the northern shore of Melville Bay who had cut off iron from a rock. Inuit had long obtained their iron supply from the meteors near Melville Bay. Most meteorites, scientists discovered, belonged to one of three categories: irons (mainly metallic iron and metal), stony meteorites (mainly silicon and magnesium oxides), and stony irons (a mix of metals and stones). In May 1894, the Greenland Inuit had shown Peary three meteors on the northern shore of Melville Bay, some thirty-five miles east of Cape York.[30] The two smaller ones were "The Woman," with an estimated bulk of twelve cubic feet and an estimated weight of six thousand pounds, and "The Dog," with an estimated weight of one thousand pounds. In August 1895, with white and Inuit assistants, Peary was able to lift both meteorites out of their beds and place them on his steamer, the *Kite*, and transport them to New York.

As work progressed on the two smaller meteorites, Peary partially excavated the larger one, "The Ahnigito." Determined to secure it, he chartered a stronger ship, the *Hope*, and in the summer of 1896 returned to the site with a group of professors, scientists, and observers. With ingenuity and effort Peary's crew and the Inuit succeeded in placing the thirty-six-ton meteor on the ship and carrying it to New York. All three of the Cape York meteorites were exhibited in the museum until 1935.[31]

Rasmussen's meteorite was not one of the three acquired by Peary. The Inuit had long sought it. They knew by tradition that it lay somewhere on Ironside Mountain, but had forgotten the exact locality, since its metal had ceased to be a source of iron for knife-blades. Rasmussen had promised a liberal reward to the finder. Koodlooktoo, one of Peary's natives, had located the prize.[32]

Koodlooktoo expected to return about 1 January to his home on Cape Melville, not far from the meteorite. MacMillan told Ekblaw to get ready to accompany him. Ekblaw and his Inuit set out and were turned back by heavy wind off the land at Cape Alexander three times before they got off without having to turn back. They sledged over the Cape Alexander glacier to Nerky, where they stopped to sleep. The merry company traversed miles over ice so springy that it sank beneath the weight of the foot.[33]

At Nerky they were welcomed by the whole population—perhaps thirty people. Ekblaw chose to stay in Inighito's big igloo, having been told that Tookey, Inighito's wife kept it spic-and-span clean. After a good night's sleep Ekblaw set out again accompanied by Oobloyah, one of Peary's most efficient men in previous expeditions, with a big strong team of dogs.[34]

On his way, Ekblaw met Rasmussen and Freuchen at North Star Bay. Rasmussen had just returned to his trading post when "Dr. Elmer Ekblaw of the Crocker Land Expedition ... a tall, husky man ... born of Swedish parents" called upon them. He was on his way "to take possession of the meteorite for the expedition." Unfortunately the hosts had nothing to eat at the time. Freuchen, concerned over shabby treatment of "such an important guest," proposed to Rasmussen that they confess an empty larder and suggest that Ekblaw bring in and prepare his own food. Rasmussen had a better idea, one that would not expose their poverty. So he greeted Ekblaw enthusiastically and said they were pleased to be able to serve Ekblaw a very rare dish—Inuit rotten food. Rasmussen brought in a walrus flipper, chopped off a chunk with an ax and handed it to Ekblaw with a flourish, never permitting Ekblaw to get in a word, assuring Ekblaw that the morsel was very good. He could see that Ekblaw appreciated good food: "rotten meat with the Eskimos, fruit in the tropics, and pâté de fois gras in Paris." The host ate a piece, leaving no way out for the guest, who said that it was quite a treat. Insisting that Ekblaw have more, Rasmussen handed him a portion of blubber green with age. Since he had no coffee, Rasmussen said it would be a pity to drink coffee after such a meal as they had enjoyed. The next morning Ekblaw asked permission to bring in his own food and do his own cooking.[35]

Ekblaw and Rasmussen left North Star Bay with a dash to look at the meteorite. Rasmussen told Ekblaw that the treasure was claimed by the Danish Museum. He offered to have a piece of it shipped to the American Museum. In about eight hours they reached the bear-cave near Petowik glacier, where they stopped for rest and coffee. The bear-cave occupied a prominent place in Inuit legends and traditions. The Inuit regarded it with superstition. Proceeding to Akpan, they stopped at an igloo where Ekblaw's party and another party, a total of nineteen people, slept in one igloo like a litter of kittens. Their host, a successful hunter, fed them with bear meat, walrus, seal, birds, narwhal blubber, and other Inuit delicacies. A long march, with a brief visit to the settlement at Cape York, brought the party to Savikseevik (or Savigsuit), the village of three igloos nearest the meteorite.

The party sledged over the Cape Alexander glacier to Nerky, where they stopped to sleep. The next day they set out again, Ekblaw having persuaded Oobloyah, one of Peary's most efficient men in previous expeditions, to accompany him. They followed the inside route to Inglefield Gulf to the mouth of Olrik's Bay, and from there sledged over the ice cap, down Grenville Bay, and up Wolstenholme Sound, a distance of about eighty miles in a little over twenty-two hours.[36]

On the following day the party reached the foot of Ironstone Mountain at noon and soon found the pillar-like boulder of white gneiss that Koodlooktoo had set up to mark the meteorite. The meteorite itself, a large rusty block of nickel-iron alloy, was buried deep under the snow. Having cleared away the snow, Ekblaw and Rasmussen uncovered and measured the meteorite and tried to get some samples. But in the intense cold—52°F below zero—their chisels and hammers broke against the chill iron. Using a heavy sledgehammer, they obtained a small sample and collected a number of sharp-edged slabs of basalt that the Inuit had used in former times to cut off the little flakes of iron that they made into their little serrated knife-blades.

The trip was "an adventure worthy of a saga," Ekblaw exulted after the fact, "this our visit to the mighty, lost hammer of old discarded Thor. Scandinavians both [i.e., Rasmussen and Ekblaw], though one came from the Old

World and one from the New, we felt a like interest in this massive ingot forged in interstellar space, which we fancied had perhaps been flung from Valhalla before the days of iconoclastic science. As we were deeply engaged in our discussion on the possible origin of this vagrant planetesimal the coffee-pot boiled over; with little regret our thoughts swung back from the realms of celestial speculation where they had been wandering, to mundane reality. We had visited the meteorite."[37]

President James learned indirectly about Ekblaw's visit to the meteorite. D.B. Böggild, the director of the Mineralogical Museum of the University of Copenhagen, wrote about it to Henry Fairfield Osborn, president of the Honorary Committee of the Crocker Land Expedition. Rasmussen had found a large meteorite at Melville Bay, Böggild related, and had brought a small specimen of it to the Mineralogical Museum, "at whose disposal he has at the same time placed the large stone at present lying on the spot where it was found." The Crocker Land Expedition had rendered Rasmussen scientific help in this matter by having the stone examined "both on the spot and in the laboratory, an examination which through the kindness of Mr. Donald MacMillan was carried out in a most excellent manner by Mr. Elmer Ekblaw, the Geologist of the Expedition. Mr. Ekblaw was not deterred by the long and difficult journey to the spot but in the interests of science investigated the facts and submitted a very complete report which is of the greatest importance to us. We are indebted not only to the Expedition in Greenland but also to the Direction in America. We therefore feel it our pleasant duty to tender our best thanks to the committee just as we have already directly thanked both Mr. Donald MacMillan and Mr. W. Elmer Ekblaw." Böggild closed with "wishes for the Expedition's scientific results and happy home coming." Hovey sent James a copy of Böggild's letter.[38]

In late January Ekblaw made a report of the meteorite to the King of Denmark. He hoped that this courtesy might lead Ramussen to help him to do the geological work in Melville Bay.[39]

By this time the expedition party had settled in at Etah and the men were about to begin their search for Crocker Land. We shall follow them in this search, which was supported by three distinguished sponsors.

3

Searching for Crocker Land

The American Museum of Natural History, the American Geographical Society, and the University of Illinois had pledged their support for the search for Crocker Land, and now the search was about to begin. During the Arctic night in 1914 MacMillan began planning the twelve hundred mile trip to Crocker Land and return. An advance party would leave Etah when the weather permitted, cross Smith Sound to Cape Sabine, and establish food depots on Ellesmere Island. A series of small parties would follow.[1] As the men pored over their maps, Panikpat, an Inuit whom Peary had employed from 1891 to 1909, advised them to worry less, "for after all, it is a great deal Torngasuasq (the Almighty Devil) will have to do with your travel."[2]

The Evil Spirit could not be ignored. Goodsell, the medical doctor on the 1908–09 Peary expedition, described the Inuit as a religious people who believed in spirits often malicious in intent. Torngasuasq, the evil spirit of the North, lurked above the ice foot, in the cracking ice, and in the blasting winds, threatening to destroy. He and his devil crew had to be appeased and pacified by gifts, incantation, and ceremony. Torngasuasq's wife was just as malicious. The hell for the unhappy departed was a never-ending night without game and without oil to replenish the lamps. The offices of medicine man and priest were combined in the angakuts (or angakoks), who presided at occasional religious meetings. Inuit were not allowed to mention any objects or beings by their regular names, since it spelled disaster for those mentioned. At such a service, Inuit sang in a melodious chant, repeating the syllables, accompanied by a small gut-covered hoop similar to a tambourine.[3] This service must have been a mumukto or much like one.

Now, having agreed on the best route for direct, rapid advance, the men estimated the position and size of provision caches. Experience had established the value of advanced divisions smoothing the way for the party that would make the final effort. MacMillan aimed at putting two white men and two natives at Cape Thomas Hubbard, each with his own team, all having traveled over a broken trail from Etah. He chose two men who were eager to go and ambitious to drive a dog-team.[4]

Elmer Ekblaw and Fitzhugh Green with attending Inuit, dogs, and sledges were to make the first trip north with loads of oil, biscuit, and pemmican to establish Depot A. Green was delighted at the prospect. "Ek," he wrote, "had proved a thoroughly enjoyable fellow on every sort of work; and his popularity and success at the University of Illinois showed that our esteem was well founded. Although professing to be a cut-and-dried man of science, his instincts were keenly adventurous.... Little had he not learned about the sea and the land and the creatures thereof." With another man of this caliber, Green confessed, he might have been at a disadvantage. "But Ek's pet aversion was ignorance, and he sought to enlighten all who came within the circle of his own brilliance, and that without the least hint of patronage." One thing comforted Green: Ekblaw could not pull an oar. But posterity would bear witness to "Ek's indefatigable assiduity in the prosecution of scientific work." Ekblaw and Jot Small had become friends, and while autumn twilight permitted, "this modern Humboldt and his would-be Dana" made excursions into the surrounding wilderness, especially to Brother John's glacier at the head of the fiord, to measure glacial movement by means of iron rods ranged across the crevassed face in a straight line, afterward to be bowed by more rapid flow near the glacier's axis.[5]

In early December Green and Ekblaw checked their equipment for the last time. Their garments were entirely native except the single suit of woolen underwear. At 5 a.m. on 11 December, with the crack of Sipsoo's whip, the five sledges, three in Ekblaw's division and two in Green's, were off. After a day of travel they camped just above the Cairn Point of Elisha Kane's expedition and made two igloos for themselves. Shortly after morning came they spotted a bear and three cubs. After a wild chase they killed four bears, skinned one, and then the men and the dogs gorged on bear meat. Two days later they returned with the report that the depot had been established and that Smith Sound was apparently frozen over from shore to shore. Consequently, MacMillan gave orders to prepare at once for crossing the Sound and transporting 1738 pounds of provisions to Depot B at Cape Rutherford in Buchanan Bay. The cache consisted of oil, biscuit, tea, condensed milk, and man and dog pemmican. Later, MacMillan realized that men remained strong with a ration of only bread and meat.[6]

During the dark months, the men used the two weeks of moonlight for traveling, either laying out caches northward or gathering meat, skins, and natives from the south, and they used the dark days to repair sledges, prepare for the northern venture, do routine scientific work, keep records, write, and tabulate. Tanquary bottled bugs, Dr. Hunt counted corpuscles, Allen fussed with his generator, Jot Small stirred soup and sawed sledge bars, while

Dinner of the expedition party on 13 December 1913 (American Museum of Natural History Library).

MacMillan measured the dolichocephalic dimensions of a dozen Inuit.[7] Green was overjoyed at getting ready for an extensive trip because he delighted in traveling, while staying home was misery.

By Christmas fresh meat had arrived from the south and the men had procured skins for full outfits. The explorers advertised their Christmas party weeks in advance in order to draw the native men whom they expected to make up their sledge caravan. Jot taught them the use of tools, and they built sledges.[8]

On Christmas Day the men popped corn and Inuit girls threaded it for decorations. Some fake evergreens and ribbons made the room seem like home. The dinner that Henry Fairfield Osborn had presented to the expedition in New York had come through in good shape except for the wine, which froze and broke the bottle. The dinner included roast turkey and cranberry sauce. After the feast, the men listened to opera music on a Victrola and gave a bite of fruit cake to each of sixty-one Inuit visitors.[9]

On the following Sunday Dr. Hunt performed the first operation of the expedition. An Inuit had a stricture and was in great pain. "I laid him on the dining room table," Green recorded, "and Hal gave him the ether."[10]

The time set for departure towards the Polar Sea was early February.

"The trip will be a hard one, with unforeseen dangers," Dr. Hunt observed. "To tell the truth, I rather dread the start. The cold, the danger, and the privations are not pleasant to look forward to, yet I know that once we are under way, the bustle and hurry of the trail will take up all our attention." He thought it possible that the adventurers might not get back from Crocker Land the same season. "Here there are no cliques as yet. The men are good companions, when we give in some to each other's idiosyncrasies. Allen and I have had no squabbles yet, which cannot be said of the other roommates."[11]

In preparation, the party sent advance supplies north to Anoritok and cached them at Cape Sabine on Ellesmere Island. Needing to hire about twenty Inuit and to acquaint them with the white men's travel methods and routine, MacMillan made a round of the tribe to choose additional men and to promote a friendly spirit toward the expedition, carrying with him small presents and other inducements, including kerosene and small burner stoves for making tea and cooking meat. News got out about the wealthy and generous white men, whereupon Inuit soon arrived at Borup Lodge bringing skins, dogs, lines, and meat. At MacMillan's suggestion, each white explorer formed a particular friendship among the visitors in order to learn their tricks and habits. Green took a fancy to Sipsoo, who was stocky and lithe, reserved but alert, and clever beyond his years. Four children, a wife, and a mother-in-law depended on his skill with harpoon and lance. Sipsoo taught Green how to build a snow house and start a native lamp with moss and blubber, how to trail a bear in both autumn and spring, how to care for his feet, and how to drive dogs. Each white man took his course. "It was not easy," Green recalled, "rotten meat and vermin could not go easily with ten centuries of culture. We stuck it out though and thereby bought our lives as later experience showed us."[12]

On 22 January MacMillan wrote that he and the exploring party were well and comfortable. He selected from the numerous visitors to Borup Lodge seventeen Inuit, many of whom were the best in the tribe and well known to him. He planned to dispatch the expedition's divisions on successive days. The smallest details could be attended to with only three or four sledges departing at a time. The advance party would pick and break the trail and build a snow house that succeeding divisions could occupy. Green and Ahpellah were to go first with seven sledges, take on loads of five hundred pounds each at a place fifteen miles north of Etah, cross Smith Sound, and proceed toward the musk ox grounds of Eureka Sound in Ellesmere Island. Here the expedition would rendezvous, send back the least desirable men and dogs, and then push on toward the Polar Sea. The first division left on 7 February 1914. Tanquary with his division left the next day. Ekblaw and his Inuit followed on 9 February, while Dr. Hunt and his division departed on 10 February.

Now nineteen men and fifteen sledges drawn by 165 dogs were headed toward the Polar Sea, by air line a distance of 485 statute miles.[13]

Days later Dr. Hunt and Tanquary with five Inuit took loads of pemmican and milk to the cache at Anoritok. South Greenland Inuit had brought mumps, coughs, and colds to Etah. They coughed and spat incessantly and were not careful where they spat. Ekblaw had the mumps. The idea at that time was for the white men to walk, with no teams, while the Inuit sleds were to carry all the provisions. Only MacMillan was to have a dog team. "I do not approve of this but cannot change it," Dr. Hunt wrote. "MacMillan is trading for fox skins to take home for himself, giving in exchange tea, sugar, biscuits, tobacco, matches, and other articles. I should prefer to have him purchase dogs and traveling outfits for the men. He does not ask advice or take any when offered by any of us." It seemed likely, Hunt added, that, barring accidents, MacMillan, Ekblaw, and Green would be the ones to go through to Crocker Land.[14]

Bad weather delayed MacMillan's departure until 12 February. His division reached Payer Harbor at Cape Sabine the next day. This cape, MacMillan observed, had played a large part in Arctic history. Seeking a shelter, MacMillan found the old hut that Peary had made the headquarters of his 1900 Polar Expedition. MacMillan proceeded the next day despite horrible weather. In a few hours he reached a big cache at Cape Rutherford, at the entrance to Buchanan Bay, where the men loaded their sledges and pressed on until they caught up with those who had preceded them encamped in igloos near Hayes Sound. Some of the natives had influenza, some had the mumps, and some had cold feet. Nearly all refused to go on: their dogs were weak and would probably die on the big glacier of Ellesmere Island, over which they had to cross. Ootaq, who had followed Peary for a quarter of a century, was the chief agitator in the strike. MacMillan's arrival ended the discussion. He took in the situation. Since it was early in the year, he could well afford to return to Etah to "eliminate the sick, the chicken-hearted, and the older and more influential Eskimos." So they started back the next day. The explorers profited from their first failure, becoming acquainted with their Inuit and learning about the difficulties of protracted sledging in painfully low temperatures.[15]

Upon arriving at Etah and in view of the probable lateness of their start, MacMillan gave up all thoughts of the *exploration* of Crocker Land and decided to concentrate on proving or disproving its existence. If it should be found, he could return the next year. He reduced the number of the party to ten: Macmillan, Ekblaw, Green, and seven Inuit. On 11 March the last sledge got away for Cape Sabine.[16]

Preparing to go out on the Polar Sea, MacMillan selected seventeen natives of the Smith Sound tribe, many of whom were the best in the tribe, and three expedition men well fitted physically for the arduous work. They

3. Searching for Crocker Land

would be in charge of their respective divisions but relieved of all care of a team. The time of the start depended upon the length of the journey: the greater the distance the earlier the start.

Accordingly, the search for Crocker Land began as the Arctic darkness turned to light. On 7 February, eleven days prior to the astronomical date of sunrise, the various divisions of the party—nineteen men, fifteen sledges, and one hundred and sixty-five dogs—left with orders to rendezvous at Eureka Sound and await MacMillan's unit, which left on 13 February. The finding of two dead dogs on the trail was MacMillan's first intimation of trouble in the advance party. Etookashoo, one of MacMillan's best men, was down with the mumps, the other men were sick and discouraged, the dogs were weak with dysentery, and nearly all agreed that it was unwise to go on. It was so early in the year that they could well afford to return to Etah, condition the men and the dogs, and repeat the attempt later. MacMillan decided to do this, ordering that all equipment and provisions be left in cache and that all retreat to Etah, except Hunt and Green, who were to remain with two Inuit who were unable to travel.

In view of the probable lateness of their start, MacMillan now decided to devote his efforts to proving or disproving the existence of Crocker Land. If it should be found, he could explore it the following year. By curtailing his plans, MacMillan could reduce the number of the party to ten: seven Inuit, Ekblaw, Green, and himself.

On 11 March, with the temperature at minus 31°F, MacMillan, Ekblaw, and Green got away soon after noon, accompanied by Minnik, Etookashoo, and Peeahwahto. They made their way through a stiff north wind to Cammowitz and occupied the old igloos for the night. The next day they crossed Smith Sound in six hours, having empty komatiks except for their personal equipment and four cans of pemmican. At Payer Harbor they found the four natives who had been sent ahead to prepare walrus meat for their dogs. On the way over that party had killed a large bear; their dogs looked fat and well. Two days of pleasant traveling to the big cache in Hayes Sound included a miserable night in the tents that they had brought along, which proved the luxury of a snow igloo. At the big cache they took on full loads and continued on. At this latitude two crossings of Ellesmere Land were available: one by the way of the old migration trail of the Inuit at the head of Flagler Bay, which Sverdrup had found to be windswept and bare of snow, the other by way of the Beitstadt Glacier at the head of Beitstadt Fiord. It was a magnificent sheet stretching across Ellesmere Land from shore to shore, fed by some forty smaller glaciers flowing down through the valleys of the neighboring hills. MacMillan chose the latter. Although considered much more difficult, it would furnish good sledging to the western shores of Ellesmere Land.

At noon on 16 March the party arrived at the foot of the glacier that stretched more than fifty miles across Ellesmere Land. The geology of it was an open book to Green, who could not resist describing its evolution until "every atavism drops away like an excrescence; until, upon the threshold of to-day, the ape form stands hairy and abrupt, with no inkling of the vast heritage that is his."[17] The problem confronting the men put a stop to such dreaming. The ten men and one hundred dogs together with about six thousand pounds of food and equipment confronted a perpendicular wall of polished ice two miles wide, flanked by unscalable cliffs. At forty feet high the icy buttress sloped back slightly, and at 600 feet high it rounded into the main glacial body, which mounted at a 30 degree angle to the ice cap over 2,000 feet high. "A sleep, and then what?" MacMillan asked Arklio. "No sleep, perhaps," he replied. "Not so often does the Almighty Devil permit cessation of his remorseless winds hereabouts."[18]

So Arklio and Peeahwahto took their ice axes and searched the glacier's front for a good place to begin. There must be room for two rows of steps and not much debris below, Arklio explained, lest someone who fell from the top be killed by lacerations. So the Inuit cut two rows of steps into the face of the ice with their hatchets to secure a good grip for the hands and a good step for the foot. Then other Inuit carried loads of from eighty to one hundred pounds by neck lines over their heads to the top, and they hauled up the dogs with howling protests. By dusk the party had transferred over four thousand pounds to the surface of the ice, ready for loading the next day. At this point Minnik, who was not doing his share of the work, decided that hard work at -50° F did not agree with him. He admitted that the expedition had treated him very squarely. With MacMillan's permission he left to return to Etah. His withdrawal led to the loss of Tauchingwa, one of MacMillan's best Inuit. He left because he had a wife at home and feared that Minnik would steal her.[19]

The departure of the natives with sixteen dogs dangerously reduced the amount of food that could be transported over the glacier. Loads were now so heavy and the gradient so steep and slippery that free use of the whip was necessary to induce the dogs to move. In three days the men advanced 40 miles, crossed a million crevasses, and camped almost at the summit, which was 4,750 feet in altitude. Far to the west they could make out Eureka Sound, but they failed to find any part of the glacier that would permit descent without risk of life.

Peeahwahto finally found an old riverbed through which they might possibly lower everything with ropes. This they did, and on reaching Bay Fiord they found it impossible to descend to the sea ice below because of the height of the vertical face of the ice upon which they stood. At length Peeahwahto discovered a crevice worn deep into the ice by a summer stream. Although it was slippery and a bit treacherous, they succeeded in lowering

Rough ice on the way to Crocker Land, April 1914 (American Museum of Natural History Library).

everything to the surface below, a riverbed covered with a light layer of snow. They pitched camp one mile distant and built two igloos with the temperature -50°F. In the morning they killed seven musk oxen, which provided the dogs and the men with plenty of red meat.[20]

Now that they were in musk ox country and with their loads safely across Ellesmere Land, MacMillan could dispense with two men and their dog teams, thus reserving the provisions they consumed daily. In ascending the glacier, Ekblaw had badly frozen both feet. Having reached Bay Fiord and the musk ox herd, MacMillan decreed that Kiotah accompany Ekblaw back to Etah. With them went Green and two Inuit with orders to load up their sledges with supplies from the big cache in Hayes Sound and meet MacMillan at Cape Thomas Hubbard, the northernmost point of Axel Heiberg island.[21]

Meanwhile, MacMillan proceeded toward Eureka Sound. His Inuit had declared that they could live on the country. MacMillan was not so sure. The next morning the footprints of a polar bear and a bloody track through the snow were evidence that the bear had captured a seal. In a few minutes a large white wolf bounded out of the ice foot and took to the side-hill. Peeahwahto seized his rifle and shot and killed the animal going at full speed about one hundred yards away. The men removed the skin as a specimen for the

American Museum. The dogs sniffed at the red flesh but walked away, recognizing their near relative from the smell.[22] The men were ready to build an igloo when Peeahwahto spotted three musk oxen alongside them. White men would have immediately made sure of their game, but not the Inuit. They cut snow blocks, built an igloo, and then went for their prey, coming upon the animals from the rear, cutting off their retreat, and killing five of them. The next morning the dogs ate to repletion while the men spent half a day in skinning and cutting up the animals and sledging the meat down to the igloo.[23]

On 29 March MacMillan and his Inuit were at 80° N, having covered a whole degree in two days. They had perfect sledging. They killed another wolf, and a blue fox crossed in front of them. To stop or control Inuit dogs with the tail of a blue fox waving in their faces would be like stopping the world from going around. The dogs took after the fox, which outran them. On 30 March, from the Fosheim Peninsula MacMillan headed across Skraelingodden, which marked the end of the party's good sledging and good weather. They plodded through ankle-deep snow all the way to Schei Island. There was land on both sides; they were either in a cul-de-sac or there were low-lying islands off the southern part of the island which Sverdrup's map did not show. Etookashoo found that the snow was suitable for building, so they built an igloo, went inside, closed the door with a snow block, and lit the stove. Their dogs needed fresh meat. The next day the Inuit harnessed their dogs and went looking for musk ox tracks. At midnight they were back, having killed thirty-five musk oxen. Like savages, MacMillan noted, they had slaughtered the whole herd for the pure love of killing, although they knew that the party could not possibly use so many. "In through the door of the igloo came hearts, tongues, livers, and juicy tenderloins. What a feast!"[24]

For five days MacMillan slept on Schei Island awaiting Green and his party and strengthening his dogs with a liberal allowance of fresh meat. Knowing that many things might have prevented a reunion with Green, MacMillan went on, leaving a note that he would await Green at Cape Thomas Hubbard. On the Axel Heiberg shore, MacMillan's Inuit discovered a small cache of pemmican and condensed milk that was undoubtedly left by Sverdrup in 1902. It was practically as good as new. For the next several days low temperatures (-20°F) and blowing and drifting snow gave MacMillan and his two natives a drubbing. To make matters worse, they had left their sleeping bags in their igloo at Schei Island. On 12 April, mingled with drifting snow came the sound of a voice. Green and his two Inuit had arrived, and with them on their sledge was everything required for work on the Polar Sea.[25]

On the eve of this great work, Green reflected on his own situation. He was alone with two men his own age, yet separated were they from what was really me by 4000 miles and 40,000 years. Their life was a sublimely simple fight for food and clothing. Mine was a cruel struggle of such labyrinthine intricacy that only the genius could be rich and none be truly contented save the shrewdest philosophers. Any average Inuit might have wealth in return for the bare skill of practice. All normal ones have a comfortable plenty. And with them enough is a song-inciting sufficiency. I, on the other hand—I the cultured, pampered ascendent of ages, knew not the contentful joy of indifference. Imbued as I was with the ugly rivalry of a white man, every irksome detail counted; the most insignificant items of living became fortuitous assets toward victory over my fellow man.

Age for instance—I knew I knew I was 25—was glad of it; I had a start on those older who were no further longer along in life than I. But my happy-go-lucky companions never gave the fleeting years a thought. Arklio could not count past 20—all his fingers and toes—but was positive he exceeded that number by at least four years. Nucarpingwah excused his ignorance by describing a certain favorite harpoon of his father's on which were notched each spring the children's ages....

A year to me was a task-space in which so much must be gained in the direction of my professional aims. To these carefree savages it meant but a few more skins or less, a series of hunts and feasts; a few famined months followed always again by hunts and feasts; a tribesman gone; another wife; a new baby.[26]

Green had both an active imagination and the ability to analyze his situation from a wide perspective. His "40,000 years" was apparently a recognition that his companions were products of a culture much older than his own. He followed this rumination by noting that the three men made camp. They had left their sleeping bags at the glacier to lighten their loads, so in their cold cramped little igloo they slept spoon fashion, taking turns in the middle. Going forward, making marches from twelve to fifteen hours long, bent on catching the other crowd or dying in the attempt, they came upon an igloo in which they found MacMillan's note saying that there were meat and skins in the igloo and thirty dead musk oxen on a hill nearby. The note indicated that Green's party was only three days behind MacMillan's party. So they regrouped, proceeding days later.

On Monday, 13 April, one of the fairest days ever made, the two parties were all together in the dugout, a very happy crowd. MacMillan concluded that four sledges could proceed as well as six, so he ordered Arklio and Nookapingwa to return to Etah the next day. MacMillan and Green spent the day searching without success for the Peary cairn and record on Cape Thomas Hubbard and for signs of land on the distant horizon seen from this very point. If Crocker Land were only 120 miles distant, as Peary had thought, MacMillan could go out in twelve days and back in seven, at the most. Thus far, in thirty-three days' continuous work they had covered 580 miles, an average of seventeen and a half miles a day, which told heavily on the dogs. Pemmican could not be relied upon for a long trip on the Polar Sea. Fortunately, the Inuit had killed four caribou. MacMillan and Green looked along the shore for the cairn that Peary had said no explorer could miss, and from the top of the hills they searched for Crocker Land for hours but failed to discover the slightest appearance of land.[27]

As MacMillan headed northwest over a hard surface of blue ice, he felt that his work had really begun. They were going toward that point where land had been drawn on a map with a question mark. MacMillan and Green, with Etookashoo and Peeahwahto, would settle the matter.

The Search

On 15 April the men traveled eighteen miles along the northern coast of Axel Heiberg, and from Cape Thomas Hubbard they took their departure the following day. They started light hearted and hopeful but soon found the Polar Sea all that had been given it in the way of condemning epithets. "The two natives," Green recorded, "could not conceal their hesitation," which grew to fear and begat mutiny. They were crossing many leads on thin ice that might break at any moment. The open water reminded Peeahwahto of his starvation days with Peary. He was not at all enthusiastic about the advance on the Polar Sea. But when MacMillan mounted a pressure ridge, took in the view ahead, and said he had seen worse, the Inuit realized that they were going on. MacMillan promised the natives more rifles and ammunition; they sulkily agreed to stay. Their first day's march netted them fourteen miles over old blue rolling ice, so smooth in places that with difficulty they prevented skidding into hollows and splitting the sides of their sledges. On 17 April they worked through rough ice on to a beautiful stretch of good going and netted eighteen miles for the day. On the following day they crossed safely over bending ice, found beyond a level stretch of good ice, and traveled at a rapid clip until held up by open water. On 19 April they met a succession of leads which bent and buckled like rubber. As they crossed the last one it came together and rose beneath their feet, lifting dogs, sledges, and men with a grinding, crushing noise. Two dogs dropped into a crack but were pulled out. MacMillan yelled to Green to hurry, but by the time he arrived their bridge was destroyed, compelling him to cross some distance below. On 20 April the men traveled for seven and one half hours with excellent going, crossing nine newly frozen leads. Two dogs dropped and were not see again.

On 21 April, a beautiful day, the party had the very best of going, advancing twenty-four miles in eight hours. Before leaving camp the next morning, Green yelled in through the igloo door that Crocker Land was in sight. "We all rushed out and up to the top of a berg," MacMillan recorded. "Sure enough! There it was as plain as day—hills, valleys, and ice cap, a tremendous land extending through 150 degrees of the horizon." They picked out the point to

3. Searching for Crocker Land   51

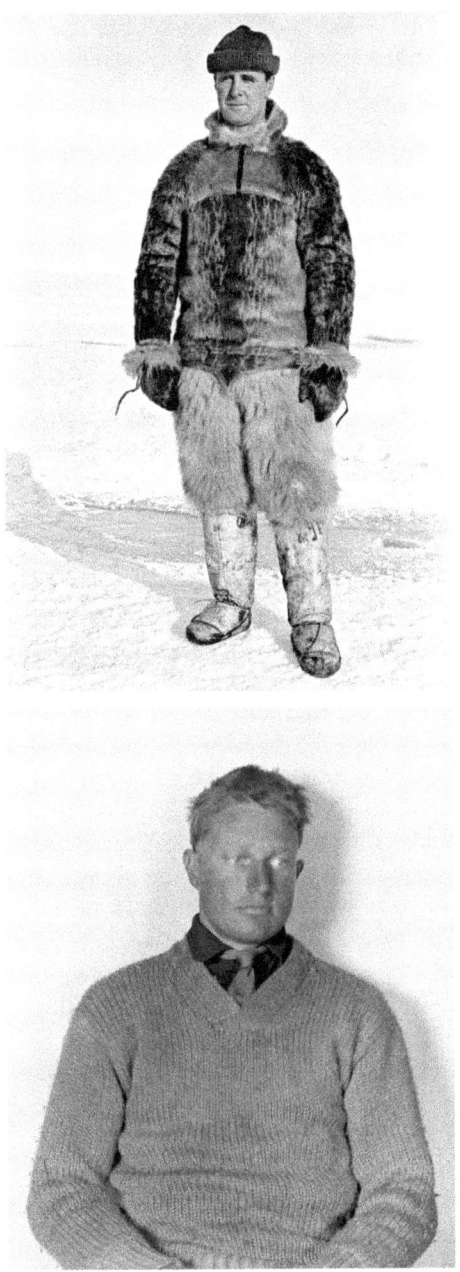

head for when Peeahwahto said that he thought it was mist in the sky resembling land. Watching it more closely, they were forced to conclude that it was a mirage of the sea ice.

On 22 April, MacMillan made it clear to the natives that he was going to the "brown spot" on the map, which he showed them, that they would not turn back until they got there, and the faster they traveled the sooner they would return toward land. As a result, the Inuit worked hard all day.

From this point onward the sea ice was a shattered mass entirely different from what they had passed over. Before them there were no parallel pressure ridges, no parallel leads, no grinding of the ice, no open water as far as they could see; simply a chaotic mass through which they could possibly work at the rate of five or six miles a day with the help of their hatchets and ice lancets. On 23 April Green's computation showed that they were already on Crocker Land. They made their last camp that day, and the next day they advanced three miles into the chaotic mass to test it and to obtain a more extended view from the tops of some of the pinnacles. It was fully as bad as it looked and with no promise of improvement. So they

Donald Macmillan (top) and Fitzhugh Green were the explorers who searched for the archipelago known as Crocker Land (American Museum of Natural History Library).

returned to camp and secured some careful sights which established their position as being 137 geographical miles due northwest of Cape Axel Heiberg. Green placed the location of the explorers in latitude 82° 30' N and longitude 108° 22'30" W.

From the summit of a pressure ridge near their last snow house they swept the horizon with a powerful pair of binoculars and saw not the slightest resemblance of land. The day was perfect—not a breath of air, the sky a cloudless blue, all mist had disappeared from the surface of the ice, indicating that all leads had frozen. MacMillan was confident that there was no land within fifty miles of their position.

When one of the leads froze, Green and an Inuit crossed it, followed by MacMillan and the other Inuit. Then they crossed nine newly frozen leads, having covered an estimated thirty miles that day. Their total distance at the end of this march was an estimated seventy-eight miles. The next day, with the sky clear blue, Green called out, "We have it." Everyone rushed to the top of the highest mound where they saw hills, valleys, and snow-capped peaks extending through at least one hundred and twenty degrees on the horizon. Peeahwahto scanned the supposed landfall for a few minutes and declared that it was mist. So it was. With the sun's movement the landscape changed appearance; at night it disappeared altogether. Could Peary have been mistaken? Had this mirage deceived Peary eight years previously?[28]

For the next few days the party set a more northerly course. Observations showed that they were 150 miles due northwest from Cape Thomas Hubbard. Peary had placed Crocker Land 150 miles out. Their latitude and longitude observations checked their dead reckoning. Suddenly a faint shadow in the northwestern horizon indicated success, but one of the natives declared that it was just a mirage. So it seemed, for the specter grew no nearer as the men advanced. Scanning the horizon, they saw nothing, not even a mirage. Now they were convinced that they were pursuing a "will-o'the wisp." Peary had said that he had seen a distant land; he left it for younger men to prove or disprove. This MacMillan had done. To see land from where Peary said that he had seen it was contrary to all scientific reasoning.[29]

The character of the ice would lead one to believe that this whole mass had been forced over shoal ground and thus had broken into small pans or had been in the grip of powerful cross currents, which exist only in the immediate vicinity of land. To test the former theory, at their farthest north and west MacMillan lowered his small pemmican hatchet, held with three-ply linen thread, through a hole in the ice to a depth of 150 fathoms (900 feet) and found no bottom. The ice that he found at this point, MacMillan believed, had been forced around the northern point of some land far to the west.

The secrets of the Polar Sea are pressure ridges and leads. Pressure ridges, piled up snow and ice, wore out the dogs, discouraged the men, and

3. Searching for Crocker Land

retarded progress. Leads, bodies of open water, were decisive: thus far and no farther. But with the temperature at twenty below zero, the leads would freeze. Seventeen miles from land the party constructed an igloo and made a sounding. They lowered nearly 2,000 fathoms of wire, but their five-pound pick was so light that it was carried off by the current, which probably flowed into Nansen Sound. To get the wire and pick back with the thermometer at twenty below took five hours. They attached a handle to the reel and relieved the operator every fifteen minutes. Peeahwahto had the last relay. He called out that the wire had broken and the pick was gone. The loss was serious. They had no other object that would serve as a weight. With the loss MacMillan wrote, "I felt as if I were a pall-bearer at a funeral as I carried the reel to the top of the highest ridge and left it there."[30]

On 25 April the men turned back toward land, contending against a strong wind and drift that covered up their outward trail. Within a few hours they could not detect the slightest sign of the trail. To find it was essential, since MacMillan had cached food at No. 4 igloo on the trail. When MacMillan was about to give orders to return to their last igloo, he heard the voice of Etookashoo telling them to come on. "That day's work by my two men, clinging to the trail in driving snow, stands out as something more than an incident in my four years' work," declared MacMillan. "It was nothing short of marvelous and a distinct credit to the keen vision and intelligence of the Polar Eskimo."

On Sunday, 26 April, they were up at 3:15 a.m. ready for the long march from No. 7 to No. 5 igloo. On this day they had their first touch of snowblindness, a warning that henceforth they must wear their snow glasses constantly. The next day they marched from No. 5 to No. 3 igloo and double-fed their dogs for their hard work. The tops of the mountains of Grant Land were now visible far inshore. As they traveled toward land on 28 April they detoured around the leads and rough ice in the vicinity of No. 2 igloo and struck straight for the top of what they judged must be Cape Thomas Hubbard. Fifteen hours later they stood upon the shore beneath the Cape.

Although very tired, MacMillan and Green took advantage of perfect weather to stand for their last examination of the Polar Sea where Peary had stood in 1906. Attaining the crest of Cape Thomas Hubbard with great difficulty, they spotted a substantial cairn, from the top of which protruded a stick. At its base they found a cocoa tin containing a section of a silk flag and a brief record that read "Peary, June 28, 1906." MacMillan replaced a copy of the record and also a small American flag and his record, which said that he and Green had arrived here on 28 April 1914 from a point on the Polar Sea 125 miles northwest true from here.

Standing beside this cairn, Peary had seen and reported Crocker Land to lie 120 miles due northwest. MacMillan and Green looked toward the distant horizon and saw land everywhere. Had they not just come from far over the horizon, they would have reported land as Peary had. Reluctantly, they were forced to conclude that what so strongly resembled land was simply a loom of the sea ice, a mirage common in the Arctic regions.

So the two explorers swallowed their disappointment and double-marched back to land with empty sledges and feelings of relief and sadness. They would have to retrace their steps and could turn to scientific research when they reached Etah.

On 29 April the two parties separated. MacMillan sent Green and Peeah-wahto along the coast of Axel Heiberg Land to look for Sverdrup's record, while he and Etookashoo went to Cape Colgate to secure the farthest-north record of Sverdrup. A storm was coming. They must move at once. They were to rejoin a few days later for the return trip to Etah. But that plan was not to be realized, as we shall see.

4

The Murder of Peeahwahto

MacMillan and Green separated on 29 April after returning from their search for Crocker Land. According to agreement, MacMillan went east with Etookashoo while Green went southwest with Peeahwahto. They were to reunite four days later on the coast east of Cape Thomas Hubbard. But as events transpired, that was not to be.

Green and Peeahwahto, advancing rapidly down the shore of Alex Heiberg Land, met considerable wind. Peeahwato, who had been with Peary and was at home in the Arctic, spoke of the scarcity of game and their exhausted teams. From this, as Green related, Peeahwahto turned to the abuse of MacMillan and his methods and to the deceitfulness and weak nature of white men in general. He did not believe he would get everything promised for his work. A gust of wind interrupted what Green viewed as his silly talk, and a seething blizzard drove them to cover. Green's dogs would not move no matter how he beat them. Peeahwahto made a small igloo. It snowed up rapidly; they could not keep an air hole open. As a result their stove would not burn and their tea was a failure. They tried to go out, but wind and snow made it impossible. Finally, in danger of being smothered, they cut a hole in the roof and Peeahwahto went out while Green stayed inside. The Inuit built a small igloo on top of the first one. When the two men finally got out during a lull on the third afternoon, Green found that his dog team had been buried under about fifteen feet of snow. Only one team of six weak and emaciated dogs remained alive. The men had more trouble with their stove. It stormed again. They tried twice before they got away. A lull in the storm was always followed by wind and snow.

Peeahwahto refused to go south or stay where they were. Green was forced to follow him, since he had no dogs or sledge. They got away at 7 a.m. the following day. Soon the weather was as bad as ever. Green could not ride as his feet were wet and several toes seemed to be frosted. Peeahwahto wanted Green to ride on the qamutik even if he risked losing toes, because losing toes was better than losing a life. And they had to find food for themselves

Peeahwahto, holding a caribou head near sled and dogs, April 1914 (American Museum of Natural History Library).

and the dogs. As they went over glare ice Peeahwahto kept whipping his dogs. When Green told him he could not keep up, Peeahwahto advised him to follow his trail. This was impossible. So, as Green related, "I then snatched the rifle from the load and warned him to keep behind me. A few minutes later I turned and saw him whipping up the dogs away from me. I shot once in the air. He did not stop. I then killed him with a shot through the shoulder and another through the head."[1]

With difficulty Green found the igloo at the Cape. When the storm abated, he went over to Peary's cairn, photographed it, and left a detailed account of events from 28 April to 1 May. This "confession" related the ineffectual attempt to locate Crocker Land, being caught in a ceaseless storm, the Inuit's refusal twice to obey Green's orders, and the Inuit's attempt to desert Green for the second time since leaving MacMillan. As Green recorded the event, "I ran after him & fired the rifle into the air; He did not stop. I then shot him. I rejoin MacMillan as soon as storm abates. I have 8 dogs, sledge and provisions for 2 days."[2]

Green gave MacMillan a slightly variant account of the murder. Hoping to find better shelter closer inland, he wrote, Peeahwahto drove on with their only stove and a quart of oil. Green caught him by hard running. "Twice I found Peeahwahto trying to get away from me by leaving the trail. Watching my chance I quickly grabbed the rifle from the sledge I asked him where the

4. The Murder of Peeahwahto

igloo was. Starting out in the direction of his pointed arm I ordered him to follow closely behind me. Looking back a few minutes later I noticed that he had left the trail. I shot over his head. He did not stop so I shot him through the body. He fell back against the upstanders. As the dogs did not stop I thought that possibly he might still be alive so I shot again splitting his head open so that his brains fell out."[3]

After returning from the Arctic, Green published an account of his search for Crocker Land that ended with the murder. In describing the trip that he and Peeahwahto had made southwest of Axel Heiberg Land, Green wrote:

> He sullenly refused to go slowly. I took the rifle from its case and ordered him to follow me. Head down in the wind I did not know he had turned aside until his whip cracked. I cried for him to stop. Without looking around he urged his dogs onward. To make sure I fired into the air. His whip sang again. I pumped in my last cartridge, knelt, and shot for my life. He toppled drunkenly and rolled into the snow.[4]

So ends Green's telling on this occasion.

A comparison of the two versions is rewarding. MacMillan had given Green and Peeahwahto food for three days when they separated after return-

On the trip in search of Crocker Land, Fitzhugh Green encountered rough ice (American Museum of Natural History Library).

ing from the search for Crocker Land. When six days had elapsed, MacMillan, wondering where they could be, saw a black dot on the horizon. As it came nearer, MacMillan thought the approaching sledge must be Peeahwahto's. But where was Green? MacMillan ran along the ice foot to meet the sledge. The dogs were Peeahwahto's. As MacMillan was about to ask "Where's Green?" he saw the strange likeness of Green, who looked as if he had risen from the grave. "This is all there is left of your southern division," Green said. "What do you mean," MacMillan inquired, "Peeahwahto dead? Your dogs and sledge gone?" "Yes," Green replied, "Peeahwahto is dead; his dogs were buried alive, his sledge is under the snow forty miles away."[5]

As MacMillan wrote in his field notes, Green proceeded to tell MacMillan the story of how they were caught in a blizzard fifteen miles down the coast, made and crawled into a dugout, which was soon covered to a depth of fifteen feet. When the storm partly cleared, Peeahwahto said he was going home. Green's dogs and sledge were left under the snow and were never seen again. The men started back with one sledge. Green's feet were freezing so he could not ride. The dogs were going so fast he could not keep up with them. Peeahwahto tried twice to get away from Green, which would mean Green's death. So Green seized his rifle from the sledge and ordered Peeahwahto to follow him. Looking back, Green saw that he was not doing so but had turned to one side. Green fired over his head first to warn him. He did not stop, so Green shot him twice, once in the body and once in the head, splitting it open. He carried the body to Cape Thomas Hubbard and left it there. It was there now lying on the ground outside the door.[6]

In a later account Green elaborated on his killing of Peeahwahto. "When I fired at Peeahwahto," he wrote,

> there were no echoes.... As I stood there with empty, smoking rifle in my hand something of that gratification of sense held me. At last I tasted of pleasure for which I starved. A moment before I had faced the end of everything. Now I beheld the beginning. I had seen dogs, clothing, fuel, food, vanishing in the gloom ahead. Here they were—mine to keep, to drive, to wear, to burn, to eat. He that had loomed hostile and a deceit between me and safety lay now crumpled and inert in the unheeding snow.
>
> For once fate was balked. I gloated over my victory, not the man—he like myself was but a pawn in the game of the gods. But I feasted on the thought that fate had played to lose the piece which, measured by all men's standards, was of the two the more finished and mature. I had baffled misfortune. The feeling sent red gladness to my anaemic humor, feeble in the gloom of eight aching weeks....
>
> Perilous uncertainty lay before me. Certain danger lay behind. But the present was perfect, ecstatic. To prolong was my impulse. I laughed, not fiendishly, but because I was glad. Then the mood passed. I went over to the Eskimo. He lay face downward, unmoving, in the snow. The dogs ... whined as the scent of fresh blood,

human blood, excited in them a strange mixture of fear and passionate retching of their pinched stomachs."⁷

The king dog barked sharply and the team jumped, eager to get at the body, Green explained, but with the whip he drove them to their places. Action startled Green out of the lethargy into which the sad affair had driven him. His object had not been to take Peeahwahto's life but to save his own. His duty now was to the Inuit. Not without tenderness, he placed the body atop his load and set out for an igloo at the cape. The dogs did poorly with their new master, but Green finally stumbled on the igloo, which he had to rebuild. He dragged Peeahwahto in, ate a little dog pemmican, and kept wanting to say, "Peeahwahto, you lucky dog, it's all over for you. For me it's hundreds of miles of hell, with all the pain and misery of hell, and not one degree of its heat!" But he would not let himself say it. He was afraid of being afraid.

Green slept. When he awoke he glanced across to where another man should have been and met a horrible sight. "Warmth of Peeahwahto's head had melted snow underneath until he nodded my way," Green wrote. "His eyes were open, glaring and indignant, fixed upon me. Unable to endure the dead man's silent loathing, I seized his wooden shoulders, dragged him without, and hid the body behind an iceberg. Perhaps the wolves and foxes did not find it for several days. Made little difference."

All of this seemed gruesome, Green admitted, but he did not write to boast "morbid delight in a truly sorrowful experience." He wished to illustrate how little removed we are from the creatures we despise. "Grip a man's heart and his reactions are inarticulate protests against the unseen force which throttles him. Let the right combination of circumstances, edged by the pitiless elements, cut a man to the quick and he will turn savage by the very logic he once boasted was his certificate of culture."⁸

Green made a little tea and concentrated on his predicament. He had a four days' supply of food and was due to meet MacMillan between thirty and forty miles east. But a blizzard raged, he was weak, and he had to subdue his suddenly vicious dogs. The white fangs of a vicious little female had cut through his mitten and into his hand. Green tried to grip the scruff of her neck but stumbled and fell. Green saw the hunger lust of the team. With the strength of madness he twisted his arm clear, seized the bitch by her throat and hind quarters, lifted her over his head, and hurled her into the king's face—"a slight *lése majesté*." After a nap he found the weather clearing, but a heavy mist hung over the sea ice. The gale had torn loose the heavy pack. Between Green and the distant floes lay "a Stygian river of inky blackness, a wide lane of open water stretching east and west as far as I could see. Thirty-six hours longer on the Polar Sea and we should never have returned. Such a break-up could not freeze again so late in the year. Something—Someone was then on our side."⁹

Green felt forced to make haste in any weather rather than miss MacMillan. "The howl of a wolf was borne down to me as I crossed the bay east of Cape Thomas Hubbard, and caused me to shudder. Death was never an alarming possibility. But the idea of being *meat*, to be gnawed, goaded me to travel as only the wolf quarry can travel when the hungry-cry of the pack is in the air."¹⁰

About noon the next day Green rounded the last cape before rejoining MacMillan.

The two men were now ready to begin making their way back to Etah. MacMillan and Etookashoo outdid themselves to make Green comfortable. From their caribou cache they brought meat and a fresh head. Green "topped off a pemmican stew with frozen brains spooned like ice cream out of the natural cup." MacMillan asked Green if he felt he could go on. Green assented, and Etookashoo broke trail at a great pace. "No attempt was made to describe the truth of Peeahwahto's disappearance," Green wrote, "and probably the younger man [i.e., Etookashoo] concluded that the sooner out of this scrape the better." Green then observed, "Although the average Eskimo's imagination is rather an inelastic piece of mechanism, I have no doubt that our man had some anxious musings as he trudged the slow miles homeward."¹¹

MacMillan, Green, and Etookashoo then began their return to Etah, working their way to Schei Island and along Fosheim Peninsula, often traveling at night. Several days out, at a cache they found a box Ekblaw had left for them with chocolate, hash, and milk in it. Pressing on, in Beitstadt Fiord Etookashoo killed a seal. The party made a beautiful run to Payer Harbor, where they found a box with marmalade, cranberry sauce, chocolate, and canned fruit. Two Inuit brought fresh meat for the dogs. The men went from Payer Harbor to Etah in one march, arriving home on 21 May. "But," Green wrote, "we would rather have kept on traveling. That is real life."¹²

After describing the death of Peeahwahto, Green resumed his narrative. As he and MacMillan returned to their home base they had a perfect view of the white ranges of Axel Heiberg Land, which they now coasted for the first time. They camped for the night. The next day they met a stiff wind that narrowed into the white funnel of Eureka Sound. They went on to Schei Island, where they saw several herds of musk oxen. But they had enough meat, and with weak dogs it was more a question of speed than of stopping for a kill. On 7–8 May they covered something like seventy-five miles down the sound. A dog, "the original dog," attacked and fed upon one of Green's weak dogs, who had eaten Nucarpingwah's dog, which had in turn gnawed clean the bones of Etookashoo's dog, "and so on through the whole story to the original protoplasmic cannibal, toothless, even gumless, and manifestly

4. The Murder of Peeahwahto

without aims—yet was attacked and eaten by 'the original dog.'" As the party crossed Alexandra Fiord on the return to their home base, Green wrote, they caught their first sight of the Greenland coast. How far north they would be compelled to go in order to cross over no one knew. After additional trials, the expedition crossed the Sound and was on the Greenland shore, headed south for Etah and Borup Lodge.[13]

At Etah, on 21 May Dr. Hunt had sent out two Inuit to meet MacMillan and Green, giving them enough dogs to supply the return party if necessary. MacMilllan and Green arrived the following day. They had met the two Inuit sent out while making camp at Payer Harbor, and with plenty of dogs they came the rest of the way on the run. Etookashoo was with them. "Peeahwahto died at Cape Hubbard," Dr. Hunt was told. As he added, "On the return to Cape Thomas Hubbard, Green and Peeahwahto started south to find Sverdrup's record. It was on this trip that Peeahwahto was lost. I do not yet know the circumstances."[14]

MacMillan hastened to publish an account of his and Green's searching for Crocker Land. In concluding his two-part story, MacMillan wrote that when he ran across the ice foot to meet the sledge when he thought that Green and his Inuit were returning to meet him, he saw Peeahwahto's dogs but not Peeahwahto. But then he saw Green, who looked as if he had risen from the grave. Green said, "This is all there is left of your southern division." What do you mean, MacMillan, inquired, "Peeahwahto dead? "Yes, Peeahwahto is dead; his dogs were buried alive, his sledge is under the snow forty miles away." This spare description of the climax of the search for Crocker Land was designed to avoid alerting readers to the fact that Green had murdered Peeahwahto.[15]

In his report to the American Museum about his Arctic experience from 1913 to 1917, MacMillan related how he and Green together searched for Crocker Land and went their separate ways thereafter, but he avoids mention of the death of Peeahwahto. Noting his anxiety over Green's absence, he wrote that Green arrived after an absence of four days and that Green's experience in the storm had been similar to his own. Then, with no further reference to the murder, MacMillan proceeded to describe the return of the two men to Etah.[16]

Later, commenting on the murder in a book intended for the general reader, MacMillan wrote, "Green, inexperienced in the handling of Eskimos, and failing to understand their motives and temperament, had felt it necessary to shoot his companion." Here he presents the death as a simple necessity. But he adds, in indirect criticism of Green, "Peeawahto was a faithful assistant to Peary for more than two years, his last trip as one of the famous starvation party to the world's record of 87° 6' N. He had been my traveling companion from the first, and one of the best."[17]

The Aftermath

What are we to make of Peeahwahto's death and the response to it? MacMillan peremptorily dismissed it. Green felt great physical and mental pain as he tried to make sense of it and then moved on. We cannot so easily dismiss the matter. MacMillan and Green viewed themselves as products of an advanced civilization who were dealing with men of a primitive culture. Nevertheless, Peeahwahto's death was murder. Should the killer of an Inuit be accountable for his deed? Was the murder justifiable as an act of self-defense? Did brutal physical conditions have their counterpart in a brutal moral climate?

Dr. Hunt, who was at Etah when the search for Crocker Land took place, learned more about what had happened to Peeahwahto after MacMillan and Green returned to their base. "The story we had been told that he [Peeahwahto] had been killed in an avalanche was not true," Dr. Hunt wrote. "Green, having no understanding whatsoever of Eskimo mentality or language, had panicked and had shot him. He did not consider it murder. Peewahto was just a savage. It was necessary that no one know of this murder so long as we were in Greenland." Dr. Hunt would have to live with and care for "a man who had killed my friend." He found his anger hard to control, but guessed that he succeeded, because Green remained friendly with him. When Dr. Hunt learned that Peter Freuchen had written that Green killed Peeahwahto because Green wanted the Inuit's wife, Dr. Hunt said, "I don't know about that."[18]

Freuchen was familiar with the Polar North. Commenting on the difficulties MacMillan had in the search for Crocker Land, Freuchen wrote, "One of the Eskimos was killed, and this made a bad impression on the natives, especially as none of us accepted the weak explanation. Many of them came to ask me what tactics to pursue, and I was unable to advise them. The country was not officially in the possession of any power at that time. Knud [Rasmussen] and I had settled there without protection and, as a result, the upper hand ruled." According to Freuchen, the only satisfactory solution would have been to arrange a pension for the widow for as long as the children were in her care. But this was difficult for MacMillan to manage under the circumstances.[19]

After the search for Crocker Land ended, Freuchen wrote, the friction between the Americans at Etah worsened. Fitzhugh Green turned up in Umanak one day and asked if he might move in. Freuchen had no objection, especially since he brought along a great deal of food. Freuchen might have turned Green away had he known why Green left Etah. The reason was that his American colleagues treated him as an outcast "due to the fact that he had shot and killed Peeahwahto, an Eskimo he had taken along on a trip, in order to take over the man's wife." Freuchen, who had been told that Peeahwahto lost his life under an avalanche, once asked Green what had happened to his Inuit companion. Green turned pale and asked Freuchen never to mention the man's name. Green's reaction, Freuchen thought, meant that he had taken the man's tragic death to heart.[20]

Years later Freuchen learned the true story as revealed by MacMillan in his travel diaries. Once the truth was known, Denmark demanded reparation from the American government on behalf of the widow and children who had been left without support. In the meantime, Freuchen averred, "Green had won national fame as an aviator and was quite a hero." But something had happened in Thule that took care of the reparation demand. One of Peary's Inuit companions, Kudlooktoo, had become a Christian, and as soon as he was baptized he went to confession. He told the minister that, on return from the North Pole with Peary, he had shot and killed Professor Marvin in order to save the life of his cousin, whom Marvin wanted to leave alone to die on the ice because he was too weak to travel. As soon as it was known that Marvin had not drowned but had been killed by an Inuit, the American government "made a counterclaim and it was decided to let the Green case cancel the Marvin case." Freuchen, who related these details about the death of one Inuit and one American, added that "later Peeahwahto's widow married my father-in-law, and thus the international dispute was settled to mutual satisfaction."[21]

Freuchen's account is similar but not identical to other descriptions of these events. In justice, however, if there were two murders, they should both have been adjudicated properly. When the truth about the murder of Peeahwahto became known after members of the Crocker Land Expedition team returned to the United States, Dr. Hunt wrote, Green was on duty in the world war. He was exonerated, Hunt understood, "as having acted in self-defense, and ... the Danes refrained from making a stir about it because Kudlooktoo, converted to Christianity, had just confessed to having killed Marvin, an American on the Peary expedition to the North Pole, also apparently in self-defense. All involved deemed it well to play down both cases."[22]

Seeking Justice or Closure

There the matter seemed to rest. But it was not yet over. On 22 March 1921, at the direction of the Danish Minister of Foreign Affairs, C. Brun, a member of the Danish Legation in Washington, D.C., wrote to Charles Evans Hughes, the American Secretary of State, about the death of Peeahwahto. MacMillan, Brun observed, openly admitted that Green shot and killed Peeahwahto. (The reference is to MacMillan's book, *Four Years in the Arctic*, published in 1917.) Brun enclosed a report of the matter written by Knud Rasmussen. "This report," Brun added, "will be found to contain all the circumstances so far known of the case and to draw certain conclusions and outline certain claims based on justice and humanity and on the peculiar conditions of the life of the natives of Greenland." Having considered the case, the Danish Minister of Foreign Affairs concluded, as pointed out in Rasmussen's report, "it is highly to be regretted that Mr. McMillan should in his report have passed over the slaying of a human being as an occurrence of small importance, and that the Expedition should have taken no measure whatsoever to repair as far as possible the consequence of the act by providing for the widow and children of the man who was slain." It must be the duty of the Expedition, "who sent Mr. Green on the trip and must have been aware of Mr. Green's lack of knowledge of the Esquimaux," the Danish Minister asserted, "to make provision for the support of the dependent relatives of the slain man." This compensation should be paid in a lump sum as soon as possible. The Minister asked that the leader of the Expedition report and explain all the circumstances in which Peeahwahto was slain, since it was of the greatest importance for the Danish Administration and the Danish Mission among the Polar-Inuit that this unfortunate occurrence should be fully elucidated.[23]

When Knud Rasmussen came to the district in 1916 and heard about Peeahwahto's death, he was given the explanation that had been given to the Inuit and others earlier. He thought it was true until he met Green at Egedesminde and told him that Peeahwahto was his friend. He was interested in hearing the details connected with his death. "At my question," Ramussen added, "Mr. Green's face suddenly changed color, and in evident confusion he replied that this was a matter which Mr. McMillan had told the members of the expedition not to talk about."

Rasmussen regarded the answer as evidence of Green's mental condition, knowing that the winters in northern Greenland had absolutely ruined Green's nerves. Rasmussen knew Peeahwahto well. He believed that Peeahwahto was a man one could trust and who was ready to make sacrifices to help his companions. Thus Rasmussen had read MacMillan's report on the murder in *Four Years in the White North* with great consternation. The report was "brief and cynical, just as if there was only question of a dog, which was shot down and thus finished and done with. But a life is a life whether Esquimau or American." Perhaps some want to take refuge in the argument that this drama was played in "No man's land," where the laws of the white man do not reach. But the white man's responsibility follows him as far north as his work takes him, especially in the case of people who travel in the name of science."

It was only "common human law" that the Crocker Land Expedition be held responsible for what happened. Rasmussen felt "indignant and scandalized at the supercilious en-passsant way in which the murder of an Esquimau is spoken of in Mr. McMillan's book." He wanted MacMillan to give information on Peeawahto's death and the Expedition to take care of those of Peeahwahto's children who could not yet support themselves. Green was most certainly a nervous wreck when he acted and cannot be regarded as responsible for his act, but the expedition was responsible to Peeahwahto's nearest family. In a grandiose conclusion, Rasmussen depicted the Inuit who was shot by an American on an American expedition as "a veteran in the American struggle for the capture of the Northpole, a capture which has justly added to the splendor of the United States' contribution to geographic research."

On 12 April, the Danish Minister in Washington requested the good offices of the U.S. State Department in obtaining from the leader of the expedition "an engagement" to provide for the support of the five children of Peeahwahto together with a report of the circumstances in which he was slain. The request was also sent to the sponsors of the Expedition—the American Museum, the American Geographical Society, and the University of Illinois.

Days later the director of the American Geographical Society replied that the matter would be brought to the attention of its Board of Trustees when it met on 21 April. At the same time, David Kinley, the president of the University of Illinois, asked O.A. Harker, the University's legal counsel, for his opinion as to the University's responsibility, if any, concerning the incident.[24]

On 6 January 1921, in a letter to the Right Reverend Dean C. Schultz Lorenzen, Secretary of the Mission of the Cape York District in Greenland, Rasmussen wrote that MacMillan had told his Inuit companion that Peeahwahto, on coming back from the search for Crocker Land, had choked to death in an avalanche of snow. None of the Inuit believed this because Itukusuk, who had been present when Green returned and reported on the event to MacMillan, understood enough English to make it clear to him that Green had shot Peeahwahto.

On 12 May 1921, George H. Sherwood informed Fitzhugh Green, who was then in the United States, that the American Museum had received an inquiry from the State Department accompanied by documents from the Danish government requesting a report concerning the death of Peeahwahto and making a claim for the support of the five children of Peeahwahto. In replying to the State Department it was necessary for the museum to have from Green a full report in regard to this regrettable occurrence.[25]

On 27 June, President Osborn of the American Museum, replying to an inquiry from the Department of State, submitted four documents "relative to the death of an Eskimo named Piuvaitsuq [Peeawahto]." They included a copy of an extract from the diary of Green, a copy of an extract from the diary of MacMillan, a copy of the official report filed by Lt. Green with the Navy Department, and a copy of a 4 May 1921 report from MacMillan to Osborn, written in reply to Rasmussen's 6 January 1921 letter to the Right Reverend Dean C. Schultz Lorenzen. From these documents, Osborn declared, it is evident that Green acted in self-defense, and that so far as it was practicable, the Crocker Land Expedition, during its stay in Greenland, made amends for this unfortunate occurrence by providing for the family of the deceased Inuit. MacMillan reported that Peeawahto had threatened to desert his party when they were out on the Polar Sea, Osborn added, but when MacMillan ordered him to advance he did not carry out the threat. The American Museum regrets that Ensign Green felt obliged to act as he did, but it feels "that in the light of all the facts his action was justifiable and that the Expedition's responsibility to the Eskimo's relatives had been discharged."[26] Thus, on the flimsy basis that Osborn erected, the American Museum absolved itself of all responsibility for the murder. Nevertheless, the controversy dragged on into November. The Danish Legation in Washington, D.C., working through the Department of State, repeatedly requested that the American Museum and the American Geographical Society provide compensation or an indemnity for the maintenance of the dead man's children or an appropriate settlement of the matter.[27]

Freuchen on the Death of Peeahwahto

Peter Freuchen, an expansive author, left an account of the murder that merits attention. Although a young man, Freuchen wrote, Green was without a smile. He demonstrated his youth mainly in his need for women. He took a beautiful girl, Alakrasina, for his sleeping partner. She was the wife of Peeahwahto. Green took her without asking the permission of the husband, who would gladly have lent him his wife as a simple act of hospitality. Peeahwahto was good-natured and did not mind Green's lack of manners. Considerate, he went on many trips in order to leave Green alone with his wife, and only occasionally asked his wife to spend the night with him. Green became so obsessed by the beautiful Alakrasina that he would not even let the man visit his own wife.[28]

After returning from the search for Crocker Land, MacMillan arranged that the inexperienced Green and the peaceful Inuit whose wife he had stolen, went off together on that fateful trip. When MacMillan asked Green what had happened to Peeahwahto, Green answered calmly, "I shot him." MacMillan was upset and afraid that the Inuit would take revenge if they knew what happened, so the two men worked out a story to tell the Inuit. The version Freuchen heard was that the men were buried in their igloo by an avalanche. Green had dug his way out but Peeahwahto had suffocated in the snow. Though improbable, the story was accepted. As long as Green stuck to it and the Inuit's body was not found, there was no way of disproving it.[29]

Green was not the same after this experience, Freuchen wrote. He no longer cared for Alakrasina and did not get along with his fellow Americans. In the late spring he sent a messenger to Umanak asking if he might come and stay there for a while. Freuchen had no reason to refuse the request. Green went there and stayed for several months.

Once, when Freuchen asked Green what had happened with Peeahwahto, Green became nervous and begged Freuchen never to mention the incident—he could not bear thinking about it. Freuchen had the impression that Green was deeply upset because he had been unable to rescue his companion. Freuchen never referred to the matter again.

Weeks later, Freuchen received a letter from the inspector in Godhavn, the highest Danish authority in northern Greenland, saying that there were ugly rumors that one of the Americans with MacMillan had killed an Inuit. Was the story true or a groundless rumor?

The rumor had no foundation at the time, according to Freuchen, and as long as Green was a guest to Umanak, Freuchen and his Inuit wife did all they could to make him enjoy his visit. Although the Inuit disliked him intensely, Green was polite and friendly, and Freuchen did not become aware of his true nature until the day he departed.

Freuchen agreed to drive Green across Melville Bay to Upernivik, and as soon as they left Umanak Green announced that he was happy to leave that terrible place. During the many months spent there, he said that he had not met a single Inuit who was better than a dog. Freuchen reminded Green that he had been the guest of his Inuit wife for four months. Unbelievably rude, said Freuchen, Green replied that nothing could change his opinion of the natives.

At that time, Freuchen did not know that Green was a murderer. He thought that Green simply wanted to ease his conscience. He had let an Inuit companion die and tried to convince himself and others that the Inuit did not count for more than dogs. Months went by before Freuchen read the book MacMillan wrote about his expedition in which he quoted Green as saying "Sure, I killed that Eskimo in Eureka Sound. I had to shoot him because he refused to obey my orders!"[30]

The confession caused a sensation in Greenland. So far as known, no Inuit had ever been killed by a white person in that part of the world. When the story became known a request was made for compensation to Peeahwahto's widow and several children. But the claim for suitable compensation was met with an equally well-founded counterclaim, and it was tacitly agreed to let the two claims cancel each other.[31]

So we know that Fitzhugh Green shot and killed Peeahwahto. It remains to be seen how and to what extent the murder figured not only in the history of the expedition but also in the later life of Fitzhugh Green.

PART II

The Expedition and Scientific Research

5

The Expedition Party in the Arctic

In 1913, after President Henry Fairfield Osborn of the American Museum bade the polar explorers Godspeed, Edmund O. Hovey, chairman of the museum's Committee in Charge, became the manager of the expedition. Communication between the Arctic and America was slow and often impossible. Nevertheless, the expedition party adjusted to life in the North, and the men pursued research in their various specialties. Their life was not easy, but they coped with various vicissitudes confident that a relief ship would arrive at year's end and return them to America. Little did they then know, that was not to be.

Wireless communication between the museum and the expedition proved to be impossible. The Canadian government did not install its wireless station at Cape Wolstenholme in the summer of 1913 as planned, and the apparatus that Jerome Allen established near Etah was ineffective. So Hovey arranged with the Marconi Wireless Telegraph Company of Canada to relay messages. On 7 March he was able to send MacMillan a message via the company's station in Fogo, Newfoundland. In May he sent a message to Etah by the same way with notes for each party member from friends, family, and well wishers.

In April 1914, A.W. "Lucky" Scott of New York, a mining man and prospector who was trying to locate commercial values in the Arctic, offered to take mail and supplies to Etah during the summer without cost, since he was going there on an expedition. Later, he said that he could not take the mail and materials unless he was paid. Hovey thought that Scott would charge not more than $1000. Since there was no money in the Crocker Land account, he asked President Osborn to authorize the expenditure. Osborn approved, not to exceed $800 for foodstuff, pending the action of the Executive Committee, but $1000 for transportation seemed very high. Hovey assembled the items sent by relatives and friends of expedition members and purchased supplies to ship to the Arctic. Hovey informed Robert Peary that the museum was sending mail and supplies to Etah this summer and would be glad to include any message that Peary had for MacMillan. Since Scott may have been interested in examining the coal beds on Disco Island with a view to exploiting them commercially, Hovey informed him that H.L. Bridgman of the Brooklyn *Standard Union*, who knew these coal beds, would be glad to assist him. But the scheme fell through. In August, Hovey held everything accumulated with a view to sending it north the following year.

Knud Ramussen carried mail from Etah to Copenhagen, which was then forwarded to New York. Hovey was pleased to receive reports sent by this means, but he should have liked longer letters from MacMillan. "An article from you for publication in Harper's Magazine," he wrote MacMillan, "would have been most acceptable to the Magazine and most helpful to the Crocker Land Expedition." The museum craved favorable publicity.[1]

Hovey was glad to know that MacMillan was carrying out the expedition's plans. The museum hoped that a comprehensive preliminary report of what the scientists of the expedition had done would be received by early fall. The men should have the principal portion of their report telegraphed to the *New York Tribune* from the nearest telegraph or wireless station. The museum was expecting the expedition to stay in the North through the field season of 1916. Hovey asked MacMillan to express to his Inuit helpers the museum's high appreciation for their faithful service in MacMillan's undertaking.[2]

President Osborn received letters from expedition members assuring him that they were not only in good health and spirits but were "working like one man" with MacMillan as leader "for the success of this great expedition." Osborn had felt the "greatest confidence in the unity and spirit" of the party ever since the memorable farewell dinner at the University Club, when he had an opportunity of judging each man individually. MacMillan's report of the organization and work done from the time of their arrival at Etah to 10 January 1914 impressed Osborn favorably. By this time you have made your long journey, Osborn wrote MacMillan in June 1914, and have returned "either with the full accomplishment or with the report that the land is not there." The continuation of your work depends more or less on "the actual presence of the Island or small Continent of Crockerland." If the objective has been reached, you will plan to return there next spring to continue your observations. Besides this, the work to the southwest of Cape Thomas Hubbard and to the north of Parry Islands remains to be done. Osborn expected the men to remain in the north during the field season of 1916; the museum would send a ship for them during that time. The letters Osborn had received from expedition members seemed to express a unanimous desire to carry out the original plans in full. "I feel very strongly," Osborn added, "that this representative American Expedition should bring back a substantial extension of our scientific knowledge of the regions to the west and southwest, even if the main objective has not been reached or should be found not to exist." *The New York Tribune* had published full reports of the expedition's work, and other newspapers had reproduced the principal movements of the expedition. "Those of your party who are Progressive in politics will be disappointed to learn that there is a strong tide steering towards the Republican party," Osborn wrote, "and results in the States of California and Pennsylvania point towards a great Republican reaction and subsidence of the Progressive Movement."[3]

President Osborn was impatient to hear the results of MacMillan's winter's work. "I trust that you are keeping a very full journal and diary from which newspaper reports may be prepared as soon as you get into communication with our part of the world.... Matters which may seem small to you, owing to your long experience, are of very great interest to the public, and we shall especially try to furnish the *Tribune* with interesting material, in response to their cooperation with the expedition." Osborn added, "I have not yet made a very determined effort to raise the large amount of money necessary to finance the return of your expedition, feeling that your success, or even news of your efforts, will be a great stimulus to our group of friends including the Crocker Land supporters."[4]

Fitzhugh Green had given Osborn a great deal of information as to MacMillan's relation with the Inuit and his ability to assemble a strong, able body of men to conduct the expedition northward. Osborn replied that Green's tributes were most generous, and "the continued reports of the friendship and goodwill prevailing among the Crocker Land men are delightful reading." Osborn was not surprised that Green and Ekblaw had been chosen to accompany MacMillan northward. All had done their very best, and whether or not you have succeeded is really less important than the fact that "you have made a great effort and have let no opportunity go for want of intelligence, foresight or courage."[5]

Two years in the Arctic was "life intensified," Green reported, a situation that every man should be granted before he is thirty. He would return far better prepared to get the best out of life if only because now he knew now what the best is. He described his travels of the last winter and spring, snowshoeing and driving a dog-team for hundreds of miles. At home in Etah, the five university men and two others had a large and well-chosen library. They kept house in turn, and with the summer had four beautiful months in which the sun never went below the horizon. "The dead land comes to life and gives us grassy spots full of daisies and buttercups where we may go and dream of the south. Can't you see why it is worthwhile!"[6]

It gave Green great pleasure to inform Hovey that MacMillan had succeeded in what he had set out to do. Green then described the search for

Crocker Land which he and MacMillan had made. His detailed account ends when he and MacMillan separated. Green makes no reference to the murder of Peeahwahto.[7]

Life at Etah

In early 1914 Ekblaw was confined to Borup Lodge waiting to learn whether Dr. Hunt would have to amputate part of his foot.[8] While waiting, he browsed upon the "rich heather of our excellent library."[9] He read volumes of the *Atlantic Monthly*, "that genuine aristocrat among magazines"; Bergson's *Creative Evolution*, "one of the profoundest books of all time despite its modernity"; *The Spirit of American Literature* by Macy; *The New Freedom* by Woodrow Wilson; *My Study Fire*, Hamilton Wright Mabie's happiest book; and Whitman's *Leaves of Grass*, the "free, strong, pure message that the clean of mind and deed hear as the message of the free, strong, pure Renaissance that we expect."[10]

Ekblaw's effusion was an expression of the Progressive moment in American thought and culture. His reading shaped his sense of humankind's possibilities, widespread at the time. Henri Bergson's book, published in English translation in 1911, "that philosophic masterpiece which is crystallizing all the thought of our time," suggested that evolution is motivated by an élan vital, humanity's natural creative impulse. John A. Macy's book surveyed nineteenth-century American authors as well as William James and Henry James. The subtitle of Woodrow Wilson's book was *A Call for the Emancipation of the Generous Energies of the People*. Hamilton Wright Mabie, an essayist and a member of the Author's Club, was well regarded.[11]

Optimism about humanity's prospects was dealt a blow with the outbreak of the world war. In his letter Ekblaw apologized for his expansiveness. He had only recently discovered that writing to friends was a passion that he indulged. His view of life had been broadened by his stay in the calm, vast Northland and its elemental conditions of life. The primitive customs of the Inuit, Ekblaw wrote, "so primeval and yet so sturdily harmonious with the environment which nature has provided them, are almost a revelation to one who has been obedient to the conventions that civilization imposes. They have given me food for mature deliberation and thought. Surely, even life is a matter of geography as truly as conscience and morals."[12] Eblaw's experience among the Inuit was widening his mental horizon.

Although the least disposed of the party to find pleasure in killing, Ekblaw had been the most fortunate in bringing in big game. Two big polar bears and five musk oxen had fallen to his rifle recently. The two finest musk oxen skins that he brought back from Ellesmere Island he hoped to see

5. The Expedition Party in the Arctic

Elmer Ekblaw, Etah, Greenland, 1915. Ekblaw's frozen feet prevented him from participating in the search for Crocker Land. He recuperated at the expedition's house in Etah, which had a considerable library. Ekblaw loved to read (American Museum of Natural History Library).

mounted "in the museum of my Alma Mater, the University of Illinois, sometime, for then I shall feel recompensed for the pains and hardship of getting them back." The men of the expedition had needed the bearskins for clothing and the musk oxen for meat. "I was not reluctant to shoot the bears; for the musk-oxen, a vanishing race, I felt genuinely sorry, but Necessity in this Northland is very stern, very insistent, so I think I was justified."[13]

Ekblaw wished that he could carry back some of the "vast solemnity of this wonderful North—the calm serenity, the naked 'elementaliness' of this world-old waste." It made him realize what the ends of the earth seemed like. He wished the world to understand the "lure of the long, lone trail, so cold under the brilliant constellations of the north, so dazzling under the low-slanting rays of the Arctic sun.... Fancy what it is like to be all alone far out on the steel-black ice at Arctic midnight, keeping your course true by Arcturus –under Great Bear it means—or by Vega, your runners singing a wild eerie song, your dogs pit-patting speedily on and on into the darkness that lies ahead; always a great silence, always a great cold, always great dangers attending your way; and yet nothing daunted, never thinking of the silence, or the cold, or the dangers, though ever sensing them, I found myself, often, breaking into the fierce old saga-songs of my Thor-worshiping ancestors that my father taught me before I even learned to speak English, songs that somehow seemed to challenge the North, to have the rhythm of elemental things."[14] As soon as his foot healed he would start on a long sledge journey along the coast of Melville Bay to make a geological reconnaissance and would not return until summer was well on its way.[15]

When MacMillan returned to Etah after searching for Crocker Land, he found that Ekblaw and Tanquary were at North Star Bay with Peter Freuchen. MacMillan was getting the power boat provisioned to run to Oomanoose to bring them back. Since returning to Etah, MacMillan had been busy with birds, eggs, flowers, and photography. He had prepared thirty-eight skins of seventeen species of birds, had blown about five hundred eggs, had taken and developed about a thousand photos, and had made prints of about two hundred. He was sending some of them to Hovey and giving some to the boys for their parents, wives, and sweethearts. Meanwhile, they were caching meat for the next winter, since their success depended on the condition of their dogs.[16]

"Fitz has been rating the chronometers," MacMillan added, "doing some magnetic work, and making a survey of the harbor. Hunt is in his kayak most of the time hunting and is a crack-a-jack. Allen is working like a nigger on wireless. Has not given up yet in getting a message. Have today finished carrying the whole equipment to an island at the mouth of the harbor. Shut in as we are by the big hills he thinks that the aerial waves may be absorbed or reflected back to the wires. Will build a new house out there large enough to shelter the equipment and two men and will fly kites for the aerial. May be a good sub-meteorological station. Allen is not a strong man and needs to be watched or he will overwork."[17]

They had plenty of everything, so Hovey should not worry about them. As for the next year, Rasmussen had forestalled them on the ice cap. A trip by them to the ice cap, as originally planned, would be a waste of energy and equipment. Peary Channel has possibilities that might be considered. The Lake Hazen region should be further explored. The Mary Minturn River district we know nothing about. But the greatest attraction was southwest of Ellef and Amund Ringnes Land. No one had been there for sixty years; much work remained to be done. It was a long hard trip, but through a game country, which means everything.[18]

The expedition party was planning to go home next summer, MacMillan wrote in August 1914, as their work would be done. A ship came every year to North Star Bay for Rasmussen from Copenhagen; Hovey might make arrangements to have the party return in that way. After his 1913 experience, MacMillan would hesitate before chartering a Newfoundland ship or crew. The crew were drunk most of the time, MacMillan added, and stole. "Consult Captain Comer about a ship." The expedition party would have everything packed and ready for home by 15 August 1915. He hoped that Hovey could come up; "we will all be glad to see you."[19] Little did he know then how such plans would be thwarted or that Hovey would be a burden.

In August 1914 MacMillan wrote Robert Peary, whom he knew and admired, describing the expedition's work in Crocker Land. "Coming so soon after the controversy in which you received so much unjust criticism and following Rasmussen's report on the Peary Channel," MacMilllan began, "it hurt very much to be obliged to deny the existence of this new land." MacMillan went on to describe some highlights of his year in the Arctic. Crossing the sound on the way to Crocker Land in February 1914, he wrote, Ootah, Sipsoo, and other Inuit declared that the salt in the pemmican was responsible for the diarrhea among the dogs and the apparent weakness of all; they would all die in a few days and we would be obliged to walk home. How much of this to believe MacMillan did not know, as Sipsoo had the mumps and did not want to go on, "and Ootah had declared before we started that he would get square with you and me and all the other white men for alleged and imaginary wrongs done him in the past. He has done so much talking that I have refused to give him anything. He is a bad article; he has been mixed up in two or three woman scrapes, and without a doubt he shot Wee-shark-obsee. He and Mee-ne [i.e., Mene Wallace] are planning to sledge down the west side and reach America! But this I did know that I had quitters and must get rid of them at once so immediately turned back for Etah."

Of the Inuit, Minnick [i.e., Mene] and Tauchingwah, who deserted when climbing the ice steps of the glacier, he wrote, "Was glad to see the former go as he is a d--- poor thing, neither Inuit nor white. Is going back to the states and has schemed to get money from Mrs. Jesup. If he ever does reach New York she should be warned against him as he is in league with a sharper there who was responsible for much that came out in the papers just before we left in 1908."[20]

MacMillan then recounted the fruitless search for Crocker Land. Returning to Cape Thomas Hubbard, he and his Inuit started north while Green and his Inuit went south. "When Green rejoined me four days later, he was alone and looking like a ghost. They had been buried alive by drifting snow. His dogs were never seen again. How Peeahwahto lost his life I cannot tell you for certain reasons." What were the reasons? The laws of established societies had no force in the Arctic, MacMillan knew, and he decided not to talk about the murder.

Arctic Research

After searching for Crocker Land, expedition members pursued scientific research. The geographical activity originally planned included an expedition to the summit of the ice cap of Greenland, the exploration of Ellesmere Island, work to the north of the Parry Islands, the collection of data and specimens in various branches of science, cooperation with the U.S. Weather Bureau, and research with a Canadian station which was to be erected in the Hudson Bay district.[21] In mid–April 1914, MacMillan, about to leave Etah to lay down cairns at six points on the Greenland coast for Ekblaw, put Green in charge of headquarters, instructing him to secure from the Inuit whatever he thought would add to their scientific collection and to keep the work shop tidy.[22]

Peter Freuchen had gone to Etah to meet MacMillan and Green on their return from Crocker Land. While there he gained the impression that there was little harmony at Etah. Ekblaw and Tanquary seemed eager to get away, so Freuchen invited them to come to Thule and stay through the summer as his guest. He assured them that he had ample food for their needs. The opportunity to study the geology and biology of the unglaciated region lying about Wolstenholm Sound seemed so good that they accepted Freuchen's offer. Dr. Hunt, whom MacMillan had left in charge of the station while he was away, insisted that it was their duty to go.[23] Ekblaw's foot was healed when he and Tanquary left on 15 May. MacMillan was not pleased when he returned to Etah and found that they were gone. He did not approve of men deserting the station in his absence.[24]

When Ekblaw and Tanquary in a train of eleven dog-sledges left Etah, the midnight sun was two weeks old; travel was easy and pleasant. Just south of Cape Alexander they met a party of thirteen sledges, northward bound. The result was probably one of the largest groups of dogs, sledges, and Inuit gathered at one time in that part of Inuit-land. Ekblaw and Tanquary stayed there for almost half a day, boiling coffee, walrus meat, seal meat, and whatever else the sledges provided. Everybody was happy and loath to proceed. The assembly broke up only when the dogs became so unruly that a general mix-up threatened.

The party stopped a few days at Nerky, where most of the Inuit tribe was assembled for the spring walrus hunt. From there they went by the outside route around Cape Parry, stopping for a day at Keatek, where the first pair of snow buntings appeared from the Southland. The ice being generally good, they made rapid progress to Umanak or North Star Bay. Except for a violent blizzard that forced them to build snow houses near Cape Parry as a shelter from the storm, they arrived there without incident.

As they drove up to the trading station they met Sechmann Rosbach, a catechist or teacher, with his family and a number of Inuit from Danish Greenland. Sechmann, a South Greenlander with both Danish and Inuit ancestry, was employed in Rasmussen's trading station. His childhood's happiest times were of days playing with Kurt Rasmussen. Ekblaw and Tanquary did not then anticipate that Sechmann would save them from starvation before the summer was over. Freuchen established them in his house and they made themselves as comfortable as the limited facilities permitted. They had a little misgiving when Freuchen told them that during his absence the Inuit had eaten nearly all of his provisions and had made way with all of his coffee, sugar, and tinned goods. They felt that they could live on meat and blubber if need be, never dreaming that in a land where game was relatively abundant they should ever lack meat.

The days passed pleasantly. Hunting was apparently poor, and it was difficult to get meat from the Inuit. The visitors made serious inroads upon the few supplies they had brought from Etah, and they made no particular effort to save anything, relying upon Peter's assurance that an abundance of meat would be available when summer arrived. By 1 June, less than a month after their arrival, most of their tinned supplies were gone, even though they had dispatched several sledges to Etah for more.

The trading post of Freuchen and Rasmussen, at North Star Bay, was a center for many activities. Rasmussen bought fur pelts from the natives and sold them to Americans, and both men were hosts for assorted visitors. Photo taken 18 July 1916 (American Museum of Natural History Library).

The plans of the scientists included the reconnaissance of Melville Bay; a study of the repopulation of a once-glaciated nunatak by the biota of the coastal regions; a study of the life and geology of a lake and its unglaciated shores lying far within the ice cap; and as thorough and extensive an exploration of this region as time and facilities permitted.[25] Ekblaw and Tanquary pursued their respective sciences zealously. Almost every day they were out on long tramps over the rough country back of the station or sledging to some place about the Sound. Birds were numerous, the vegetation relatively luxuriant, and the geology varied. Of the 122 plants listed by "Simons and Porsild" as possibly growing here, Ekblaw found at least 95.[26] Ekblaw catalogued thirty-five birds and studied some very little known ones. He found the nest, never before found, and collected and banded the young of the Knot, *Tringa Canutus*. He studied the nesting habits of *Lobipes lobatus* and the summer history of *Plectreophenax nivalis nivalis*. He also did some good work in geology. Tanquary found the region well worth an entomologist's research.

The two explorers collected insects of the order Collembola that consisted of eight species. Although none of these species were new, all but *Orchesella cincta* were described and illustrated in a report that was printed and distributed in 1919. Justus W. Folsom, the author of the report, was on the University of Illinois faculty. The expedition brought back the little-known *Onychirus groenlandicus* and the interesting *Tetracanthella wahlgreni*, and added four species to the faunal list of Greenland.[27]

By late July the summer was passing. The birds were leaving and the burden of the botanical work—becoming acquainted with all the floristic of the region—was over. Ekblaw had done all he could in geology and was ready to leave as soon as a ship arrived. He had enjoyed the work at Thule. He found the glad, free life there, without restraint of custom, rule or schedule, very pleasant, and the rich field for scientific research, though not offering all the possibilities of Grant Land and Ellesmere Land, had kept him busy and interested enough to prevent his becoming homesick.[28]

However, in late May Ekblaw had had an attack of snow-blindness when he went for a seal-hunt with Mene Wallace, "the New York Eskimo celebrity."[29] They hunted steadily for over thirty hours, using no sunglasses and not fearing snow-blindness. When they finally made camp, they hunted ptarmigan, finding several flocks. After seal meat for lunch they started home. Ekblaw's eyes were heavy and tired, but he thought nothing of it until almost halfway home. Coming out of Grenville Bay and turning up Wolstenholme Sound toward North Star Bay, Ekblaw began to feel sharp pain in his eyes and his sight became blurred. The pain increased and his eyes became so bloodshot that what little he could see looked red. Soon after arriving at the station late in the afternoon, he went to bed. By midnight Ekblaw was almost raving mad with the pain. He called Tanquary and Freuchen for help. For nearly three days they dropped cocaine into his eyes at frequent intervals and gave him occasional morphine hypodermics. Whenever the effect of the drugs waned, the pain became excruciating. Ekblaw thought he would never regain his sight. But the pain finally abated and he began to see again. In a few days his eyes were clear and apparently as strong as ever.

Before Ekblaw recovered, Freuchen decided that he would leave for a bear hunt on Melville Bay and get some supplies he had cached at Cape Seddon. He had proposed this trip a month earlier but had postponed going. Now Freuchen departed with two Inuit, and Ekblaw and Tanquary had trouble in subsisting. Their supplies were gone, their Inuit were short of meat, and they had no dogs with which to go hunting. Mene Wallace helped them by killing occasional seals. Finally, they accepted Sechmann's invitation to share the mission station with him. His wife arranged one of the largest rooms in the station for them. They moved in, and for the remainder of their time at North Star Bay were most comfortably situated.

Freuchen returned from his bear-hunt about mid-June. He stayed at his house a few days and then went to Saunders Island, ostensibly to get eider eggs, taking with him the few remaining supplies in the house. Ekblaw and Tanquary had previously realized that they could not depend on Freuchen for assistance. Peter apparently meant well, "but he shed responsibility as a seal sheds water."[30]

So the Americans were thrown upon Sechmann's bounty. Though "only an Eskimo," he proved to be a gentleman and true friend. He shared his food with them, hunted every day, and was never sullen, discouraged, or angry. Many times the visitors were without food in his house for days at a time, but his hospitality and kindness never changed. In Ekblaw's view, "he measured up to a high standard as a man and as a Christian. Many a white man would not have been so truly hospitable and generous."[31]

But the shortage of food worried them. Starvation stared them in the face. During the summer conditions grew worse and worse and then critical. Sledging to Etah was impossible after early June; they had to wait until relief came by boat. They nearly wore out their field glasses watching the horizon near the sound for sight of a ship. The strain on their stomachs was hardly worse than the strain on their tempers. Irritable, sensitive, and quarrelsome, the two Americans were hardly on speaking terms for a week.

When it first became evident that they faced a food shortage. Ekblaw and Tanquary took stock of what they had, which included part of a small tin of prunes. They counted the prunes and concluded that if a relief ship reached them by August, they could make the prunes last if they each ate four a day. So after their long daily tramps, they brewed tea, drank it without sugar or milk, since they had neither, and ate their prunes. Tanquary gathered the seeds, took them out to a big flat rock, cracked them, and ate the kernels. They ate their last prune almost two weeks before relief came.

The only untoward event of the summer was Ekblaw's near-drowning. On the last day of June he was returning from Saunders Island over a route used safely two days earlier. In the interval a warm sun and high tides had rotted the ice. Ekblaw had to pick his way carefully among the pools of open water and thin ice. At a treacherous reach he thought he saw a long stretch of good going between two icebergs about a hundred yards apart. He started across and had just about reached the middle when everything—Ekblaw, his dogs, and his sledge—fell into the water. He thought his time had come. His king-dog, a big, shaggy, white fellow with Newfoundland blood, did not give up. Finally, with Ekblaw's help, the dog got to the edge of pool, and so too Ekblaw.

The trading station fur-house was one of the most interesting sights at North Star Bay. When Ekblaw and Tanquary were there it was hung with about 3,000 blue-fox skins in bunches of fifty, graded according to color, and 300 white skins in bunches of fifty. "The soft, glossy, fluffy furs ready for market," Ekblaw exclaimed, "were wealth and luxury that a queen might have desired to add to her wardrobe."[32] Before the summer was over the furs ceased to interest the visitors. They wanted to get away.

MacMillan suspected that all was not quite well at Umanak, so on 9 August, with the harbor free of ice, he headed for North Star Bay in the *George Borup*, their thirty-foot power boat. At the village of Nerkre, six hours along the way, his party found six tupiks inhabited by twenty-two people, "all of whom, ill-clothed, dirty, and greasy, were in marked contrast to our hair-combed, face-washed, cloth-clad, cigar-smoking Inuit. The change brought about by a year's contact with white men was hardly credible." Skirting the shore below Cape Parry, the rescuers passed but a few yards from the hut at Booth Inlet erected by the retreat party from Kane's *Advance*, where they had been locked in the ice of Rensselaer Harbor. These men, MacMillan wrote, lacked the moral strength to stand by their leader when hardships came. They preferred the risks of a southward journey in two small boats rather than remain for another winter. But at last, confronted by the consequences of their poor judgment, they returned to the ship to be fed and administered to by Kane and those who had remained loyal.[33]

MacMillan arrived at North Star Bay on 12 August. From the crest of the divide back of the station Ekblaw saw the Danish colors waving from the flagstaff of a ship, and in the little bay he saw the *George Borup* lying at anchor. He hurried down the mountain toward her. Dr. Hunt and Jot Small met Ekblaw in a whaleboat at the shore and took him to the motorboat. After Ekblaw had eaten a can of pears, he and Tanquary ate buckwheat cakes as fast as Jot Small baked them. They ate a hundred, Jot insisted, Ekblaw taking the lion's share.

5. The Expedition Party in the Arctic

Except for near-starvation, Ekblaw and Tanquary found the summer at North Star Bay pleasant enough. But they were glad to get away. They gave Sechmann Rosbach all that could be spared from the motorboat, packed their equipment and put it aboard the *George Borup*. Then MacMillan gave the signal to start. Without regret that the summer was over, they were soon back at headquarters once more.[34]

The rewards of their visit were abundant. They sent the American Museum a number of precious *tringa canutus* eggs, and Ekblaw had found a hundred and two varieties of flowers in the North Star Bay area.

Freuchen watched the *George Borup* disappear with a great sense of loss. It had been a rare treat for him to live with the Americans and to learn about America. Ekblaw was much interested in college life, Freuchen observed, especially intramural activities. He had been the editor of his college newspaper and still received copies of it. Freuchen tried to read them, but even when he could read the English he could not understand what was meant. At any rate, he corrected his earlier impression of "Americans as rather wild men whose favorite pastime was training horses and shooting off revolvers in saloons."[35]

By October Ekblaw and Tanquary were back at Etah. Ekblaw spent several weeks shooting walrus for dog meat, while Tanquary spent a fortnight hunting caribou near Rensellaer Harbor. Life went on, and the men began preparing for the next season. Ekblaw's new komatik (sledge) was being constructed. He intended to name it *Polaris* after the star and the polar exploration ship commanded by the ill-fated Charles Francis Hall. Ekblaw had called his former sledge Vega after the well-beloved star of Scandinavians and the brave ship in which Nordenskold made his memorable voyage.[36]

Ekblaw then described the plans for the next season. MacMillan and Green with two Inuit would cross Ellesmere Island, turn southward into Eureka Sound, and push on to the unexplored reaches of Sverdrup Islands. Time permitting, they would push on to the Parry Islands and return by way of Hill Cate, Jones Sound, and the east coast of Ellesmereland.

Ekblaw anticipated for himself a far richer field in another direction. He would accompany MacMillan and his party to Bay Fiord, study the geology of that region (whose limestones were rich in fossils and where a coal seam eighteen feet thick outcropped near the base of one of the cliffs), and then turn northward into Eureka Sound to explore Greely and Canon Fiords, the Lake Hazen Valley, and the east coast of Grinnell Land. He outlined in detail a journey that he would take with two Inuit, during which he would be gone three months and would travel over 1,000 miles. Tanquary with his two Inuit would come to Ekblaw's relief as Ekblaw's party returned on the east coast in May, and Dr. Hunt with two Inuit would go southward to the support of MacMillan's party. Ekblaw admitted that the results might vary considerably from the original design, but in fact he had outlined an expedition he took the following year.[37]

MacMillan the Ornithologist

MacMillan regarded the bird life as one of the great surprises of the Northland. He found many ornithological specimens in the territory he covered, and combined with those Ekblaw and Tanquary gathered they had a grand collection. The big burgomaster, or glaucous gull (*Larus hyperboreus*), seemed to be part of the area. With outstretched wings he was fully conscious of his power to secure subsistence and to battle against the wind and snow. The remains of black guillemots, ptarmigan, and eider ducks testified to the appetite, strength, swiftness, and aggressiveness of this bird, the first to come and the last to go each season. Another white bird, the gyrfalcon (*Falco islandius*), fearless, aggressive, and the swiftest of all, was the king of Northern bird-land. The chief characteristic of the sea pigeon or Mandt's guillemot (*Cepphus manditi*) was vivacity. Dabbling, diving, and perking their heads, these sprightly birds were found in every pool and all along the edge of the ice. The sea pigeon remained in the open waters of Smith Sound throughout the dark winter night, seemingly the only animate thing in that frozen world outside of the dogs and the men of the expedition. The northern eider duck (*Somateria mollissima borealis*), each of which weighed three and a half pounds, and a single egg of which weighed three and a half ounces, was of considerable food value. Incredible numbers of these birds arrived at Etah about 13 May, dotting the waters, the edge of the ice, and the surrounding islands.

The men once gathered 4,000 fresh eider duck eggs in a few hours on one small island. Cached beneath the rocks, away from the rays of the distant sun, these "golden nuggets" were appreciated during the long winter months. MacMillan and his colleagues also found many brant (*Branta bernicia*) on Sutherland Island near Cape Alexander and upon islands north of Etah. The brant's nest, containing from four to six white eggs, resembled that of the eider. And yet the true representative of the bird life of the Arctic was the dovekie or little auk (*Alle alle*). It meant so much to the Smith Sound native. As numbers of black-and-white bodies wheeled out from the talus-covered cliffs into the fiord, their breasts reflected the rays of the sun and they resembled a swarm of bees. Inuit women and children, anticipating a feast, swept the air with nets, often gathering ten or twelve birds with one sweep. The Inuit ate many of these birds raw on the spot, and they cached thousands, uncleaned, for midwinter feasts.[38]

In *Four Years in the White North* MacMillan included an appendix on ornithology in which he gave the scientific name and the English name of thirty-five birds. He added to the entries details about where and when the birds bred, which ones he had seen, their nests and their eggs, what they fed on, and the length of their season in the Far North. Two entries well illustrate his catalog. His entry number 14 reads:

> *Sterna paradisaea.* Arctic tern. Sea-swallow. Inuit name, Emuckkotailya.
> I found this species nesting on the northern shore of Grant Land on July 7, 1909. Lat. 82° 33′ N. Nest contained one egg. Very common in vicinity of Etah; flocks continually passing north and south. Breeds extensively at head of Inglefield Gulf and at North Star Bay.

MacMillan's entry number 23 reads:

> *Tringa canutus.* Knot. The robin snipe. Beach robin. Gray-back. Red-breasted sandpiper. Ash-colored sandpiper. Inuit name, Ting-may-tée-a. Very common on eastern and western shores of Smith Sound as far north as 82° 30′. Two nests containing three eggs each found by Polar Peary Expedition on July 1, 1909, at Cape Sheridan. Two nests of three and four eggs found by Crocker Land Expedition at North Star Bay in June 1917. Nest a slight depression in soil on rolling ground about one mile from the sea.[39]

Ekblaw the Botanist

While in the Arctic, Ekblaw studied its natural history. His descriptions of the plant life of northwest Greenland are both charming and valuable scientific documents. He found a relatively luxuriant vegetation in northwest Greenland between the glaciers of Melville Bay on the south and the Humboldt Glacier on the north. Within these limits he collected over one hundred and twenty-five species of vascular plants. In the summer, he wrote, after the snow disappears and before killing frosts come, when the warmest noonday temperature is never higher than sixty degrees, the rocky slopes and ledges are dotted with brilliant blossoms or carpeted with low, soft growths of grass or sedge. The plants are adapted to make the most of the twenty-four hour sunlight that shines upon them and to survive a blanket of snow if it does not last too long.[40]

The climate of northwest Greenland is insular in character, much milder than most lands so far north because the strong tides and currents in Smith Sound keep open water along the shore or not far away, usually throughout the year, and open water means warmer, moister air. This climate is the principal reason why the vegetation is relatively so luxuriant. That the flowering plants succeed so well is also because the sun shines twenty-four hours of every day. Even with this favorable climate and continuous sunlight, the vegetation must be fitted to endure the long frozen period and the destructive changes from warmth to blighting cold. The plants that respond to these conditions are usually low creeping or tufted forms with tough, hard tissue, and nearly all are perennials.

Some of the plants that constitute the vegetation of northwest Greenland are widely and generally distributed. The purple saxifrage (*Saxifraga oppositifolia*) grows, and the Arctic poppy (*Papaver radicatum*) flourishes. The alpine chickweed of the north (*Cerastium alpinum*) and the Kentucky blue grass (*Poa pratensis*) are common. The pretty little Arctic heather (*Cassiope tetragona*) and the mountain avens (*Dryas integrifolia*) are perhaps the most numerous plants of the region. They seemed to be able to grow almost everywhere.

Ekblaw found many widely scattered plants. Of several species he discovered a single station or collecting place. Growing on a little gravel slope just west of Borup Lodge, he came upon *Androsace septentrionalis*, a delicate, inconspicuous little flower never before recorded from Greenland. In 1898, Ekblaw observed, Simons, the noted Swedish botanist, when traveling along this coast with Sverdrup's expedition, had visited the delta on which the Crocker Land Expedition built their house, and they must have passed over the path beside which Ekblaw found this little plant and also a beautiful, luxuriantly growing fern, *Dryopteris fragrans*. That these two plants had eluded Ekblaw's careful search illustrated how easily even a specialist might fail to notice some of the small plants of the North.

To illustrate how a plant might escape discovery, Ekblaw cited his experience at North Star Bay throughout the summer of 1914 when he lived at the little mission station there, studying the vegetation of the large area of ice-free land lying about Wolstenholme Sound. Ekblaw had collected numerous plants and had helped Tanquary collect insects and bugs from the small bog that lay a few feet from the front door. Ekblaw thought that he had observed carefully every plant that grew in the bog, but when he spent the summer of 1916 at North Star Bay, he found there, growing in profusion and in full bloom, the little red-stemmed, red-leaved *Montia lamprospermum*, which he had eagerly sought in 1914 without success. North Star Bay was the best place in the region to study plants. Within half a mile of the station, Ekblaw found eighty plants. The habitats were so varied and the general conditions so favorable that it was a botanist's paradise. It was also a splendid place in which to make a careful study of the much-discussed *Drabae*; almost every northern form of this genus was found there in abundance and in confusing variation.

Ekblaw found the study of plant association and plant societies in this region fascinating. A slight change in the quantity of one factor produced a change in the vegetation that was all the more easily recognized because of the simplicity of the association or the society. The struggle for survival in the North was not so much one of competition between plants for light or food as one against the climatic conditions. Generally speaking, there was no crowding of individual plants as there is in regions of denser vegetation. "Light and room enough there are for all that can withstand and survive the stern climatic conditions."[41]

Among the groups of plants that might be readily distinguished were the luxuriant grasses (*Alopecurus. Poa*, etc.) and the scurvy grass (*Cochlearia offficinalis) on* the cliffs and slopes where the numerous Arctic birds nest. Also found were the sedge (*Carex*) and the cotton grass (*Eriophorum polystachium*), association of seepage-water swales; and the heathlike association, on warm, airy, sunny slopes, of cat's paw (*Antennaria alpine*), arnica (*Arnica alpine*), and reed-bent grass (*Calamagrostis*). Many other similar distinctive groups helped to form a vegetation as interesting as one finds anywhere, even though the number of species was not so large and the interrelationships not so common as in that of more favored lands.

"Of Northwest Greenland," Ekblaw wrote, "it can hardly be said that one cannot see the forest for the trees."[42] The tallest tree did not rise more than three inches from the ground. This tallest and most common tree was the Arctic willow (*Salix arctica*). Although it grew so low, it often spread over about a square yard or more of ground. Some of these trees, the trunk of which was no thicker than one's thumb, were more than fifty years old, as determined by counting the rings. The soft, fuzzy catkins on these trees rose above the ground farther than the trees themselves and tempted the swiftly flying, nervous Arctic bumblebees as few other flowers could. Another willow (*Salix herbacea*) was about as tiny a tree as one could imagine. It rarely grew more than an inch high and had but two little leaves and a tiny catkin each summer. The dwarf birch (*Betula nana*) had been recorded from near Borup Lodge, but Ekblaw had not found it.[43]

The little Lapland form of the rhododendron that flourished on the warm, sunny, well-watered slopes interested the botanist Ekblaw. "Its pretty little rose-purple, plumelike blossoms star the brown basalt rocks about North Star Bay, first cousins to the gorgeous forms that color the ledges of the Appalachians."[44] Two northern species of the cranberry family (*Myrtillus uliginosa* and *Vaccinium Vitis-Idoea*) bore numerous little pink-shaped flowers, as sweet and delicate as lilies of the valley; but they rarely saw fruit, except on the warmest slopes where the summer snows melted as fast as they fell. The curlewberry (*Empetrum nigrum*) grew in a few favored spots, where its pretty, purple, velvet flowers made it conspicuous, but it bore few berries. The Inuit liked to use it and the fragrant branches of the heather (*Cassiope tetragona*) to make outdoor fires over which to boil their tea or coffee.

One of the prettiest flowers of the northland, the so-called Arctic heather (*Cassiope tetragona*), grew almost everywhere. Its dainty, cream-white bells colored some of the rocky slopes. This item and *Dryas integrifolia*, a starry blossom of the same hue, were perhaps the most numerous of the conspicuous

Arctic flowers. These two flowers began blooming early and continued until August arrived with its frosts and freezes.

A group of pretty flowers usually found on rocky ledges that the ptarmigan frequented included several beauties. One was the northern arnica (*Arnica alpine*), with a smiling, bright, golden-face not unlike a diminutive Kansas sunflower, smaller than its cousins of the far southland, but otherwise quite like them. Another was the dainty pink and white shinleaf (*Pyrola rotundifolia*), its thick, glossy leaves and fair blossoms seemingly modeled from wax. Still another was the modest and lonely little bluebell (*Campanula uniflora*) rising blue and gentian-like on its fragile stem. With the foregoing was a strikingly beautiful, dark purple grass (*Trisetum spicatum*), of which the plumed tufts were noticeable rods away. This group of plants often included one or another of the other sun-loving plants of the dry slopes, but they were not so definitely confined to the one habitat.

Ekblaw inventoried three representatives of the lousewort or beefsteak family. Of these (*Pedicularis hirsuta*) grew everywhere along the coast. Its first cousin, *Pedicularis lanata,* a much prettier rose-red cluster of flowers, was not so generally distributed, but at Life-boat Cove, north of Etah, its bright blossoms dotted the moors. At Etah, *Pedicularis capitata*, a plumelike golden cluster grew. It had been found nowhere else in Greenland.

The botanist found bluebells (*Mertensia martima*) in profusion in but one place, the little Inuit village at Sonntag Bay. There the delta of a small mountain torrent was carpeted with them. On that delta Ekblaw found the most abundant growth of *Statice maritime*, a beautiful, dark pink goblet of florets. Of the cinquefoils (*Potentillae*) of the rose family, Ekblaw found six species, all profuse-flowering and golden. Vahl's cinquefoil was the cheeriest of all, because its inch-wide blossoms with their saffron centers shone from every dry slope.

The early purple saxifrage (*Saxifraga oppositfolia*) ushered in a succession of ten of the family, of which none was so beautiful as the leader. It is the earliest of Arctic flowers to burst into bloom. Often purple pennants of its gorgeous blooms bordered the snowdrifts.

Sixteen species of the cress family inhabited the region. Nearly all of them were white-flowered, but one notable exception was the purple rocked (*Hesperis pallasii*), sweet with the odor of plum blossoms, the only fragrant flower in the North. The *Drabae* comprised ten of the sixteen cress species. To this family scurvy grass (*Cochlearia officinalis*) belonged, that far-famed, reputed preventive of the dread disease, scurvy, which had decimated so many Arctic expeditions. It tasted bitter, like cress.

Ekblaw discovered that buttercups, waxy golden and bright, were numerous and varied. Most of them were yellow, but one tiny form (*Batrachium paucistamineum*) grew in ponds. During about two weeks of midsummer its starlike little flowers floated on the water. Many explorers rated as their favorite flower the dainty pink *Silene acaulis* that grew in dense clumps on gravelly slopes, but Ekblaw thought that its hard stems were too stiff. The Alpine chickweed grew everywhere, seemingly undaunted by the most unfavorable conditions. One of its near cousins (*Melandrium triflorum*), an Arctic catchfly, was found only in Greenland.

The dandelion, so despised in the southland, merited respect and consideration in the northland. Besides the bright, golden forms, closely resembling those known to Americans, a white-flowered form (*Taraxacum arctogenum*) with pink border grew in profusion about Etah and nowhere else in the world so far as known. It would attract attention anywhere as a pretty flower.

And yet the explorer was always ready to give the highest praise to the sunny-faced Arctic poppy. This fragile but hardy little blossom had preceded man to the farthest northland yet attained. On the most lonely and desolate coasts it greeted him all summer long. Along the icebound seashores, upon the bleakest plateaus, in every lonely valley, wherever a crevice in the rocks or a pocket in the cliffs gave a foothold, it was sure to establish itself. Great fields of it flamed about Etah, and it grew abundantly about Borup Lodge.

No green meadows or pastures carpeted any part of the far northland, but on the sunny slopes where some of the numerous Arctic birds had formed a rich guano soil the turf had become thick and soft. The frequent summer frosts seared the delicate tips of the grasses so that they never appeared verdant; a real green slope was a rarity in the Far North. The most lush-growing grass was the misnamed Arctic timothy (*Alopecurus alpinus*), upon which the Inuit depended for padding between their stockings and boot-soles and under the skins of their bed platforms and for dishcloths or towels with which to wipe their few pots and pans. Many blue grasses grew in Greenland, but about the Inuit villages Kentucky blue grass (*Poa pratensis*), tall and thick, was the most common form. In a few of the shallower ponds along the coast grew the beautiful little *Pleuropogon sabinii*, unique in its genus.

Pretty, plumy cotton grasses (*Eriophorum polystachium* and *E. Scheuchzeri*) waved their white tassels along the banks of the streams and pools and in the wet swales; graceful little rushes and reeds (*Juncus* and *Luzula*) grew with the numerous sedges (*Carex*) to form mats of turf where no grass grew; harsh scouring rushes (*Equisetum arvense* and *E. variegatum*) formed mats on some of the flatter stream beds, and a yellow-green club moss (*Lycopodium selago*) dotted the upland swales, all of which helped to create variety in the Arctic vegetation.

Rather unexpected but none the less welcome were four diminutive ferns that grew on the rock ledges, reminding one of the southland. *Cystopteris fragilis*, the commonest fern of the North, grew abundant and luxuriant in moist crevices on the steep cliffs. *Apsidium fragrans*, rigid but beautiful bronze-green, a sweet-smelling fern, was found on sunny shelves. Completing the list of ferns were two little woodsias, *Woodsia glabella*, a Lilliputian form scarcely an inch high, and *Woodsia silvensis*, not much larger.

The vegetation of the northland included the large, edible mushrooms at Etah. They were of a species probably not hitherto known. Some of them grew as large as dinner plates. They could stand for days, unspoiled and untouched by insects, and still be almost as edible as when fresh. Ekblaw and Dr. Hunt gathered many, cooked and ate them, and considered them excellent.

The plants and flowers of northwest Greenland had hardly two months in which to grow. As soon as the snow melted, the first flowers began to appear, usually only a few days before 1 June. At that time the midnight sun was a month and a half high and gave almost as much heat at midnight as at noonday. Even so, frequent summer snows and cloudy weather often retarded the development of the plants so that they could not blossom before the killing frosts arrived in early August, while the midnight sun still graced the northern sky. Even in mid-July, the little willow leaves began to turn yellow, and a week or two later the autumnal golds, tans, and browns indicate that the season of growth was ended.

The flora of Greenland, Ekblaw concluded, was a mixture of European and American forms. Many interesting problems presented themselves in the occurrence and distribution of many of these forms, and much work had been done toward their solution. As yet, however, the evidence for definite conclusions was not available. It was to be hoped that the collections and data obtained by the Crocker Land Expedition would make a considerable contribution to the knowledge needed.[45]

Existence in the far north was precarious for the Smith Sound Inuit, Ekblaw wrote, because the margin of safety in their food supply was always narrow, Famine did not often actually face the tribe, but several times game had failed them so completely and for so long that many Inuit had succumbed to starvation. The times of stress usually came in the spring when the sun first rose above the horizon, before the birds had come back. The oldest members of the tribe recalled that starvation would have overtaken them many times except for the timely arrival of the first birds. After a famine accompanied by a plague in which most of the tribe died, the survivors lost the art of making the kayak for summer hunting. As a result, during the open season they were unable to kill any sea food. And since caribou formed no part of their diet then, they had to depend on the millions of birds that frequented the cliffs and islands off the coast. Before the ice went out of the fiords, the Inuit repaired to the cliffs of the great rookeries where they obtained all the birds they needed for food. They stayed there until the ice froze again and permitted the killing of seal and other sea game.

Ekblaw and the Smith Sound Inuit

Ekblaw was a keen observer of all that he met in the Arctic, and he left valuable accounts of his experience. "Of all the interesting things in the Northland," he wrote, "this little anarchy of the Smith Sound Inuit is as pure a type of government as can be found, if my conception of anarchy is correct." He went on with a fuller description:

> They are absolutely ungoverned, as far as chiefs, or representatives, or laws, is concerned. Every individual is free, and equal to his neighbor, and a law unto himself. Actually, there is no wealth, so to speak, for, since the Eskimo's motive in life is acquisition and not possession, he is not provident, accumulates no worldly goods except those immediately necessary to his existence, and gives of his surplus to anyone who has not so much as he. Their moral and ethical standards are rigid, and conform to the conditions under which so limited a number as the tribe comprises, exists. The relationship of sex, the home life, the communal life are, I believe, better adapted to the preservation and progress of the tribe than our similar institutions are to those of our race. Their religion, such as it is, is vaguely Pantheistic, though the devil to them is a very personal being.[46]

Ekblaw could not go into detail about "our Eskimo, our adventures, or our daily life" when he wrote. He would save that for later.

Meanwhile, he wrote that existence in the far north was precarious for the Smith Sound Inuit because the margin of safety in their food supply was always narrow. Famine did not often actually face the tribe, but several times game had failed them so completely and for so long that many Inuit had succumbed to starvation. The times of stress usually came in the spring when the sun first rose above the horizon, before the birds had come back. The oldest members of the tribe recalled that starvation would have overtaken them many times except for the timely arrival of the first birds. After a famine accompanied by a plague in which most of the tribe died, the survivors lost the art of making the kayak for summer hunting. As a result, during the open season they were unable to kill any sea food. And since caribou formed no part of their diet then, they had to depend on the millions of birds that frequented the cliffs and islands off the coast. Before the ice went out of the fiords, the Inuit repaired to the cliffs of the great rookeries where they obtained all the birds they needed for food. They stayed there until the ice froze again and permitted the killing of seal and other sea game.

Fitzhugh Green and "Joy Forever"

After Fitzhugh Green returned from Crocker Land, he and Jerome Allen lived together in a small house built for the wireless that was set apart from

Borup Lodge. Green named the place "Joy Forever." He was there, according to Freuchen, because he was under a cloud for the murder of Peeahwahto. Writing to Hovey, Green said that MacMillan was planning extensive work for the next spring. Ekblaw would go up Eureka Sound to Greeley Fiord and return by way of Lake Hazen country, while he looked forward to another long trip in which MacMillan would aim for the region west of Axel Heiberg Land. Tanquary and Hunt would make independent trips of great importance to the success of other exploring projects. The Committee in Charge at the American Museum should recognize how difficult it had been to establish wireless communication; moreover, the seismograph had not been working. "It seems that we must really go home next summer. I am not in love with the scientific work but all my life I shall be hankering for a dog team and the white miles ahead. I expect that I have this fever worse than any of the others, and it is a fever that the coldest weather cannot cool."

"By this mail," Green wrote to Robert Peary in December, "MacMillan reports his failure to find Crocker Land. And he shows clearly that a mistake as to its existence was not only possible but indeed very probable under the circumstances of his own extended investigation." Green and MacMillan were happy to bring back records that Peary had left in cairns at the Cape. "After nearly two years of this life, I have come to realize your own delight in it. But when I consider your difficulties and when I recall the toil of even our comparatively short and easy trip over the Polar Sea I truly grasp the significance of your work." This letter, in which Green never mentions the murder of Peeahwahto, is a fine example of Green's ability to ingratiate himself with dignitaries who might be useful to him some day.

Some entries in Green's diary when he and Jerome Allen lived together apart from the other expedition members merit attention. Allen was not much of a talker while Green was a compulsive writer. Describing two Inuit who visited the house, one over twenty-five, the other over thirty-five, Green wrote that "any continued confinement palls on their energetic spirits." He listed twenty diversions by which his visitors amused themselves. For example, they drew pictures of animals on the wall and shot darts to kill them, they threw rocks into the air to represent birds in flight and threw other rocks to kill the birds.[47] Of a young Inuit who visited the house, Green wrote, "He is a nice boy in that he is a real boy." Green confessed, "I miss the children out here, like the music box they do grate a little sometimes but they do with their smiles and round puppy-like eyes somehow get into one's heart and cheer it."[48]

One evening Ahdukahingwah appeared at "Joy Forever" with her baby on her back. She had started out for a walk, Green related, and just happened to come here, "which sounds feminine enough." He entertained her by offering some prunes, and she entertained him by reciting various family troubles, "a habit with her." She said that Ahnokiah (her son Sammy) didn't like her and told her so every day, that she wished she didn't have Peter (her baby), and that she was very unhappy. "I suppose that some people would find these tales of woe very boring," Green related, "but I get the keenest pleasure out of them. She never repeats, never had the same sorrow two days in succession; and whatever the tragic circumstances may be she relates them with such wide-eyed pathos that I involuntarily sympathize and thereby stimulate this fountain of sorrow to the extent of leaving me such a stock of human interest as can amuse me for days afterward."[49]

Green described Inaloo, an Inuit woman who sewed for Ekblaw, as having an almost terrifying look, even when she smiled. At regular intervals she "cuts up high jinx in her attack of piblokto. The children are all afraid of her appeals to the devil and the walrus."[50]

One beautiful January day a sudden gale that arose about suppertime detained three Inuit at "Joy Forever." Everyone spent the evening singing and playing with biscuits and other eatables "every little while." By this means, "We got rid of considerable stale bread and other odds and ends." Green added, "The Eskimos are just like dogs, always hungry."[51]

Green redeemed his time at "Joy Forever" in countless ways. Hating idleness, he spent considerable time reading. Occasionally he listened to the Victrola. He kept daily records of temperature and wind, taught himself Gregg shorthand, and practiced building a snow-house (igloo). For a time he studied psychology and evolution but found neither subject appealing.

The Committee in Charge, Green wrote in late 1914, should recognize how difficult it had been to establish wireless communication; moreover, the seismograph had not been working. "It seems that we must really go home next summer. I am not in love with the scientific work but all my life I shall be hankering for a dog team and the white miles ahead. I expect that I have this fever worse than any of the others, and it is a fever that the coldest weather cannot cool."[52]

Looking Forward

Along with their scientific studies, the explorers accumulated fresh meat for the coming winter. Necessity for meat was the only excuse for the slaughter of walrus, who could inflict casualties. Each year the party's natives secured between fifty and one hundred of these brutes, the best of rich red meat for themselves and the dogs, a guarantee of strength for the trail to unexplored lands, and now the main object of the expedition. Hal Hunt and Jot Small were keen hunters. Dr. Hunt supplied their table with seal meat, and Jot Small with eider duck, black guillemot, and murre, many of which were prepared as specimen skins for the American Museum. On 20 June Dr. Hunt appeared at midnight with the hindquarters of a caribou around his neck. A week later the party's Inuit arrived from the region of the Humboldt Glacier bringing with them four polar bears, a long-tailed jaeger which Akpoodashah had caught by hand when the bird was feeding, and the highly prized egg of an ivory gull.[53]

Ahnoka brought the expedition party the best gift—a yellow, faded record of the Elisha Kent Kane Expedition bearing the date 24 August 1853. MacMillan, who knew Kane's book on the subject, explained that on that day the little brig *Advance* was being tracked along the ice foot on her way north. A day earlier, Kane recorded that he had sent out Wilson, Petersen, and Bonsall to inspect a harbor. MacMillan was able to decipher the name of Bonsall, which indicated that the record was placed there by the Kane party. Days later Akpoodashaho gave MacMillan two valuable Kane records—an old cap-lining and a sheet of heavy paper on which was cut with the point of a knife: "All well. Kane. Aug. 29, '53. Gone south. 78° 40'." Across the bottom of the page, with difficulty MacMillan deciphered a large "Kane," which might have been made with a pointed stick or the point of a bullet. MacMillan quoted some extracts from Kane's book that aided him in understanding what he found. Kane had written that he had scratched "O.K." with a pointed bullet on his cap lining and had hoisted it as the flag's representative. Seeing this "O.K.," MacMillan exclaimed: "To think that we held in our hands a record and the cap lining of the first American Arctic explorer! Actual relics of the author of a book which has caused many a lad to neglect his studies and dream of sledges, dogs, snow-shoes, and the North trail! I felt that we were almost shaking hands with the immortal Kane." MacMillan was intoxicated with Arctic fever.[54]

Miserable weather prevented the Americans from celebrating the Fourth of July in 1914 with a planned program of races, but they raised the flag in recognition of Independence Day. Jot Small and two Inuit caught seventeen salmon trout (*Salvelinus stagnalis*) in Alida Lake; the largest one measured twenty-eight inches and weighed four and three-quarter pounds. By the middle of July the ground was fairly dotted with flowers. MacMillan counted eighteen different varieties within a minute's walk from the door.

On 23 August Jot Small and Ekblaw proceeded south with the party's Inuit to Sulwuddy to hunt walrus and seal and to bring all the meat in cache to Etah. Just below Cape Alexander the boys met Freuchen, who was bound for Etah with Ekblaw's dogs, which Ekblaw had left at Umanak, and with mail from the U.S. via Copenhagen by means of Rasmussen's ship, which had recently arrived at the trading station 120 miles to the south. Freuchen transferred the letters and the newspapers, the first the party had received for a year, to MacMillan's boat. A few days later nearly every man in the expedition party contracted a severe cold. The germs of civilization had reached farthest north.[55]

In early September Dr. Hunt and the Inuit made the annual pilgrimage to the caribou grounds some fifty miles north. They returned nearly two weeks later with forty-two warm skins, invaluable for bed-robes, coats, and sleeping bags for the extreme temperatures. Such good luck inspired Tanquary and Jot Small to start north the next day with two Inuit. They reached home sixteen days later with empty arms.

The sun appeared for the last time on 14 October. The coming of the great night was part of the Inuit's life. They looked forward to it with pleasure. Ever since arriving, the expedition party had planned to entertain their northern friends with a vaudeville show. They gave it on 19 December. The Inuit left the room to discover on their return an auditorium with seats, stage, and drawn curtain. On the stage when the curtain opened were a "hideous, leering row of imported masks." The Inuit children gasped and fled in terror. In the second act Dr. Hunt performed a mock operation, etherizing Jot Small and removing from his stomach a six-pound can of pemmican, a ball of twine, a box of cigarettes, and a large piece of walrus liver. In the finale the doctor appeared to sever the head of the body and throw it to the audience. Gasps of horror turned to shrieks of laughter upon discovering that the act was a joke.[56]

With Crocker Land proved a myth and the expedition's plans for Arctic work curtailed, MacMillan thought it necessary to inform the American Museum that a relief ship might be sent for them in 1915. Thinking it imprudent to trust so valuable a mail to Freuchen, who journeyed south every spring, he planned to sledge across Melville Bay to Upernavik in South Greenland during the moonlight of December and January, some 500 miles from Etah. He could add considerable ethnological data along the way by getting in touch with every man, woman, and child in the Smith Sound tribe. Freuchen agreed to a December start and promised to make the arrangements for drivers and meat. Tanquary requested to go along. MacMillan agreed to the request. They left the day before Christmas with fourteen Inuit headed south to visit friends and relatives. Along the way they met a howling wind and low temperatures. A section of the ice foot cracked beneath their sledge and fell seaward, leaving Tanquary, who was guiding the sledge, with one foot over the crevice, tottering on the edge. He barely avoided serious results. They spent a night in snow houses in the village of Ittibloo, renewed their strength with hot tea and biscuit, and arrived at Thule (Umanak), North Star Bay, a distance of fifty miles, in twelve hours. Freuchen welcomed them warmly. They had a ball with the Inuit girls on two nights and visited the igloos. Ahnahdoo, one of the oldest Inuit in the tribe, spoke of the mysterious death of the astronomer of the Hayes Expedition of 1860–61. Isaac Israel

Hayes, in *The Open Polar Sea*, hinted at foul play. Ahnahdoo averred that the sledge on which the astronomer was riding plunged down an embankment into the sea, and that Hans, the Inuit driver, did not warn the man of the danger or try to save him. When MacMillan asked why Hans should be guilty of this treachery, Ahnahdoo told him that Hans wanted all the white man's things for himself. Macmillan doubted the story. Such an accident might easily happen. Hans declared that he had tried to get the freezing man to safety, but the man had died on the way.[57]

Proceeding, they arrived at Upernavik, where the Inuit, glad to see them, brought them frozen murres (*Uria lomvia lomvia*) and fetid seal, part of the summer harvest. The birds, not exactly fresh, were banquet food to the northern gourmands. After their evening meal, Freuchen discoursed upon the merits of socialism. He had renounced civilization as being unfit for man, had married an Inuit woman, and had settled down at the top of the world among what he described as ideal socialists.

Ooblooya, another host, offered his guests what resembled a fat frozen seal. It was squeezed through the small circular entrance in the floor, then, with a sharp knife a slit about one foot long was made in its belly and the man of the house rolled back his sleeve, plunged his arm in up to the elbow, and withdrew it, smeared with grease and clutching black strips of meat. What looked like sausages packed in lard were strips of sun-dried narwhal packed in narwhal oil. Was anything ever better? By this time MacMillan had misgivings as to the probable success of the jaunt. Freuchen had poorly planned the trip from Cape York across Melville Bay to Cape Seddon, a distance of 170 miles. Depending upon ideal conditions, he had provided neither sufficient food nor good equipment.

Nevertheless, MacMillan plodded on, finally throwing off everything from the sledges and making a dash for two Inuit igloos. He made his way along the covered passage and stuck his head up through the hole in the floor. To the Inuit, the dirty-faced, full whiskered object at the entrance—MacMillan— was his conception of the Devil himself. MacMillan had never beheld such abject fear upon a man's countenance. But the Inuit's wife, who had been on the S.S. *Roosevelt* on Peary's North Pole trip, recognized MacMillan. Tanquary, who soon arrived, devoured raw bear meat like the wildest aborigine. MacMillan and Tanquary remained there for eight days. Tanquary was an ideal traveling companion, MacMillan observed. He possessed an even temperament, never got excited, was always in good humor, and seemed by far the healthiest of the Crocker Land personnel. Thus far he had withstood the trip admirably.[58]

During their sojourn at Upernavik, they learned much in their conversation with the Inuit. They heard about a twelve-year-old Inuit boy and his mother who, years ago, were starving. In such circumstances it was customary to kill a small child rather than permit it to suffer. But the mother let the boy, outside with the dogs, fight for his life by eating dung and refuse. This he did, scouring the hills for rabbit-droppings and whatever he could snatch from the dogs. His head was covered with scars inflicted in his struggles near the door for whatever was thrown from the entrance.[59]

MacMillan put a letter to the American Museum in the mail-pouch going south requesting, according to agreement in case Crocker Land did not exist, that a ship be sent in 1915 to transport the expedition back to civilization. He placed another letter in the mail-pouch informing the museum that he would remain another year in the Arctic alone, independent of museum help, and he sent another letter to a friend in Kingston, New York, requesting that he send provisions in case the museum failed to do so.[60]

Maurice Tanquary, an entomologist by training, was somewhat out of place on the Crocker Land Expedition (American Museum of Natural History Library).

Tanquary, Freuchen, and one companion left for the south with instructions to proceed with the mail to Upernavik, secure twenty dogs and other articles, and return to Etah. MacMillan and Etookashoo headed north across Melville Bay for a quick run up the coast, with little in the way of supplies. They crossed Melville Bay in four marches and enjoyed the hospitality of genial Ahngodablaho, who filled them to repletion with bear, narwhal skin, little auks, seal, tea, coffee, sugar, milk, and biscuit.[61]

It was now late in the year. MacMillan sent word to the American Museum that the members of the party, except himself, were ready to return home.

The men of the expedition had made good use of their time. They had studied many dimensions of life in the Arctic and had left evidence of their findings from which others would reap the profit. Surely the time was ripe for them to return home.

6

More Research, More Adventures

Despite believing that the time was ripe for them to return home, circumstances forced the expedition members to spend a third year in the Far North. Imprisoned and uncertain as to when a relief ship might arrive, the men labored under both physical and psychological stress. Food supplies were low and tempers irritable. But the explorers carried on their scientific research and had their share of adventures. In fact, the enforced layover happily enabled the expedition to contribute to the advancement of man's knowledge of science.

In early 1915 Ekblaw was planning to study the geology of Ellesmere Land in order to solve some scientific questions. His proposed route would take him to the Lake Hazen region in Grant Land. The Greely Fiord-Lake Hazen portion of the route was most promising for scientific investigation. Long stretches of it had never been explored. The route would be about 1,200 miles and the venture would take about three months. Ekblaw would return via Fort Conger, Kennedy Channel, and the Kane Basin. MacMillan thought that Ekblaw should go with two Inuit companions to Lake Hazen and that Tanquary would sledge along the east coast of Ellesmere Island to meet Ekblaw. He left the preparations to Ekblaw and promised to furnish him with a good team of dogs.[1]

Ekblaw chose Esayoo and Etookashoo as his assistants. As support parties, he chose Oobloyah and Okpuddyshao to go to the divide of Ellesmere Island, and Arklio and Nukapingwa to help as conditions necessitated. Because his route was circuitous, Ekblaw would have to depend upon the country for game to feed the men and the dogs.

The party set out on 24 March, but the men were turned back by a gale and a driving blizzard. They proceeded again on 30 March, but rather than going up Beitstad Fiord as intended, they crossed Buchanan Bay, went up Flagler Fiord, and along Bache Peninsula they found a real Arctic boulevard.

6. More Research, More Adventures 99

They made camp at the point of Knud Peninsula. Ekblaw named the place Camp Small because they reached it in the first hour of Jot Small's birthday. Jot was born on April first and always said he was Cape Cod's April fool. The Inuit went bear hunting, and after a few hours returned with the meat and the skins of two bears.

Dashing along after breaking camp, Esayoo pointed out the big cairn on the isthmus of Bache Peninsula that Peary and Esayoo had built years earlier. On the next day, Easter Sunday, Ekblaw was impressed with the view that lay before them. As he described it:

> Like great walls on either side, the precipitous mountains rose to guard the pass that we intended to go through. Never in all my Arctic experience have I been so thrilled, so excited, so exhilarated as I was during our drive up that valley to the pass, that glorious Easter Sunday. The sun shone clear, and the weather was so warm that we drove all day without our caribou-skin kooletahs; the ease and pleasure of this route, compared with the Beitstadt Fiord way of the year before, delighted me; the going was good, the scenery unsurpassed; on every side we saw game or traces of game; and late in the afternoon, just after we had passed through the narrow gateway into a broad valley in the heart of the hills, we saw and killed our first musk-ox, a fitting close to an explorer's lucky day. I could have hugged Esayoo for guiding me by this pass. I named the gateway Sverdrup Pass, in honor of the stalwart old Norwegian explorer who had first seen it.[2]

A storm kept the party in this valley at Camp Green (named, no doubt, for Fitzhugh Green) until 7 April. Then Oobloyah and Okpuddyshao helped them up the glacier as a last evidence of kindly regard and turned back toward Etah. Ekblaw and the Inuit crossed the ice cap in a few hours, and suddenly the black, serrated cordillera north of Bay Fiord burst into view. The descent to Bay Fiord was rapid and easy. When they reached the low land, Nukapingwa discerned a large herd of musk oxen near Camp Ekblaw and shot them. Then they established Camp Tanquary and stayed there until they had consumed the eleven musk oxen.

Proceeding leisurely down Bay Fiord, they stopped at Camp MacMillan. Near here Ekblaw investigated a thick seam of lignitic coal. In crossing the fiord, Nukapingwa set off after a bear while the others killed fourteen musk oxen, the finest Ekblaw had ever seen. "They were thick padded with fat as golden and sweet as butter; their coats glistened bright and well-kept in the bright sunshine; and their horns were smooth and polished."[3] Their splendid condition was no doubt due to the excellent pasturage on the grassy meadows among the mountains and along the fiord. There were sixty-seven in the herd.

The west coast of Ellesmere Island near Bay Fiord was not generally so precipitous and bleak as the east coast. It was more maturely dissected, the valleys wider, the slopes less steep, and the mountains did not rise so abruptly.

Large tracts supported a relatively luxuriant growth of willow, sedge, and grass—the chief foods of the musk oxen.

Early on 14 April, Arklio and Nukapingwa turned back with sledges laden with skins and meat. Ekblaw sent with them to Etah an account of his experience thus far.

Down Bay Fiord and up Eureka Sound, in four marches they attained the northern end of Fosheim Peninsula at the mouth of Greely Fiord. Along the way they killed all the musk oxen they needed for food, and at midnight on 18 April, seeing the midnight sun for first time, they named their stopping-place Midnight Sun Camp. The next morning they saw a big herd of musk oxen. The Inuit killed twenty-one of them. Since they had three teams of hungry dogs, and since a team of eight or ten dogs easily devoured a musk oxen at a meal, all the meat was gone in a week, except for a little they carried on their sledges.

They stayed until 26 April at this place, Camp Etookashoo. Here Etookashoo built a roomy snow house, which they lined with the skins of the musk oxen. Tramping about the plain at the northern end of the peninsula, Ekblaw collected dry plants and fossils. He found many Paleozoic and Mesozoic fossils. The peninsula teemed with life: hares, ptarmigan, and musk oxen fed on the slopes and the plains. From the top of Mt. Hovey Ekblaw counted over 200 musk oxen. Wolves, foxes, ermine, and lemming were common. The snow along the coast was beaten down by passing bears.

Setting out again, they made their way to Camp Fosheim, which they reached in eight hours. With musk oxen numerous about, they stayed here two days, during which they had their first sight of the cheery little snow bunting, the only songster of the Northland.

Ekblaw and Etookashoo built a big cairn on the sandstone ledge of a cape that ran out into the head of the fiord. In a bottle in the foot of the cairn they left a record of their expedition to date. On the back of the record Ekblaw wrote a stanza of the most popular University of Illinois song. He did not name it, but most likely it was "Hail, Alma Mater."

In a day's march the men returned to Camp Fosheim, and from here they set out toward the unexplored coast of Grant Land. They made camp at the mouth of the fiord, entered it the next morning, and just after noon, with his Leitz glasses, Ekblaw descried over sixty musk oxen on the crest of a ridge. He uttered a brief prayer, "Lord, Thou has done well with us," and went on with renewed strength.[4]

The musk oxen were at the top of the mountain, two miles from their sledges and 2,000 feet high. Snow lay deep everywhere. Walking single file, Etookashoo, Esayoo, and Ekblaw advanced. Just before reaching the animals, Ekblaw thought, "Lord, Thou hast done well, but for the sake of my legs, Thou couldst have done better." They stalked the herd, shot all they needed, and rolled them over the cliff down to their sledges. As he crept into his sleeping bag, Ekblaw thought, "Lord, Thou hast done splendidly."[5]

They spent two days exploring the fiord, which Ekblaw named Borup Fiord in honor of George Borup, to whom their expedition was a memorial. The fiord was a magnificent bay sixteen miles deep flanked by high mountains. Seeing some seals basking on the ice in the golden sunshine, they tried for them with no success. They saw numerous fresh bear tracks but no bears. A snowy owl swooped for a lemming but failed to get him. Spring was coming to the Northland.

Near Greely Fiord the men killed two musk oxen and made camp. With rare good luck they were on a richly fossiliferous limestone cliff from which Ekblaw collected a group of corals and brachiopods. Ekblaw named the place Tanquary Fiord, and he named the range of high mountains about the head of the fiord, Osborn Mountains, "in honor of my friend and patron, President Henry Fairfield Osborn of the American Museum of Natural History, and the former in honor of my fellow in science on the expedition, the true friend of many years. Dr. M.C. Tanquary." The bold headland at the mouth of the fiord he named "in honor of 'Prexy' Edmund Janes James of the University of Illinois, who has been my inspiring friend; and the mountain opposite, Mt. Bayley, to honor my friend and mentor, Dr. W.S. Bayley, also of the university." Naming these places was some of the best fun Ekblaw had on his "lonely trip."[6] He was repeating Robert Peary's practice of naming geographical landmarks in honor of friends and donors.

The exploration of Tanquary Fiord was the most important work of the venture. The fiord is deep and extends in the general direction of Lake Hazen almost thirty miles northwest into the heart of Grant Land. Bordered on both sides by high mountains, those on the south are sharp and steep, while those on the north are sloping and rounded. Numerous glaciers reach the waters of the fiord but do not discharge many icebergs. The scenery about the head of the fiord is wild and picturesque. A large valley extending toward Lake Hazen opens out at the head of the fiord. Near here Ekblaw found the ruins of ancient Inuit habitations. Musk oxen were plentiful along the shores of the fiords. They killed six of them. On the plateau nearby they found the ruins of Inuit caches and fox-traps, evidence that the Inuit had at one time lived on the shore of this fiord.

On 16 May the party reached the head of Greely Fiord and camped beside a little lake. One of the dreariest, loneliest, coldest spots on the globe, it was about fifteen miles long and two miles wide, bounded on the south and north by almost vertical cliffs over 1,500 high and terminated at both ends by bleak, blue glaciers. "In my four years' experience of silent vastnesses, and lonely distances, in the North," Ekblaw wrote, "I never felt so submerged in the forsakenness of the Arctic as I did in this prison-like lake-bed.

I cannot imagine anything lonelier than this far northern crypt at Arctic midnight when a northern blizzard rages. It would be the best hiding place on earth."[7]

At the head of the lake a canyon-like pass afforded Ekblaw and his Inuit escape from the prison, but they were forced to make a way with icepicks over the debris broken from the glacier. They worked at this several hours and then entered a canyon whose cliffs towered 1,000 feet above them. They sledged along on the frozen stream at the bottom of the canyon for several hours and, at last, coming to a fork where a tributary gorge entered, they stopped to consider whether to attempt the tributary or the main canyon. Etookashoo felt sure that they could easily exit by way of the little gorge.

After tea, they started up the narrow gorge. But the going was so difficult that they had to retreat. Their situation concerned them. They could find no way out. Ekblaw had a slight attack of snow-blindness and could not travel. But Esayoo and Etookashoo found a place where the three of them might possibly get up on the plateau, and after toiling all day they finally got up onto it. Unless they found meat quickly, their position would be precarious. They made camp in the intense cold. Ekblaw and Esayoo set out in search of musk oxen but found no trace of game. By the next morning nearly all of their dogs had eaten their traces and were almost too weak to move. Ekblaw and Esayoo started out over the hills, reached the top of the divide and started down, and near the bottom nearly collided with a big musk ox. The dogs set wildly after him. The men finally saw a herd of eight bunched up to fight off their assailants. Their dogs rushed in upon them, the men shot them, and their ordeal was over.

They stayed at Camp Remington for a day to rest and feed their dogs, and then headed due north, traveling along the left bank of the Veery River until they passed Mt. Arthur. Here they searched for but could not find the cairn that Maj. A.W. Greely built at its foot in 1882. From the top of a large mountain north of Mt. Arthur, Ekblaw saw Lake Hazen, some ten miles to the northwest. The Conger Mountains lay in the foreground like a snow wall, Mt. Connell and Mt. Biederbick rising above the rest. Farther behind them rose the peaks of the United States range. To the northeast lay Lake Hazen, a snow-white plain set among the snow-clad hills. In all the landscape, the wide valley at the head of the lake flanked by steep walls was the most spectacular feature. As from a witches' caldron, white steam rose from the upper reaches of the lake and the pools of the plain. The dark valley set among the white, calm hills looked like a veritable inferno.

Ekblaw and the Inuit decided to try to get to the head of the valley if not to the lake that day. Eighteen times they unloaded their sledges and carried their equipment over high rock barriers. By the time they reached the end of the gorge, they were fatigued and cross. Even their dogs were in bad humor. They pitched camp on the flat at the mouth of the gorge. Esayoo's team of dogs broke loose and chased up the mountainside after the Arctic hares feeding there. Supper that evening was one of the best meals Ekblaw had ever eaten.

The next day was hard. Their sledging was the most unpleasant they had experienced since leaving Etah. Another day's march brought them to the source of the Ruggles River. Here they expected to find a pool of open water in which they might catch some Lake Hazen salmon, but the lake was frozen. So Ekblaw and Etookashoo dug two holes over eight feet deep but struck gravel instead of water. They gave up fishing and killed three fat musk oxen near the mouth of the lake.

Ekblaw was suddenly seized with cramps. He thought he would die. Lying in his sleeping bag, he recalled a tale of an Inuit who had eaten warm caribou tallow and had drunk ice water, with the result that the tallow stiffened in his pyloric sphincter and killed him. Ekblaw had committed the same indiscretion and was certain that he would die. He wrote some farewell notes, told Esayoo what to do with his equipment, and resigned himself to the mercy of his sphincter. Still alive the next morning, he happily took the trail.

Ruggles River, the outlet of Lake Hazen, was a splendid thoroughfare—some quarter of a mile wide, forty feet deep, and frozen solid. Ekblaw and his Inuit drove in a canyon about twenty feet deep, cut in the ice by the water from the lake, and with good going soon reached salt water. They had successfully crossed Grant Land from salt water to salt water.

With the snow deep and soft, the going down Chandler Fiord and up to Lady Franklin Bay was hard. Summer was coming. Seals were numerous. From Lake Hazen to Lady Franklin Bay they made four marches. At Camp Marvin, on the point of a little peninsula north of Sun Bay, when a great polar bear came calling the men cut the traces of the dogs, the bear headed for an iceberg nearby and made it before the dogs reached him. Ekblaw and the Inuit threw on their underclothes and pursued Mr. Bear. Ekblaw photographed him and then put a bullet through his skull. His soft, golden-white pelt was beautiful.

From Camp Marvin the men proceeded to Fort Conger, previously the site of Major Greely's headquarters. Searching the ruins, Ekblaw found the tablet put up in memory of men of the North Greenland Exploration Party of Nares who had died of scurvy while out on the trail. In one of the shanties Ekblaw found a series of records left by MacMillan when he was there in 1909 taking tidal observations. The records had been written in one of Greely's notebooks. Ekblaw made copies of them. It was now Memorial Day, and Ekblaw added to his note a quotation in memory of the brave fellows of Greely's party who had lived here for two years and were left to die on the bleak rocks of Cape Sabine.

And only the Master shall praise us, and only the Master shall blame,
And no one shall work for money, and no one shall work for fame,
But each for the joy of the working, and each in his own separate sphere,
Shall draw the thing as he sees it for the God of things as they are.

Ekblaw had cited these lines from Kipling, "When Earth's Last Picture is Painted," when he first learned that he was to be a member of the Crocker Land Expedition.[8]

Ekblaw was disappointed that no one had come to Fort Conger to meet his party. But he saw a herd of musk oxen on the mountainside, scaled the mountain to reach them, and let his dogs go when they were a quarter-mile from their quarry. Rather than grouping to fight off the dogs, the musk oxen ran up the crest. Fearing that they might lose them, Esayoo dropped one with his Winchester, and Ekblaw got another with his Remington. Then, shooting alternately, they killed the herd of eleven. The men fed their dogs the meat of three animals and cut up the rest, reserving the tenderloins, porterhouses, hearts, and other choice pieces for themselves. Esayoo cracked the marrow bones and kept the marrow to take home to his wife. To get as much of the remaining meat as possible down to their sledges, they lashed it into the three biggest musk ox skins, hitched their teams to the load, and skidded down the mountain side. The dogs seemed to enjoy the mad dash as much as did the men.

After reloading their sledges, the party returned to Camp Marvin, where they slept before starting their homeward journey. Early on 3 June they headed directly across Lady Franklin Bay to Cape Baird. The ice was rough, but Etookashoo was adept at picking out the smoothest trail possible. Late in the afternoon they struck smooth ice that extended the length of Kennedy Channel. About nine o'clock that evening they made camp, Camp Archer. They broke camp early the next day, eager to get to Cape Constitution, where MacMillan had promised to make the first cache for their return. They were in no need of supplies but expected to find letters there. Two wide leads, over which they ferried on ice-cake, indicated that the ice was breaking up.

A mile or so north of Hans Island a pressure ridge about forty feet high extending across the channel stopped their progress. So they tumped their loads and sledges over the first barrier ridge [to tump is to drag or carry by means of a tump line, which is a strap placed across the forehead to assist a man in carrying a pack on his back], hitched their dogs to the sledges again, and proceeded toward Hans Island. They made camp on a flat floeberg [a floeberg is a berg composed of a sheet of floating ice, a detached portion of a field of ice], and after supper climbed to the top of the island to survey the route ahead. What they saw was ice as rough as that through which they had just passed. So they drove around the west end of the island and headed for Franklin Island.

The next day, in seven hours of utmost exertion, the party made only three miles. Just as they were about to make camp they struck smooth ice and decided to try for Cape Constitution, which they reached in two hours. They looked for the flag that was to mark the cache but saw none.

Starting out again, they found sledge tracks that had been made that day. Crossing Lafayette Bay after a half-hour's drive, they heard a rifle shot nearby. They headed for the bay, and at the foot of the cliffs came upon a tantalite tent with sledges, a white man, and some Inuit grouped around it. Fitzhugh Green rushed out to greet Ekblaw and his Inuit.

They stayed there a day, then headed back across Peabody Bay and in due time reached Cape Kent, south of the Humboldt Glacier. They made no camp until they reached the mouth of the Mary Minturn River, where three Inuit families were encamped. They stayed there a day, which gave Ekblaw an opportunity to survey the plants beginning to bloom on the warm, sheltered ledges where the snow had melted. The vegetation of the place was luxuriant, and the ruins of large Inuit stone houses indicated that at one time many people had lived there.

They soon set out again, stopping only at Rensselaer Harbor to visit the site of Dr. Kane's expedition. From there in one march they arrived at Anoritok. Jot Small had been there hunting a few days earlier, and Hal Hunt had been there to doctor a sick Inuit. The Ekblaw party stayed at Anoritok one day and then started for home. At Lifeboat Cove, about ten miles from Etah, they went up overland, and in their drive down the valley met the worst weather they had experienced on their venture. But now they were veterans of the trail, and the weather did not seriously affect them. They almost tumbled down the slope to the house. MacMillan, Tanquary, Hal Hunt, Jot Small, Jerome Allen, and all the Inuit welcomed them home.

The trip had been eminently successful. In addition to his notes, Ekblaw brought back valuable collections. He closed his "modest chronicle" with a tribute to his companions. He gave the lion's share of the credit to "old Esayoo," a kind, pleasant companion throughout the journey, and he gave due credit to Etookashoo for his unfailing good humor, rare hunting ability, and excellent driving.[9]

Green's Trip to Cape Constitution

On 22 May 1915, MacMillan instructed Fitzhugh Green to proceed north to Cape Constitution in command of a support party to meet Ekblaw, who was returning from a thousand mile trip by way of Lady Franklin Bay, Kennedy Channel, and Peabody Bay. On his way northward, Green was to make caches of food and supplies at Cairn Point, Cape Leiper, Cape Russell, Cape Scott, Cape Calhoun, and Cape Constitution. Ekblaw had been instructed to cross the channel no later than 15 June. If he had not arrived by that date, Green was to delay no longer than 20 June. Upon departure, he was to leave a cairn containing instructions as to caches to the south and locations of encampments of Inuit en route to Etah. As time and conditions permitted, Green was also to survey the coast, bring back skulls and skins of bears shot, and photograph points of interest. Green would find at Cape William Wood a cache of supplies which MacMillan described. He was to take whatever he might need. MacMillan set no date for Green's return to Etah, but he would look for him about 20 June.[10]

On Sunday, 23 May, Green left Etah with Ooloyah and Aklio and the latter's wife, Ahlningwah. Each person had his (and her?) own komotik and share of the supplies. Several Inuit families who were migrating northward accompanied the party to Anorotok, where they arrived after two short marches. On 25 May they experienced good going. Even with considerable loads they soon reached Cape Ingersoll, where Jot Small and his two Inuit were hunting. Somewhat later they met with heavier going, which increased until they began to plow the soft snow of Peabody Bay.

In order to carry out his orders, which called for a survey of the coast, Green planned to check the available maps of the region. According to the legends upon those prepared by Charles Francis Hall, Elisha Kent Kane, and Robert Peary, no general triangulation had ever been attempted. Their work was no more than the result of a series of widely separated astronomical observations connected by sketched and roughly measured contours of the shoreline. Green assumed the observed latitudes to be correct, so he endeavored only to reconcile with them the plotted longitudes. He measured the distance between headlands with fair accuracy by combining the party's rate of travel with the elapsed time, allowing for delays.

As an additional check he hoped to observe a complete set of azimuths, but limited time and unlimited variation of weather confined him to a few watch-sun bearings. With the exception of the coast between Cape Calhoun and Cape Constitution, he found no considerable discrepancy in the position of prominent landmarks. With fair weather, he was able to revise the delineation of several minor traverses. The drawing that he appended to his report was substantially correct. Green preferred to avoid belittling the work of his predecessors or emphasizing his own results by pretending that anything less than a rigorous triangulation of the coast could yield a strict projection. For convenience of travel, his revision of the local charts was adequate. For most scientific reference a mathematical precision would be required for which no expedition had yet been prepared, except at its headquarters. In this connection, those features of the coast that depended upon longitude were necessarily approximate. In high latitudes, azimuth and time could be obtained with a great deal of repetition, which alone could eliminate errors. This process was impracticable in Arctic fieldwork. The longitude of the main stations alone could be relied upon, as in North Star Bay, Etah, Elisha Kent Kane's winter quarters, and the other situations of previous expeditions.

The inscription on the rock at Cape Leiper and many dilapidated cairns were constant reminders of Dr. Kane's two terrible years in this desolate country, but the sight of gulls and ravens nesting among the sunny cliffs, the rabbits that they gathered on the talus slopes, and the fat, well-fed dogs dispelled any gruesome images of famine and disease. Except tea and biscuit, they depended on the country for their staples.

By the end of the first week they had made most of the caches for Ekblaw. Their loads were light and their dogs were in shape; they were prepared for bear hunting in Peabody Bay, which contained the famous Humboldt Glacier. Green was impressed by the maze of bear tracks that netted the snow fields of Hall Basin and festooned the majestic tabular bergs scattered in profusion before their mother glacier. Bear tracks they saw everywhere, but they traveled three days before sighting a mother and her two cubs. The engagement that followed was short, and the victory went to Green's party. The delicious short ribs of the small bears held the sweetest morsels to be found among the many meats they had in the Arctic.

After five days on the monotonous snow stretches of Peabody Bay they were glad to find a gravelly spot in Wright Bay for their camp. From then on they found the ice foot excellent. Near Cape Madison they pursued a bear out through the wild ice of Kennedy Channel. Very thin but well coated, the bear was worth the rough and tumble steeple-chase he led them. In Lafayette Bay they killed three more bears and added their skins and skulls to their precious cargoes, making seven in all.

On 5 June they camped at Cape Independence, and went on the next morning to Cape Constitution. Here they found an opening lead, happy for the sea pigeons but not for dogs or men. Green found a cairn at the Cape and left a note but no food, since he believed that the water would prevent Ekblaw's party from reaching that point. Although Green had been ordered to wait at Cape Constitution, he decided to move to the cove just east of Cape Independence, where they had shelter from the wind and a tent site on land.

The arrival of what Green describes as "the other party" put an end to useless planning. In the morning of 6 April Green saw komatiks swing around the Cape. He fired a gun to guide them. Both men and dogs were in excellent shape. Their sledges carried quantities of musk ox meat, skins, and fuel. In fact, Ekblaw entertained his relief party throughout the trip home. He had used his supplies sparingly and was well-prepared to winter upon his own resources.

They journeyed home in the luxury of perfect weather. After the loneliness of travel with no other white man, Green and Ekblaw found companionship very welcome. For Ekblaw's tales of musk ox kills and great discoveries in new lands Green had to trade some meager news of international war. From his point of view, Green had easily the better part of the barter. The two men spent a day with the Inuit in Marshall Bay and another at Anoritok to give their dogs deserved rest. On the last day they met all the evils of summer Arctic travel—snow, fog, rain, rocks, and open water—impediments which sought in vain to depress their spirits, for this was the home stretch, which ended at the bottom of Etah hill.[11]

Ekblaw the Ecologist

While in the North, Ekblaw made a study of the Polar Inuit that described the adaptation of the human animal to the circumstances of his habitat. The people who inhabited the northwest portion of Greenland contiguous to the waters of Smith Sound, he wrote, were the northernmost people in the world. Along eight hundred miles of desolate shore they had persisted for centuries as a unique social group of about two hundred and fifty individuals. Their homeland was small in area because the Greenland ice cap restricted all life to a narrow belt along the shore, free of ice and snow during the short summer. Their climate, though Arctic, was essentially oceanic. Their periods of continuous day and continuous night were longer than those with other people. The relationship between the Polar Inuit and their environment was fast becoming obscured by external factors. Closer and more continuous contact with foreign people was changing the character and culture of the Polar Inuit.[12]

As to racial status, Ekblaw observed that the Inuit were a distinct race with a distinct character, language, and culture. They possessed some characteristics of the North American Indian in form and figure, and some characteristics link them with the Mongolian. At the same time they were a distinct race with their own distinctive language and peculiar culture. Their total number Ekblaw estimated at no more than 40,000 people scattered around almost half the earth's circumference, though the area of their occupancy was small because everywhere they frequented only a narrow strip of coastal territory. By character and culture the Inuit were a shore-dwelling people.

Despite their sparse and widespread distribution, the Inuit presented a remarkable homogeneity in character, language, and culture. This racial homogeneity was probably due to a relatively recent dispersal from the home center, but probably the most powerful factor was the restrictive influence of the monotonously rigorous environment throughout their range. The Polar Inuit differed so slightly from the rest of the race that any variance could be ascribed to a corresponding variance in local habitat.[13]

Viewing the subject in historical perspective, Ekblaw wrote that the weight of opinion inclined to the theory that the ancestral home of the Inuit was in America, either on the mainland between the Mackenzie River and Hudson Bay or in the archipelago just to the north. The Polar Inuit constituted a relic of the last wave of migrants that swept down the west Greenland coast after A.D. 1000, displacing the Norse settlements established there, and a later element introduced in the mid-nineteenth century by an immigration of several families from Baffin Land, who introduced new elements into the culture and modified the mode of life of the natives.

As a consequence of these two elements, the Polar Inuit exhibited two distinct types. The one represented by the descendants of the earlier settlement was characteristically Inuit—short and stocky of stature, round and flat of face, flat of nose, stolid of countenance, and with a tendency to *piblokto*, a form of Arctic hysteria. The other type, represented by the descendants of the immigration from Baffin Land, was suggestive of the Indian—taller, lither body, higher cheek-bones, longer face, almost aquiline nose, alert countenance, and absence of *piblokto*.

Until discovered by Ross in 1818, the Polar Inuit had been separated from the rest of the world for centuries and had not been affected by any influence foreign to their homeland. Transient contact with whalers, traders, and explorers produced no visible effect in their character or culture, but since 1910 there had been rapid change as a result of connection with the external world through successive Arctic expeditions, the establishment of a trading station at North Star Bay, the arrival of Danish Greenland Inuit, including missionaries and teachers, and the extension of Danish authority to the Smith Sound Region.[14]

In his survey of the Polar Inuit, Ekblaw turned next to edaphic factors, that is, those pertaining to the salinity, alkalinity, or drainage of the soil. The homeland of the Polar Inuit, he wrote, comprised the peninsular portion of the Greenland coast lying between the great glaciers two hundred miles wide, which debouch upon Melville Bay to the south and the Humboldt glacier sixty miles wide, which debouches upon Kane Basin to the north.[15] These glaciers served as formidable barriers to habitation north and south and to ready travel and intercourse with the Inuit to the south. This area, the permanent and distinctive home of the group, is bisected by Inglefield Gulf. Wolstenholme Sound bisects the southern half and Foulke Fiord bisects the northern half. The entire coastline, indented by small bays, is between eight hundred and one thousand miles long.

The waters of Kane Basin on the north and of Baffin Bay on the south wash the shores of this land, with Smith Sound connecting the two. Kane Basin is frozen over from October to July, and throughout the summer it is filled with more or less drifting ice. Baffin Bay is more or less open throughout the year. Inglefield Gulf, Wolstenholme Sound, Melville Bay, and numerous smaller bays are usually frozen over from November to June. In Smith Sound the water does not freeze over. Open water rarely lies far from the shore, and in some places it extends in to the ice foot. The islands off the mouths of the gulfs and bays are an important factor in the freezing of the waters, which they help enclose.

Everywhere along the coast the ice foot begins forming in late August or early September and persists into July or August of the following year. The ice foot is that part of the sea ice which freezes fast to the shore and does not move up and down with the tides or float away when the ice goes out before the winds or with the tides. The ice foot varies in width from only a yard or two along high precipitous shores to a hundred yards or more on a gently sloping beach.

The tides play an important part in the formation and permanence of the ice. Throughout the winter the ice is solidest and safest during the neap tides and most broken and treacherous during the spring tides. The high, narrow plateau between the ice cap and the sea which becomes free of ice and snow in summer is nowhere more than forty miles wide. Parts of this area are Laurentian gneiss and granite, while other parts are Huronian sandstones, limestones and shales intersected by dark traps and diabases. Everywhere the topography is comparatively rugged. This coastal belt is intersected by numerous glaciers, of which the larger and more active ones discharge great numbers of huge icebergs into the waters on which they debouch.

The mineral resources of this land are negligible. Except for small deposits of pyrites and soapstone, and the iron-nickel meteorites, none are available for use by the Inuit.[16]

Continuing, Ekblaw turned to the climatic factors in the area about which he wrote. With the large extent of open water along the coast even in midwinter, the temperature rarely drops to more than minus 50° Fahrenheit. Even with an extensive ice lay, the temperature is modified by the water. The highest summer temperature is 55° to 60° above zero Fahrenheit. About mid–June the temperature rises high enough to melt the ice and snow; melting ceases about mid–August. By mid–September the sea ice begins to form permanently in the fiords and deeper bays, which are generally occupied throughout the summer by drifting fields of ice. Rarely are they free of icebergs.

Snow falls in every month of the year. The summer snows that do not melt are those of late August or early September. The depth of the snow is rarely over two or three feet because a great deal of snow evaporates even in the coldest weather. When the snow begins melting in June, every canyon and valley holds a torrential mountain stream until melting ceases. Rain rarely falls, but when the chinook comes down off the ice cap, rain may fall in January. The region is one of low humidity.

6. More Research, More Adventures

The winds are cyclonic in character. The heaviest storms come from the southwest with destructive on-shore winds. In the bays and fiords the winds invariably blow down to the sea from the ice cap.

The period of continuous night begins about mid-October and ends about mid-February. Continuous sunlight begins about mid-April and lasts until mid-August. Between mid-February and mid-April the days lengthen and the nights shorten; between mid-August and mid-October the days shorten and the nights lengthen. The night is rarely so dark as to stop traveling or sledging entirely. Throughout the periods in which the moonlight is continuous, all activities can be carried on without difficulty. During the period of continuous sunshine, noon and midnight do not differ greatly in temperature or intensity of light. The air is always fresh and clean.[17]

In his account of the ecological relations of the Polar Inuit, Ekblaw turned next to biotic factors, those pertaining to living things. Owing to the short growing season and the long dry cold period, no trees or shrubs grow in the Polar Inuit's homeland. The tallest tree is the Arctic willow, a scant three inches in height. Over a hundred species of vascular plants grow in the region. Sedges, blues grasses, and similar grassy plants grow in the region. Two are particularly abundant—*Poa pratensis* and *Aloppecurs alpinus.* On some of the talus slopes manured by nesting birds, the mat of grasses is thick and heavy. Mushrooms are common and lichens clothe the rocks. Flowering plants, though small and relatively inconspicuous, grow in dense mats on favorable slopes where the sun shines warmly and moisture is ample.

The plankton development in the sea is incredibly rich throughout the summer, and the heavy growths of luminaria and other sea weeds on every shoal ledge are luxuriant.

The bird life is incredibly abundant, not in species but in individuals. Of the land birds, the ptarmigan and snow bunting are the most common. Shore birds, ravens, snowy owls and falcons are rather numerous. The ptarmigans, ravens, and snowy owls are permanent residents. Of the sea birds, the dovekies are the most numerous. They nest in suitable slopes of easy gradient along the entire coast in such numbers that they cover the sea when feeding and darken the sky when in flight. Almost as numerous as the dovekies are the murres that nest on the ledges of the steeper shore cliffs along the coast. The eider duck frequents the coast in thousands, and the black brant is common. Kittiwakes, guillemots, gulls, jaegers, and fulmars are numerous. All the seabirds find an abundant supply of food in the small life of the cold, well-lighted waters off the shore.

Animal life on land is relatively scarce. The musk ox is extinct along the Greenland shores of Smith Sound, though still common in Ellesmere Island, Grantland, and westward. The caribou, though still fairly abundant, is generally restricted to a few isolated areas not readily accessible. The Arctic hare is widely distributed and common. The blue fox and the white fox are abundant in the bird-cliff localities where they feed upon both the eggs and the birds. The Arctic wolf is almost extinct, and the lemming and the ermine do not frequent this part of the Greenland coast. The musk ox, caribou, and hare feed upon the willows, grasses, and small herbs; the wolf and fox feed upon the birds and the hare; the wolf also feeds upon the musk ox and the caribou.

The sea animals are very numerous because of the ample supply of food. Four species of seal—the ring seal, the bearded seal, the hooded seal, and the harp seal—are all rather common, though the ring seal is by far the most abundant. The walrus frequents the coast during the whole year, especially when the mussel-shoals furnish good feeding grounds. The narwhal and the white whale are numerous. The killer whale and the bowhead, and at times the right whale, visit the coast. The sleeper shark feeds over the deeper bottom.

The polar bear, both a land and sea animal, is as much at home out on the open sea among the icebergs as on the shore. He avoids all habitations of man, particularly when dogs are about. Keen of scent and of all perceptions, as well as of intelligence, the polar bear is certainly the most superb animal of the North, though not nearly so dangerous as the walrus.[18]

Proceeding, Ekblaw described how the Polar Inuit related to their environment. Having no tribal organization, they had an ideal anarchy. Their villages consisted of two to four families gathered together in places accessible to the sea or at the mouth of some valley which furnishes a stream of water and opens into the hills or up to the ice cap. The families usually stay one or two years in any village because the nearby hunting grounds offer limited game for food and clothing. The villages are from thirty to sixty miles apart.

The Inuit travel from village to village as soon as the sea ice along the coast becomes strong enough. When necessary, they sledge over the ice cap or along the coastal valleys. In summer the men travel in kayaks; as a rule they do not venture far from home.

The Polar Inuit family is based upon economic factors rather than on reciprocal sexual monopoly. The woman requires a husband to provide basic necessities—food, clothing, shelter—for herself and her children, and the man requires a wife to sew his clothing and cook his food. He provides for his wife's children, whether his or some other man's.

The home of the Polar Inuit is adapted to the season. In summer they live in tupiks, roomy sealskin tents, and in winter they live in stone houses covered with turf and snow known as igloos. An ordinary igloo is maintained at a temperature of from 60 to 70 degrees. On the trail, and on occasion when the igloos are too few in number, the Inuit build snow houses or temporary shelters. Built of blocks of snow, these houses are admirable temporary homes, especially when lined with furs or skins.

The Inuit dress exclusively in skins and furs. The men wear birdskin shirts made from the breasts of dovekies, murres, guillemots, or eiders; they wear rabbitskin stockings and boots of sealskin, cariboukin, or bearskin. In summer they wear a sealskin coat; in winter they wear a foxskin or cariboukin coat. They wear bearskin trousers in summer and winter and sealskin or bearskin mittens. The rabbitskin stockings are essential to prevent frozen feet.

The Inuit women tan the skins and furs used for clothing by chewing, which they begin when they are four or five years old. They continue chewing for the rest of their lives. The clothing is sewed with sinew-thread from the flanks of the caribou or narwhal. The needle is made from a hare's tooth ground thin or small bones from birds.

The secret of keeping warm in the far North lies in keeping dry. Fur clothes are much more easily kept dry than are woolens. Snow can readily be beaten out of fur clothing.

The Polar Inuit obtains food and fuel almost solely from animals. Only rarely do the Inuit eat any of their native plants. Every animal supplies part of the diet. Nothing of an animal carcass is thrown away. The land animals constitute a relatively small part of the Inuit food supply, and of the land birds only the ptarmigan plays a part in the diet.

The Inuit depend upon the sea birds and the sea animals for much of their clothing and all of their food and fuel. The dovekies, murres, eiders, and guillemots that frequent the coast supply meat and eggs. The ring seal, the staff of life, can be obtained along the whole coast throughout the year, furnishing skins for clothing, tents, and boats, meat for food, and blubber for fuel. The bearded seal supplies the splendid leather for boot-soles, dog traces, sledge lashings, and harpoon lines. The walrus furnishes the great supply of dog-food, and his tusks furnish the ivory for harpoon heads and points and other essential artifacts. The white whale and narwhal furnish meat for food, blubber for fuel, and sinew for thread. The tusk of ivory of the narwhal is shaped to implements for household and hunting use.

With the exception of pyrites for lighting fire, soapstone for lamps and pots, and meteoritic iron for small knife blades, the sole resources for the living and culture of the Inuit come from animals. Consequently, the sole occupation of the Polar Inuit is hunting the animals that afford these supplies and preparing them for use. The men and the women share the work in the family and the village without any thought of men's rights or women's rights. Life is simple and direct.

The character of the Inuit accords with this simplicity and directness. He is essentially kind, soft-spoken and gentle, hospitable to a fault, care free and independent, and honest beyond our understanding. His psychology of time differs radically from that of civilized society. Because of the long day and night in the Far North, the Inuit views time as a continuous flow not a succession of defined intervals. Without schedule, he eats when hungry, drinks when thirsty, and sleeps when sleepy.[19]

Concluding, Ekblaw observed that recent contact with the white race had changed the mode of life, culture, and character of the Inuit so that these matters were no longer the effect of his environment. By contact with foreigners. Ekblaw wrote, the Inuit is losing his native honesty, independence, and sterling character. He is changing so fast that in another decade or two he will be quite another person. The demoralization of the Polar Inuit as a distinct social unit is imminent and inevitable.[20]

As his essay on ecology illustrates, Ekblaw saw his opportunity to enlarge the world's knowledge of the Arctic, and he took full advantage of it.

Inuit Dogs

A keen observer, Ekblaw paid tribute to Inuit dogs, these "forgotten heroes" of the far North, in an article published years after he returned to

A team of fourteen dogs pulling one sled, Cape Leiper, May 1915 (American Museum of Natural History Library).

America. The Polar Inuit of Thule, or Northwestern Greenland, he wrote, was dependent on the dog, the dog-sledge, and dog driving for getting about on their hunting and fishing grounds and for getting from village to village. Prosperity and welfare might be measured in terms of dogs. Thus the dog team rigorously determined the economic status of the Polar Inuit.[21]

The Inuit dog was a marvelous adaptation to Far Arctic conditions of terrain and food supply. He is light enough to travel over ice and strong enough to pull a heavy burden by sledge. He lives by flesh alone, the only food available in the Arctic, and he can go without food for several days and still draw the sledge to which he is hitched. His heavy coat of warm hair keeps him active and comfortable at fifty or more degrees below zero, and if fed regularly about once every three days he can endure the most bitter cold for weeks on the hardest trail.

Best of all he is intelligent enough to turn every advantage to his own good. He cooperates with his driver, makes the most of opportunities for comfort, rest, or food, is loyal and happiest when in the harness and on the hunting trail. He quarrels constantly with his teammates in a semi-friendly rivalry and when occasion arises he pulls together with them as a unit.[22]

The outstanding attributes of the dog of the Polar Inuit are his devotion to his driver or master and his gentleness as compared with the dogs of the Labrador, the Hudson Bay region, and the native Alaskan and Aleutian dogs.

Sledges and dogs on the ice, from west, Etah, Greenland, April 1917 (American Museum of Natural History Library).

He dies of starvation and overstrain in the harness, lapping the hand of the driver who must desert him when there is no other course.[23]

The best balance between dogs, efficiency, and food seems to limit the team to eight or ten. In every team one dog, superior because of strength, intelligence, and fighting ability, establishes his supreme authority over the other dogs and becomes "the king dog." He maintains this authority by going through the team several times a day, reasserting his sovereignty by forcing every male dog to subject himself to the king dog's punishment. The king dog maintains order and discipline in the team and carries out the commands of the driver.[24]

Among the Polar Inuit the dogs in a team are driven fan-fashion—with an individual trace back to the sledge from every dog in the team. Such a system of driving is necessitated by the rough ice of the Thule coast. The disadvantages of the fan-fashion hitching are that the dogs on the wings of the team cannot pull forward with their maximum power, and some of their strength is lost. In guiding the team, the driver uses a long whip with a handle one-half to two feet long and with a lash tapering down to cord thickness wrapping, the cracker. "Huk, Huk" and cracking the whip is the signal for starting the dogs. Strips of ringed seal skin form the harness. The sledge is from six to eight or ten feet in length, two or more feet wide, and capable of bearing large loads.[25]

The time and effort required to kill game to feed the dogs imposes upon the Inuit a regime of hunting that occupies almost every moment of every day when weather and ice are favorable. Much of the supply of dog-food comes from walrus. Seal supplies a secondary measure of dog-meat, while relatively insignificant stores of dog food are obtained by bear, caribou, and smaller creatures. In terrain where game is abundant the Polar Inuit makes a kill and feeds his dogs about every third day.[26]

The season of sledging ends when the ice becomes rotten and unsafe. During the summer the dogs wander about the tupiks (sealskin tents) seeking such waste food as the Inuit cast away. Only occasionally are they fed, and most of the time they are ravenously hungry. Even so, they are playful though mischievous. Most of the puppies are born in the summer. Training begins when the dog is a puppy. After taking part in the first kill, he realizes that sledging means the excitement of the chase and food. The Inuit dogs vary significantly in their individual qualities and traits. Very few are surly. Most are responsive, especially when on the trail. The period of a dog's active service in the team depends in part upon the driver.[27]

The history of the Polar Inuit is a long record of dependence upon his dog. Hunting upon the ice rather than in open water is the chief activity of this group, and for this pursuit, as for the hunting of bear, musk ox, and caribou, the dog and sledge are essential. The dog constitutes perhaps the most important link in the long chain of environmental factors that make human life possible in Thule. "Perhaps nowhere else in the world is the bond of interdependence and loyalty between man and dog stronger than among these people of the North and their dogs!"[28]

Thin Ice

At the same time as he wrote about ecology, Ekblaw left a moving account of his harrowing experience on thin ice. Ice and ice floes are realities in the Polar North, and they should not be taken for granted.[29] In Ekblaw's account, he was in Thule with Mene, the Inuit boy, and Sechmann Rosbach, the catechist of both Danish and Inuit ancestry, when spring arrived. The trio set out from North Star Bay for a hunting trip at Cape Parry. Arriving there, they stayed with other hunters in snow houses for three days and then started back toward North Star Bay, hunting along the edge of the ice as they sledged southward toward Saunders Island in the mouth of Wolstenholme Sound. Halfway between Beechwood Point and the northern point of Saunders Island they came upon a large herd of walrus along the edge of a patch of hummocky old ice—an irresistible lure for Mene and Sechmann. Mene sank his harpoon into the flank of a big cow walrus. They "landed" the huge carcass, fed the dogs all they could eat, set up their tent, and made ready to turn in for a sleep.

Continuing, Ekblaw became lyrical as he contemplated the situation. "It was well after midnight," he wrote. "The sun had hardly set. In the soft night light, the pale moon swung high in the sky, almost invisible. Flocks of fulmars, guillemots and eiders, but lately returned to the north, winged their ways still further northward. The sky was well-nigh cloudless, the water rippled calm and dark before our tent and the ice gleamed solid and white as far as we could see." But Sechmann shook his head; he seemed uneasy. The sky in the south did not please him. Mene and Ekblaw detected nothing dubious and made light of his fears. They rested but kept vigil.[30]

When the sun had risen well into the sky the men turned out. The dogs stirred uneasily; not a bird was in sight. Sechmann called attention to a horizontal pennant of cloud rising high above the plateau back of North Star Bay. Polar Inuit viewed this manifestation as a dread warning of the approach of a violent southerly gale and storm that would carry the ice out to the sea. Mene knew its grave import; he yelled to his companions to waste no time in getting away.

So they untied their dogs, hitched them to the sledges, left everything behind, and headed straight for North Star Bay. For an hour or more they raced along—Mene, with the biggest and best dogs, in the lead; Sechmann, with poorer dogs but a better driver, close behind, and Ekblaw behind Sechmann.

Then came the crisis. Black and threatening before them was a dark lead of new, thin ice stretched across the entire sound. They could not see how wide it was but could readily see how thin it was because their killing-irons broke through it of their own weight. As to how far it extended, they guessed that it reached from shore to shore. There it lay, a thin film of ice that no frost had yet whitened, a dark, treacherous band that they had to cross.

Then Sechmann, Mene, and Ekblaw each drew their dogs back from the lead at increasingly large intervals so that they would not strike the ice at the same time or near together. As Sechmann's dogs struck out across the thin ice, he cracked his whip, encouraging but not striking his dogs. Both Sechmann and his dogs realized the danger they faced. Beneath the runners of his sledge the yielding ice bent. Before Sechmann's dogs had got well out on the thin ice, Mene's team was on its way toward the edge. The rounded front part of the runners was holding up as the dogs sped along. The runners cut two narrow lanes through the ice. As Ekblaw's sledge neared the black, thin ice, he hardly dared to hope that it would hold him because he weighed at least fifty pounds more than each of the others. But his runners were shod a quarter of an inch wider, and though the ice bent deep under the sledge, this extra width carried his greater weight. Heart in mouth, Ekblaw sat rigid, watching the water spray out from the sides of both runners. Not a dog faltered. The first moments were the most perilous. The young ice was thin and smooth as glass. Ekblaw and his team gathered momentum as they raced on. The lead proved to be over half a mile wide. To Ekblaw it seemed an age before he and his dogs got across. As Sechmann struck the solid ice he gave a wild yell of relief, as did Mene a moment later. Ekblaw could not even whisper. The men could not take time to congratulate each other on the safe outcomes. The storm still raged; they could lose no time. They drove relentlessly through the gathering blizzard and finally made shore just within Cape Abernathy. There they built a snow shelter and stayed until the storm swept by them.

Life in the Arctic challenged the expedition members in many ways. At the basic level the challenge was simply one of survival in a harsh and unforgiving physical environment. At a higher level the challenge was to learn about and understand the physical environment of which they were a part. The members of the expedition had met both challenges.

7

MacMillan's Arctic Research

The Arctic was a vast area about which much was known and unknown. Members of the Crocker Land Expedition were eager to learn more about the fabled North. While waiting for a relief ship to carry the expedition party home, MacMillan made a trip that resulted in what he viewed as an important discovery. He decided to explore the region north of the Parry Islands, hoping to attain Finlay Island (King Christian Island), which had been seen in about 1850 by the Sir John Franklin search expedition and in 1901 by the Sverdrup Expedition. This island, located at 100° to 105° W and 77° 30' N, was five hundred miles from Etah by sledge. MacMillan also planned to visit Ellef Ringnes and Amund Ringnes Islands. So far as MacMillan knew, white men had never visited these neighboring islands. He planned to go light and fast, living largely upon the game of the country, in order to return before Smith Sound broke out in the spring.[1]

On 22 March 1916, MacMillan left Etah with seven Inuit, eight sledges, and ninety dogs. To avoid the rough ice near Cape Sabine, the party headed for Cape Camperdown on Bache Peninsula. At the end of their fifth march they encamped at the entrance of Flagler Fiord, a spot known among the Smith Sound Inuit as a favorite hunting ground for seal. They crossed Ellesmere Island by an old Inuit pass, ascended a riverbed at the head of Flagler Bay to the height of the land, and went to the summit of a glacier at an altitude of 4,000 feet. The ascent was at a gentle angle and easy going, but the descent into Bay Fiord was discomforting. Here they discovered musk oxen tracks, and within an hour the Inuit had killed fifteen musk oxen. After feeding their dogs to repletion, MacMillan made a cache of skins for the American Museum and of meat for their return trip.

MacMillan found good bituminous coal in this region in large lumps lying in the riverbeds, evidence of recent uplift of land on all shores. On 2 April the men killed a bear and three large musk oxen, but a bull tossed and killed a fine dog. They drove from a point on the shore just inside of Storaen Island of Eureka Sound diagonally across to the Stolz Peninsula and on to

Bjornesundet. There they built an igloo on the northern shore of Ulvingen, a dumb-bell-shaped island at the lower end of Eureka Sound. At this point MacMillan sent two Inuit back to Etah with instructions to pick up all skins cached on the trail and deliver them to Jot Small at Borup Lodge. Rounding Hyperit Point, they saw typical musk oxen country, with ptarmigan and Arctic hare also numerous. There they remained for two sleeps. Careful sights for longitude, latitude, and compass variation checked up almost exactly with Sverdrup's work. Interestingly, MacMillan's compass variation steadily increased as he proceeded westward into the region between the North and the Magnetic North Poles. From 104° W it increased to 128° 15' W.

Proceeding westward, they encountered deep snow. Within sight of Cape South West they built their igloo for the night. In five hours on the next day they reached Cape South West. Everything thus far had made for a successful trip. They had killed thirty musk oxen, sixteen Arctic hare, thirteen seals, and seven polar bears, only once deviating from their course for game. They had lost only four dogs. With the addition of a trip to Gletscher Fiord they had covered 345 statute miles, an average of seventeen miles a day. "All my men were very anxious to go on," MacMillan exulted. "They were as happy as a crowd of schoolboys as we gathered in our snow house at night, had our tea,

Donald MacMillan taking observations on Polar Sea, April 1914 (American Museum of Natural History Library).

biscuit, and meat, and lit their pipes for the after-dinner story. What ideal traveling companions they are!"

Nevertheless, convinced that it was wise to limit their number to four men and their dogs to forty, MacMillan told two of the Inuit to return to Etah.

From their camp, MacMillan saw about due southwest a rounded dome that he judged to be a headland of North Cornwall. Nothing was visible in the direction of Amund Ringnes Island. A day later MacMillan reached Amund Ringnes, some five miles north of Cape Ludvig. This uncharted coast trended to the west into a large bay, then swung east to a point of land ten miles distant. The island that he had passed a day earlier could now be seen extending in a southeasterly direction from this point.

The tops of the highest peaks of Amund Ringnes Island might possibly reach 2,000 feet, MacMillan thought, but as a whole the land was extremely flat and uninteresting. It sloped from the interior at such an easy gradient that it was impossible to define the shore accurately. Land and sea merged into one.

The explorers next made camp on a small uncharted island one mile off shore, almost exactly between the Magnetic and the North Poles at 96° 30' W. They killed a polar bear and two small cubs, which helped their meat supply and justified a day of rest for the dogs. By now the party had been on the road twenty-five days since leaving Etah. The dogs trotted forty miles to the middle of Hassel Sound, from which the men should have seen the eastern shores of Ellef Ringnes Island, but owing to a heavy mist and low shores nothing could be seen to the west. The next day they encamped at Cape Nathorst. They needed to provide fresh meat for their dogs in order to explore King Christian Island. On the following day, after reaching the most southern point of Ellef Ringnes Island, they crossed over to King Christian Island in just over six hours.

Although challenged by wind, drift, and the lack of game, they killed a bear and filled their dogs to repletion before arriving at their camp on the southern shore of Ellef Ringnes Island. Soon thereafter they added two more bears to their larder. MacMillan would have liked to explore King Christian Island further, but had no time to do so. He headed across for the shores of North Cornwall and was the first to step upon the island for sixty years. Sir Edward Belcher had been there on 30 August 1852 in his search for Sir John Franklin. They ascended to the summit, 1,200 feet high, constructed a cairn, and in a little bottle left a record of their visit.

MacMillan then saw three small flat islands off to the west and northwest, one of which they passed when crossing Hendriksen Sound. To the south they saw the sea ice stretching off into Belcher Channel. On the southwestern shore was an island with its cliffs rising sheer from the sea ice. The northern and eastern shores of the island were quite different from what was plotted on their latest maps. Sledging along the ice foot for the next six days revealed the land extending due east, not southeast, well beyond the 93rd meridian before trending southward. They built a second cairn upon the shore at the foot of McLeod Head and deposited a record. Then they proceeded eastward, following the coastline and taking observations of salient points with a Brunton compass and the altitude of the sun with a sextant. (The Brunton compass was widely used to make accurate degree and angle measurements.) MacMillan discovered that the sloping northern, eastern, and southern shores of North Cornwall were besprinkled with various kinds of shells, one of which was *Mya truncate*, and bits of excellent quality coal. Proceeding, they rounded the southeast point of Cornwall Island and headed due west, noting the entire absence of the two large indentations shown on their latest maps. On the southeastern shore they discovered and passed over an island two miles long and a half-mile wide. MacMillan named it Belcher Island in honor of the first man to land there. When they reached their last camp, they plainly saw Exmouth and Table Islands to the south. Grinnell Peninsula loomed on the southern horizon.

Now, at what MacMillan reckoned as 77° 22' N and 93° 50' W and with a lack of food, he felt justified in departing. After a nearly twelve hours' march across Norwegian Bay he arrived at Cape South West. A lack of fresh meat in cache revealed that the other two Inuit had retreated eastward, moving on to the party's cache at Gletscher Fiord. MacMillan built another cairn at Cape South West and enclosed a record in a chocolate tin.

On 4 May the explorers headed eastward and homeward. That night the whole party was together again in an igloo at Gletscher Fiord. Proceeding, on the next day they reached their big cache at Bjornesundet. Two days later, traveling fifty miles while facing a cold wind for nearly twelve hours, they found their old igloo filled with frozen bear meat placed there by the two Inuit who had returned from Cape South West. Another surprise at this camp in Eureka Sound was the discovery of a caterpillar at eight above zero. This was their second sign of spring, the first being a snow bunting that had flown across their trail ten days earlier.

They remained at the head of Bay Fiord for two sleeps in order to feed and rest their dogs for the ascent of Ellesmere Land Glacier. Soft deep snow overlying a rough and rocky riverbed was tough for a heavily loaded sledge. Finally, gaining the back of the glacier they ran into a thick fog. Forced to camp for the night, the next day they ascended the summit of the glacier and descended for a mile or so before encountering a heavy mist. Uncertain as to how to find the only descent into the old Inuit Pass leading to Flagler Bay, they pitched their tent and delayed until 4 a.m. the next day and then made a fast run to the sea ice, arriving at 2:30 p.m. On the trail again at 11 p.m. they proceeded down Flagler Fiord to the water hole at the entrance, where they captured four seals in about as many minutes.

Then they headed directly for Cape Sabine. The dogs reeled off thirty miles, they camped, and making their way they reached Etah on 16 May. They had been on the road fifty-seven days. They had covered 1,140 statute miles, an average of twenty miles a day.[2]

On 4 June, Henry Fairfield Osborn of the American Museum received through the American Minister in Copenhagen a cablegram from MacMillan that reported the spring trip to Finlay Land as very successful. The message added that MacMillan planned further exploration in March 1917. The *American Museum Journal* reported this welcome news in May 1917.[3]

By means of a message taken from Greenland to Copenhagen by Dr. Hunt and cabled thence to America by the U.S. Minister to Denmark, word of this journey was obtained from MacMillan and published along with a map of the venture in the *Geographical Review*.[4] The *Review* was encouraged to have so promising a report of actual results accomplished. The determination of the geographical positions of new islands and of hitherto uncharted portions of coasts, known only through distant sights by much earlier explorers, was a real contribution. And if the published accounts were correct in assigning a latitude of 78° 18' to the large island just east of Amund Rigness Island, some of the best maps of this region would have to be remade. Among the important results achieved in the journey across Ellesmere Island were observations on the extent of the glacier ice, the abundance of game, and the existence of much coal. Finlay Island and adjacent land masses were reported to show evidences of recent uplift on all shores—"a valuable observation when ultimately shown on the maps of the expedition, since it will give us an important basis of comparison with the raised beaches and terraces of northwestern North America and particularly Labrador. The extent of the rise of the land since the removal of the great ice load of glacial times is one of the significant problems of glaciology."[5]

Ellesmere Island Trip

While still waiting for a relief ship, MacMillan made other discoveries. On 26 March 1917 he left Etah with three Inuit on an exploratory trip along the southeastern coast of Ellesmere Island from Cape Sabine to Clarence Head. The American Geographical Society advocated the work, which had been carried out previously by Inglefield in 1852, Kane in 1854, and more accurately by I.I. Hayes in 1861. But all of these delineations were based on surveys made from the decks of vessels, often miles from shore, and thus were not always accurate as to details. Due to severe weather, the party was four days in crossing Smith Sound. Open water extending north as far as Clarence Head and well into Buchanan Bay compelled the party to go south by way of Rice Straight, an interior channel separating Pim Island from the main body of Ellesmere Island. Blocked again at Cape Herschel, MacMillan turned inland again and cut across the intervening promontory to Baird Inlet. There, at Inuit Point, at the northern entrance to the inlet, the walls of three stone houses and the remains of a boat were found on the site of the first encampment of Greely's starvation party in 1883.

Continuing south, MacMillan was stopped at Cape Isabella by open water and an impassable ice foot. Before turning back he searched the cape carefully and was fortunate in discovering records left by Sir George Nares, who commanded the *Alert* and the *Discovery* in the British Arctic Expedition of 1875–76, and also mail for the *Discovery* and *Alert* left by Sir Allen Young of the *Pandora* in 1874. They were legible and in fairly good condition. MacMillan mapped Baird Inlet on his return to his base.

Starting from Etah again on 3 May in zero degree temperature, MacMillan encountered ice conditions that were little changed. Since he could not go around Cape Isabella, he decided to go over it. He climbed the glacier leading over John Ross Mountain, then turned the party into Cadogan Inlet and up over the glacier back of Paget Point. Proceeding, the explorers advanced on sea ice covered with deep snow. Without good snowshoes the trip would have been impossible.

Between Paget Point and Cape Faraday, MacMillan discovered a very large glacier, which he named the American Museum Glacier. It was formed by the ice cap pushing over the edge of the land into the sea and was second in size only to the Humboldt Glacier, which was located between 79° and 80° N. The coast they traversed was quite different from the one on the map. MacMillan discovered two islands—one south of Paget Point, the other in Talbot Inlet, just south of Cape Faraday. He also discovered that, despite reports of early navigators, Lecante Island and Saunders Island did not exist.

There had been tremendous glacial activity all along the coast since 1850, MacMillan observed. The land was fairly buried in ice, which was flowing over and around the headlands and filling all the fiords. He obtained good sights for longitude, latitude, and azimuth at all salient points. Five polar bears and a number of seals furnished meat for the dogs and the men. On his return, MacMillan camped in Peary's old hut at Cape Sabine and visited the second camp of Greely's starvation party on the north shore of the cape. He made a survey and took photographs of the locality.[6]

W.L.G. Joerg, the associate editor of the *Geographical Review*, critiqued MacMillan's account of his venture north of the Parry Islands, not intending his comments for publication. First, MacMillan's manuscript gave less specific information on the trip than did the press dispatches that were summarized and published in the *Geographical Review* in October 1917. Second, the author showed unfamiliarity with the circumstances connected with the dispatches of the Nares expedition of 1875–76, which described what Nares found at Cape Isabella. Joerg illustrated his point as follows: MacMillan's comment (MS p. 10) on Sir Allen Young's letter is not to the point. It was not Captain Nares but Commander Markham who stood on that spot, and he did find the mail deposited there although not Sir Allen Young's letter. The mail that he failed to find was on the other side of Smith Sound, at Littleton Island. See the account in "Discovery of New Islands in the Arctic Archipelago by Stefansson" accompanied by a map of Stefansson's and MacMillan's "Recent Explorations in the American Arctic Archipelago" in the March *Geographical Review*.[7] MacMillan left incomplete, Joerg added, the signature at the end of the postscript of Sir Allen Young's letter (MS p.10), presumably because it is illegible in the original. Perusal of the literature would show the signature to be that of Lieut. Charles R. Arbuthnot of Sir Allen's expedition. Third, MacMillan created the impression that he visited the Ellesmere Island coast as far south as Clarence Head, latitude 76° 40' N (MS p. 16, and press telegram from Sydney, C.B., 27 August 1917), for which see the October *Geographical Review*. Joerg cited MS, p. 17, "On May 15 we camped at Roger Point," and p. 19, "On the 16th we started back." It would seem that the farthest point reached was Roger Point, latitude 77° 25'. The claim of having surveyed the coast as far as Clarence Head would seem to be based on sights taken from Roger Point (MS, p. 18), which, for Clarence Head, would imply a sight about fifty-five miles long.[8] Joerg wrote with authority. He doubted MacMillan's ability to report his achievement accurately.

MacMillan furnished the Geographical Society with additional details about his trip to Ellesmere Island together with photographs taken on the trip. The *Geographical Review* published "Notes on MacMillan's Ellesmere Island Trip" In March 1918.[9] MacMillan was presumably the author, although the *Review* does not name him as such. One can only speculate as to the reason for the omission. The photographs are the main value of the article.

Comer's Midden

When the *Cluett* was trapped in the ice, Captain George Comer put his imprisonment to productive use. Born in Quebec in 1858, Comer had grown up in Connecticut. At seventeen he had shipped out on a New London whaler. Between 1895 and 1912 Comer had made six Hudson Bay whaling voyages. When his whaling ships were immobilized in winter harbor, he collected samples of Inuit material culture. He had published an article on this subject,[10] and the anthropologist Franz Boas had used Comer's information in his book,

The Central Eskimo. With equipment provided by the American Museum, Comer had photographed the Inuit, made plaster casts of their faces and hands and sound recordings of their dances, songs, and stories.[11] His journals revealed his genuine affection and concern for the Inuit.[12]

While in the Arctic, Captain Comer kept a record of tides at Etah from 3 May to 15 June 1917, while First Officer Nielson of the *Danmark* kept a record of tides from 1 May to 6 July 1917 near Umank, Wolstenholme Sound. These records, kept in field notebooks, were sent to the U.S. Coast and Geodetic Survey, where the results from reductions of high and low waters at both sites were compiled. "The observations appear to have been taken with a great deal of care," the superintendent of the Coast and Geodetic Survey wrote, "and reflect much credit upon those who were engaged in the work."[13]

Comer also carried out archaeological excavations at Umanaq. Although neither equipped nor prepared for such work, he wished to make the most of the opportunity. So he located old house sites and dug away the débris covering the original floors. He plotted and excavated fifty-three such sites located from Parker Snow Bay to Rensselaer Harbor and examined some twenty graves.[14] It was unlikely, he thought, that a single site would be occupied continuously or for appreciable periods at intervals. Such conditions were decidedly unfavorable to archaeological research, the successful outcome of which depended upon the establishment of chronologies as interpretations of observed stratifications or superpositions. Nevertheless, Comer found little difficulty in distinguishing sites belonging to Inuit of the last fifty years and those of an earlier date. His collections showed that reasonably old sites were represented.[15]

Comer's most important discovery was a considerable deposit of camp refuse at a site near North Star Bay, the small harbor within Wolstenholme Sound. Since the mere location of such a site was unique in Inuit archeology, he named it Comer's Midden.[16] Seeing what Comer had struck, Peter Freuchen and Lauge Koch, a geologist and a foremost Arctic explorer who was in the North at the time, set to work on the opposite end of the refuse pile. They found it difficult work, since the ground was frozen solid an inch from the surface. It required many days for them to reach any depth, digging a few inches and then waiting for more earth to thaw out. Freuchen named the site Comers Kitchen Midden.[17]

Comer and perhaps his colleagues communicated their findings to Clark Wissler, an anthropologist at the American Museum. Wissler published them in a long article that began with Dr. Hovey's description of the location and physical characteristics of the site dug into by Comer. Wissler described the excavations in Comer's Midden, the age of the deposit, and the methods of working bone and ivory. He devoted most of the article to a discussion of specific objects—knives, the woman's knife, whetstones, spoke shaves, snow knives, the adze, ice picks, hammers, mattocks, sledges, toggles, kayaks, bows and arrows, bird and fish spears, harpoons, lamps and kettles, household utensils, work in whalebone, stone and bone points, decorated objects, and house plans. Wissler also commented on the relation of Comer's Midden to other sites and profusely illustrated his article with drawings.

A problem that arose from the excavation was the respectable age and extensiveness of an iron culture among the Inuit with no satisfactory data as to native sources of supply. Dr. Hovey, a geologist, denied the presence of telluric iron in the Cape York-Smith Sound region, which made it reasonably certain that the iron first used by the Polar Inuit was of meteoric origin. Hovey contributed to Wissler's article on the archaeology of the Polar Inuit a paper on "The Use of Meteoric Iron by the Polar Eskimo."[18]

MacMillan the Author

Beginning life with humble origins, Isaiah Bowman had been on the faculty at Yale before becoming the secretary and main operating officer of the American Geographical Society (American Geographical Society Library, University of Wisconsin–Milwaukee Libraries).

After returning home in 1917, MacMillan published *Four Years in the White North* (1918) about his experience in the Arctic. In preparing the manuscript he asked Isaiah Bowman of the American Geographical Society if Bowman could tell him who first saw and reported on a visit to Finlay Land, the King Christian Island of Sverdrup. Bowman replied with precision, quoting his sources. From these statements, Bowman added, it would appear that no one had set foot on it, though "we have not taken the trouble to look up original sources."[19]

Months later MacMillan asked Bowman where he could find an article on the first sighting of Finlay Land. He would like to speak of it in his narrative. Bowman referred the query to W.L.G. Joerg of the American Geographic Society. Joerg replied that Finlay Land was first sighted by Sherard Osborn on 29 April 1853. He cited his source.

MacMillan thanked Joerg; it was just what he wanted.[20] MacMillan was cleaning up his act.

By the time that MacMillan explored the area north of the Parry Islands, the members of the Crocker Land Expedition were winding up their affairs in the Arctic and were eager to return home. The story of their homecoming, which is related in the following chapter, is full of surprises and adventures.

8

Returning Home

The contract committed the Crocker Land Expedition to remain in the Arctic two years. When circumstances locked the men into place longer, they carried on their research and made out as well as possible while awaiting relief. The return of the party was kaleidoscopic. To follow the mishaps and adventures of seven men who were eager to get home is complicated, and the records of their escape are incomplete.

In May 1915 the American Museum received letters from the expedition via Denmark asking that a relief ship be sent northward in the summer. Accordingly, the Crocker Land Committee chartered the *George B. Cluett* from the Grenfell Association. The schooner left New York on 9 June with Captain George Comer of East Haddam, Connecticut, as the ice pilot. Dr. Edmund O. Hovey, Chairman of the Crocker Land Committee and Curator of Geology in the American Museum, was also on board, being sent to oversee the return of the expedition. The ship was expected to return in September or October. When Hovey departed, Assistant Secretary George H. Sherwood became acting chairman of the Committee in Charge of the Expedition.[1,2]

The *Cluett*, after being delayed thirty-five days in Melville Bay by ice and a disabled engine, arrived at North Star Bay in Wolstenholme Sound on 12 September. It then had the misfortune of being held fast in the ice, unable either to reach her goal or to return. Peter Freuchen, a Dane at the Thule trading station, which was near Inglefield Gulf to the north, went to the *Cluett* in his motorboat, boarded the vessel, and gave his name. An elderly gentleman stepped forward, grabbed Freuchen's hands, and told him how pleased he was to see him. Now, he said, all his worries were over. The man was Dr. Hovey.[3]

Since the Cluett was unable to proceed, Freuchen offered to take Dr. Hovey in his motorboat if Hovey furnished the kerosene. Hovey agreed, eager to contact his party and dreading the possibility of having to spend a winter in North Greenland. With Hovey, Captain Comer, and two natives, Freuchen set out for Etah. When forced to put in to repair their boat, the tide went out, leaving them high and dry. Hovey was furious. A mild little man at home, he found it no vacation to run into such dullards as he considered Freuchen. It took some time for Freuchen to calm him. Hovey betrayed his petty economies by showing Freuchen the gifts he had brought to please the natives and to pay them for their favors. The gifts were of no account. Waiting for the tide, Hovey wanted to have coffee. Some natives followed them into the cabin, and when the cook poured the coffee for them Hovey asked, "Do you allow him to give coffee to the Eskimos?" "Why not?" Freuchen asked. "But that's different," Hovey replied. "Your cook has no right to serve the ship's provisions to the natives. The museum has to pay for everything, and I have to see that expenses are kept to a minimum." Comer and Freuchen explained to Hovey that he was in the Artic now, not at an accountant's desk. How, Freuchen wondered, could a well-known scientist be so lacking in understanding human nature.

Setting out again, the travelers encountered a storm and had to put up for the night at Cape Alexander, much to the doctor's dissatisfaction. Captain Comer told Freuchen about the trip north and the politics he had to use to get around Dr. Hovey. It was not easy, he said. Dr. Hovey explained that he had come north to untangle certain difficulties that had arisen. He complained about the terrible expenses that MacMillan had incurred for the museum. The Eskimos need only to be told what to do, said Hovey, not paid to do it.[4]

When Dr. Hovey reached Etah, he found that the expedition's supplies and findings had been packed awaiting his arrival. MacMillan and Jot Small were not there; they had gone to Nerky. Dr. Hunt also was not there. Hovey proposed to take Ekblaw, Green, Allen, Tanquary and important records with him back to the *Cluett*. He supervised the loading of the supplies into the motorboat and a second boat they were to tow. Hovey took from the Inuit many things that MacMillan had either sold or given them. Reaching Nerky early in the morning, Hovey roused MacMillan from sleep. He could not go home yet, the sleeper insisted, since he had not accomplished half of the work he had hoped to do. Hovey agreed to permit MacMillan, Dr. Hunt, and Small to remain in Greenland another year, since it was not feasible at that time to take out the expedition's collections and equipment. Freuchen thought it would reflect discredit upon the museum for the leader to leave behind the major portion of his treasures.[5]

On the return from Etah, Dr. Hovey, grateful for Freuchen's help, asked Freuchen what crime he had committed that had banished him to the Arctic. Even if guilty of a misdemeanor, Freuchen ought to be able to find a decent job in the outside world. Hovey would be glad to recommend him. Freuchen was touched by Hovey's kindness.[6]

When Dr. Hovey returned to the *George B. Cluett*, he discovered that

8. Returning Home

the ship had been forced to winter in Parker Snow Bay.[7] Unless it was necessary to prolong the search another month, the *New York Times* reported, the *Cluett* might send a report on her voyage homeward almost any day.[8] Provisions soon ran short, however, and in January 1916 Dr. Hovey and Captain Comer were forced to leave the ship and the expedition party separated. Hovey, along with Tanquary, Green, and Allen, began a sledge journey across Melville Bay with the object of reaching the southern Danish settlements. Owing to his physical condition, Hovey could not proceed farther than Cape York. So he returned to North Star Bay.

As a result of these developments, both the main party and the relief party were now in need of assistance. Accordingly, the Crocker Land Committee arranged to send the steamer *Danmark* to the relief of the expedition. The ship, then in south Greenland, was to proceed to Etah. After picking up the members of the expedition it would land them either at St. John's Newfoundland, or Sydney, Cape Breton, late in August or early in September.

Unfortunately, the *Danmark* was having trouble. According to a cablegram the museum received from Copenhagen on 15 November 1916, the ship was observed in Melville Bay on 20 August 1916, bound northward. Apparently the steamer had made only 150 miles northward in seventeen days, since previous advices reported her as being off Upernivik on 3 August 1916. This report and the ship's failure to arrive either at Sydney or St. Johns indicated that the ice conditions were severe and that the vessel had probably been delayed by ice on her southward voyage. It was still possible that the *Danmark* might reach America before the end of the year, but even should she be caught in the ice and be compelled to winter in the north, no anxiety need be felt for the safety of the party, since the vessel was staunch, well equipped, and well provisioned.[9]

The first relief ship, the *George B. Cluett*, had finally left its winter quarters in North Star Bay the latter part of July and arrived at Battle Harbor, Labrador, on 7 September 1916. She brought out a letter from Dr. Hovey, dated 10 July 1916, stating that he was in touch with Knud Rasmussen, that the members of the Crocker Land Expedition were well, that MacMillan had returned to Etah on 6 May 1916 from his 1,500 mile sledge journey to the westward, and that all were looking forward to the arrival of the second relief ship, the *Danmark*.[10]

Meanwhile, Fitzhugh Green had come across the ice cap from Etah to Thule with a letter from Hovey asking Freuchen for help. Green remained there while Freuchen hurried down to the ship. He found Dr. Hovey, who had never considered remaining in the Arctic through the winter, in a bad frame of mind. Hovey asked Freuchen to furnish him and his men with clothes and to help him get in touch with MacMillan. When Captain Comer said that it would be difficult to stretch his provisions to last nine more months, Hovey reminded him of the contract and remained on board eating his fill, though he knew that what he ate would be subtracted from the crew's mess in the coming winter.[11]

MacMillan went to Thule when he learned of the ship's plight and took Hovey back to Etah with him. Hovey insisted that no food be sent to the ship from Etah, since the ship's captain had a contract to supply all the rations. Less relentless, MacMillan sent a great deal of food to the boat. Freuchen told Hovey that he could not trade with the natives if Freuchen helped him, since that would put him in competition with Freuchen. "He whined and expostulated over the poverty of the museum and the drain of this expensive expedition on it." Freuchen had a grand time with Green, who was "gentle and understanding, and fit comfortably into the household." He was considerate of Navarana, Freuchen's Inuit wife, kind to the natives, and occupied himself largely in reading.[12]

Now, locked into the Arctic, the explorers could not count on speedy relief. On 17 May Dr. Hovey informed the American Museum by cable that the *Cluett* had failed to reach Etah. He had got Green, Ekblaw, Tanquary, and Allen with Rasmussen's power boat commanded by Freuchen from North Star Bay, while MacMillan, Small, and Hunt were absent hunting for food. The Cluett was wintering at Parker Snow Bay with its engine disabled. As Dr. Hovey reported, "Food supply inadequate. Charter violated. My party forced to leave vessel in January to obtain subsistence." Green, Tanquary, Allen, and Dr. Hovey had started southward by sledge on 16 January, but the others left Dr. Hovey at Cape York because it was unwise for him to cross Melville Bay "on account of physical condition which developed next day." Tanquary was on the *Hans Egede* from Holstenborg to Copenhagen; the museum should cable him, in care of Rasmussen's address, $500 to cover his expenses to New York. MacMillan was on an expedition to King Christian Island; Jot Small was in charge in Etah. Ekblaw, Hunt, Comer, and Hovey were at North Star Bay, and all were well. The captain of the *Cluett* said that he would sail directly homeward without attempting Etah again. Therefore it was necessary for the museum to send a reliable steamer with a competent, experienced master, adequate accommodations, and a full year's provisions for six passengers. The vessel was to leave St. John's, Newfoundland, by 10 July for Etah, North Star Bay, and other Greenland points as desired, with instructions to attempt Cape Sabine to relieve MacMillan if necessary. The vessel was to load cargo from the beaches. "Send me written authority over property and control over movements of vessel," wrote Hovey, who closed by saying he was sending a full report by mail and messenger and asking the museum to inform all friends.[13]

Thus prompted, Henry Fairfield Osborn attempted to secure aid for the beleaguered party. In a telegram to President James, he said that all the members of the Crocker Land Expedition were alive and well and that important scientific results had been secured. But owing to unprecedented weather on Greenland's west coast, a costly effort to insure the relief of the widely scattered party during the summer, and to dispatch a full year's provisions to provide against a second defeat of our plans, he was negotiating with shipping countries in America, Denmark, and Norway to secure the lowest estimate before making a contract. Osborn estimated that $15,000 would be necessary to close one of the contracts. "I trust you will authorize me to depend upon the University of Illinois for one third of this amount." A telegram from President James's secretary replied, "President away. Appropriation improbable as budget of trustees very rigid."[14]

President Osborn also wrote to Dr. Hugh M. Smith, head of the Bureau of Fisheries in the Department of Commerce in Washington, D.C., asking if the bureau could detail the ship *Roosevelt* in command of Robert Bartlett for relief. Coal for the vessel and Bartlett's salary would be at the museum's expense. Smith replied that the *Roosevelt* could not go to sea without extensive repairs. He regretted not being able to assist in the emergency. Days later Osborn informed Smith that he was experiencing great difficulty in finding an absolutely reliable vessel either in the U.S., Denmark, or Norway. He trusted that Smith would consider dispatching the *Roosevelt* by 1 July. "I can of course," Osborn added, "secure the necessary support of your action through my personal relations with Secretary [William C.] Redfield [of Commerce] and President [Woodrow] Wilson. Will inform you immediately if alternative vessel is secured."[15] Smith desired to assist Osborn, but the *Roosevelt* was not in position to go to sea. He would interpose no objection to the ship's detail if Osborn cared to take up the matter with the president and the secretary.[16]

Meanwhile, in January, owing to the shortage of provisions on the *Cluett*, Hovey, Green, Allen, and Tanquary had set out on the 1,300-mile sledge journey over the sea ice to the Danish settlements in southern Greenland. On their first day out they covered about sixty miles, but the physical exertion proved too much for Dr. Hovey. Unable to proceed farther than Cape York, he returned to winter quarters at North Star Bay. Days later, the other three set out again with sledges and finally reached Egedsminde on the south side of Disko Bay.[17]

Conditions made it advisable for only one man to proceed from Egedsminde to Holstenborg, so Green and Allen remained at Egedesminde while Tanquary sailed for Copenhagen on the *Hans Egede*. When it stopped at Thorshavn, the capitol of the Faroe Islands, he sent a cablegram to the American Museum reporting that the expedition members were well but it would be necessary to send a powerful steam vessel to Etah to relieve them and to pick up the collection and the equipment. In late May, in a message sent through the American State Department, Tanquary wrote that the cheapest offer for the Danish steamer *Danmark* was about $16,080 for about four months, and it was necessary to get several guarantees from the Canadian government for the owner of the *Danmark* to proceed. Osborn immediately wrote to the Canadian prime minister describing the situation and asking for a reply by wire as to the probable attitude of the Canadian and English governments to the described arrangements.[18]

These negotiations enabled the Crocker Land Committee to charter the *Danmark* with the Greenland Mining Company. Authorities hoped that it would be able to pick up the first relief party at Parker Snow Bay, proceed to Etah to relieve other expedition members and return them and their equipment to Sydney, Nova Scotia, or to St. John's, Newfoundland. The committee cabled instructions to Fitzhugh Green, who had worked his way over the Greenland ice down to Egedsminde, to represent the Crocker Land Committee on the *Danmark* until Hovey or MacMilllan arrived. The charter for this ship was $18,300; other expenses incurred made the total cost from $34,000 to $40,000. It would be necessary for the museum to raise to raise that sum to insure the safe return of the explorers.[19] If the voyage of the *Danmark* was successful, the *New York Times* reported, "one of the most dangerous and, in many ways, unfortunate polar expeditions ever sent out will be brought to an end. It may, in its fruits, compensate for the disappointments and disasters already suffered by the explorers and their backers."[20]

The *Danmark* labored for three days to depart on its mission but could not get through the ice. So the ship prepared to lay over for the winter. Hovey tried to put the best face on his predicament. "If no relief comes next year," he wrote, "we shall be unable to heat the house, our supply of white man's food will be exceedingly limited, if not exhausted, and we shall be obliged to distribute ourselves among Inuit igloos, here and elsewhere, and live with and like them." Their white biscuit (army bread) was damaged by mold, but Hovey and MacMillan preferred the whole wheat, whose makers provided against breakage by mixing in a little cement.[21]

Ekblaw and Dr. Hunt Return

Ekblaw and Dr. Hunt had been aboard the *Cluett* since it arrived. The ship's officers welcomed them, the food was abundant, and the cooking was good. But under Hovey's authorization and MacMillan's instructions to proceed home, they left North Star Bay in mid–December 1916 on a 1,400-mile journey with six sledges and five Inuit, Rasmussen accompanying them.[22]

The first night out the party encamped in two tents. The going was heavy from Parker Snow Bay to Cape York. The men hoped to cross Melville Bay in two or three days, but for centuries the bay had been a barrier between the Smith Sound Inuit and the Inuit of Danish Greenland. The sledges were not connected by ropes, but every man had a coil of rope which he could throw for assistance in case the ice gave way. The conditions for sledging were the worst Rasmussen had ever seen. Despite many narrow escapes, only one sledge was thrown in the water. Its Inuit driver was rescued and the sledge was recovered. Toward the end of the journey supplies ran very low and five dogs died of starvation. Food was eked out by polar bear and narwhal meat obtained from Inuit caches.

Crossing along the coast from Cape York to Cape Seddon, with the temperature more than -40°F, they made fairly good time despite the deep snows because their dogs were fresh and rested. When they struck the "pootenook"—heavy snow with water on thin ice—the going became fearful. The following day they got no farther than Cape Melville. In the next four marches they made little distance. Men and dogs were discouraged, food was scarce, Dr. Hunt had chafed the tendons of his ankles, while Ekblaw had frozen both big toes. Nearly exhausted, they found the lee of an iceberg in which to shelter their tents from the wind and made camp.

Huddled together on Christmas Eve, they cooked bear meat and made tea. Rasmussen provided two boxes of canned pears, Ekblaw a package of dates, and with bear meat, a little frozen pemmican and tea, they made their supper. Cuddled down in sleeping bags, Ekblaw and a Danish Greenlander, whistled "Stille Nacht, Heilige Nacht," exchanged Christmas greetings, and fell asleep.[23]

The following days were a nightmare. The going was hard, the weather was cold, the food was scarce, and the dogs were on short rations. And they were still miles from Cape Seddon. So Rasmussen adopted relief measures. With two teams of the best dogs and the two best Inuit drivers, Knud set out at midnight on a forced march to Cape Seddon, promising to have relief ships to them by daylight. When no relief appeared, they waited a day or two. Then Ekblaw, Hunt, and the Inuit sledged their way toward Cape Seddon with weak dogs. The afternoon was nearly gone when Ootah appeared. They made tea, boiled some meat, and passed from despair to delight. While they ate, Rasmussen caught up with them and they went on to Tooktooliksuah, the Inuit village on Cape Seddon. Many of their dogs died. Due to the frosted lining of his nasal passages Ekblaw had a nose bleed and lost considerable blood. Weak and disabled, he was "a worn, broken specimen of Arctic explorer."[24]

Ekblaw and Dr. Hunt reached Upernavik on 11 January and departed on 18 January. Rasmussen accompanied them as far as Augpalartok and then turned back to North Star Bay.[25]

The others went on to South Upernavik, where, confronted by open water and lack of dog food, the men and the sledges they had engaged at Pröven to accompany them to Igalorawit returned to Pröven, while Hunt and

Ekblaw waited at South Upernavik for new ice to form. On 9 February the ice was strong enough to warrant their leaving. On the next day they were forced to turn back because of open water in Umanak Fiord south of Iglorssuit Peninsula. The season had been the most open within the memory of the oldest natives, none of whom thought that ice would form over the mountains of Iglorssuit Peninsula. The voyagers were unable to procure enough sledges to take their whole party by this route. The Inuit, reluctant to attempt the proposed route, gave as their main reason the poor condition of their dogs. Both here and at Pröven the hunt had been so poor because of bad ice conditions that the dogs were but few and poorly nourished.

Since their whole party could not get through, Ekblaw sent Dr. Hunt and their interpreter on. Ekblaw viewed Hunt's reasons for getting home as more urgent than his; he hoped to proceed later if new ice formed, engaging sledges for the purpose. Taking precaution to ensure that one would succeed, they arranged to part at Sarkok, on the south side of Nugsuak Peninsula. Dr. Hunt was to proceed by way of Ritenbenk, Christianshab, and Egedesminde; Ekblaw by way of Godhavn. Thinking it likely that he might be unable to get beyond Godhavn, Ekblaw was reconciled to a considerable stay with Morten P. Porsild, Director of the Danish Arctic Station in Disko, Greenland. Porsild had a splendid English library. But Ekblaw was unprepared for a protracted stay without any literature or equipment for scientific work.

After resting at Tooktooliksuah, the companions went on to Upernavik, the capital of the colony. Here Governor Vinterberg, Pastor Rosen, and Doctor Bryder made them welcome. When they reached South Upernavik they met open water that prevented their continuing farther south. For over a month they stayed at the home of a factor waiting for colder weather and new ice. When such conditions appeared, the local dogs were in such wretched condition as to prevent their proceeding. For both men to travel might mean that neither would succeed. Then their message asking for relief might arrive too late. To insure as much certainty as possible they decided that Dr. Hunt should proceed southward with the best dogs and equipment while Ekblaw awaited relief at South Upernavik.[26]

On 16 February Dr. Hunt left for Holstensborg to catch the *Hans Egede*, which plied between Greenland and Denmark during the open season. Because of thin ice, he went by a new route over the mountains and succeeded despite almost insurmountable obstacles. After he departed, Ekblaw turned back with a heavy heart to begin a five-month's wait for a means of getting home.

At the little sod-walled trading station Hans Kintrup-Jensen assured Ekblaw that he was welcome. The Danish cooper had gone to Greenland twenty-three years earlier in the employ of the Royal Danish Company. He had married an Inuit woman who had died years earlier and left him with six children. He had sent two children to Denmark for their education and had made a home for the other four. A genial fellow, Kintrup-Jensen was fond of ale, coffee, and tobacco. He ruled the village despotically, dispensing his station's stores as profitably as he could. Whenever the mood seized him, he gave a dance to which he invited favored Inuit. His house was a three-room cottage, snug and comfortable but poorly ventilated. He kept six servants—three men to hunt and look after his dogs and three women to cook, brew his ale, and look after the house. Pauletta, his Inuit cook, managed her master and his household. During his five-month stay, Ekblaw was not once reminded that he was almost a self-imposed guest or that he made serious inroads on the Danish provisions.

With eight dogs and a sledge, Ekblaw sledged about the colony and went seal hunting. He caught almost two-score seals and half a hundred sharks during the season. In Danish Greenland the Inuit caught seals in nets throughout the length of the coast every fall and spring. In the most favorable season, when an Inuit often found half a dozen or more seals each day, he lived well, using the meat for food and exchanging the skin and blubber with the trader for sugar, coffee, and other commodities. The shark fishery was unusual. The shark caught was the sluggish sleeper-shark; its liver yielded an illuminating oil. Thousands of pounds of shark-liver oil were obtained annually. At South Upernavik the shark fishery was not very profitable, but at Pröven, hundreds, even thousands, were caught each year. Usually, the liver was the only part used. Ekblaw also went caribou hunting with the factor at Pröven, and on occasion he went to Upernavik to visit Governor Vinterberg, his family, and the Danes there.[27]

Ekblaw learned to like the Inuit of the little village. Their lot was hard, and yet they were happy and usually hopeful. Consumption was rampant among them.

In mid-July the chief magistrate of this part of Greenland picked up Ekblaw in his motorboat and took him to visit Upernavik, Pröven, Nuksuah, and Godhavn. At Godhavn, Ekblaw stayed with Porsild, the director of the Danish Arctic Station. For a month Ekblaw reveled in his splendid library, well-equipped laboratory, and the flora near the village. Here he found the exquisite courtesy and generous hospitality that characterized the Danes throughout Greenland. In mid-August Captain Bartlett arrived in the *Neptune*. With him were MacMillan and Jot Small. Ekblaw bade goodbye to the kind people and steamed away. His Far Northern venture was over.[28]

Dr. Hovey and Others Return

While Dr. Hunt and Ekblaw sought to cope with the vicissitudes of their return home, Dr. Hovey, Green, Tanquary, and Allen were on the stricken

Cluett. With as many as nine or eleven men crowded at times into a small, poorly ventilated cabin intended for six people, friction was inevitable. From the ship the explorers removed to Thule, the trading post of Rasmussen and Freuchen. One day Freuchen drove across the glacier to Parker Snow Bay only to discover that the *George B. Cluett* had finally departed. He returned to find the Americans more upset than ever. Dr. Hovey regretted that he had ever left the ship, and he blamed Rasmussen for bringing him to Thule. From the look of the ice in Melville Bay it seemed fairly certain that no ship would be able to reach them this year. But just as Dr. Hovey and his companions gave up, they saw a boat coming around Cape Atholl. Dr. Hovey went almost mad with joy, yelling and shouting like a boy. The ship was the *Danmark*, an old tub that had been forty-five days crossing Melville Bay. The Americans boarded the ship, which labored for three days to get through the ice, but had to turn back and lay over for the winter.[29]

Perhaps it was early 1917 when the stranded party decided that they should return home on sledges by way of South Greenland. Freuchen was to take them as far as he could, with Dr. Hovey riding on Freuchen's sledge. A number of reliable boys and a complete outfit would accompany them. According to Freuchen, "the old doctor irritated us all, especially me," by fussing over everything, inquiring about the cost and complaining because it could not be done for less. Dr. Hovey wanted Freuchen to assure him that he and his fellow travelers could stop as guests with the Danes down the coast—surely the Danes would be delighted to have such important and interesting guests. Freuchen could not promise that, and would not have wanted to bother his countrymen and friends with visitors who represented the richest museum in the world, especially as Dr. Hovey was such a tactless, impolite person. He preferred not to comprehend Freuchen's point of view, and asked favor after favor, for none of which was Freuchen to be paid. The ship's captain asked Freuchen to buy more tobacco for his men. Dr. Hovey cantankerously objected, saying that he had paid the boys for their trip and he controlled their return voyage. Since Dr. Hovey had hired Freuchen, he wanted Freuchen to do the captain no favors. This was too much for Freuchen, who told the "quaking old man" exactly what he thought of him and made it clear that only his age protected him for physical violence.[30]

The party proceeded. After passing Cape York the passage became bad. Green, the most experienced traveler among the Americans, saw that they would have to turn back and wait for colder weather. Dr. Hovey grumbled at the delay, but walking from the sledges to the houses he fell into a dead faint. His companions sent for Dr. Hunt, who was on the ship. Dr. Hovey admitted that the trip had been a great strain on him. Freuchen now realized that Dr. Hovey rode on the sledge because he could not walk. Dr. Hovey pleaded with Freuchen to take him along. Dr. Hovey loathed the Arctic and realized that he was much disliked there. The poor man assured Freuchen that he had only done his duty. Dr. Hunt confirmed the decision to leave Dr. Hovey behind because his heart could not stand the hardships of a long outdoor trip at this time of year. So Green, Tanqueray, and Allen left without Dr. Hovey. For Freuchen, it was a great pleasure to be associated with the three Americans, but the natives did not care for them, especially since they used their discretion about travel details and were great on discipline and routine. At Tassiussak, in the home of the trader Nielsen, the Americans delighted the Danes. Tanqueray's beautiful baritone voice was a joy to them. Freuchen was prepared to bid farewell to the Americans at Ikerask. They could secure safe passage with natives to Egedesminde and then drive south with the mail carriers and catch the first steamer to Denmark. Freuchen had the fondest memories of their stay in his district.[31]

After Freuchen returned to Thule, Rasmussen arrived. He had come up to Greenland on the first boat permitted through the North Sea during the war, had bought a sledge, and had worried his way north to Egedesminde, where he met the three Americans whom Freuchen had piloted south. They were stuck there. Tanqueray had lost two of his toes through frost. Rasmussen brought word that the American Museum was going to try to force another boat through to pick up its expedition and Dr. Hovey's first rescuing outfit. They notified MacMillan; Rasmussen carried the news to Dr. Hovey at Parker Snow Bay. He had been in a quandary over whether to order the *Cluett* to proceed to Etah for the supplies and findings and then sail back to New York or whether they should go south at once. Captain Comer resolved the matter by saying that if the ship went anywhere it would go home. Rasmussen brought Freuchen a letter from President Osborn thanking him for his assistance. Osborn did not yet know how Freuchen had been fighting with Dr. Hovey. Rasmussen invited Dr. Hovey, Captain Comer, Dr. Hunt, and Ekblaw to come to Thule and stay with him and Freuchen until the new ship arrived.[32]

In late May a third relief ship was being fitted out to rescue MacMillan, who was at Etah. The remaining expedition members were somewhere in the neighborhood. Museum officials were confident that the marooned adventurers were in good health and could be brought back to St. John's by September. Perhaps the third relief ship could give some aid to the *Danmark*, which was supposedly frozen up.[33]

A week later, the American Museum received from the Faroe Islands a cable which said that MacMillan, Comer, Small and Hovey were at Etah, the *Danmark* was at North Star Bay, Ekblaw was at Godhavan, and Hunt was on the *Hans Egede*. Arrange credit and a passport in Copenhagen through the American Minister, the message added. The sender was Dr. Hunt. As Sherwood explained, the cablegram meant that the *Danmark* was caught in the ice and forced to winter in North Star Bay. The last previous word received from the expedition was dated 10 July 1916 and written by Dr. Hovey, who was then not far from North Star Bay. That letter was brought out by the *George B. Cluett*, which was to return to America as soon as she could. All of the men named in the cable had been marooned in North Greenland for two years. The cable meant that Ekblaw and Dr. Hunt had sledged from Etah or North Star Bay over 1,500 miles of snow and ice, and had reached Godhaven on Disco Island. For some reason, Ekblaw remained behind, while Dr. Hunt went on, probably to Holstenborg. From there he evidently caught the *Hans Egede* and set sail for Copenhagen, which he would probably reach within a week and be in New York within a month.

Now, with the *Cluett* trapped in the ice and the *Danmark* undoubtedly frozen in in north Greenland, Mr. Nyboe, the president of the company that owned the *Danmark*, proposed to send his motor schooner, the *Kap York*, to Greenland with supplies for his stations as soon as navigation opened. For $7,500 he offered to have his boat await news from the Crocker Land Expedition. If a third ship was needed, the *Kap York* would proceed to a Canadian port and the museum could then charter another steamer.[34]

With this information in hand, Sherwood suggested that if the news was favorable spending $7,500 would save the need to pay from $20,000 to $30,000 for a third ship. If the news was unfavorable, the museum would have to charter a third vessel at approximately $25,000 in addition to the $7,500. "With the lives of our six explorers in north Greenland possibly at stake, the risks far outweigh the chance of saving $25,000." The wisest course was to charter a third ship and send her to North Greenland in the summer and apply the $7,500 for the *Kap York* to the larger vessel. Owing to shipping conditions, the charter fee for a suitable vessel might be from $30,000 to $40,000. Sherwood recommended that the executive committee authorize the Committee in Charge to charter an adequate steamer and to dispatch her to north Greenland as soon as practicable.

On 4 April 1917, Sherwood wrote to W. & S. Job & Co. in New York stating his desire to charter a powerful steam vessel to proceed from Sydney or St. John's about 1 July to north Greenland to bring back the six members of our Crocker Land Expedition. The charter period would begin sometime between 1 July and 15 July and would cover not less than two months and probably not more than three. The Crocker Land Committee desired to have the vessel commanded by Captain Robert Bartlett, who was experienced in Arctic waters. Sherwood requested a list of the boats available, their net tonnage, and the charter fee on a Government basis.[35] W. & S. Job & Co. could not immediately reply because it had to communicate with underwriters in London about special insurance on ships. They feared that they might have to ask $12,000 a month to equal other prospective employment. The museum quickly engaged Bartlett to command the relief ship at $500 for his services, regardless of the length of time.³⁶ The effort to secure a relief ship became more difficult. Job Brothers was unwilling to offer or to commit themselves to any of their vessels, whereupon Bowring and Company offered the *Viking* at $30,000 for five weeks, while Baine, Johnston and Company offered the *Bloodhound* and the *Njord* at $500 per day. Osborn, Sherwood, and Bartlett accepted the charter terms for the latter.³⁷

Unfortunately, satisfactory terms could not be agreed upon for the *Njord*, so officials chartered the *Neptune* for $15,000 a month, having to take it for not less than two months. The vessel would be made available the first week in July at St. John's; it should be ready to sail from Sydney on 10 July. To guard against being caught in the ice, the museum was sending full rations for their explorers for a period of fourteen months. Austin, Nichols and Company was putting up six tons of provisions at a cost of approximately $3,500. The cost of the vessel was excessive, and the means of financing the relief expedition had not yet been provided. The museum was advancing the money for contingencies as they arose.³⁸

As these details were being arranged, Dr. Hunt at Thorshaven sent to the American Museum the cablegram reporting the location of the various expedition members. In light of this news, the Committee in Charge was anxious to send the *Neptune* to the relief of the Crocker Land Expedition party as soon as possible. The Expedition had been very costly, said Sherwood, but had yielded results entirely commensurate with the expense.³⁹

Meanwhile, Green, Tanqueray, and Allen had left the *George B. Cluett*, perhaps at Upernavik, intending to proceed along the Greenland coast to South Greenland. Their way was carried out under the usual hardships attending Artic travel. Early in this trip, Green was stranded on an ice floe with his dogs and sledge when an Inuit, coming upon him, feared that Green was the Devil. As described by Green, the two parties went "crashing and tearing [their] way through rough up-ended floes, spinning around bergs, stumbling and capsizing in the darkness, and all the time both of us keeping up a steady stream of breathless objurgations (and other profanity) at our dogs—even a Kennedy Channel bear hunt wasn't in it." Green suddenly lost control of his dogs and sledge, wriggled in mid-air, and landed on his shoulders. The Inuit had apparently driven around a low tilted berg while Green's team had cut across it and dropped about six feet. Green untangled his traces, went 200 yards farther, and found the rest of his party. "We thought you passed a few minutes ago," Tanqueray said, "but the Inuit declared it was either the Devil or a pibloqtok native from one of the inner settlements. He was going like an express train and making twice as much noise." Green assured the others that the Devil had pretty nearly got a compound fracture of his neck bone.⁴⁰

While the party met unusual hardships, there were compensations for the scientific observer when they entered south Greenland, which had been modified by Danish influence. The sharp change at Cape Holm marked the beginning of a sequence of progressive cultural changes which seemed to result from human interference and geographical influences, most particularly climate, which limits the time possible for the various native occupations. In Greenland, white intervention aroused particular interest because of the policy by which it was controlled. Nearly half a century earlier the Danish government had closed the country to outsiders, in part for economic reasons but chiefly for the protection of the natives and for the maintenance of native initiative.[41]

The Americans arrived at Pröven, a trading station, late at night. Natives greeted them, and Nilsen, the trader, filled the visitors "chock to the nozzle" with seal meat and broth and spread their skins on the floor of the little cabin. While the travelers sat naked on the parlor floor and picked a new generation of body lice out of their undershirts, Nilsen provided a little accordion music. Such informality as sitting naked and picking cooties from their lairs was possible in trading stations but not in the colonies.[42]

The colonies were officially distinguished from the trading stations by the presence of a governor or executive. Socially the difference lay in the relations between the whites and the Inuit. Nearly every trader had either an Inuit wife or mistress who was housekeeper and nurse. This intermarriage encouraged greater familiarity between races. As viewed from a later perspective, it slightly elevated the brown man's propensities for a civilized environment and naturally lowered the white man's propensities for the same. Green observed a kind of snobbishness among the Danes living in colonies. It was the natural superiority of their culture, said Green, but it was not permitted to dampen kindness toward the natives or to deepen the loneliness of the isolation. The governor's staff included an assistant, a doctor, a pastor, and in the largest colonies a carpenter. Usually each of these functionaries had a Danish wife and children. The colonies were a set socially independent of native pastimes and entertainment. The governor was king of his district, answerable only to the inspector at Godhavn.[43]

The governor's assistant was a young man who made about one-third of the salary of the governor. His house was free; his servants did his domestic chores. He could not marry. He had to lead a moral life lest reports to Denmark end his career in the colony. The doctor was the most unhappy man in the colony. Perhaps wanderlust or failure at home had driven him to accept a colonial appointment. He almost never got a fair opportunity for professional work. He was little better than a first-aid artist. A white man could not ask an Inuit to change his diet, wash, or sleep in opposition to the wishes of the Almighty Devil. As the tribes became more civilized the need for medical attention increased, but few natives lived to any great age to be attacked by tumors and cancers. At Etah in 1914, however, a grandmother had died, supposedly of cancer. Dr. Hunt thought that some good might come from investigating the case. To do so he would need a specimen from her body, which lay under the rocks on a hillside. He bribed the victim's son in order to proceed, and then turned to his task with a saw, chisel, and hammer. The loving son held his parent while the doctor sawed her in half. When it came to hacking the desired lump out of her middle, the son fled. The doctor returned to his task, but the specimen never reached the laboratory. The dog pack broke in and the specimen disappeared.[44]

The pastor was a member of the governor's staff in the colonies. Green viewed the pastors as real missionaries, men of fundamental goodness, faith, and zeal. They strove to convert the natives to Christian belief and to achieve a mental and moral uplift of the race. Although native superstition was unyielding, the fight went on. No more inspiring sight could be encountered than a poor, half-fed Danish priest imploring a mob of filthy, "vermined" Inuit, not to believe as he believes, but to join him in little kindnesses to others to the end that everyday evils be cast out. The name of Hans Egede was perpetuated in the colony of Egedesminde, where his spirit abided.[45]

The native religion, animistic, was an obstacle to the Christian religion. The natives believed that there was a separate spirit for each item of their life, abstract and concrete. Even after the Inuit had been practically Christianized, their original beliefs persisted. The younger generation, owing to wider education, have less faith in the existence of supernatural beings. However, superstition was not far off. In the dark months a vague uneasiness sometimes arrived. The native meets dead friends, personified deeds, manlike animals, or other of the many forms that lie within the power of the superior devils. Sipsoo, Green's foster father and a man of the highest character, witnessed the brilliant descent of a well-known planet. He even heard the spitting steam that rose in clouds wherein the star's return was concealed. One could ridicule the poor barbarian's Almighty Devil, but some day, when one was agonizingly fatigued, one would see the Almighty Devil and all his court. Mr. Balle, the "High Priest" of all the Danish colonies in Greenland, knew the psychology of these things that impeded his work and exasperated his common sense.[46]

The carpenter, or general handyman, was the lowliest white inhabitant in any Greenland settlement. Some of them, addicted to Danish schnapps, often poured "the Devil's own breath" into their bellies at any hour of the day or night. In sum, the organization of the colonies proved very effective.[47]

At Pröven, the trader Nilsen permitted his American visitors to pay for board and lodging, which made them free to remain a convenient length of time. They determined to stay two days, during which they enjoyed the irregularity of bachelordom. Allen gave a dance, which the Inuit declared highly satisfactory. In the afternoon, Pastor Rossen, who had come down from the north, performed a marriage ceremony. The natives, who had nothing of this sort among themselves, were without morals in regard to sex except that they were careful not to permit children from those too closely related. This custom has nothing to do with possible degeneracy but with the inevitable displeasure of a certain devil. Pastor Rossen's performance was rather crude even for the frontier. He made a short speech on getting married in whiteman style, and then a disciple went among the crowd and extracted a man and a woman and brought them before the pastor. The man strongly objected to the proceedings, as did the woman, and the recalcitrant lovers fled.[48]

The Americans' next stop was South Upernavik. Jensen, the trader there, had a Danish wife and several children. When the wife died, Jensen took an Inuit wife, who was a good mother and an excellent housekeeper. Pastor Rossen was eager to marry the two, but Jensen needed no help of a minister. Jensen, having heard of the Americans coming, had collected a supply of meat, fish, eggs, and other delicacies and had made his beer usually potent for the visit. After a lavish dinner, followed by coffee and Danish tobacco, Jensen gave a dance attended by the pick of the village belles. It lasted until 3:00 a.m. Jensen traded every morning between 10 and 11. The natives used Greenland currency to buy various commodities. In the afternoon the hunters who had skins or blubber to sell met, being paid according to a schedule of prices set by the government.

Use of money made it possible to make each exchange separate. Each summer Jensen's station was supplied with a stated amount of trading material, most of which was recorded and sold by weight. Jensen's trade featured sugar and flour. If he was charged by the government for 100 pounds of flour and could make that same flour weigh 110 pounds by the time it was sold, he would have a considerable profit. Tampering with the scales would not work because high-grade scales were used and the local authorities inspected the scales. So Jensen exposed his flour and sugar to dampness and sold it at a good 10 percent profit on the original weight.[49]

Fitzhugh Green described Jensen's "ruthless bleeding" of the natives in order to offset it with his true generosity because it illustrated the character of a certain type of trader. Jensen used the money he made by crooked means to entertain the village. "As a wealthy, powerful individual among simpleminded peaceful people," Green added, "a trader caters to his own weak vanity and feeds upon the adulation and ignorant respect of those about him."[50]

Proceeding from South Upernavik to Umanak, the Americans took a roundabout way in order to avoid open water. With a native guide, they took the pass, a depression that led over Svartenhuk, or Black Cape. After an hour or so the party of six sledges halted while the Inuit debated turning back. The Americans insisted on driving on. They soon had to climb more than

3,000 feet to reach the summit of the land mass. Luckily they stumbled on a place to descend, but Green's sledge struck an invisible nubble and capsized. After several days of heavy going and one long march, the Americans reached the trading station at Igdlorsuit.[51]

Here they found a single frame building, a large shed for the storage of fat and skins, a small chapel, and a shop. Native igloos clustered about in disorder. Nilsen, the trader, a man of sixty-six years, was small, brown, and unkempt. Born in Greenland, the son of a carpenter, he was sent to Denmark, given ten years' apprenticeship at barrel work, and in 1865 returned as a cooper. He married a native woman, by whom he had nearly three-score children, grandchildren, and great-grandchildren. He dealt absolutely fairly in his trading station, and Igdlorsuit was known as next to the happiest district in Greenland. The one or two in the neighborhood not related to Jensen were almost outcasts, doing all the dirty work. Nilsen, who ate all meals with his guests, gave a ball in their honor the night of their arrival.[52]

On 2 March the Americans bought one new team of twelve dogs, hired extra drivers, and went on to Umanak, a colony of several hundred Inuit on the eastern side of an island whose top was 3,274 feet above the sea ice. The visitors stayed with the governor, who arranged for them to continue their trip with "High Priest" Balle, his brother-in-law, who was on his way to Egedesminde.[53]

Despite the High Priest's chaperonage, the trip southward was hazardous. For fifteen hours the men either scaled a vertical wall of snow and glacial ice or dove from dizzy heights into a cauldron of swirling drift. At Kekerdat, an island about five miles from shore, they encountered Mr. Fleischer, a little-crazy trader. Over seventy years of age, he could remember the retreat of Elisha Kent Kane's party down the coast. His native wife put him out of the room whenever he started to talk to his guests. When the visitors offered to intercede on his behalf, the High Priest advised them not to, because the wife cooked splendidly and would not do so if they lost her friendship.[54]

The Americans proceeded another twenty miles to Ritenbenk. Here the governor had a native wife. The visitors were treated to a dance, candles, accordion, figs, and so forth. But the way onward was impossible. Looking south across Disco Bay, the men saw open water as far as the eye could reach. If the Americans were cut off here, they might not get to Denmark in time to send help to their friends. Nevertheless, they organized an expedition and left on 9 March. After a week of solid land work, over the ice, the mountains, and the ice cap, and twice in native boats, they arrived at Rodebay, a cluster of igloos that provided shelter and a chance to recuperate for the lap to the next colony.[55]

Continuing their journey, the party arrived at Jacobshavn on 18 March 1916. Since leaving Umanak they had traveled more than 250 miles in 15 days, an average of over 16 miles a day. The explorers came in from the cold to the governor's warm house. Green was trying to explain to the governor why the word "though" was spelled as it was, but the governor was utterly perplexed when suddenly the door opened. The sight that met Green's eyes was too much. He swooned. When he regained consciousness he realized that once more, after three years, he was looking on "a flesh and blood, pink-cheeked, blue-eyed, be-skirted, be-waisted, be-flirtable girl." Green insisted that he was not overdoing the incident. "Thank God I'm married," said Allen. "Thank God I'm going to be married," said Tanquery. "Thank God," said Green. The Americans found it necessary to stop at Jacobshavn for a few days. Here they had a pleasant visit.[56]

Home Again

Jerome Allen, the electrician, was the first member of the Crocker Land Expedition to return to the United States. He arrived in Washington on 23 August 1916.

Fitzhugh Green arrived in Copenhagen on 19 August. The American Consul General in Copenhagen announced Green's return from the expedition,[57] and the Navy Department instructed him to report to Washington at once. He intended to sail for New York next day.[58]

On his return trip, Green had written to Admiral Peary from Sydney, Nova Scotia. "We had a wonderful experience in the north," he exulted. He hoped that the expedition's reports would show some results of scientific value. "I am grateful to believe that you will join us in regarding the Crocker Land question of minor importance compared with the true exploration and diligent research for which all explorers have sacrificed time and labor and life itself." He hoped to call on Peary after he returned to Washington.[59]

Henry Fairfield Osborn wrote to welcome Green home and to express his appreciation of "the fine service which you have rendered to the Crocker Land Expedition ... and the valiant part that you took in the trip to the north." He also desired to "welcome you personally and to renew our acquaintance before you returned to your naval duties." Osborn hoped to meet Green in New York, after which he should take great pleasure in writing to the Secretary of the Navy giving his testimony as to the service Green had rendered science, especially the part Green had taken in the expedition. Osborn approved of Green's action in returning. "It was undoubtedly the wisest course for you to come home immediately, since by remaining you could not contribute further to the rescue of the northern party, which was assured through the arrangements with the *Danmark* and the *Cap York*, and you might have been compelled to remain another year among a people who were already in want of provisions."[60]

8. Returning Home

Green described himself as arriving in Copenhagen "more empty handed than Ulysses and twice as dirty." His books, papers, and diaries were still in Greenland. He enjoyed the luxury of clean sheets, a good bed, and delicious food, but an "indescribable loneliness" suddenly seized him. He yearned to tell others "of the beauty of the Great White North" and of his longing for it. Yet he knew that they would never understand.

He proceeded to explain why we go to the Arctic. It must be adventure. As a boy he admittedly knew Arctic literature as the theologian knows his Bible. Most Arctic explorers, he perceived, had been naval officers: Barrow, Franklin, Kane, Nares, Abruzzi, Shackleton, Scott, and Peary. He had seen Peary when Peary's last expedition had sailed, and he recalled how Peary had seen a distant land that he named Crocker Land. So it came about, Green surmised, that the Crocker Land Expedition was based upon a controversy, the eyes of the traveler pitted against the theories of the scientist. But cause for mystification remained. MacMillan and Green had penetrated the Polar Sea well beyond the point marked land by Peary and found only "a white desolation of the ruptured ice."[61] Yet on their return they too saw from the heights of the northeastern cape a land or something so like land. Green went on to tease a "tempting legend" of the Inuit inhabiting a distant oasis. This fanciful and opaque excursus was the type of thing that delighted Green.[62]

Dr. Hovey returned to the museum on 27 August after an absence of over two years during which he had made observations on the geology and glaciers of the Greenland coast from Cape York to Etah, supplementing the studies made by Ekblaw.[63] His "enforced exile in the frozen Arctic" ended with important geological, geographical, and ethnological discoveries, the *New York Times* wrote. According to Hovey, the scientific value of the Crocker Land Expedition would be more than commensurate with the expense, estimated at $250,000.[64]

MacMillan reached New York on 30 August. He went on to Freeport, Maine, to visit his sister, and from there he planned to go to New York to begin classifying the specimens that he had obtained for the American Museum.

Ekblaw had arrived in Godhaven on the *Neptune*. There he joined MacMillan for the return trip. He arrived in New York on 30 August and almost immediately left for Illinois.

A Curious Conference

On 1 May 1917, before all expedition members were back home, an important event occurred. George Sherwood of the American Museum had invited Isaiah Bowman of the American Geographical Society to a luncheon.

On this occasion Sherwood revealed information not previously known to the Geographical Society about "divided authority and dissension among the various parties." The "various parties" are not identified. Sherwood stated what he knew only to Bowman, and offered to show him a report from Dr. Hovey in regard to the matter that only Sherwood and President Osborn had seen. Bowman advised against doing this: such a document ought to be exhibited only after the return of the expedition and to an investigating committee assigned judicial functions. Osborn had agreed.[65]

Nevertheless, Sherwood related the essential facts in the document. "It is thought by everyone," wrote Bowman after seeing the document, "that MacMillan is the nigger in the wood pile[,] because when Lieutenant Green and Messrs. Allen and Tanquary returned, they agreed among themselves not to criticize any of the men or measures of the expedition until the leaders had returned and could speak for themselves. A penciled note on the document adds: 'Details of later date show that Hovey is responsible for the entire mismanagement of the relief expeditions. I can give details[.]'" It appears, the document adds, that hardly had the relief ship *Cluett* left New York before the captain refused to listen to the advice of the ice pilot who was supposed to be in chief command, the captain falling back upon admiralty law. When the ship became frozen in in Parker Snow Bay trouble arose between Dr. Hovey and MacMillan on the one hand and between Dr. Hovey and the captain of the *Cluett* on the other.

The whole purpose of sending Dr. Hovey on the relief expedition was to put in charge of the operation in the field the man who was in supreme authority in the office, but neither MacMillan nor the captain of the *Cluett* recognized his authority. In addition, difficulties had broken out among MacMillan's men, who were dissatisfied with his conduct of the expedition and with his plans for the future. The result was that both on this occasion and when the *Danmark* reached Greenland, there was no coordination among the various parties, which explains why there occurs in the statement of the Committee in Charge under date of 21 March the peculiar sentence, "The reason why he and other members did not come on the *Cluett* is that they expected that the second ship with steam power would reach home sooner than the *Cluett* which must depend on sail power alone."[66] This document describes troubles and tensions that are important but not easily understood or explained.

Bowman suggested that to avoid having the relief expedition of 1917 meet the same fate as the one described, it would be imperative to clothe Captain Bartlett with supreme authority as the leader of the entire relief expedition to put on board his ship the instruments, collections, and men and bring them back to New York, and to do this in whatever manner and at whatever time he chose, without reference to the wishes of any member of the expedition in Greenland. President Osborn thought that was a wise thing

8. Returning Home

to do. On an archival copy of this document, President Greenough of the Geographical Society penciled this note: "Mr. Ford: This whole memo of a talk with Sherwood & Osborn is important." The reference is to Dr. James B. Ford, a member of both the council of the Geographical Society and the museum's Supervisory Committee for the Crocker Land Committee. Ford, a generous benefactor of the geographical society, hid his light under a bushel. In August, after Dr. Ford had made another gift to the geographers, Greenough thanked him and told Bowman that "his [Ford's] action will close the mouth of the Nat. Hist. people (I hope) and will set an example and standard for their own Trustees. He is great."[67] Bowman agreed, and added, "The whole attitude of the Museum people has been so patronizing, not only in this but in other matters. If the Museum people have not lost all sense of proportion, they can not do less than acknowledge that their previous strictures were ill-timed and ungracious."[68]

Bowman was invited to become a member of the museum's Committee in Charge of the Crocker Land Expedition. He declined because he would be coming in at the eleventh hour, and to give advice on the administration of the expedition would require examination of every detail of the expedition from its beginning to the present. He did not care to undertake this task, having faith that Osborn and his associates would handle any future matters in a manner that would meet with Bowman's approval. Osborn respected Bowman's reasons.

The Geographical Society had raised $1,100 for the third relief expedition, Bowman told Osborn. Osborn reported that the museum's trustees had authorized him to obligate the museum to the extent of $30,000, which was the amount the Crocker Land Expedition was in debt up to the formation of the third relief expedition. Osborn thought that the geographical society ought not draw out of the Crocker Land Expedition on account of the unfavorable effect it would have on the public. Bowman agreed.

Osborn asked Bowman if the Geographical Society's council wished Bowman to stay off of the Committee in Charge. The council had taken no official action, Bowman replied, but their sentiment was against the idea. In view of this, Osborn would omit both Greenough's and Bowman's names from the letterheads of the stationery that the museum was about to print.

"To my surprise," Bowman added, Osborn said it was an article in the original agreement between the museum and the geographical society that the society was to receive all of the geographical results and the popular results were at MacMillan's disposition. The society would receive the material in due time. Upon the return of the Crocker Land Expedition Osborn would ask the participants to meet him, go over the entire matter, and report the difficulties that had arisen so as to get at the reasons for the division of authority. Osborn said that he understood the difficulties to surmount to secure the assistance of the American Geographical Society, whose board contained a number of very old men who were naturally conservative. In time, he added, younger men would make up the board and it would become more progressive.[69]

The preceding account raises questions about matters related to the conduct of individuals and the relations between the American Museum and the Geographical Society, but, sad to say, these questions are not answerable.

9

MacMillan's Geographical Report

Early in 1917 the American Museum of Natural History and the American Geographical Society were preparing to deal with the return home of the last members of the Crocker Land Expedition. Both were headed by presidents who worked closely with a council. Henry Fairfield Osborn, a patrician, scholar, and Princeton graduate, was president of the American Museum. His council included men of affairs. John Greenough, a Harvard graduate, former banker, broker, and railroad executive, had retired in 1898 to devote himself to benevolent and charitable pursuits. He was the president of the American Geographical Society from 1916 to 1925. His council included men of affairs. Chandler Robbins and Dr. Walter B. James were councilors who served on the Supervisory Committee in Charge of the Crocker Land Expedition.

Isaiah Bowman was the director of the Geographical Society. Born in Canada, Bowman spent his early years on a farm near Brown City, Michigan. He graduated from the Normal School at Ypsilanti, Michigan. After earning a BS at Harvard (1905), he studied geography at Yale, where he earned a PhD and was on the faculty until 1915. He then became the executive secretary of the Geographical Society.

In early 1917 Osborn urged upon Greenough the desirability of sharing the responsibility in meeting with the delays and accidents of the Crocker Land Expedition. If it had been a great success, the geographical society would have had its full share of credit, and it should share in "the disaster which has befallen this expedition, the last obstacle arising from war conditions."[1] Greenough differed. A dispute over the matter lasted for years.

When Hovey and MacMillan arrived in New York in late August 1917,[2] Greenough congratulated them on their safe return and expressed satisfaction that no loss of life had attended the venture. It had afforded "an example of gallantry and persistent courage in full accord with Arctic tradition. Our society will look forward with eagerness to receiving the promised reports of the geographical results attained by the expedition." Greenough sympathized with Osborn's financial burden. "I mentioned to you when we dined at my house the attempt I was making to enlist further financial aid from my associates, and I have the pleasure to announce that I expect to be able to hand you $15,800 as an additional contribution from our Society."[3] This substantial sum might serve as a stimulus to others to assist in lifting the weight of the liabilities arising from the rescue expeditions.[4]

Noting the safe return of the explorers, Osborn wrote that the geographical results were to be exclusively and first reported in the journal of the geographical society. Osborn praised American science and the work of young explorers and was grateful for the addition to the generous previous contributions.[5]

The disposition of the geographical results was embedded in a larger problem—MacMillan's alleged "right" to publish accounts of his Arctic experience. In mid–September, he discussed the matter with Bowman. In the spring of 1913, MacMillan related, he had agreed to give *Harper's* all of the popular rights "both in magazine and book form," and on the day of sailing he signed an agreement with museum authorities that gave him the "popular" rights, to include not only the narrative of his journeys from his base camp but also his geographical discoveries and conclusions. Although he had this agreement with the museum, on several occasions the geographical society had been promised the geographical results. MacMillan had told Bowman that, at the suggestion of President Osborn, Mary Cynthia Dickerson, editor of the *American Museum Journal*, had asked him to prepare an article on his journey to Cape Thomas Hubbard, "the most interesting geographically of his various journeys." MacMillan did not write the proposed article because of the contract with *Harper's*. But, Bowman countered, "this does not diminish the importance of Miss Dickerson's extraordinary request." In sum, the museum had promised to give the geographical society what MacMillan now said it was impossible to give. Unless some change was made, the geographical society would receive no return for its $34,800 investment in the Crocker Land Expedition.[6]

Thus alerted, Greenough informed Osborn that a review of the correspondence about MacMillan's expedition and his interview with Bowman demonstrated a marked departure from the society's understanding as to its compensation for its financial contribution. He would have to ask his council to act. To prevent any misunderstandings he summarized the record, as follows.[7]

The society's original contribution of $9,000 was made with an implied understanding that it was to have the first publication of the geographical results of the expedition. Greenough recited confirmatory details and quoted

Osborn's letter of 2 September 1917. The departure from these understandings first became evident on 11 September, when MacMillan made a statement to Bowman, initialed by both, in which three principal points of difference arose.[8]

The resulting conflicts impelled Greenough to ask for an interpretation of the meaning of Osborn's declarations and "to point out in what manner it seems to you that our Society is to receive any equivalent from the MacMillan expedition for the part that it has played therein." According to Greenough, MacMillan contracted with *Harper's* for practically all of his geographical products, the museum contracted with the geographical society for the same products, and the editor of the museum's *Journal* demanded from MacMillan an essential part of the product already under contract to two institutions.[9] Not wanting to invite controversy, Greenough wished to learn whether some publishable result could be secured which should seem to justify the attitude and action of the council throughout this undertaking.[10]

It appeared to him, Osborn replied, that the misunderstanding had arisen largely through the failure to distinguish between popular and scientific publication. The museum's agreements with MacMillan were that he would have "the exclusive privilege" of popular publication of lectures, articles, etc., for what little he could get from these sources. The other members of the party received pay from the Crocker Land Committee or from the Government and were not given the privilege of popular publication without MacMillan's consent.[11]

Osborn had instructed MacMillan and Ekblaw that the scientific publication and the priority of their geographic results belonged by the museum's agreement exclusively and originally to the American Geographical Society.[12]

As for reference to the *American Museum Journal*, Osborn explained that the article requested for it and the popular results to be published in the narrative volume were designed to be of a very general character and not to anticipate the careful and documentary history, maps, place names, etc., all of which should be reserved for the geographical society. America was so large that the more widely this popular information could be distributed the better.[13]

Nevertheless, Osborn wished to make the publication arrangements agreeable to the geographical society. He cited article ten in the 1913 contract, which gave MacMillan certain rights of popular publication and the exclusive right "to prepare and deliver, or publish, such popular accounts, whether in lectures, book form or in magazines, as he chooses, after the first declaration of scientific and other results through the party of the first part." Osborn hoped that a meeting of Bowman and MacMillan would lead to a satisfactory understanding.[14]

This contretemps had not yet run its course. Bowman contested seven paragraphs in Osborn's letter. For example, re: no. 7: The arrangement that is "entirely satisfactory and agreeable to the American Geographical Society" is that all geographic results of whatever nature be submitted to us for publication as we choose. As now administered by the museum, the only institution that wins publicity from the Crocker Land enterprise is the museum. And re: no. 9: MacMillan and Bowman have met and discussed the matter without result. A second conference would serve no purpose. "We stand on our rights. Let the museum produce the promised results."[15] When MacMillan said that he wanted to talk over the whole matter with President Greenough, Bowman replied that the society had invested $34,800 in his expedition and expected to get the results promised at the beginning. In closing his letter to Greenough, Bowman said that they were face to face with a decision that would determine whether we are a vassal or an independent society. "*All of the geographic results of the Crocker Land Expedition are ours.*" Shall we not ask the museum to deliver them?[16]

John Greenough was a graduate of Harvard who had a successful business career and served for many years as president of the American Geographical Society (American Geographical Society Library, University of Wisconsin–Milwaukee Libraries).

Despite Bowman's strictures, Greenough wished to preserve an interrogation attitude. "We must not have a row which will leave a sting, although we have been badly used." He hoped that Bowman did not think him unduly placid, but he tried to regard the issue as he understood it—that is, what amends can they make? They clearly wished to do so. Osborn was conciliatory and earnest in his desire to see justice done.[17]

In a skillful reply to Osborn, Greenough summarized the geographical society's case. "Like everything from your pen," he began, referring to Osborn's letter of 19 September, "its general comment and declarations are interesting, but in so far as they refer to the past, they tend to invite controversy which I deprecate. Our quest is simply for information as to what we are to receive in consideration of our payment and contract. We have been informed of material which we are not to receive, but we are without knowledge of the converse of this. We understood that we were entitled to all the geographical results of the expedition, and it is now apparent that this aggregate is to be materially diminished. This it seems is the result of a limitation to '*scientific*' results and the construction placed upon this phrase, which has no place in the society's original contract or in its interpretation until the present discussion." What he sought to know was what residuum they were to look for. If confined to "the careful and documentary history, maps, names of places, mountains, peaks, etc." as Osborn stated in his letter, Osborn would hardly expect the geographical society to approve such a catalogue as the equivalent of their $34,800 outlay.[18]

Greenough would be pleased to confer with MacMillan and Osborn to arrange for publication satisfactory to the geographical society. He suggested that MacMillan bring to the proposed conference an outline of such information as he intended to furnish the others, which would enable Greenough to answer the question, "What are we to receive in discharge of our contract paid for in advance?"[19]

The relations of the two societies were so intimate and their altruistic purposes so in unison, Greenough added, that he did not want the harmony disturbed. It seemed, however, that MacMillan's affairs had resulted in a tangle, which called for a spirit of accommodation and possible sacrifice in order to solve it satisfactorily. "It is bootless now to observe that the difficulties would have been avoided if our Society had been consulted whilst modifications of our presumed rights were being arranged."[20]

Greenough's chief concern in the matter was that it tended to discourage the society's financial backers and to impair the value of the society's imprimatur on an enterprise. He did not wish to write this to Osborn, but would say it to him. Hence the importance of making as good a show as they could. Greenough did not doubt that Osborn was heartily sick of the whole business, but he must not let his troubles make him indifferent to those of the American Geographical Society. "He must bring all pressure possible on MacMillan who is likely to get 'raw' under fire."[21]

Pending a meeting with Greenough, Osborn pleaded his case with his pen. He did not believe it possible for any sponsor of the expedition to secure anything like the equivalent of their outlay. The lion's share for scientific publication, pledged to the Geographical Society, would hardly be equivalent to its $34,800 outlay. All that was reserved to the American Museum, which might amount to a much larger sum than its cash contribution to date of $35,344, was Ekblaw's geological and botanical work, the archaeological work of Captain Comer, and the limited zoological and ethnological collections.[22]

In conferences with MacMillan, Osborn understood that in MacMillan's and Ekblaw's journeys there was a great deal of important new matter, all of which belonged exclusively to the Geographical Society. The proceeds of a popular narrative of the expedition and popular lectures were all that MacMillan reserved in the way of financial return. He was the only member of the expedition who did not receive a regular salary.[23]

Presumably, MacMillan was preparing his geographical results while the two presidents discussed their disposition. In early October Greenough wished to know what steps the expedition's promoters proposed to take in fulfillment of their contractual obligations, and he recapitulated the agreements between the two organizations. First, Chandler Robbins had stated in writing that our payment would entitle us to the literary and geographical results of the expedition. Second, Osborn's letters to Greenough since the return of the expedition had confirmed the latter clause of this agreement, namely, the geographical results, without, however, referring to the former part. Third, the contract with MacMillan authorizing him to convey to Harper & Brothers the rights which had previously been contracted for by the society was an error that Greenough believed would not have occurred had Osborn been personally cognizant of the situation or had the geographical society had a representative in the expedition's preliminaries.[24]

Greenough was not disposed to dwell upon these matters. The society must, he said, await a knowledge of MacMillan's reports before arriving at a decision forced upon him by reason of the conditions under which the society held a deposit of $15,800. Those conditions declared that the deposit was made upon the condition that the expedition had been sufficiently fulfilled to secure to the society its geographical results. Otherwise, the deposit was to be held subject to the wish of the subscribers.[25] Were it not for the stated obligation, Greenough would be prepared to dismiss further discussion with respect to the $19,000 contributed on behalf of this society in the early stages of the expedition. He should, Greenough thought, return the conditional subscription to the contributors for them to decide what action to take with respect to it.[26] Greenough hoped that the agreeable relations between their societies should not be impaired by the incidents connected with this expedition.[27]

At this point MacMillan submitted to Osborn a report upon the Crocker Land Expedition. In twenty-six typewritten pages he traced the history of the venture from 2 July 1913 to 26 August 1917, closing by listing sixteen results of the expedition.[28] Having read MacMilllan's narrative with an eye for its geographical features, Greenough wrote, "It is to laugh!! Even the supply of 'names peaks & inlets' is scanty. Parturunt montes nascitur ridiculus muus."[29]

On 29 October, Osborn informed Greenough that he had just received MacMillan's report. He was having it copied and sent to Greenough.[30] Writing also to MacMillan, Osborn trusted that he would take pains not to violate "our agreement" with the geographical society that the first announcement of geographic names, discoveries, etc., would be made to them.[31]

MacMillan was apparently working on his report. On 24 October he had written to Hovey at the American Museum requesting the loan of "the Arctic records."[32]

Pending news about the report, museum officials were trying to wind up the expedition's financial affairs. Net receipts to date were $91,945.40, and net expenditures were $165,953, leaving a deficiency of $74,007.60. Osborn asked Greenough if it would be convenient to send the additional subscription which the geographical society had contributed, as stated in Greenough's letter of 28 August 1917 to Osborn.[33]

His letter expressed a hope, not an accomplishment, Greenough replied. Having canvassed his associates, he had received a conditional assurance of support based upon an understanding as to the contractual relations of the geographical society with the promoters of the expedition. "As there seems reason to believe that the interests referred to may not be realized, I am not in a position to demand from my contributors that they shall release the conditions attached to their contributions and make them good at once. I still cherish the hope that the funds may become available in the near future but you will readily appreciate the difficulties with which I am confronted as a solicitor."[34]

The disposition of MacMillan's report was the ghost at the banquet. Osborn requested that MacMillan write an article for the geographical society on the geographical results of the expedition. MacMillan was sorry that at the time of promising this material to the geographical society Osborn had not stated definitely that MacMillan's book and a series of articles had been contracted for by Harper's publishing company. Had Osborn done so, the present trouble, "due apparently to a difference of opinion as to just what constitutes geographical results," would have been avoided. The geographical society had planned for and had appropriated money for the publication of MacMilllan's book. Both the society and the museum must realize that there was only one decision for MacMillan, namely, to fulfill his contract made in 1913. MacMillan sent Bowman a copy of his letter to Osborn. MacMillan had been expecting to hear from Osborn, but had not heard. "Evidently," he concluded, "the whole matter is to be dropped."[35] Clearly, that was not the case.

Days later Osborn sent Bowman "a very interesting article" that MacMillan had prepared for the *American Museum Journal* but which belonged to the Geographical Society. MacMillan was not a scientific man in a technical sense, Osborn explained, and it seemed to be difficult to get in his mind just what their respective institutions desired. With tact and patience, Osborn felt confident, they could secure a full and really valuable geographic report.[36]

In January 1918 Osborn learned that that MacMillan had a diary of his

Arctic journeys that covered all of the expedition's geographic work except that in Ekblaw's separate venture. Osborn had arranged for MacMillan to work in Boston with a stenographer to take down his geographic report. It was to be supplemented with maps and astronomical observations, the work being done at the expense of the American Museum. MacMillan's contract gave him the right of popular publication and lecturing, while the geographical results were to be assigned to the institutions concerned. MacMillan had been instructed not to do any of the naming, the correction of coastlines, etc., in his popular work.

A misunderstanding had arisen between the geographical society and the museum because Bowman had been unaware of the publication agreement. The contract had been drawn with the American Museum exclusively because it was necessary for one corporation to assume the legal liability for chartering vessels and making business arrangements. Bowman would set the matter before the geographical society's board, Osborn trusted, because it was important that the two institutions work harmoniously in the advance of science. Osborn believed that MacMillan would be able to produce a very valuable report, a credit to himself and to both institutions.[37]

Obtaining from MacMillan a report of his geographical results was preliminary to any discussion of the matter, Greenough replied. Osborn agreed and suggested appointing a Special Committee on Publication of Crocker Land Reports, with MacMillan and Ekblaw as members. Since neither was experienced in the preparation of scientific reports, Osborn wanted Bowman to represent the geographical society on the committee. Greenough demurred: His society had not taken part in administrative matters connected with the expedition and had better adhere to that position, "especially since we are to accept the geographical results in conformity with our contractual relations with the promoters."[38]

In mid–January Osborn sent Bowman an article "from Mr. MacMillan." In responding, Bowman wrote, "MacMilllan tells us" that this article is one of several which he could place with *Harper's* and that according to his contract with them it belongs to them. Under the circumstances, Bowman was not sure that the geographical society should keep it lest they should deprive MacMillan of a considerable sum. "I think we mentioned $500. Your advice in this matter would help us to make an ethical decision."[39]

In late January Osborn and Greenough tried to prod MacMillan to act. Osborn was willing to wait until MacMillan had submitted his geographical reports before further discussing the results of the Crocker Land Expedition. To assist MacMillan and Ekblaw in the preparation of their reports, Osborn proposed to appoint a Special Committee on Publication of the Crocker Land Reports chaired by the editor of certain museum publications. Osborn named Sherwood, MacMillan, and Ekblaw as members of this committee, although neither MacMillan nor Ekblaw had had much experience in the preparation of scientific reports. The committee would supposedly stimulate the preparation of the reports and insure their scientific character.[40]

Thus matters stood for a time. Then a tempest blew. Writing to Bowman on 20 March, Osborn said that he regretted to find a reference in the March issue of the *Geographical Review* to Fitzhugh Green's articles on *Arctic Duty with the Crocker Land Expedition* and a narrative of the expedition. "We have had a great deal of trouble on account of these articles," Osborn confided, "because Lieutenant Green has not kept the terms of the contract by which Mr. MacMillan was given exclusive rights in the publication of a popular narrative of the Crocker Land Expedition, and this has made it increasingly difficult to secure from Mr. MacMillan his full reports." The publication of the last two articles by Green was a distinct violation of Osborn's understanding with him.

Osborn considered the matter so serious that he notified Green that his articles must cease. At Osborn's request the U.S. *Naval Institute Proceedings* had withdrawn Green's article from its February issue. Osborn regretted the prominence that the *Geographical Review* had given Green's articles. Surely this was inadvertence by Bowman. Osborn trusted that it would not lead to further difficulties with MacMillan. The gratifying news was that MacMillan had nearly finished his book for Harper's and promised soon to devote his entire time and energy to his geographical report. Osborn was doing all in his power to secure a complete scientific report.[41] On 15 April 1918 Osborn informed Greenough that MacMillan had completed the manuscript of his book with *Harper's* and was now giving undivided attention to his geographical report.[42]

The American Museum archives contains two handwritten documents that shed light on MacMillan's purported geographical report. One is a four-page account of events from 1914 to 1917 whose author has not been identified. This document concludes, "More valuable observations proportionately in this part than in the other parts of the report. Whole is padded and thin. Some important data are given but more are omitted. Report should be accompanied with maps showing routes traversed and bearing discoveries, new names & other data as far as practicable 2) tables of observations of several kinds, e.g., temperature, weather, altitudes, soundings, character of land crossed, etc[.] Meteorological and strictly geographical work at Etah, North Star Bay and Parker Snow Bay should be given. Brother John's Glacier, Foulke Fjord map & soundings &c[.] Extraneous matter shld be omitted."[43]

The other document is a comment on MacMillan's report made by Hovey at Osborn's request. It is an interesting popular account of the three exploratory sledge journeys that MacMillan undertook during the field life of the expedition, Hovey wrote, but it failed to do justice to the subject or to give an adequate idea of what was actually accomplished. To be of full value, the report should be accompanied by (1) maps showing the routes traversed, the land forms observed and charted, the altitudes of principal points, soundings as far as made; (2) tables showing the thermometric, barometric and meteorological observations day by day; and (3) data regarding the nature of the country passed over when the journey was on land. The geographical work done at Etah and the results should be included in any comprehensive report on the geographical results of the expedition. Although the report contained many items of scientific value, it failed to do justice to the subject or to give an adequate idea of what was actually accomplished.[44] This report was not the one anticipated by Greenough and the geographical society.[45]

In early November, having learned that the geographical society had not yet received MacMillan's report, Osborn assured Greenough that he had extended to MacMillan every facility for its completion. The original data were all in his hands. The society would have received it by now, Osborn thought, had it not been for the war. (MacMillan had been in the Aviation Service.) Osborn trusted that the geographical society would not act until receipt of these reports.[46] Greenough replied that he had postponed asking the society to take action with respect to the funds deposited with it as trustees. Osborn appreciated Greenough's decision. Osborn hoped to put MacMillan in a room with a secretary where he might prepare his report. He hoped that Greenough would present the situation to his colleagues.[47]

Time flew. On 4 June 1919 Osborn informed Greenough of the conference he had had with MacMillan. Relieved from the Naval Aviation Service two months ago, he had completed all but one section of his reports. Having examined them, Osborn believed that there was a great deal of geographical material as well as astronomical and meteorological records. In a week MacMillan would deposit the documentary evidence with the American Museum and bring the final section of his report. Osborn was confident that the Geographical Society would be able to publish a highly creditable and well-documented account of this expedition.[48]

At long last the day arrived. On 26 June 1919, Secretary Sherwood of the museum transmitted MacMillan's *Geographical Report* to President Osborn. Its three sections with eighty-eight pages of text, five pages of astronomical observations, and five maps were supported by five field notebooks, four journals, and one volume each of astronomic observations, barometric and temperature records, a vocabulary of Inuit words and phrases compiled by MacMillan, the Journal of both Fitzhugh Green and Jerome Allen, and several boxes containing thermograph and barograph records.[49]

Days later, according to the agreement of 9 February 1912 and the correspondence between the two presidents, Osborn forwarded the report to Greenough. To Osborn, it seemed appropriate that MacMillan's report and

9. MacMillan's Geographical Report

Ekblaw's report of his trip through Ellesmere Land in 1915 should bear the names of the American Museum, the American Geological Society, and the University of Illinois. Final disposition of the original records and journals awaited further consideration. Meantime, they were placed at the disposal of the American Geographical Society for the purpose of verification of the report.[50]

MacMillan's report begins with a covering letter from Freeport, Maine, dated 2 April 1919, addressed to the three sponsoring institutions. Its first section starts in the year 1913, traces the settling in at Etah, and describes some experiences in Greenland. Most of this part chronicles the trip over Ellesmere Island, the arrival of MacMillan and Fitzhugh Green, each with an Inuit, at Cape Thomas Hubbard on Axel Heiberg Land, and their search for Crocker Land. When forced to conclude that what resembled land was a mirage, they retraced their steps. A storm was brewing; the two parties separated. Within the hour they experienced a raging blizzard. Every day increased MacMillan's anxiety over Green and his companion. When Green arrived alone, driving the Inuit's dogs, his story was quickly told. His dogs were buried under the drift and were never seen again. The Inuit refused to proceed down the coast with one team only and declared that he was going north to rejoin MacMillan and his Inuit. Green with rifle walked ahead of the dogs and ordered Peeawahto to drive slowly and keep behind him. Twice Green discovered that the Inuit was bearing to the right; therefore he shot him. "I am exceedingly sorry that Green felt it necessary to do this," MacMillan wrote, "for these northern natives are as a rule most excellent travelling companions, faithful and loyal. We cannot place ourselves in Green's position, and therefore cannot judge as to whether or not the act was justifiable."[51] With this comment MacMillan dismissed the murder.

The next section of MacMillan's report, "Astronomical Observations," consisted of five pages of figures dealing with his spring sledge trip on the Polar Sea in 1914. Following is a twenty-two-page account of the "Winter and Spring Work of 1915–1916." With the coming of the party's fourth year, little exploratory work remained to be done. The verification of the existence of Peary Channel seemed to be the most important problem to be solved, but MacMillan learned that Rasmussen had arrived with this object in view. Arctic etiquette demanded that MacMillan relinquish his own plans and help Rasmussen. He did so, instructing Captain Comer to supply Rasmussen with everything he needed. The remainder of this section of twenty-eight pages described MacMillan's survey of the eastern shores of Ellesmere Land between Cape Sabine and Clarence Head.[52]

So, the impasse over submission of the report was finally over. Or was it? "After talking with Bowman," an undated note signed by D.B.M. [MacMillan] declares, "I have concluded that there is no possible way in which *all* of the geographical results can be turned over to the Society as promised by the Museum through President Osborn in various letters." On the archival copy of this document is Bowman's penciled comment: "Sept 11/19 Our first intimation of departure from agreement with us."[53]

A letter from Osborn to Greenough accompanied MacMillan's report. In accordance with the agreement between the three institutions, Osborn wrote, the report represented the fulfillment of the contract. As a matter of fact, a geographical society spokesman replied, "this in no sense fulfills the contract." The author (Bowman?) explained that MacMillan had published "the narrative and geographical results of his expedition serially in Harper's Magazine[,] and his book 'Four Years in the White North' contains the complete results of his journey both narrative and geographical. The report forwarded to us consists of a few odds and ends, some of which have been published before and others of which could not be published anywhere as a worthy contribution to knowledge." The society had contributed $19,000, for which it had to show a "meagre and unworthy report, so poor in my judgment we can not publish it. In fact, I would go further and say that it would be absurd for the Society to publish it." The subscriptions in the treasury should be returned to the donors, it said.[54]

As for the conduct of the expedition and MacMillan being allowed to sign a contract for the publication of his material subsequent to the museum's understanding that the society was to receive all of the geographical results, these matters were handled by Hovey, "whose attitude in my judgment has been incorrect throughout, to say the least." The author, presumably Bowman, assumed that his comment would be circulated only among trustees of the geographical society.[55]

The American Museum received MacMillan's report at about this time. On 20 November 1919 the Geographical Society appointed a committee to consider it. The members were John Greenough, Edwin Swift Balch, and Isaiah Bowman. Balch was born in Philadelphia, had received much of his education in France and Germany, and after graduating from Harvard he began to practice law.

The committee was given three instructions. First, to advise the council what disposition it should make of MacMillan's report of 3 July 1919. Having read and compared the report with publications by MacMillan and other expedition members, the committee concluded that the report contained "nothing of sufficient novelty or importance to justify the Society in printing it."[56] Second, the committee was to recommend what action to take with regard to the funds deposited in trust with the society upon condition that the expedition had been sufficiently fulfilled to secure to the society the geographical results. The committee cited MacMillan's statement of 11 September 1917 to the effect that he could not turn over to the society all the geographical

9. MacMillan's Geographical Report 163

results. It also cited MacMillan's 1918 book [*Four Years in the White North*]; Ekblaw's accounts in appendices to MacMillan's book; and Fitzhugh Green's articles in the *United States Naval Institute Proceedings*, all of which reported geographical matters. The residuum was offered as fulfilling the understanding of the promoters. The agreement had not been sufficiently fulfilled to secure to the society its geographical results. Moreover, an attempt to create a distinction between popular and scientific geographic results could not be maintained. No such distinction was recognized in the contract, and the facts did not support such a hypothesis of distribution. MacMillan's publications through *Harper's* contained many essential scientific (geographical) data, as MacMillan frankly admitted.[57]

Third, during "all this time" the society was ignorant of the fact that "the commander had contracted with Harper's for the delivery of important matter previously purchased and paid for by us, and not until January 1920 were we furnished with a copy of his agreement with the promoters of the expedition under which he claimed the right to partition his geographical discoveries." Therefore, the special committee recommended that the $15,800 held in trust by the society be returned to the depositors because the society had not received the geographical results of the expedition.[58]

This report might have ended the matter, but it did not. Early in 1920 Osborn sent Madison Grant, a member of both the geographical society's council and the museum's Special Crocker Land Committee, some valuable papers related to the matters at issue. MacMillan had followed precedent in putting certain scientific information into his popular work, reserving for the geographical society his complete scientific report. "It is," Osborn added, "the best and only geographic work that has come from the Crocker Land Expedition." Osborn had had two conferences with Greenough and one with Allison Armour, a member of the geographical society's council, on the subject. He hoped that Madison Grant's committee would waive technicalities and consider all the very difficult circumstances when he cleared up the matter. The society entered into a gentleman's agreement, added Osborn, who did not feel that he could recommend that the museum's trustees alone assume the burden of paying off this $16,500 debt. Osborn called Grant's attention to Dr. Hovey's letter to Dr. Kinley of 27 February 1913. It clearly stated that the popular results belonged to MacMillan, the geographical results to the Geographical Society.[59]

A copy of the agreement between the museum and the participants in the Crocker Land Expedition mentioned by Osborn is in the geographical society's archives. In the upper left corner of the first page of the document is this penciled notation: "Communicated to AGS for the first time!! Jan 8/20." The handwriting is that of Isaiah Bowman.[60]

"Uneasy lies the head that wears crown," Osborn began a letter to Greenough on 8 January 1920. Madison Grant and Allison Armour had resigned from the Special Crocker Land Committee, he reported. He sent along an epitome of the correspondence between the museum and the society. "You will observe," Osborn added, "that as early as February 27, 1913, the agreement with MacMillan was very clearly stated, and I do not think that he has departed from this in any particular. Certain general scientific information crept into his popular book, just as in the case of all his predecessors in Arctic and Antarctic exploration." Osborn trusted that Greenough would find someone to replace Grant on the committee, someone who would take "a wholly dispassionate view of this question, for I am confident that careful inquiry into all the circumstances, with an entirely unbiased view, will result in the conviction that Mr. Ford's contribution should be applied to the reduction of the Crocker Land indebtedness."[61]

The substance of the correspondence, which documented agreements allegedly made from 18 January 1912 to 29 October 1917, was a variation on the theme that first publication of the strictly geographical results of the expedition was pledged to the American Geographical Society. And yet the contract between the American Museum and MacMillan conveying publication rights was first submitted to the Geographical Society on 8 January 1920.

On 11 January 1920, an unidentified person wrote to MacMillan, then in Boston, "We cannot give your letter of 7 January full consideration before the next council meeting on 20 January." At the bottom of the page a note added, "Since writing the above, the matter had to be considered, and I am obliged to say we find it impossible at this time to give any further assistance much as we are interested in your work and well as we wish it. Please accept our regrets but also our good wishes." Who wrote this cryptic but intriguing message? A likely author is someone in the American Museum writing at Osborn's request.[62]

At this point Greenough wrote to Osborn as follows: "The whole matter of the funds now temporarily in our possession is an exceedingly simple one but has become confused by the introduction of irrelevant matters which have led to unnecessary discussion and to misapprehension even on the part of some of our own Council." The sole issue was one of fact, determined by written evidence and leading to action in which the society had no discretion. First, the money did not belong to the society. It was deposited with the society under an obligation to return it to the depositor except in one contingency, namely, that the society receive all the geographical results of the Crocker Land Expedition. This was the beginning and the end of the business. Beyond this conclusion, the society had no complaint and no desire to discuss the expedition or its results. This determination of fact was a dispassionate declaration concerning which there could be no difference of opinion.[63]

Replying on 19 January, Osborn accepted any decision Greenough reached and renewed his desire to continue cooperation with the geographical society. Then he picked at details. Macmillan had fulfilled both the letter and the spirit of this contract, Osborn declared, and the only financial return for his four years' work was his honorarium as a writer and a lecturer. On his return he refused the special honorarium offered by Osborn. When he finally completed his geographical report, with maps, and deposited his diaries and documents, he fulfilled his agreement to the letter. The report containing all the geographical results was turned over to the American Geographical Society on 3 July 1919.[64]

Unfortunately, Osborn replied, Greenough's decision left the museum without the means of clearing the debt incurred by the Crocker Land Committee in their efforts to rescue the party from the North. This debt amounted to $16,350, since the committee had recently spent $650 for stenographic service for MacMillan to complete his geographic report. Osborn thought it necessary to make a fresh start to raise this fund by subscription. Meanwhile, he itemized the contributions from various groups interested in the expedition, which came to a total of $153,610. In response to the suggestion that Osborn address the depositors personally, Osborn said he did not know who they were and would appreciate Greenough sending each of them a copy of his letter.[65] A month later Greenough informed Osborn that his society's council had voted unanimously that the funds should be returned to the depositors inasmuch as the conditions of the trust had not been fulfilled.[66]

The continuing problem of MacMillan's report prompted an anonymous author (surely Isaiah Bowman) to describe the facts regarding the geographical society's relation to the Crocker Land Expedition. After stating that the subscriptions of geological society members were based upon the condition that the society would receive all of the geographical results, the author reported that during the summer of 1919 the society received a manuscript report prepared by MacMillan purporting to contain the geographical results of the expedition that "consists of a very meagre and poorly constructed narrative of portions of the expedition.... It is so bald and inconsequential in character that though we greatly desire material at this time for publication in the *Geographical Review*, it is out of the question for us to print it. As geography it amounts to nothing."

Relations between the museum and the society were now difficult, to say the least. Early in 1920 Osborn worked at conciliation. He sent to Madison Grant, a member of the geographical society's council, the Agreement with MacMillan and a resume of the conferences and correspondence between the museum and the society regarding the expedition. He put certain scientific information into his popular work and reserved for the geographical society his complete scientific report.

Osborn had conferred twice with Greenough and once with Allison

Armour of the geographical society's council on the subject at issue. He hoped that Madison Grant's committee—presumably of the geographical society—would waive technicalities and consider all the difficult circumstances when they cleared up the matter. "It was a gentlemen's agreement that we entered into," Osborn pleaded, "and I do not feel that I can honorably recommend to the Trustees of the American Museum of Natural History that they assume alone the burden of paying off the debt of $16,350."[67]

Osborn was troubled by the situation, he confessed to Greenough in January 1920. He quoted the agreement made by Dr. Hovey and Dr. Kinley of the University of Illinois on 27 February 1913, which said, "the first popular results (magazine articles, books, lectures) of the Expedition are already pledged to Mr. MacMillan, and the first publication of the strictly geographical results are pledged to the American Geographical Society." The agreement with MacMillan was clearly stated. Osborn did not think that MacMillan had departed from it in any particular. Certain general scientific information crept into his popular book, just as with all his predecessors in Arctic exploration.

On a copy of Osborn's letter Bowman wrote near the 27 February entry: "Not reported to us." The contract between the museum and MacMillan conveying publication rights was first submitted to the geographical society on 8 January 1920, Bowman added. Reporting that Madison Grant had just resigned from the Special Crocker Land Committee, Osborn hoped that Greenough would find a replacement who would take a dispassionate view of this question.[68]

Masterly in responding, Greenough did not regard Grant's resignation as of any significance "except in so far as it would have been a gratification to yourself. This whole matter of funds now temporarily in our possession is an exceedingly simple one, but has become confused by irrelevant matters which have led to unnecessary discussion and to misapprehension even on the part of some of our council. The sole issue is one of fact, determined by written evidence and leading to action on our part wherein we have no discretion. Our thought has been to deal equitably and ethically with everyone concerned. The money does not belong to us. It has been deposited with us under an obligation to return it to the depositor, except it should be demonstrated that our society has received all the geographical results of the Crocker Land Expedition. We have no volition in the disposal of the money except to return it to the depositor in any other event than the contingency described. We are concerned only with the disposal of the geographical information, which rests exclusively upon written evidence.... As regards ourselves," Greenough concluded, "deeply as we regret the circumstances, you will have seen that our function is purely a mechanical one and does not admit of variation or discussion."[69]

9. MacMillan's Geographical Report

If the funds were subscribed in the belief that prior publication of the geographic results could be secured for the geographical society, they were subscribed under a misapprehension of the wording or the spirit of the joint Crocker Land Committee and MacMillan as to publication of the geographical results. The committee extended to MacMillan all the rights of popular publication and lectures, reserving the right of final scientific publication for the museum and the geographical society.

This vexatious development finally came to an end with a whimper more than a bang. The American Museum finally received MacMillan's geographical report in 1919. A committee of the Geographical Society lambasted it. Museum officials had pondered whether and when to publish the document. MacMillan's "Geographical Report of the Crocker Land Expedition, 1913–1917" was belatedly published in the *Bulletin of the American Museum* in 1930.[70] Of the report, one might say, as John Greenough had said of a related document, "Mountains will labor, what's born? A ridiculous mouse."

10

Full Circle

So the Crocker Land Expedition had come full circle. The American Museum of Natural History, the American Geographical Society, and the University of Illinois had collaborated in sending a party to search for Crocker Land and to do scientific research in the Arctic. After discovering that Crocker Land did not exist, the voyagers remained in the Arctic pursuing research. They had planned to be away for two years, but circumstances intervened and they were in the Far North for three or four years.

"If Crocker Land had existed," the American Museum declared, "the expedition would have been acclaimed a brilliant success, would have attained world-wide fame, and no difficulty would have been experienced in meeting the heavy financial losses caused by the shipwreck of the first steamer, the failure of the first and relief vessels to reach their objective and rescue the party, and the high cost of the third relief steamer secured during the war." As it turned out, while the credit of the work accomplished by the expedition was equally divided among the American Museum, the American Geographical Society, and the University of Illinois, the burden of financing the expedition and conducting the rescue had fallen upon the museum. It had borne $86,045.07 of the total expenditure of $169,260, of which $153,660 had been paid, leaving a deficiency of $15,597 at the close of 1921.[1]

When, at long last, MacMillan submitted his "Geographical Report" to the American Geographical Society, it was harshly received. The museum did not publish it until 1930.[2]

MacMillan described the Crocker Land Expedition for general readers in *Four Years in the White North* (1918). According to Herbert Bridgman, this book was "one of the most instructive and entertaining contributions to the literature of the North." Although MacMillan avoided a scientific inquest, he invited it by listing the expedition's records and achievements. One might doubt whether any Arctic expedition was more persistently dogged by ill luck than the Crocker Land Expedition. Delayed by Borup's tragic death, wrecked the second night out of port, navigation entrusted to a hesitant master, the expedition party made up in enthusiasm what it lacked in training. The reason for its being dissolved like a dream, with no sight of relief ships the first or second summer, the incompetence of men and the perversity of nature conspired to prevent ships from effecting a rescue, each man making his way homeward, until in late 1916 only two of the original party remained in the North.[3]

According to Bridgman, MacMillan was remarkable in his understanding and sympathy with the natives. He had a considerable understanding of the language and customs of the Inuit, which was doubtless the fruitage of MacMillan's years of association with that great leader Peary. MacMillan was able to hold the Inuit loyal and attached throughout the expedition's long stay in the Arctic. In his book, MacMillan thoroughly demonstrated his affection for and loyalty to the Arctic.[4]

Bridgman's celebration of MacMillan was of a piece with his celebration of Peary. Bridgman was Peary's friend, secretary of the Peary Arctic Club, and a supporter of Polar work. When Peary died in 1920, Bridgman wrote fulsomely about his hero.[5]

In his book *Four Years* MacMillan recycled much of what he had written in letters, articles, and his "Geographical Report." He listed what he viewed as the geographic and scientific results of the expedition and cited a number of miscellaneous discoveries.[6] Under the contract, he alone of the expedition party was permitted to publish on the experience in the North. Knowing that books and articles on the Arctic sold, he exploited his advantage.[7]

MacMillan: After the Expedition

On returning from the North, MacMillan was a reserve navy officer during the world war, after which he continued his Arctic adventures. In 1920 his backers incorporated to finance an expedition to Baffin Land,[8] and in July 1921, in the *Bowdoin*, a two-masted auxiliary schooner with a crew of six, MacMillan sailed to explore Baffin Land.[9] Damaged while taking on supplies at North Sydney, the ship went on to explore the coast of Baffin Land during the winter and to penetrate the interior the following summer. The three scientists of the party included an observer of terrestrial magnetism. Another scientist tried to determine whether a new ice age was beginning, as the movements of glaciers in the last seventy years seemed to indicate. The men returned in September 1922 with what was described as "the greatest collection of scientific and magnetic observations ever made in the Arctic."[10]

Continuing to explore, in June 1923 MacMillan sailed again in the *Bowdoin*. Departing from Wiscasset, Maine, he planned to investigate the theory that an ice age was impending. He established winter quarters in Refuge Harbor, and on 18 August began unloading the vessel. Although soon locked in by snow and ice, the *Bowdoin* was electrically lighted, had a good library and all kinds of games. The ship had a radio with which it kept in touch with the world. The men made meteorological observations for the U.S. Government and conducted magnetic work for the Department of Terrestrial Magnetism of the Carnegie Institution in Washington, D.C. At the request of the Board of Trustees of the National Geographic Society, MacMillan placed a tablet at Cape Sabine on the eastern shore of Ellesmere Island in memory of the members of the Greely Expedition who had died there of starvation in the spring of 1884. That done, the men on the expedition killed a white wolf and a herd of musk oxen and MacMillan made the first motion pictures of musk oxen. On 29 July 1924, the *Bowdoin* freed itself from a 330-day imprisonment in the ice and sailed for home.[11]

Indefatigable, early in 1925 MacMillan announced plans to set out on another Arctic expedition. He hoped to search northwestern Greenland, the vast unexplored area between Alaska and the Pole, using seaplanes. At the same time Richard E. Byrd, a navy officer eager to undertake an aerial expedition into the Arctic, and Captain Bob Bartlett made plans to establish a base at Etah and strike out from there for the Pole by means of intermediate bases. Byrd went to Detroit to see Edsel Ford and emerged with a promise of $15,000 in support. When Byrd learned that MacMillan had asked the navy for a plane, Byrd asked for two planes. The Navy Department insisted that the men join forces. MacMillan was granted seniority, with Byrd second in command. MacMillan was to direct his expedition from the schooner *Bowdoin*. The navy unit on the steamer *Peary* was to be under the command of Eugene F. McDonald, MacMillan's friend, who was president of the Zenith Corporation and an investor in the expedition. The combined party was organized under the auspices of the National Geographic Society of Washington, D.C.[12]

Byrd came into conflict with both MacMillan and McDonald. He had expected to be second-in-command of the expedition, but MacMillan accorded that position to McDonald. In addition, Byrd and McDonald were at odds over the use of the radio for communication, and Byrd disagreed with both MacMillan and McDonald over the ships' speed, the party's course, and the proper conditions for air exploration. Moreover, Byrd and MacMillan had incompatible objectives. Byrd wanted to test aircraft in the Arctic with a view to making a flight over the North Pole. MacMillan was mainly interested in scientific investigation and making a survey of northern Greenland and the Arctic.[13]

In mid–June the two ships left Wiscasset, Maine, with MacMillan in command of the *Bowdoin* and McDonald in command of the *Peary*. With McDonald were Byrd and three amphibian planes, NA-1, 2, and 3 (NA=Navy

Aircraft). Despite encountering ice floes and various hazards, they reached their base at Etah. Here, with great difficulty they transferred the planes to the shore, built a runway, and by 4 August had the planes ready to make their first reconnaissance flight. Held up by a snowstorm, on 8 August they flew to Ellesmere Island to build an advance base. The pilot and the mechanic in the NA-2 were navy men; MacMillan was a passenger. The pilot in the NA-3 was a navy man; Byrd was the relief pilot and navigator.[14]

Tension between MacMillan and Byrd was constant. "MacMillan seems to be in [a] great hurry to pack up and go back," Byrd recorded in his diary on 13 August. Days later he wrote that MacMillan's hurry was due to coal shortage, adding, "I do not invite any confidence as long as McDonald is in power. He seems to be suspicious of everything and every one." The next day Byrd wrote, "Begged MacMillan to let Bennett and me go today to Cannon Fjord but he would not agree."[15]

Nevertheless, the planes set a course for Cannon Fiord, a point on the western coast of Ellesmere Island where they hoped to create a substation between Etah and Cape Thomas Hubbard. The flight carried them over Flagler Fiord; then, with a storm rising, the two planes raced for Etah. The next day, with the situation becoming grave owing to a gale, Byrd urged that a base be established on the northwestern tip of Ellesmere Island if the exploration of the Polar Sea was to be carried out. Byrd and his companions continued to fly for several more days, but the weather was against them and two of their planes (NA-1 and NA-2) were damaged and had to be abandoned. MacMillan opposed further flights. With winter drawing near, he was eager to embark upon his expedition in Greenland. McDonald concurred. But the navy men with Byrd were determined to push forward. On 20 May, when Byrd told MacMillan that he proposed to fly with the fully repaired NA-3 unescorted across Ellesmere Island to Cape Hubbard, MacMillan vetoed the idea. Heavier-than-air planes could not be relied on in the Arctic, MacMillan argued, while lighter-than-air machines, dirigibles, could and should do it. Byrd countered that Arctic work with airplanes was not only feasible but logical. Secretary of the Navy Wilbur radioed Byrd to desist from further attempts to reach Axel Heiberg Land. He was to withdraw with MacMillan and make such flights in a secondary exploration. So the last hope of discovering new land in the Arctic vanished. The explorers arrived home in mid–October.[16] Convinced that aviation could conquer the Arctic, Byrd wrote an account of the effort of the navy planes to fly over the Pole.[17]

With this effort accomplished, Byrd planned to fly across the Pole the following spring. He was eager to do this before Roald Amundsen, who had recently been forced down only 150 miles from the Pole, could try again.[18] He selected for his flight a Fokker monoplane with three engines and named it the *Josephine Ford* in honor of Edsel Ford's three-year old daughter. Edsel

Ford was a financial supporter of the expedition. Securing the steamer *Chantier,* Byrd put the party's flying gear on deck, the plane's wings and bodies in the hold, and with a score or more of men eager to assist in facilitating a polar flight, they sailed from New York for Spitzbergen on 5 April 1926. Arriving in the little harbor of King's Bay, Byrd risked danger in transferring the plane from ship to shore. Having done this by floating the plane on a makeshift raft to the shore, on 9 May Byrd took off in a three-engine Fokker monoplane with his chief assistant, Floyd Bennett. They flew for fifteen hours, taking turns piloting, circling the Pole for the first time in history, and returning safely. A National Geographic Society committee that went over their data concluded that the observations of the men were correct. First to fly over the Pole, Byrd and Bennett were showered with honors. On 23 June, in Washington, D.C., President Coolidge awarded the National Geographic Society's Hubbard Gold Medal to both Byrd and Bennett. Large and enthusiastic crowds in New York and Boston hailed the conquering heroes.[19]

A few observers were more willing to question than to cheer. For many years Byrd's navigation charts were unavailable and his log entries for the flight were disorganized and sometimes erased. Moreover, the speed of the Fokker aircraft seemed unrealistic. Reaching the pole required a round-trip of at least 1,330 nautical miles, and the fliers were gone 15 hours in fairly calm air. This would mean that the plane flew at about 86 knots. Yet the same plane, in her triumphant round-the-country flight in 1927, averaged only 72 knots, even after all the engines had been overhauled. Bert Balchen, who later flew with Byrd on various flights and had joined Floyd Bennett on the countrywide tour of the Fokker, led Bennett through the arithmetic of the speed and distance relationships of the North Pole flight. When Balchen suggested that the plane must have turned around short of the pole, Bennett shrugged the statement off with the reply, "Well, it doesn't matter now."[20]

Late in 1926, excited by legends about Viking exploration, MacMillan planned to lead an expedition financed by Frederick H. Rawson, a Chicago banker. MacMillan would again sail in the *Bowdoin,* and along with it was the schooner *Sachem,* built for this venture and launched in April by Rowe B. Metcalf of Providence, Rhode Island. The party was to include a group of eminent scientists, a crew of seasoned men, and three teen-aged boys—one, Rawson's fifteen-year-old son, and another the fourteen-year-old son of the head of Chicago's Field Museum, which was sponsoring the venture. Three women were part of the entourage. The purpose of the MacMillan-Rawson expedition was to seek the lost Norse colony at Godthaab in southern Greenland and to collect material in Labrador and Baffin Land for the Field Museum. The Danish Government authorized MacMillan to land in Greenland, provided that all ethnographic material collected there be shipped to the University of Copenhagen for examination before being made available to the Field Museum. MacMillan spent two and a half months investigating the legends about Norse settlements at Godthaab and on Baffin Island. In addition, he collected rare specimens of fauna and flora and obtained important facts about animal life in the frozen North. It was probable, he concluded, that the ancient ruins of an island near Nain, Labrador, were the remains of a Norse settlement, but no evidence would prove that they had been built by the Vikings. MacMillan returned home in early September.[21]

Two years later MacMillan ventured again, this time on behalf of the Field Museum. Sailing from Wiscasset, Maine, in June, the party made its base at Anetalak, Labrador. Although unable to discover any conclusive evidence that Norsemen ever reached Labrador, MacMillan believed that they probably did reach it. Inuit legends were that the Norsemen went to Labrador presumably from Greenland, where there were indisputable Viking ruins. The explorers conducted the first scientific survey in the northern Labrador wilds. They gathered thousands of specimens and species of plants, animals, game, and fish, found the northland teeming with mineral wealth, and mapped and charted a large area.[22]

Indefatigable or restless, MacMillan planned to explore the northern coast of Labrador during the summer of 1929. His two goals were to survey three hundred miles of unmapped coastline that ships could not traverse because of dangerous shoals and to establish Inuit schools in five native villages. Leaving Maine on 22 June for a fifteen-month journey, MacMillan sailed in the *Maravel*, owned by a Chicagoan, taking along a tri-motored amphibian plane to take aerial photographs. The aerial camera would enable the party to do as much work in one summer as a dog-sled expedition could do in five years. Eugene F. McDonald, the president of the Zenith Radio Company, was to accompany MacMillan. McDonald had gone north with MacMillan in 1923 as a member of the crew and in 1925 in command of the *Peary*, of which expedition Commander Byrd was also a member. McDonald had bought the *Allegro*, a handsomely furnished yacht with eight staterooms, in order to accompany MacMillan on this trip. On 4 July 1929 MacMillan in the *Bowdoin* and Albert Gould in the *Maravel* sailed for Labrador. When the party arrived back in Maine on 10 September, MacMillan admitted that the trip was more a pleasure cruise than for gathering scientific data.

The dispute as to whether Cook or Peary discovered the North Pole had never expired. It resurfaced in the mid–1920s. Roald Amundsen was in the news at the time with respect to his flight to the North Pole. He had been on the Belgian Antarctic expedition with Dr. Cook in the early twentieth century; now he declared that Cook's discovery of the North Pole was just as plausible as Peary's. It was possible, he added, that neither actually reached the Pole.[23] In Amundsen's autobiography, published in 1927, he admitted that Peary could have faked his records, but, he added, Peary was not that kind of man.

Amundsen's only comment on the Cook-Peary controversy was that "Polar records must be read in the light of the antecedents of the explorers."[24] This cryptic statement opens up many possibilities. MacMillan, however, was certain that Peary had reached the Pole. Peary's observations at the Pole, he declared, were sufficient to convince anybody that he had been as near as it was possible to get to that mathematical point at the top of the earth. MacMillan based his conviction on Peary's word. He could not understand Amundsen's criticisms.[25]

While MacMillan was still in the Arctic, "An Englishmen in the Street," who identified himself as W. Henry Lewin, published a small volume, *Did Peary Reach the Pole?* (London, 1911). As Lewin wrote, Peary had difficulty in making his reported speeds agree with his scientific observations, but no one was more fully convinced than Peary that he had reached the Pole. Lewin disagreed with Peary's claim. Then why did the Royal Geographical Society present its gold medal to Peary? The society's action, Lewin explained, may have been not altogether determined by its acceptance or otherwise of Peary's story. The society may have been influenced by certain diplomatic considerations. Could the society have refused its gold medal to Peary in the face of worldwide recognition and rewards which he had received, even if it held legitimate doubts as to the alleged achievement? "The weight of the evidence," Lewin concluded, "is all against the possibility of Commander Peary having been to the Pole."[26]

Unaware of Lewin's book and heedless of the problem of Robert Peary's veracity, MacMillan defended his hero in his book, *How Peary Reached the Pole: The Personal Story of His Assistant* (1934).[27] According to Lewin, this is "the book that failed." Only 21 of its 300 pages are devoted to the actual expedition. The remainder is part anthology and part autobiography, with chapters covering the preparations for and aftermath of the expedition, but lacking entirely any new evidence, and thus without the slightest attempt to justify its "impudent title." The book appears to have been compiled with the specific object of building up in the reader's mind a favorable psychology which will ensure the reader's approval despite the lack of evidence. "Cutting out its title, eliminating all references to Peary and overlooking a few careless statements in other directions, it may be otherwise regarded as a readable and not uninteresting contribution to polar literature. But for his own sake, Mr. MacMillan should allow the world to forget his association with Peary. To do so will be to add to, rather than detract from the value of his life's work."[28]

Lewin dealt with Peary and the North Pole in *The Great North Pole Fraud* (London, 1935). As the author admits, this work destroys without recreating. Part 1 rehearses the evidence as to whether Peary reached the Pole. Lewin had already done this. Part 2 describes at length the evidence offered from 1911 to 1931 as to whether Peary reached the Pole. Lewin concluded this section by saying that we cannot afford to believe that men who occupy responsible positions in life always tell the truth. Part 3 asks how do you know when you are at the North Pole? Lewin describes how two Peary acolytes dealt with this question and labels MacMillan's *How Peary Reached the Pole* as the book that failed. Part 4 of Lewin's book discussed a case of murder in the Arctic, which is no part of the present work.

In 1935 MacMillan published a magazine article that described the lure of "The Great White North." The real value of Arctic work, he explained, was to gather facts pertaining to the world in which we live and to enrich the sum total of human knowledge.[29] This bland assertion was incontestable.

In 1935, at the age of sixty, MacMillan married Miriam Norton Look, the twenty-nine-year-old daughter of his friends, Jerome and Amy Look. Jerome had contributed money to MacMillan's ventures. At first MacMillan refused to let Miriam accompany him north, but in time he relented and she participated in his explorations. Miriam MacMillan published a valuable and interesting book about her experience, *I Married an Explorer* (1951).

MacMillan, a Reserve Navy commander, was dispatched to the Arctic with a ship and four planes during the Second World War. With the War Department he established a Northern radar network, and he also served on a secret defense board. Posted to the Hydrographic Office of the Navy in Washington, D.C., later, there he compiled *Eskimo Place Names and Aid to Conversation*, published in 1943 by the Hydrographic Office for use by army and navy men assigned to the Sub-Arctic and the Arctic. The typewritten document includes a translation of 1,500 Inuit place names, sections on conversational Inuit for the captain of a ship, a ship's doctor, and a botanist, and a section on general conversation.

MacMillan lived the last years of his life in Provincetown with his wife. He remained hale and mentally active until 1970. He died at the age of 95.

The Return of Other Expedition Members

President Osborn once questioned Dr. Hovey about the attitude of the men of the Crocker Land Expedition toward Hovey. In response, Hovey described conditions in the Far North. The four months on the *Cluett* with the expedition men were trying in some respects, he admitted, and it was not always easy to make allowances for the nerve-straining effects of an unexpectedly extended stay in the Arctic. "I honestly tried to do my best and treat my party right, but I do not claim to be perfect."[30]

Disappointed over the failure to return home, Hovey added, our men were severely critical of the museum and bitterly denunciatory of the authorities for having chartered a vessel like the *Cluett* for relief work. They complained of the unfairness, inefficiency, and obstructiveness, which they charged against their leader (MacMillan), and their hostility toward him extended to the museum (whom Hovey personified in their eyes) and everyone concerned with the management of the expedition. Hovey had assured the men that the museum would do its utmost to adjust satisfactorily all matters at issue, and he had hoped that enough steam had been let off to ensure a reasonable degree of good nature when the men reached home. Hovey feared that his efforts had not been successful.[31]

At all stages Hovey took the men of his party—Green, Ekblaw, Tanquary, and Allen—into his confidence in making arrangements for the outward trip in the winter of 1915–1916, and the plans seemed to meet the full approval or consent of all concerned. Captain Comer said that Hovey went too far in consulting the men and trying to meet their wishes.[32]

Four white men was the limit set for the party that Peter Freuchen and his Inuit could take across Melville Bay. All agreed that Hovey, if he could stand the trip, should be one of them. Ekblaw was willing to remain in the Arctic in view of Hovey's approval, which he gave subject to MacMillan's authorization of plans for work he was to do in the 1916 season. In fact, MacMillan and Ekblaw had offered to stay behind in order that Hovey might go.[33]

In January 1916, when Hovey collapsed temporarily at Cape York on the way out, he gave up the trip with good grace rather than jeopardize the success of the others, though he could have been brought out in a sleeping bag had he insisted upon it. When Green, Tanquary, and Allen left Hovey there, he gave them what they wished of his equipment, more than three-fourths of his money, and all the food that had been provided for his trip across Melville Bay. They took it, giving Ekblaw and Hovey about two pounds of biscuit for their stay at Cape York and journey back to Parker Snow Bay.[34]

During the remainder of his time in the Far North, Hovey had done everything in his power to help the men of the expedition. He was surprised and hurt that any of them, aside from MacMillan and Dr. Hunt, gave any other impression. Hunt was homesick, realizing that he ought not have gone on the expedition. His view of almost every act and word was warped and unreliable. MacMillan charged that Hovey exceeded his authority and interfered with MacMillan's prerogatives. Hovey denied the charge.[35]

Hovey mentioned the plan for going south by sledge in the 1916–1917 winter. When it seemed that no ship would reach them at North Star Bay in 1916, Knud Rasmussen offered to take Hovey across Melville Bay by sledge while at the same time arranging for the outward journey of Ekblaw and Hunt. Hovey laid the plans before the men and asked whether his going would jeopardize their success. They said that it would. So Hovey declined Rasmussen's invitation for himself.[36]

Personal likes and dislikes were of minor importance in the events described, Hovey noted. The main question was whether he had done all that he could to discharge the museum's obligations to the men of the Crocker Land Expedition.[37]

Replying to Hovey's self-exculpation, Osborn said he knew that Hovey had the interests of the expedition and of the men individually at heart. "There seems to have been some evil spirit at work which we can hardly account for and which has not ceased to operate even at the present time; there was none of the essential *esprit de corps* and 'pulling all together' spirit." Osborn hoped that they might forget all that was unpleasant in the past and make the sound and enduring results of the expedition as widely and favorably known as possible.[38]

Hovey, now an expert on the Arctic as a result of his time on a rescue mission, shared his knowledge of the place little known to most Americans. On 19 November 1917 he read a paper before the New York Academy of Sciences on "The Geology of the Greenland Coast from North Star Bay to Cape York."[39] The following May he published a paper on child-life among the Smith Sound Inuit. This delightful account included charming photographs.[40]

Harrison (Hal) Hunt, the expedition's medical doctor, arrived in New York on 20 June 1917. His kept records were published as a book.[41] In it, Hunt reported that Captain Comer valued Hunt and Tanquary above the other members of the party. According to Comer, the whole expedition was founded on selfishness. Peary thought he had seen land, resulting in the Crocker Land fiasco. MacMillan used the expedition as his plaything. Hovey, penny-wise and pound-foolish, paid poorly and did not treat people right. The museum contract that Hovey asked the men to sign was childish, unfair, and improperly prepared. The *Cluett* was a sailing vessel not fit for a relief ship. The *Danmark* was a relief ship, but it had taken on two tons of graphite to deliver on its way north. The last two years in the Arctic were the hardest and were unnecessary.

Hunt agreed with Comer about MacMillan's leadership. Upon return, Hunt reported in person to President Osborn. He thought that MacMillan had hoodwinked Osborn and that Hovey had misled him. Hunt requested additional pay for eighteen months' care of Dr. Hovey and the crew of the *Cluett*, months not covered by his contract, and for his prolonged stay in Greenland due to the inadequacy of the relief ships. Hunt's wife had received $500 from Osborn for the services that Dr. Hunt rendered to Dr. Hovey and the crew and a letter to the effect that he should receive further compensation. Osborn consulted Hovey about the matter and then informed Hunt that his prolonged stay had been voluntary, the committee recommended no further payments, and a report on Hunt by MacMillan and Hovey would lead to hard feelings.[42]

Rebuffed, on 16 May 1918 Hunt wrote a long, angry letter to the Honorary Committee of the Crocker Land Expedition. His prolonged stay in the North was not voluntary, he related, MacMillan had ordered it. Moreover, Osborn had discouraged Hunt from reporting his grievance because Osborn would have to submit his report to MacMillan and Hovey, who would then report on Hunt's management of his division. Enraged, Hunt reminded Osborn that in the past Osborn had praised him. If the committee could not agree on further compensation, Hunt asked that the matter be put in the hands of Theodore Roosevelt or "Chas. A. Hughes."[43] Charles Evans Hughes, a former governor of New York and a former associate justice of the U.S. Supreme Court, had narrowly lost to Woodrow Wilson in the 1916 presidential election. In 1918 he was in private law practice in New York City.

Dr. Hunt's letter sparked an angry letter from Hovey to Osborn, in which Hovey maintained that Ekblaw had the authority to give Hal Hunt permission to depart on the *Cluett* in the summer of 1916, and had done so. Hunt, Hovey charged, was a general troublemaker. He openly and unreasonably criticized the expedition, spread exaggerated statements regarding the expedition's trading in fox skins, and went so far as to tell Rasmussen and Freuchen that MacMillan was a hypocrite and unreliable. Hunt's attitude while in southern Greenland, Hovey alleged, was that the museum had barrels of money and could be mulcted to any amount for the expenses of getting out.[44]

MacMillan informed Osborn that Hunt's claim for further compensation was based upon his enforced stay in the Arctic, not upon MacMillan's report on his work or his relations to the expedition. MacMillan's orders to Hunt to remain at North Star Bay were given with the approval of Dr. Hovey. The orders referred to, written on 3 January 1916, said that Hunt was to remain at Umanak under the command of Ekblaw until the arrival of the relief ship *Danmark* in July or August of 1916 or until further orders. The *Danmark* having been frozen in, Hunt received further orders in December 1916. Accordingly, he left by dog sledge. Nevertheless, on 17 May 1918, George Sherwood of the museum's Crocker Land Committee informed Osborn that Hunt had stayed on voluntarily, since he had been under Ekblaw's command at Umanak and had had Ekblaw's permission to sail on the *Cluett*.

In sum, the expedition had set out with high hopes and in relatively good humor and was ending with discord and rancor. Considering the matter, Hunt wanted nothing more to do with the museum or the expedition. He settled in Bangor, gradually built up a successful medical practice, inaugurated the Urological Section at the Eastern Maine General Hospital, and ran one of the first Public Health Clinics for venereal disease in the state of Maine.[45]

Maurice Tanquary, the zoologist of the Crocker Land Expedition, brought back several species of marine teleost fishes from the northwest coast of Greenland. John Treadwell Nichols wrote a paper on these fishes that the

American Museum published in 1918.[46] The oligochaeta collections of the Crocker Land Expedition assembled by Tanquary were sent to Paul S. Welch of the zoological laboratory of the University of Michigan, who published a paper on the collections.[47]

Tanquary had also made collections of bryozoan fauna at Etah and at Umanak in 1914. Bryozoa from collections made by various expeditions to Greenland had been dealt with previously by different authors in separate contributions, but few were in English. Raymond C. Osburn of Ohio State University published a paper on the subject that met the need.[48]

Back from the Arctic, Tanquary returned to the Kansas State Agricultural College as an instructor in entomology and zoology. He later rose to the rank of associate professor in the college. From 1920 to 1924 he was the chief of the entomology division at the Texas Agricultural Station and the Texas State Entomologist. Then, for four years he engaged in commercial beekeeping in Fargo, North Dakota. He was one of the first to place beekeeping on a scientific basis and to produce honey in carload lots. In 1928 Tanquary went to the University of Minnesota as a professor of entomology. While there he became an advisor to the American beekeeping industry. Tanquary died in Minneapolis on 25 October 1944.

W. Elmer Ekblaw returned from the Far North and went to the University of Illinois. President Osborn wrote admiringly about him to President James—"one of the most able members of the expedition." The museum's 1917 annual report listed Ekblaw as a Research Associate in Geology.[49] At the same time President James appointed Ekblaw a Staff Fellow at the University at $1800 a year on Graduate School funds. James also appointed a committee of supervision under whom Ekblaw would carry on his research in close connection with the Arctic collection that the University was to receive under its arrangement with the museum. Professor Bayley of the committee thought that the University should receive in the shape of collections full value for the money appropriated for the Crocker Land Expedition. Dean Kinley of the Graduate School assigned $2,500 from Graduate School funds to cover Ekblaw's salary and expenses incidental to the preparation of his report on the Arctic expedition and its scientific results. In 1918 the University renewed Ekblaw's appointment for another year on the same terms,[50] and the American Museum carried Ekblaw on its staff as a Research Associate. After returning from the Arctic, Ekblaw published a number of articles on the geology, botany, and other aspects of the Far North.

An unidentified member of the expedition (most likely Tanquary) had collected various insects in the Arctic, among them forty-four specimens of Bremidae (=Bombidae). The author of an article on the subject drew on Ekblaw for data concerning the environmental conditions under which bumblebees live in western Greenland.[51]

Ekblaw and Tanquary brought back from the neighborhood of Etah a collection of mollusks consisting of several hundred specimens, both dry and preserved in alcohol. Despite the handicaps incident to an Arctic expedition, they obtained many species not before recorded from this northern land. Ekblaw wrote the introduction to an article on the subject by Frank C. Baker of the University of Illinois. Baker added considerably to what was known concerning the distribution of Arctic mollusks.[52]

The two Illinois explorers had collected insects of the order Collembola in Greenland. After they had returned home, Justin Folsom, an assistant professor of entomology at the University of Illinois, wrote a report on the eight species of this order, which the American Museum published in 1919.[53]

In 1920, Ekblaw directed a drive to raise funds to erect a football stadium at the University of Illinois and headed a campaign to elect the Republican William B. McKinley, owner of the central Illinois railway traction company, to the U.S. Senate. At that time Ekblaw maintained an office in Champaign as a consulting geologist. He was the consulting engineer of the Illinois Petroleum Trust, organized by local entrepreneurs to develop oil lands in Arkansas.

At Isaiah Bowman's request, Ekblaw reviewed books for the *Geographical Review*. Paid a small sum for each task, he reviewed four books in the April 1922 issue of the *Geographical Review*. One was by Otto Nordenskjöld, Polarnaturen (1918), a book on the phenomena of the polar worlds for the layman. Another, Carl Skottsberg, *Till Robinson—ön och Varldens Ande* (1918), was a narrative of the explorer's visit to the Juan Fernandez group and Easter Island. Still another, H. Blink, *Nederland als Tuinbvouwland: Historisch en Economisch-Geographisch Beschreven* (1916), was on Holland's horticultural importance, and also H.P. Steensby, *Danmarks Natur* (1919–21), a brief geographical study.[54] Ekblaw reviewed Knud Rasmussen's, *Myter og Saga fra Grönland* (1921), a book about myths and tales from Greenland, and also *Greenland by the Polar Sea: The Story of the Thule Expedition from Melville Bay to Cape Morris Jesup* (1921).[55] Ekblaw was probably the unidentified author of "The Origin of the Eskimo," an article based on H.P. Steensby, *An Anthropological Study of the Origin of the Eskimo Culture* (1916).[56]

In 1924, Ekblaw went to Clark University in Worcester, Massachusetts, to join the faculty of the Graduate School of Geography. Here Ellen Churchill Semple, a pioneer who broadened the disciplinary focus beyond the physical to the human aspects of geography, gave further emphasis to his thinking.[57] While at Clark, Ekblaw was the editor of *Home Geographic Monthly*, a children's magazine. In March 1925, Clark University initiated a new quarterly journal, *Economic Geography*. Ekblaw was the managing editor. He also wrote a Sunday feature column and a Monday editorial for the *Worcester Telegram*.

In 1927, with the permission of the American Museum of Natural History, Ekblaw published a long, impressive article on the material response of the Polar Inuit to their Far Arctic environment. In it quoted liberally from the manuscript of his geographic work on the work of the Crocker Land Expedition. Ellen C. Semple had critically scrutinized much of the manuscript.[58]

Ekblaw began this essay by describing Thule as the land of the Polar Inuit and the Polar Inuit as Arctic frontiersmen. He then systematically delineated various aspects of the Polar Inuit in the Far North. First, their villages, both summer and winter villages. Second, their habitations, including tupik or sealskin tent, igloo or stone house, and iglooyak or snow house. Third, dress. Here Ekblaw dealt with materials, tanning and sewing, and the effect of climate, and he described costumes. Fourth, food: its sources and character, its storage, and cooking. Then hunting. Ekblaw described weather and ice conditions, land hunting, ice hunting, and open-sea hunting. And last, travel. Under this heading he discussed dogs, sledges and harness, care of dogs, and sledging.[59]

In concluding, Ekblaw observed that the Polar Inuit had fully adapted themselves to the rigor of their conditions and the paucity and monotony of the available resources. "Their food, clothing, fuel, equipment, and homes have for centuries been derived from their own land; and their physical character, mental attributes, social and economic organization, and religion, have been modified only by their own environment, without alien influence. Their relation to their land is simple, direct, and native."[60]

"But the isolation of Thule and the self-sufficiency of the Polar Eskimo are now at an end. The establishment of the trading station at North Star Bay, the mission at Kangerdluksuak, and the sovereignty of the Danish government, have terminated the long dominance of solely local conditions. Hereafter the simple and direct relation of the people to their land will be modified by the subtle and impelling influence of the white man's wares and ideas and their culture will lose its distinction and their character its primitive charm. Exterior materials, alien ideas, and strange blood must inevitably submerge the native culture and character of this unique little Eskimo society on the uttermost Arctic frontier."[61]

After visiting Russia for six weeks in the summer of 1930, Ekblaw was not optimistic about the ultimate success of the Communist government. In 1949 the king of Sweden conferred upon Ekblaw the degree of Knight of the Order of the North Star for service to the Swedes and the Swedish residents of the United States and to Sweden in the way of literary and scientific achievement, knowledge about the structure of the earth and its effects on the history of mankind, knowledge about trees and flowers, and knowledge about birds and other life. An able (but sometimes diffuse) writer, Ekblaw died on 6 June 1949.

In September 1916, Minnick or Mene Wallace, having walked from North

Star Bay to Parker Snow Bay, where he found the *George B. Cluett* of the Crocker Land Expedition ready to sail, worked his way to St. John's, Newfoundland, as a sailor. With his earnings he went to New York as a ship's passenger. Arriving in New York City, he placed his clothes in a storeroom of the McAlpin Hotel, took a bath with a lump of ice in the water, and inspected Broadway. Early in 1917 he appeared at the County Clerk's office in New York City, said that he planned to become a citizen of the United States and would return the following day for his first papers.[62] He had talked with the Inuit who accompanied both Cook and Peary on their expeditions; he knew the truth of their claims bearing on the North Pole. However, he did not intend to divulge his information unless the newspapers or a weekly newsmagazine would pay him a few thousand dollars for the story.[63] Mene died of bronchial pneumonia in North Stratford, New Hampshire, on 29 October 1918.

Fitzhugh Green returned from the Arctic and resumed his career as a navy officer. The dramatic and ultimately sad story of his life in these years unfolds in the following chapter.

11

Fitzhugh Green: After Crocker Land

Fitzhugh Green arrived in Copenhagen on 19 August 1916 after three and a half years of detached duty in the Arctic. He had turned twenty-eight three days earlier. He immediately went on to Washington, D.C., and the navy detailed him to duty on the U.S.S. *Texas*. On 27 November Green married Natalie Wheeler Elliott, a Philadelphia socialite. They had three children.

After returning from Greenland, Green went through several stages in his life. In the first stage, he had a distinguished navy career, during which he combined his commitment to the service with his compulsion to write. His literary output was impressive in its range and quantity. In the second stage, after a crisis about his future, he retired from the navy, became an assistant to the New York publisher George P. Putnam, and continued to write. In the third stage he divorced his wife, became the fourth husband of a wealthy woman, and joined a circle of celebrities. At some point along the way he fell into an abyss. As the Roman poet Vergil wrote, "Facilis descensus Averno."[1]

Fitzhugh Green and Murder

In 1926, while on navy duty, Fitzhugh Green read a long article in the *New York Times* by George Putnam that referred to Green as having killed an Inuit while he was with the Crocker Land Expedition. However, Putnam was writing not about Green but about the murder by his Inuit companion of an American who was with Peary on his 1908–09 attempt to reach the North Pole.[2] The tangled skein of circumstances, Putnam wrote, had oddly unraveled during the last twelve months at the hands of a missioner and a trader. Putnam had happened on the scene just as the facts came into focus.

As Putnam related, Ross Marvin had been a member of Peary's 1908–09 quest to attain the Pole. Kudlooktoo, Marvin's Inuit companion, reported Marvin's death as due to his falling into a lead on his return from opening a way for Peary. In fact, however, Kudlooktoo, fearing that he himself might not return to safety, had shot and killed Marvin. Years elapsed, and early in 1925, at Karnah, in Inglefield Gulf, the missionary Jens Olsen persuaded Kudlooktoo to embrace the Christian religion. Olsen baptized the Inuit and asked him to confess his sins before taking communion. Kudlooktoo then publicly confessed that he had murdered Marvin and that the story of his drowning was false. An attempt had been made to keep this information from the United States, but by 1924 it had become known to a few.

Green was not much surprised to hear that an Inuit had shot Marvin. Inuit, he wrote, are kind, generous, and peace-loving people. He had known many men of many races in his more than twenty-one years of naval service, and none surpassed the average young Inuit hunter in amiability and endurance. But the brown native of the Far North has certain childlike qualities, Green added. Under pressure of hardship and anxiety he becomes panicky. Peary often spoke of this trait; other explorers have remarked upon it.

Fitzhugh Green at Peary's Cairn, Cape Thomas Hubbard, Axel Heiberg Island, Canada, May 1914. Inside the cairn, Green and MacMillan found a letter from Peary with no mention of Crocker Land (American Museum of Natural History Library).

Under such circumstances the Inuit will behave in an altogether unnatural way.

Green went on to recount his own experience. "I shot Pewahtoq [i.e., Peeahwahto] on the shores of the Polar Sea to save my own life," he declared. Continuing, he described his experience from the time he and MacMillan parted after searching for Crocker Land until they rejoined after Green had shot and killed Peeahwahto.

"I do not believe that Ross Marvin 'cracked' as the native said he did," Green declared. "I knew Marvin well. I have seen a good many men crack. Psychologically Marvin was not the type who would go to pieces noisily. His morale would disintegrate slowly. He would sit down and ask the others to go on and leave him. He might weep quietly at the bitterness of his fate." Green reconstructed the scene as follows: The two natives with Marvin realized that their small party had little food left. They were, like other Inuit, frightened at being out on the Polar Sea. Marvin wanted to follow the old trail back to land. He refused to lighten his sledges by throwing away important scientific instruments and records. The natives finally went into one of their fits of despair that come under such circumstances and disposed of the white man, who was both the cause of their plight and, to their minds, the obstacle to their safe return. Green's account is convincing. He had had an experience on the Polar Sea that the other critics lacked.[3]

News of the killing of Marvin in the icy north had not reached the State Department, the Danish Legation in Washington, or the National Geographic Society before 25 September 1926, when the *New York Times* published Putnam's article. Frank B. Kellogg, the U.S. Secretary of State, was reticent to discuss the subject in the absence of an official report. What action the department would take was uncertain. Apart from the lapse of time since the murder, no constituted authority existed where the crime was committed; therefore there could be no violation of statutory law. The site of the crime was not the property of Denmark at the time of the killing. International legal experts agreed that Kudlooktoo could not be brought to trial for the killing of Marvin.[4]

In April 1928, Thomas Hall, the author of a manuscript, "The Confession of the Murder of Prof. Marvin," responded to recent letters he had received from Fitzhugh Green. In 1927, Hall wrote, Knud Rasmussen had told Isaiah Bowman, then the director of the American Geographical Society, about the murder of Marvin. "This was a year before the Putnam Article appeared giving the news to the public," Hall added. "The fact of keeping the matter secret during that time is in itself significant. It seems to me that Bowman must know from Rasmussen just exactly what Kudlooktoo confessed."[5]

Hall was not keeping confidential matter from Green. He had none to withhold. "I have been unable to get a word from Rasmussen, who knows, or a word as to where in Washington he filed the *so-called confession*. I presume with the National Geographic Society, to bury it." Hall knew nothing that was not open to anybody. He hoped that Green would manage to see what Hall had written. "I can then perhaps in some way help you otherwise.... If you can see my article, you may admit that I have followed Kudlooktoo's tracks in the snow to Peary's tent door in the Arctic, and that possibly the indications may seem to you, that if Kudlooktoo premeditated the murder, it was in that tent."[6]

Hall was not gifted in any way, he added, but he enjoyed searching for the truth. "I evolved the facts in this case as I went along, and I was perfectly confident at every step of what I WOULD find. The situation was clear to me from start to finish. I think the truth, if it can be evolved is this, Marvin was an obstacle to Peary's ambition. (This could not be brought out in a letter.) If you read Peary's book from Cape Sheridan to Marvin's farthest north, you will, I think, see it. Even though Peary has of course carefully censored his own book. Kudlooktoo was a great favorite with Peary. They slept in the same tent all the way. There is no evidence that Kudlooktoo ever was near enough to Marvin to speak to him on the trip north. When you have all this clear, then re-read Peary's report of Marvin's "DROWNING"!"[7]

Hall's conclusions were not confidential. They were personal opinions. He could not see how anyone could read Peary's statement of Marvin's drowning without seeing serious inconsistencies even though the reader did not have the light to guide him that Hall had at his reading. Peary's recital of his trip to his farthest north in 1906 and of his trip to the North Pole in 1909 are both "unmistakably invention," as Hall thought he had proven beyond the possibility of refutation. Peary, having dared that much, it was but natural (whether true or not), that he would remove every possible means of exposure.[8]

Green was fortunate in knowing Kudlooktoo, Bowman, and Rasmussen, Hall added. If Green could meet the party who induced Kudkooktoo to confess, he could, Hall was sure, draw out the exact truth. "It saddens me to disappoint you," Hall added. "You may have been misinformed as to the nature of what I have written. My recollection is that the reason I was unwilling for it to be published was, because I thought the matter too grave, and the process of attempting to prove that the contents of Kudlooktoo's confession by circumstantial evidence too difficult, and too unsatisfactory." Hall's object was only to call attention to the indications in the "ambiguous incongruous report of Putnam" that it was misleading if not actually untrue. I hoped that I might induce someone to procure the Kudlooktoo confession itself and therefore unfold the truth. What I may personally think or believe about the matter was immaterial, Hall added, "but facts will stand against the world, whoever unfolds them."[9] The preceding details held clarify events in the Arctic, but they shed no new light on Green's murder of Peeahwato.

Fitzhugh Green: Author of Articles

After returning from the Arctic, Green tried to balance his commitment to the navy with his determination to write, which for him was a form of relaxation. He believed that men who had the good luck to make interesting journeys were duty bound to relate their experiences. In September 1917 Green published two articles. In "Running the British Blockade," published in *Sea Power*, Green described his perilous journey to Copenhagen during the world war when he returned from the Crocker Land Expedition. "Our New Navy," an overview of the subject, appeared in the *Saturday Evening Post*. And then in November 1917 Green published a wordy, frivolous account of how sailors found food and drink while briefly on shore leave. The piece revealed his conservative cast of mind.[10]

At the same time Green also wrote for the George Matthew Adams newspaper syndicate. Adams, who first flourished in Chicago and later in New York, featured pictures, inspirational matter, and humor. By 1910 over 150 newspapers depended on Adams for material.[11] In 1917 Green wrote "Facts About Our Navy," a promotional package for the George Mathew Adams Service. Soon thereafter Josephus Daniels, the Secretary of the Navy, informed Green that Navy Regulations required him to submit to the Navy Department for examination and approval anything that he might desire to publish. The samples of articles published by Green contained no information which the Department considered undesirable to have known, but this might not be the case with other articles. The Department did not feel justified in dispensing Lieutenant Green from complying with the Navy Regulations in the same manner as other naval officers.[12]

Accordingly, Green notified the Adams Newspaper Service that the regularity of his contributions must be canceled. He could neither contract for nor promise to furnish 500 words or any other amount daily for publication. Without conflicting with his regular duties, his writing had been of great value. "It is almost necessary ... that an officer have some form of relaxation." He found pleasure in light literary work. It afforded him mental exhilaration without which his professional work must suffer He could run off little articles in twenty to thirty minutes, and no other occupation could relieve so well the fatigue of concentrated effort. To the criticism of his style, Green replied that no levity was intended. He hoped only to impart an "agreeable vivacity" to serious subjects.[13]

Having been warned, Green resorted to a pseudonym. As Fait Garros, he published five articles in the journal *Sea Power* from November 1917 to March 1919. One, "Getting in the First Shot," described competitive shooting on navy vessels and what it had done for the fleet. Another suggested that the navy clothe its sailors like Inuit. The third article described how a navy first lieutenant kept his ship clean, the fourth described the duties of a ship's executive officer, and the final article was about a navy officer in a navy yard.

After this interruption, Green published in his own name in many magazines. His most frequent outlets were the *American Mercury, Century, Collier's, Popular Science Monthly,* and the *Saturday Evening Post.* He published less often in the *American Magazine, Ladies Home Journal, Outlook, Scientific American,* and *Woman's Home Companion.* Green's articles also appeared in *Boy's Life, Delineator, Home Geographic, International Aeronautics, Motor Boat, Open Road, The Sphere, World's Work,* and *Youth's Companion.*

Green wrote an account of the Crocker Land Expedition that appeared in the *United States Naval Institute Proceedings.* Its four parts, a total of 137 pages, were published from October 1917 to January 1918, after he had returned from the Arctic.[14] When he came across one of these pieces, President Osborn of the American Museum sent Green, who was then on duty on the U.S.S. *Utah,* the following message through the Bureau of Navigation of the Navy Department: "January thirty publication your article in December Naval Institute proceedings violations of your promise to myself and breach of contract with MacMillan[.] I desire immediate explanation[.] publication of Crocker Land articles must stop[.]"

Green did not stop. He placed many other articles in the *United States Naval Institute Proceedings.* One called for close cooperation between the American navy and the American Merchant Marine, and it described three colorful merchant skippers.[15] Another celebrated Robert Peary as a scientist and Arctic explorer. The editor's preface to that effusion noted that Green had enjoyed the friendship of Amundsen, Shackleton, Steffanson, Rasmussen and others who had blazed "the long white trail to the ends of the earth."[16] In an article on science and the navy, Green described the features peculiar to all coastlines. The mechanical agents that have the most to do with the fashioning of coastline, he observed, are earthquakes and seaquakes, the rise of molten rock to the earth's surface, an attack of weather, sea waves and tides, the rise and fall of land, and glaciers past and present.[17]

Green was a transitional figure in the history of Arctic exploration. At one time a driver of dogs and sledges, he was present at the dawn of air travel to the Pole. Granting that an air route from Europe to the Orient by way of the North Pole cuts the distance from 10,000 miles to 5,000 miles, Green wondered if such an air route was worth developing in light of the risk and the other obstacles.[18] Nevertheless, Green made a case for the navy to continue the work in the North by air. The Arctic venture being proposed at the time was a stunt, he said, but the broad scientific research that could be carried on by such an expedition established the justification for it.[19] While dealing with large issues, Green also made a plea for use of the slide rule on board ship.[20]

Green's articles in popular magazines, most numerous from 1926 to 1930, illustrate his remarkable versatility. In writing about the U.S. Navy, for example, he commented on the perils of polar flight, the sky sports of tomorrow, nations racing for the Pole, going to Paris by air, and thrills he had never had. In other, miscellaneous articles he wrote about armchair explorers, building bridges, flying in the future, and sky sports.

Green also wrote about real explorers. In 1927 he published in the *American Mercury* an article about Roy Chapman Andrews, an explorer and naturalist who gained world fame in the 1920s through a series of expeditions to Central Asia. Andrews wrote several books and was at one time the director of the American Museum of Natural History. Green also penned an article about Martin Johnson, who explored the wildlife and the people of East and Central Africa and other exotic lands. Green may have written one of the books attributed to Martin Johnson. He wrote articles and a book about Richard E. Byrd, an aviator, explorer, and fellow Naval Academy midshipmen.

Green was a ghostwriter, as we know from articles he wrote for Martin Johnson on African safari adventures.[21] By the nature of the case it is often hard to determine what fits such an ill-defined category. Green was probably the ghostwriter for articles on Arctic exploration and adventure by his friend Richard E. Byrd. Green wrote the articles on puzzles by an author known as Sam Loyd that were published in *Liberty* magazine in 1927.

In 1928 Green published an account of "The Crocker Land Expedition." This brief article, illustrated with photos, told the story of the last extensive dog-sledge expedition in the Arctic. The chief success of the expedition came in 1914, Green wrote, when MacMillan and he sledged across Ellesmere Land and out over the Polar Sea but failed to discover Crocker Land at or near its supposed location. Nothing in the article was new, except its failure to mention Green's murder of his Inuit companion, Peeahwahto.[22]

Fitzhugh Green: Naval Officer

On 13 May 1917, while stationed on the U.S.S. *Texas*, Green requested duty on any vessel going into the war zone. While cruising in Arctic waters, he wrote in pleading his case, he had acquired much information that might be of value on such duty. He had been on the Danish vessel *Godthaab* in August 1916 when she ran the British blockade. He described how the ship reached Danish waters successfully. Germany had extended her blockade zone to Greenland. Only a few Danes and three Americans besides Green had the experience to run the blockade. Two years in the northern waters had established Green's peculiar fitness for the requested detail.[23]

On 5 June 1917 Green was promoted to lieutenant; later that year he was ordered to the U.S.S. *Utah* as radio officer and aide on the staff of Rear Admiral Augustus Fechteler. Early in 1918 Green was promoted to lieutenant com-

Fitzhugh Green, looking out from top of a ship's mast in Melville Bay, August 1913, continued to serve in the Navy until 1927 (American Museum of Natural History Library).

mander, and Josephus Daniels, the Secretary of the Navy Department, ordered him to report to Admiral Thomas S. Rodgers as Aid and Flag Lieutenant on his staff during the world war.[24] In 1919, Green was assigned to duty in charge of ordnance testing at the Naval Proving Grounds at Indian Head, Maryland. While there he received a special Letter of Commendation and was awarded a Silver Star from the Bureau of Navigation of the Navy Department for services rendered during the world war.[25]

While at Indian Head, Green sent to the Chief of the Bureau of Ordnance the rough draft of an address he had in mind on naval policy. In 1917, he began, when he was a member of the War Council's staff of lecturers, his ostensible mission was to entertain soldiers and sailors with an illustrated talk on Arctic exploration, but he was instructed to appeal for public interest and sympathy in naval matters. With suddenness, he discovered that a "stereotyped speech" was a snare and a delusion. In one fortnight he faced three disparate audiences, and in each case only the message was stereotyped. His addresses were vastly different. The Navy Department must choose the message, Green declared, the audience alone could fix the address. Danger lay in both the choice of message and its delivery. As a result, whether his plan was or was not to combat Radicalism, in some quarters it would be so construed.

Utmost care must be taken to avoid an encounter with the Radicals. How ignorant the public was of naval matters was astounding. As a result the public had no conception of why a navy was needed. He wrote that the public looks upon an adequate navy as a needless extravagance. Should we have to go to the mat with Radicalism, we shall encounter a dull lack of public understanding. The Navy Department must therefore select the message, and it must be impeccably American. Assume that the message chosen aims at popularizing the navy, the lecturer must be profoundly acquainted with the navy. He must consort with all types of people and views with almost superhuman adaptability. A skillful wielding of the sword of truth against the lawlessness of the world was desired. Most vital was the platform personality of the speaker. He must have emotional poise and a mastery of human interest to be effective against the ignorance the speaker was bound to meet in a university auditorium or town hall.

After this preface Green outlined the address he had in mind: "Our Navy: The Great American Tonic." Its theme was that our navy was at once a weapon, an insurance policy, a stimulant, a work of art, and the greatest educational institution in the world. The address had six parts: How we came to have a Navy; our Navy of today; our Merchant Marine; inseparability of Navy and Merchant Marine; what the Navy means to the country at large; why the Navy means what it does. The last part asserted that the Navy and naval policy epitomize America in the eyes of the world.[26]

Green's proposal reveals much about both the man and the times. Alert to the Russian revolution, post-war radicalism, and the government's deportation of putative radicals, he identified himself not merely as a loyal American but as a superpatriot.

Leaving Indian Head, Green was detailed as the gunnery officer on the U.S.S. *Texas* and later as the gunnery officer on the U.S.S. *Chaumont*. In 1923, when the *Chaumont* arrived in New York, Green was ordered to the Naval War College at Newport, Rhode Island. Here he was aide to Admiral C.S. Williams, who headed the college. He graduated from the junior course in 1924. When Green left Newport, the navy assigned him to special temporary intelligence duty in New York. This phase of his career is described later.

Fitzhugh Green: Author of Books

While churning out articles and serving at sea, Green authored more than a score of books. Among them were *Arctic Duty* (1917); *Clear the Decks* (1919); *Won for the Fleet: A Story of Annapolis* (1922); *The Mystery of the Erik* (1923), a novel that draws on his Arctic experience; *Z R Wins* (1924), a novel; *Fought for Annapolis* (1925), 271 pages in which Green describes the transformation of a willful, headstrong boy into a thoughtful midshipman; *Our Naval Heritage* (1925), about which more later; *Hold 'Em Navy* (1926); *I'll Never Move Again* (1926); *Uncle Sam's Sailors* (1926); *Anchors Aweigh* (1927), with a foreword by Rear Admiral Charles P. Plunkett, who testified that Green gave an "accurate and entertaining" picture of Annapolis life and impressed the reader with the need for putting the welfare of the many above that of the individual; *Midshipmen All* (1927), with a foreword by Rear Admiral William S. Sims, who objected to its inaccuracies; *Some Famous Sea Fights* (1927), co-authored with Holloway Frost, a 1900 Naval Academy graduate; *Dick Byrd: Air Explorer* (1928), on Green's friend and Annapolis classmate, the naval officer Richard Byrd, who, with Floyd Bennett, said that he flew over the North Pole in 1926; *Martin Johnson: Lion Hunter* (1928); *Bob Bartlett: Master Mariner* (1929); *The Film Finds Its Tongue* (1929), an account of the early history of Hollywood; *The Romance of Modern Exploration* (1929), a book on adventure, explorers, aeronautics, and voyages published by the American Library Association. Green, who had written an article about Andrews, also published *Roy Chapman Andrews: Dragon Hunter* (1930). Green's book, *Peary: The Man Who Refused to Fail* (1926), published by G.P. Putnam's Sons, was favorably reviewed in April 1926 on the front page of the *New York Times Book Review*. "Green's 'Peary' could not be more timely," the reviewer gushed. Arctic exploration by aircraft, the review noted, was about to be put to the test by Richard Byrd among others.

Fitzhugh Green: "Our Naval Heritage"

In 1924, while at the Naval War College, Green wrote Captain R.H. Leigh in the Bureau of Navigation about talking with Admiral Williams of the war college about a plan he had. The admiral "thinks highly of my opportunity," he added, and under the circumstances was willing that Green should be detached for other duty on his graduation on 29 May. Therefore, Green suggested, appropriate orders for him would be something like, "To the Office of Naval Intelligence for special temporary intelligence duty in New York and for work connected with the compilation of a History of the American Navy." Through press friends, Green thought he could secure free office space in New York at 40th Street and Fifth Avenue, an ideal location, across the street from the Public Library, just around the corner from his publishers, and midway between the navy historical centers, Boston and Washington. Green's relations with the Office of Naval Intelligence would be very specific. He would be considered an extra officer "on their allowance" due to "the peculiar nature" of his duties. He would keep in touch with the Office of Navy Intelligence for guidance in his lectures and his historical themes. Aside from occasional "Arctic-navy lectures" he would attempt no publicity work. Finally, no expense for travel or other matters would devolve upon the government, and he would keep the Navy Department apprised of the progress of his work. In a word, he sought sufficient freedom to give his plan a fair trial without straining the indulgence of the Navy Department.[27]

Captain Leigh told Halsey Powell, a commander in the Information Section of the Office of the Secretary of the Navy, about Green's plans. Powell wrote Green that the navy needed Green's "sort of work" if we were to maintain our navy. One of the most valuable ways of making the navy popular was through history, especially history that young people could read. Powell offered the assistance of his office to promote publicity for the naval profession in this country.[28]

The day after Green wrote to Captain Leigh, Leigh sent Green change of duty orders. When directed by the President, the orders read, Green was to regard himself detached from duty at the Naval War College and from such other duty as may have been assigned to him, proceed to Washington, D.C., and report to the Director of Naval Intelligence for special temporary intelligence duty in New York, NY, and for work in connection with the compilation of a history of the American Navy.[29]

Thanking Powell for his 13 May letter, Green wrote that the two men shared the same mission, viz. "to gain for our Navy the support and sympathy of the American people by educating them on naval matters." Green criticized "the notorious mustiness" of naval histories drawn out of "dark and gloomy" libraries. He had secured office space at 40th St. and Fifth Avenue in the thick of the press and publishing district and could write "with one finger on naval archives and one on the public pulse." Another feature of his plan was his Arctic lecture. He had given it in Washington in February and had been called on to deliver it twice at the War College and six times in Newport. The Harvard Club of Boston liked it so well that they had reserved a speaking date for Green the following winter on any subject he chose. The lecture was not all Arctic; it was 40 percent navy stuff. As to the financial side of this, Green added, "this kind of writing" does not pay. From his boy's books he had averaged about $150 apiece. From his lectures he received free transportation and $10 each time for depreciation on his slides. Incidental expenses ate up what profit there was. The true profit lay in the fact that "*I am and have been gradually winning an audience that ... will accept my navy propaganda as child takes medicine from a trusted parent.*" This was the important point. Officers had been voicing their enthusiasm for "the whole scheme." Green's orders were to report to ONI before going to New York. He planned to go to Washington in early June and hoped to see Powell. "As I have a wife and three children to settle in New York besides my writing arrangements," Green would be in Washington only one day.[30]

Later that year Green skirted danger. In November he published in the *New York Times* a long article titled "The Worst Menace of Another War." Its subtitle was "Swarms of Pilotless Planes, With Huge Gas Bombs Aboard, Threatening a Whole Nation With Deadly Vapors, Are Pictured—No Defense Yet Found."[31] The text spelled out the dangers in detail. The Secretary of the Navy Curtis D. Wilbur wrote Green about "the matter" before the Office of Naval Intelligence knew that the secretary planned to do so. While the Director of Naval Intelligence agreed with the secretary that this article should not have been written, he appreciated Green's other work and believed that this would be all that is necessary to cause him to watch more carefully in the future. In fact, the Director tried hard to get the Secretary to let him handle the whole matter. Halsey Powell, writing to Green about the matter, was "just as sorry that official methods were used in this as I am that you wrote the article." Try to remain cheerful, Powell counseled, and keep up the good work. "We all down here appreciate what you are doing, and Admiral Hough has told the Secretary much of your work."[32]

Nevertheless, Green had to eat crow. Writing to the Secretary of the Navy, Green regretted the appearance of the article. It was the result of a hurry-up call from the editor of the *New York Times* "with whom I have built up a friendship for the sake of future favorable Naval publicity. The scarehead was the paper's own invention. This does not excuse, but in some measure explains my error in judgment which, I assure you, will not occur again."[33]

Despite his abject submission, on the day that he wrote to the Director of Intelligence (9 December 1924) Green wrote a Memo for his own records. "The truth behind this tempest in a teapot was that Wilbur had a statement already to go before the Senate proving that the battleship was the finest weapon in the world, and that all of our old junk should be put into proper shape for operation with the fleet. My article therefore did not accord with what he was trying to prove. The Senate passed his bill this day." But Green was not willing to concede. "As a matter of fact," he added, "it is likely that there is more truth in my article than there is in his statement to the Senate. However, I am forced to take an apologetic position or risk being sent to sea, which for a variety of reasons I cannot afford to do. Hence the absurdity of the whole thing, and the derision it gives rise to." On the Memo, Green penciled in the following observation: "Dec. 26 Dietrich says that the Sec. Nav. Wanted to court martial me."[34]

While this tempest raged, Green had been working on his history. On 9 April 1925 he reported that the first volume would go to the press in June. Besides the history, he had been living behind the scenes in the world of publicity. By keeping clear of naval affiliation he had not been looked upon as an agent of the navy and yet had been in touch with the department's policies. He got into the New York Newspaper Club as an accredited journalist, built up friendships with a number of publishers, advertising men, editors and syndicates, and as a result had been able to get the "inside" reaction to Navy Department efforts. One of Green's greatest ambitions was to leave New York with the ground prepared for a regular "P.G. [Post Graduate] course." He hoped that the navy would send one young officer to New York each year for twelve months divided between a big newspaper, a big advertising agency, a publishing house, a syndicate, and a national magazine. As a result, the navy should have a small but well-informed corps of educated publicists in its own ranks. Another interesting though limited phase of his work was the moving picture game, as witnessed by films that Hollywood moguls were making including *Shipmates*, *Shore Leave*, and one based on Peary's account of his discovery of the North Pole. Green described himself as valuable to the navy as long as he remained in New York, ostensibly just a "mildly-intelligent historian" and not another "Navy Publicity Agent."[35]

On 3 July Green wrote to navy officer John Stapler, surprised by his friend's letter of the previous day, because to date Green had accomplished about twice what his publishers or friends in the department thought he could. He was forwarding under separate cover the first proofs of "Volume I of my history. More to follow." For twelve months he had worked ten to sixteen hours a day and was pretty tired. It would be a long story to list all the snags and complications he had struck. Green had always understood that another year was allowed him, and in good faith the publishers had gone ahead with publicity for volume two. It would be bad tactics to stop them.

Since Green had been ashore only two years, there should be no trouble on that score, especially since he had real results to show for his time.[36]

Fitzhugh Green's labor led to the publication of *Our Naval Heritage* (1925). His goal was "a succinct and vivid recital of our country's past afloat, and of her newly won world leadership at sea."[37] With an Introduction, thirty-two chapters, forty-eight illustrations, and an index, the book ran to 459 pages. The author avoided Scylla, the "notorious mustiness" of earlier naval histories, but foundered on Charybdis. A reader of the book penciled on the title page an expletive followed by the declaration, "He knows neither History Ships nor The Sea!"[38]

In March 1926, Green proposed that he stay in New York for another year. For the first time in his life he felt that he was of 100 percent value to the navy and was doing something that no other naval officer had ever been able to do, and doing it well. His work was divided into two parts: writing and conniving. In writing, during the winter he had produced one volume of history, an Annapolis book, a naval biography, and a recruiter's aid. In conniving he had been military adviser to four big publishers, had made speeches, and had, he thought, "killed General Mitchell's book." (This was a reference to Billy Mitchell, an army officer who was an early advocate of air power.) Just when Green's plans were fully matured, he was scheduled for sea service. Yet publishers, four of whom he named, had signed him up for books, and the heirs of two naval heroes wanted him to do biographies of their ancestors. The writing could not possibly be done at sea.

It was hard enough to do it in New York, where all the extra money he made and half of his time went into the intricate game a writer and publicist had to play in order to move along. Green believed that he was ten times more useful in New York than aboard ship. Then too he could not go to sea because "some damn thing is the matter with my heart." Doctors said that it originated with the long spell of rheumatic fever he had had after his last 1,200-mile sledge journey in Greenland. The previous year he had had a mild stroke, which he had managed to keep off his record. Navy doctors and civilian specialists said that he must go into a hospital for three or four months of surveillance, perhaps longer, before he changes from sedentary to ship life. Another year of careful living in New York would enable him to get physically by the navy selection board when he went up for commander's rank the following year. Stapler could see what a delicate position Green was in and what a futile conclusion it might come to if either the navy or Green failed to take into account all aspects of the situation. Green was trying to put professional interests before personal ones because "my heart is now and always in the Navy."[39]

Perhaps his heart was fickle, perhaps pressures weighed on him, or perhaps enticements attracted him. In any case, in March 1927 he faced what he described as "The Big Crisis." As he confessed, he had walked a tightrope for

11. Fitzhugh Green: After Crocker Land

three stiff years. From the War College he had got himself ordered to Washington for duty in New York. In carrying out regular naval duty while at the same time acquiring commercial experience, he could not risk being dragged off for one of the collateral duties to which a naval officer on shore duty was obligated—e.g., a parade, a funeral, a court-martial. At any moment from 1924 to 1927 he had never known when catastrophe would crash upon him. He salved his conscience by working hard at laying the foundation for a "Public Relations" system for the Navy Department and at the same time he gave the best in him to serve his "commercial masters."

His financial position was the keynote to this desperate time in his life. His family resources were small. The total outlook for his parents, soon to retire, was less than $500 a month income. His wife's family had a background of wealth, but the wealth was distributed over a large family and too confused by mismanagement to permit him any money hopes in that direction. His wife received $100 a month allowance, but it was neither dependable nor adequate in case of trouble. Thus he had to take stock of his economic circumstances and was largely bound to the standard of living to which he and his wife and friends were accustomed. "It's perfectly nauseating," his wife cried one evening, "for you to talk about how much money people in our family have." "But I have to," he countered. "It's low and mean. It's *dirty*, I dare say." Did she have any suggestions? "You're making more in business than you make in the Navy," his wife replied, "and you can't do your work and worry like this." To which Green replied, "I'm not worrying. I'm analyzing. I'm making an 'Estimate of the Situation.'" And so on far into the night.

For years Green had been relying on the assurance that the government paid his salary. If he became ill or permanently disabled, he could look forward to about $3,000 a year in retired pay. His navy financial figures—$500 a month and an assured fine pension—were large in comparison with the vast majority of American family men.

An older businessman friend told Green that he and his wife had a standard of living equivalent of $10,000 a year while he was in navy, and that his financial future was assured even if his income wasn't large. "But there is no future in the Navy," Green countered. "What do you mean by 'future'?" "Oh, getting somewhere in life. Making more money so that my family can have two cars instead of one; a bigger house to live in; more travel and better schools than I can afford now." What are you going to do, the friend countered, if your health breaks down, you haven't enough capital to live on, and there are no family resources to fall back on. Green suddenly realized the struggle his friend had gone through in his climb to the upper level of his business. "But there's no future," Green kept repeating. "Well," the friend asked, "what *do* you want out of life?" Suddenly, Green asked himself, what do we want out of life? He still did not know, twenty years later. From a later perspective we know that Green was caught up in the race for riches that characterized the 1920s—until 1929.

Finally, the inevitable day came. Green heard that he was to be ordered to sea. He had had four years of shore duty: one at the Naval War College in Newport and three in New York. This was a feat in itself, getting four years ashore when even three years was considered good. On the other hand he had had only his brief postgraduate course in high explosives and his two years at the Naval Proving Ground, Indian Head, Maryland, ashore since he had graduated from Annapolis in 1909. He had not been dodging professional duty at sea.

So he quickly prepared a prospectus of the work he was doing in New York. The central idea was that he should build up contacts with writers, editors, and publishers who would keep the public continually in touch with what the navy was planning and doing. A great mass of the American people saw and heard almost nothing of naval matters, and there was in Washington a proper unwillingness to risk divulging military secrets. There was a great need for a strong navy, so Green proposed to institute a public relations mechanism in the navy department that would keep the American public aware of the needs and propriety of a suitably strong American navy.

Alas, Green wrote, it was heartbreaking to establish anything new in the government. In the beginning, Green had persuaded Theodore Roosevelt, Jr., Assistant Secretary of the Navy, five admirals, and a score of captains and commanders of the intrinsic desirability of his plan. When Green said that it would take time and work to get officers who would take an interest in something far removed from purely professional work, Roosevelt replied that Green must pick another person to follow on after him. Roosevelt agreed to see that a suitable officer and staff were set up in the department before Green went to sea. Green did not mention his resigning because he did not think it would help matters or him.

Green had gone to Washington to see if there were any chance that he might stay on another year in New York. When he reached his hotel he had a call waiting for him from George Putnam, his New York boss. "Get back here as soon as you can! Martin Johnson is up on his ear about his manuscript." Green went back, but he also saw the admiral involved with Green's orders to sea. The admiral had been told that Green had been in New York three years, and all he could find out was that Green had written a lot of books. The admiral who had been Chief of Bureau when Green left the War College had gone to sea; the new admiral had never been properly informed about Green's status. He told Green to go down the hall and get his orders. The Asiatic Chief of Staff had informed this admiral to get Green to Shanghai as soon as possible. He was to be Flag Secretary of the Asiatic Commander-in-Chief, "a nice enough job for any normal naval officer." But Green was not normal.

His orders were to catch a transport sailing from San Francisco the following week. Everywhere he found a vague attitude of "well, you've worked your graft long enough. Now go back to work." It did not seem possible that his plan had not made some sort of dent in the consciousness of the navy department. It was a good sample of how the taxpayer's money was wasted. His salary alone was over $15,000 during his years in New York, and the same work would have to be done over again by someone else. No individual was to blame. It was the system.

In addition to these problems was Green's "volcanic association" with his business bosses, especially George Putnam. "He was like a six foot three wire spring, constantly in vibration. He didn't care what my association with the navy was so long as I gave my life's blood to his needs. That I was in Washington making a profound change in my career was of not the slightest importance to him. In his mind I must 'get to hell' back to Forty-Fifth Street. Admirals and Asiatic Fleets were nothing in his young life."

Green found it difficult to describe the intense strain of that forty-eight hours in Washington. He had thought it would be easy after three years to decide whether he should leave the navy. He had a job in both civilian life and navy life. Dare he risk burning his bridges behind him in the shape of the security that went with a government job? Could he face "the impecunious monotony of military service?" He felt the need of some sort of supernatural tip that would guide him. The "tip" came when, lunching at the Army-Navy Club, he heard some fellows from the Bureau of Aeronautics discussing future transatlantic flights. One of them mentioned the flying-boat enterprise that the navy had carried out sometime before. It set off in Green a chain of thinking. He had already helped Dick Byrd with his Greenland flight and later his trans-polar flight from Spitzbergen. Byrd hoped to try the Atlantic in a few months. Noel Davis had spoken to Green about raising funds for a similar try. "An obscure mail pilot, named Lindbergh, was mentioned as a possible contender if he could get a ship. A friend of Green had asked him if he would cooperate with René Fonck, "the great French ace of World War I," in a New York to Paris hop.

"There was my tip!" Green exclaimed. The publishing end of these proposed flights was as much his as anyone else's. "The man who succeeded would be a national hero. If I could get his book and serial rights I would not only make some money, but I would for the first time establish my own name in the line of business I had chosen as my civilian career. Certainly I was up against a lot of professional publicity men. But if I kept on my toes and watched the great Race carefully in advance I might very well associate myself with the winner." So Green chocked down his last few mouthfuls and hurried back to the navy department. He had made his Great Decision. He resigned from the naval service.

"Seclusion of the Soul" described what happened next to Green. Suddenly, cut off from the people and diversions that make up the life of a naval officer, he felt bereft, desolate, and depressed. At last he had arrived at being able permanently "to live with my wife and babies." He could have a home and mold domestic life to suit his personal tastes. But nothing could ever take the place of the navy. It was a kind of grief, but while he grieved life closed in around him like a swarm of angry bees. The stable of writers in that branch of Putnam's to which Green was assigned kept him busy day and night. "Some got drunk, some got married; some rushed in with fiery indignation that we didn't make more money for them; others demanded literary nursing to a degree that a young mother never achieved over her newest-born. There were rows, fracases and fisticuffs." This sort of thing diverted Green from his personal economic problems.

Green then elaborated on the "hunch" that swayed him, in the spring of 1927, when he reached what seemed like the Big Crisis in his life—to resign from the navy. He had entered the publishing world and had to do something that would establish himself firmly in that world. In pushing forward, he said, a man has to be egocentric if he is to succeed. Green had associated with Dick Byrd in 1926 when Byrd flew over the North Pole. On Byrd's return to New York, Green met him in Gravesend Bay and discussed his plans the night before Byrd's triumphal parade up lower Broadway.

The following March Byrd asked Green to meet him in the Wanamaker department store on Eighth Street. Grover Whalen, the city's official welcomer, was there. Byrd introduced Green to Mr. Wanamaker, who was always on the lookout for something that would provide a clean, decent, and effective means of capturing public interest in the Wanamaker stores in Philadelphia and New York City. Byrd confided to Green that Mr. Wanamaker wished to back the first non-stop flight from New York to Paris. Whalen said that this summer someone was going to make the first full trans-oceanic plane flight as forerunner of what in a few years would be commercial air travel to Europe. "What a trip—what a trip!" Mr. Wanamaker exclaimed. How could he help? Green asked. "Fitz," Byrd replied, "Mr. Wanamaker wants to know if you would go to France and England and make arrangements for me at that end of the flight. We don't know, of course, exactly what our destination will be, Paris or London. Paris, we hope; but weather may decide for us." Green asked, "When will you hop off?" Byrd replied that several contestants were already making secret preparations. One was Noel Davis, who still needed a plane. "And a young chap named Lindbergh, backed by a St. Louis group. He has been a very successful air-mail pilot. He plans to go alone, I hear." Byrd wanted to use a multi-engine ship, more in line with what would be commercially used in the future. There were two or three other fellows in the field. Anthony Fokker was working on a special design of plane for the flight. Fokker had built the most successful planes the Germans had in the recent war. At this point Green ends his account of "The Big Crisis."[40]

On 25 March 1927 Green tendered his resignation from the navy. It took effect on 31 May.[41] Seemingly at loose ends, he thought of establishing a new sort of business with a group of explorers who would go to any part of the globe. The modern explorer, he said, faces the most difficult problem. "He has to be a military leader, a business executive, writer, technician and publicist. At the same time he is often temperamentally a genius. And genius is usually impractical. Only mediocrity is altogether practical. No mediocre man ever becomes a successful explorer." When to these details are added facing death in the wilderness and the collection of scientific specimens under the most perilous circumstances, little wonder that only a man with strong nerves and wide experience would attempt any kind of exploration. It was probable that his new firm would guide anything of an adventurous nature, anywhere. No doubt much of the work would be done by air, but there were inaccessible parts of the world where the traveler would be compelled to use old-fashioned methods.[42] Observers were likely to view Green's proposals as fanciful. In any case, he grounded himself.

From 1926 to 1931 Fitzhugh Green placed twelve articles in the *New York Times*. Whether he was on the staff or a free-lance author is not known. His pieces dealt with miscellaneous subjects: polar routes, units of the fleet, submarines, battleships, Bob Bartlett, Richard Byrd, and Greenland. Eight of the articles appeared in 1929 and 1930.[43]

Fitzhugh Green and the Glitterati

At some unidentifiable point in time, perhaps before he resigned from the navy, Green became an assistant to George P. Putnam, the director of G.P. Putnam's Sons, a New York publisher. Born in 1887 in Rye, New York, Putnam attended Harvard for one year, then went west, where he attended the University of California for one term and then struck out on his own. In 1908, as a guide on a Sierra Club outing, George met Dorothy Binney, the daughter of Edwin Binney, the inventor of Crayola crayons and co-owner of the company that made them. On 26 October 1911, after a two-year courtship, the couple were married at the Binney home on Sound Beach, Long Island, New York. Early in 1912, the bride and groom went west, settling in Bend, Oregon, a town of six hundred souls, where Putnam was the publisher and editor of the *Bend Bulletin* and for a year the mayor of Bend. In 1915 he became the private secretary to the governor of Oregon.

After eight years in Oregon, the couple returned to the East and purchased a house in Rye, New York. By 1922, at the age of thirty-five, Putnam had become the visible spokesman for G.P. Putnam's Sons. Dorothy Binney Putnam was relegated to suburban domesticity while George was thrust into the limelight of the publisher's world. Strains in the marriage, now evident, became more pronounced over time.

When Green worked for Putnam, both were caught up in the frenzy after Charles Lindbergh, a young mail pilot, made history with his solo flight across the Atlantic in 1927. Putnam hastened to reach Lindbergh in Paris to make an offer to publish the pilot's story, but Lindbergh had already asked Carlisle MacDonald, an American newspaper man, to ghost-write his story. Lindbergh accepted Putnam's offer, and Putnam wrote him a check for $100,000. MacDonald moved in with the Putnams to write an account of the historic flight. By the time he finished, Lindbergh had a change of heart. Dorothy Binney Putnam, who was close to these events, observed that "Fitz is dog tired and very worried over the Lindbergh book. There is difficulty and Lindbergh doesn't want to accept it, now that it's written for him."[44]

Who wrote Lindbergh's book *We* (1927), the story of the aviator's solo flight across the Atlantic? According to Dorothy Putnam, Lindbergh wrote it in longhand and delivered the manuscript in time for July publication. But the matter is more complicated. Lindbergh accepted an offer from George Putnam to write a book about his transatlantic flight and his early life. Fitzhugh Green may have been the author or the co-author of the book.[45] In the published work, Green is credited as the author of "A Little of What the World Thought of Lindbergh," the section that describes the post-flight receptions for Lindbergh in Paris, Brussels, Berlin, London, Washington, D.C., and New York. Putnam paid Green four thousand dollars for his contribution to the book.[46]

After returning home by ship, Lindbergh made a triumphal tour across the country. With Lindbergh's consent, Fitzhugh Green was paid ten thousand dollars to chart the hero's progress from the moment he reached America. Green celebrated the occasion with especially florid oratory.[47]

Fitzhugh Green had assisted George Putnam for nearly two years while still in the navy, as his correspondence with Isaiah Bowman, Director of the America Geographical Society, reveals. In August 1926, Putnam, then on an expedition to Baffin Land on the schooner *Morrissey*, whose captain was Bob Bartlett, radioed to inform Green that Knud Rasmussen, who was with Putnam, wanted Bowman to write a foreword to Rasmussen's book about his trip from Greenland to Alaska. The manuscript needed to be cut about 30 percent. Green took on the editing and asked Bowman if he would write a foreword to the book.[48]

On 19 August, the *New York Times* ran a front-page story about the Putnam expedition's encounter with a walrus herd the previous day. Writing to Bowman about the event, Green boasted that Putnam had shown resourcefulness and unadulterated grit in the affair. Having spent nearly four years in that country, Green understood Putnam's splendid work.[49]

Green corresponded with Bowman about Rasmussen's plans for a lecture tour and Richard Byrd's desire to find a publisher for a book about his polar flight.[50]

The most complicated story Green handled at this time was the murder of Ross Marvin, described earlier. Green sheds more light on it now, but questions still remain. On 8 September 1926, Green sent Bowman a telegram which is reproduced exactly as follows:

> PUTNAM WIRES FULLY ADVISES MARIN MATTER PER RASMUSSEN LETTER AUGUST FOURTEEN LAST YEAR HAVE PREPARED AUTHORITATIVE STORY PROPOSE SEND TIMES BELIEVING WISE RASMUSSEN STANDPOINT SIMULTANEOUSLY HE ADVISES DANISH
> MINISTER WASHINGTON THUS AMERICAN OBSERVER STRESSES RASMUSSEN
> FIVE ATTITUDE SO MANY NOW INFORMED BREAK SOON INEVITABLE POSSIBLE UNFRIENDLY RASMUSSEN VISEES THIDS MESSAGE QUERIES YOU AGREEMENT OUR JUDGMENT UNQUOTE PLEASE WIRE REPLY CARE PUTNAM COMPANY.[51]

Days later Green informed Bowman that he had sent Putnam a message as coming from Bowman in connection with Putnam's dispatch about Marvin. The reference is presumably to Putnam's proposed article on the subject for the *New York Times*, published on 25 September 1926. The message read, "Bowman approves general details your plan to release Marvin story and sees no objection or complication that might later arise. He believes the story should be released by Rasmussen rather than be allowed to trickle out." Putnam was due in Sydney about the last week in the month and would no doubt see the story when it appeared.[52]

When Green heard from Putnam a day or so later, he received this dispatch: "For Bowman this message. Hope you join us stop. Statement will eminate [sic] from Rasmussen giving me representing Times on ground enables tactical presentation. Also Times sends expedition much reciprocation equitable[.] He send story Denmark paper. Official report Washington."[53]

The preceding details shed light on the murder of Ross Marvin. But not enough. It seems clear that the main actors in the drama are covering up something. What? Thomas F. Hall unraveled this mystery in an article he wrote, as described earlier, but the matter is still not clear and the Marvin murder is not our main concern.

Writing on 26 September, when the *Morrissey* was off Nova Scotia, Putnam suggested that Bowman honor Rasmussen's book with a foreword. Rasmussen had prepared a statement of what he had done and sought to do with his Thule Station in North Greenland; he wanted Bowman and Putnam to have the statement as a matter of record. Putnam welcomed it as ammunition "to combat any such malicious slanders as were offered to me some time since regarding our friend Rasmussen by another Arctic explorer perhaps especially distinguished for his *abundance* of jealousy and lack of probity."[54] The unnamed explorer was Peter Freuchen.

Green informed Bowman that the *Encyclopaedia Britannica* would pay $125 for 5,000 words about the Antarctic. The article was to be signed by Richard Byrd, who was willing to do so. Bowman thought that Constance Lindsay Skinner was just the person to prepare the article for Byrd's signature. A very thorough person who had rather specialized in polar things, whatever she prepared would be sincere and accurate. Bowman sent Green her address.[55]

In 1928 Bowman asked Fitzhugh Green about a book by Hall, *Has the North Pole Been Discovered?* The best way to identify Hall, Green replied, was to send Bowman Hall's book, "one of the most extraordinary I have ever read."[56] Thomas F. Hall's analysis of the narratives of Cook and Peary on the subject had been published in 1917, followed in 1920 with a second volume. The geographical society had a copy in their library. Green had previously discussed the substance of the book with its author.

In late 1928 Green exchanged correspondence with Lincoln Ellsworth, who was then living in New York City.[57] In 1913 Ellsworth had applied to become a member of the Crocker Land Expedition, but had not been chosen. He had gone on to have a noteworthy career in Arctic exploration and later became an Antarctic explorer.

Green's role in a publishing house is hard to reconcile with what seems to be his simultaneous navy career, whereas Putnam's life is open and accessible. Early in 1928 he had a priceless opportunity. Mrs. Frederick E. Guest, of London, the former Amy Phipps of Pittsburgh, had hoped to be the first woman to cross the Atlantic by air. Dissuaded by her family from doing so, she secretly transferred ownership of a trimotor Fokker floatplane, the *Friendship*, from Commander Richard E. Byrd to herself, eager to have her plans consummated with an American woman on board.

George Putnam had heard of Amelia Earhart. Born in 1897 in Atchison, Kansas, Amelia had grown up in various places in the Midwest, had graduated from the Hyde Park High School in Chicago, and for a time had been somewhat unsettled. In the fall of 1927 she became a resident of Denison House in Boston and a full-time social worker.

Meanwhile, Earhart had taken her first airplane ride, had made her first solo flight, and had bought her first plane, a Kinner Canary. In early May 1928 Putnam interviewed her, having been commissioned by Mrs. Guest to find an American girl who measured up to adequate standards of American womanhood. Putnam was impressed by Amelia's striking resemblance to his hero, Lindberg, and he promoted "Lady Lindy" as his choice for the secret crossing. Putnam immediately left for Boston, where the plane and the crew were waiting. After repeated delays owing to poor weather, Amelia Earhart lifted off in the pontooned *Friendship* from Trepassey Bay, Newfoundland, for the transatlantic flight. With her were Wilmer Stultz, the pilot, and Lou Gordon, the flight mechanic. Twenty hours and forty minutes later the plane set down at Burry Port, Wales. Although her role had been merely to keep the log, she was immediately catapulted into fame. After being celebrated in London, in New York by a Fifth Avenue ticker-tape parade, and in Boston, Chicago, and other cities, Earhart secluded herself in the home of George and Dorothy Putnam in Rye and wrote *20 HRS. 40 MIN.: Our Flight in the Friendship*, an account of her achievement. G.P. Putnam's Sons published the book in 1928.[58]

At about the same time, Putnam published three books by Fitzhugh Green. Two of them were part of Putnam's adventure series: *Martin Johnson: Lion Hunter* (1928) and *Roy Chapman Andrews: Dragon Hunter* (1930). The other one was *The Film Finds Its Tongue* (1929).

Following her flight and the publication of her book, Amelia Earhart, the celebrated "Lady Lindy," lectured extensively, became the aviation editor of *Cosmopolitan* magazine, the vice-president of Ludington Airlines, and made several transcontinental flights in an autogiro, a forerunner of the helicopter. She depended more and more upon George Putnam in literary, financial, and social matters. GP, as she called him, and his wife, Dorothy, had separated in 1929. A year later Dorothy obtained a divorce. Putnam, now free to court Amelia, pursued her ardently. On 7 February 1931 they were married at Putnam's mother's home in Noank, Connecticut. Putnam was ten years older than his bride. On their wedding morning, Amelia wrote in penciled longhand about her reluctance to marry Putnam, which might thereby shatter her chances. "In our life together," she wrote, "I shall not hold you to any medieval code of faithfulness to me, nor shall I consider myself bound to you similarly." She exacted a cruel promise, "and that is you will let me go in a year if we find no happiness together."[59]

Thereafter Putnam handled his wife's flights and public appearances. He initiated various commercial ventures that capitalized on her name and arranged for the publication of her book, *The Fun of It* (1932). Determined to demonstrate that she deserved the fame her earlier flight had won her, she became the first woman to solo across the Atlantic. On 21 May 1932 she lifted off from Harbor Grace, Newfoundland, and slightly under fifteen hours later she landed in a field in Culmore, Ireland. For her achievement the U.S. Congress awarded her the Distinguished Flying Cross and the National Geographic Society awarded her a gold medal.

Amelia Earhart won a place in aviation history because of her solo flight.

She is well remembered because she vanished years later while trying to circumnavigate the globe. She is part of the story told here because of her ties with Fitzhugh Green.

Easy Is the Descent

For forty years Fitzhugh Green lived a seemingly exemplary life. After graduating from the U.S. Naval Academy and briefly doing sea duty, he became a member of the Crocker Land Expedition. From 1917 to 1928 he was both a naval officer and a prolific author. On retiring from the navy, Green became an assistant in Putnam's publishing house. Often a guest in the Putnam home, it was probably here that Green and Earhart met. Earhart may have introduced Fitzhugh Green and Margery Durant, also a pilot, to each other, or perhaps Durant introduced Green to Earhart.

Margery Durant was born on 24 May 1887 in Flint, Michigan. She and her father, William Crapo Durant, the founder of the General Motors Corporation, were close. On 18 April 1906, Margery married Edwin R. Campbell in St. Paul's Episcopal Church in Flint, Michigan. She was then eighteen and he was thirty-eight.[60] A Flint physician, Campbell became William Durant's personal doctor, and he joined Billy in the automobile business. Margery and Edwin Campbell had two children.

In 1919 Margery Durant divorced Campbell. In 1923 she married Robert W. Daniel, the divorced president of the Liberty National Bank of New York, which William Durant owned. A handsome, black-haired descendant of the Virginia planter-aristocrat John Randolph, Daniel was three years her senior and the owner of Brandon, an aging mansion on the James River. Margery, who had a large trust fund, spent generously in redecorating and refurbishing the place. But the marriage did not last. In 1928, after the birth of a daughter, Margery divorced her husband. "Daniel kept his job at the bank and consoled himself with raising race horses until he found another wife with money."[61]

Margery went to Reno, Nevada, to obtain a divorce from Daniel. While in Reno, Mitchell Kennerley, an English-born publisher and New York art dealer visited her. They may have become engaged. He was then negotiating for the control of the American Art Association Gallery and the Anderson Gallery, both in New York City. His ability to purchase the galleries depended on his forthcoming marriage to Margery. An impediment to that union was removed when Kennerley's wife obtained a divorce in Paris.[62]

On 3 May 1929, however, Margery Durant unexpectedly married John Hampton Cooper, "a younger and handsomer man," in Newark, New Jersey. Even so, a Kennerley–Durant union still seemed possible in 1930. In the late teens Billy Durant's fortune was variously estimated at between $50,000,000 and $100,000,000.[63] In 1929, however, he was wiped out financially in the Crash, while Margery remained wealthy in her own right. Her impulsive third marriage to Cooper, the "playboy and ginger-ale salesman," was over. In March 1930 the *New York Daily Mirror* reported that the thrice-freed Durant heiress would wed Mitchell Kennerley, a wealthy art connoisseur.[64] But that was not to be.

Margery Durant wrote a biography of her father, William Crapo Durant. In the foreword she wrote, "In order that this book should be thoroughly accurate, and to that experienced writer, Commander Fitzhugh Green, who has helped me make this book possible, I am sincerely grateful." The Knickerbocker Press of G.P. Putnam's Sons published *My Father* (1929) in a limited edition of 250 signed and numbered copies and a privately printed edition of fifty copies.[65]

Margery Durant, a pilot, was emboldened by the cross-Atlantic flights of Lindbergh and Earhart. Eager to popularize private air travel, she took her own plane across the Atlantic on an ocean liner on 22 April 1931 and then flew around Europe, the Middle East, and Africa in a plane piloted by Charles La Jotte. When Earhart introduced Green and Durant to each other (as was probably the case), Durant was rich and restless while Green was talented and rootless. On 13 November 1933, Green's wife, Natalie Wheeler Elliot, sued for divorce, charging cruelty.

On 20 November 1933 Fitzhugh Green and Margery Durant were married by a justice of the peace in East Chester, near Bronxville, New York. Amelia Earhart and Margery Durant had become friends through their common interest in flying. The newlyweds immediately left on a wedding trip to Palm Beach, Florida. While there they announced plans for an aerial expedition into Central Africa to gather material for a book they planned to write. Neither Fitzhugh Green nor Margery Durant was a pilot, although Mrs. Green had taken air trips of thousands of miles, including one to unexplored regions of the Nile Valley in Africa accompanied by her pilot. On the forthcoming trip the pilot would be Mrs. Green's son by a former marriage, Lt. William C. Campbell of Hamble, England, "a noted British flier." The couple were to leave Palm Beach for New York, from which they would sail on 15 December on the North German Lloyd liner Bremen for the Channel Ports.[66]

Fitzhugh Green and Margery Durant spent three months in Africa. They traveled by air from Cairo to Luxor and thence to Mombasa. Green said he had been making an aerial survey of the Riff Valley extending through East Africa in the hope of discovering the source of the wealth that flowed into Jerusalem at the time of King Solomon. He believed that the precious metals and other wealth came from this valley, and he was planning an expedition to survey the prospects by land.[67]

After returning from the Middle East the couple lived in luxury at 54

East 58th Street in New York City. A compulsive writer, Green took up his pen again. He wrote a weird story about an Inuit from Lapland who, while part of exhibit at the Chicago World's Fair, became entangled with a wealthy young couple. This fancy appeared in a popular magazine in 1935.[68]

Green and his wife became newsworthy again in the autumn of 1947. In the U.S. District Court in New Haven, Connecticut, in late September, Fitzhugh Green, Margery Durant, and a private detective were indicted on charges of buying and selling narcotic drugs. The two men were arraigned before a federal judge on secret indictments voted earlier in the week. At the time, she was a patient at the Institute for Living in Hartford, Connecticut, a private mental hospital. She was to be arraigned when her condition permitted. Although the sale involved in the indictment had occurred on 21 June, narcotics agents said that the Greens had been buying drugs for several years and that the total involved in their transactions probably came close to $75,000. Green pleaded innocent and was released on $2,500 bail pending a hearing on 27 October. The other man was Clemens Deisler, the employee of a detective agency. Arrested in New York City on 10 July, he pleaded guilty to the transportation, sale, and exchange of narcotics. Narcotics agents told U.S. Attorney Adrian W. Maher that they had seized a large quantity of the drugs in the Greens' New Haven home.

Green later pleaded guilty to violation of the Federal narcotics act and was placed on "strict" probation for five years.[69] On 28 November, Dick Byrd, having learned that Fitz had gotten into difficulties, wrote, "nothing anyone says or nothing anyone prints will cause me to lose faith in your fundamental manhood, integrity and fineness." Whatever circumstances led to the headlines, Byrd added, "I would understand and sympathize with you," and it would not "lessen the friendship I feel for you." Byrd feared that "this whole business has been very tough for you." He hoped that from now on things would be better for Green.[70]

He hoped in vain. On the night of 1 December 1947 family members took Green to Easy Acres, a private sanitarium at Newtown, Connecticut, conducted by an Alcoholics Anonymous group. Three hours later he was transferred to the Danbury Hospital for medical treatment. At that time Margery Green was a patient in a private hospital in Hartford, having been committed there on 18 August by the New Canaan Probate Court. According to the police, Green's removal from his home to East Acres was the result of overindulgence in alcohol. Fitzhugh Green died in the Danbury Hospital on 2 December 1947.[71] An autopsy revealed that his death resulted from a chronic heart condition and lung congestion.[72] On 9 February 1948 Margery Durant Green pleaded guilty in the U.S. District Court to illegal traffic in narcotics and was placed on strict probation for five years, the same sentence that had been imposed on her husband.[73]

Margery Durant Green of New Canaan, Connecticut, died on 3 February 1969 at Palm Beach, Florida. As her obituary noted, she was the wife of the late Commander Fitzhugh Green USN, the mother of three children, and was survived by eleven grandchildren and two great-grandchildren. A memorial service was to be held in New York City at the Chapel of St. James Church, Madison Avenue at 71st Street on 18 February. It was requested that no flowers be sent.[74]

How can we understand the life of Fitzhugh Green? His service on the Crocker Land Expedition was blighted by his murder of Peeahwahto. Enormously gifted, he used his friends and his talent to vault himself forward and resigned from the navy when he saw opportunities elsewhere. Captivated by the lure of the Golden Twenties, he feared radicals, worshipped wealth, and used his talent and his friends to vault himself forward. His entry into a circle of rich celebrities may have significantly shaped his conduct. Easy is the descent to Hell, as Virgil reminds us.

Epilogue

The Crocker Land Expedition went out with two objectives. One was to test the vision of Robert Peary, who said that he had seen a vast archipelago northwest of Axel Heiberg Island. The other was to make a scientific study of the Arctic.

The expedition party left New York in July 1913, made its headquarters at Etah on the northwest coast of Greenland, and the following spring MacMillan and Green, each with a native, searched for Crocker Land. They discovered that it does not exist. Returning from the search, the two parties went their own ways for an intended brief time. While separated, Green shot and killed his Inuit companion. His motive is neither easily understood nor explained. Both Green and MacMillan were eager not to talk about the murder.

After this tragic beginning, the expedition party turned to the scientific study of the Arctic. Among his other pursuits, Donald MacMillan investigated the region north of the Parry Islands and the southern coast of Ellesmere Island. The value of some of his work has been questioned. His major scientific achievement was a study of the geography of the Polar North. Experts who have studied his report on this matter have regarded it as without value.

Ekblaw and Tanquary, especially Ekblaw, made notable contributions in botany, entomology, geology, and ornithology. Although not the first to unravel the secrets of the Far North, they widened and deepened our knowledge of the Arctic, laying foundations on which other scientists could build.

Green, a keen observer with a facile pen, published valuable accounts of Inuit life and culture. Returning to America, he flooded the market with articles and books, resigned from the navy, allied with the publisher George Putnam, and became the fourth husband of a wealthy woman. His life then spiraled downward, and he died unexpectedly at an early age.

Life in the Far North was a challenge to the expedition members. Internal tensions were acute and constant. Perhaps worse was the uncertainty as to when the explorers would be able to return to civilization. Every member of the party did eventually return home.

The Crocker Land Expedition deserves recognition in Arctic history for two important achievements. First, it settled the question as to whether a vast archipelago existed in the northwest Arctic. A negative finding has positive value. Second, and of great and lasting importance, the expedition party contributed significantly to what mankind knows about the physical and material conditions in the Arctic. After the other members of the expedition party had returned home, MacMillan participated in the attempt to attain the North Pole by air, thus demonstrating that the Crocker Land Expedition came at a transitional stage in the history of Arctic exploration.

Chapter Notes

Prologue

1. Roald Amundsen, *The Northwest Passage* (New York, 1908); *My Life As An Explorer* (Garden City, NY: Doubleday, Page & Co. 1927), 37–63, especially 61.
2. Herbert L. Bridgman, "Peary: An Appreciation," *Geographical Review*, 9 (March 1920), 161–69, a brief, glowing tribute.
3. Donald B. MacMillan, the leader of the Crocker Land Expedition, had been with Peary in 1909-10 when Peary made his last assault on the North Pole. Devoted to Peary, in 1918 he defended his hero and attacked Cook in "New Evidence That Cook Did Not Reach the Pole," *Geographical Review* 5 (February 1918), 140–41. Thomas D. Davies, a retired rear admiral, argued that Peary reached the Pole in 1909 in "New Evidence Places Peary at the Pole," *National Geographic* 177 (January 1990), 44–61.
4. George Crocker was the son of Charles Crocker (1822–1888), who was born in Troy, New York. He joined the nineteenth-century migration westward, invested in the new railroad business after moving to California, made a fortune, and died with an estate of $30 million. He left his son George $6 million on condition that the then reckless young man was not to come into it until he had reformed his life. George reformed, moved to New York City, engaged in several businesses, and by 1909 was valued at between $10 million and $20 million.
5. Geoffrey Hellman, *Bankers, Bones & Beetles: The First Century of the American Museum of Natural History* (Garden City, NY: Natural History Press, 1968), passim; William A. Brown, *Morris Ketchum Jesup: A Character Sketch* (New York: Charles Scribner's Sons, 1910), passim.

Chapter 1

1. Edmund O. Hovey, "In Search of Crocker Land," *American Museum Journal* 12 (March 1912), 83–88; Donald B. MacMillan, *Four Years in the White North* (New York: Harper & Brothers, 1918), Appendix, 412–13.
2. "George Borup—In Memoriam," *American Museum Journal* 12 (May 1912), 154–58. See also "The Reorganized Crocker Land Expedition," *American Museum Journal*, 12 (309); and "The Reorganized Crocker Land Expedition," *Bulletin of the American Geographical Society* 45, No. 2 (1913), 137.
3. Joseph Barrell to E.O. Hovey, 24 October 1912, Crocker Land Expedition Papers, Mss. C76, American Museum of Natural History, New York, New York.
4. W.S. Bayley to Hovey, 25 October 1912, Crocker Land Expedition Papers, Mss. C76, American Museum of Natural History, New York, New York.
5. Hovey to the Members of the Honorary Committee, 8 November 1912, Crocker Land Expedition Papers, Mss. C76, American Museum of Natural History, New York.
6. Hovey to Ekblaw, 19 November 1912, Crocker Land Expedition Papers, Mss. C76, American Museum of Natural History, New York, New York.
7. Lincoln Ellsworth's father funded the 1925 attempt by Roald Amundsen and Lincoln Ellsworth to fly from Svalbard to the North Pole. These two published *Our Polar*

Flight (1925). Lincoln Ellsworth wrote "Arctic Flying Experiences by Airplane and Airship," *Problems of Polar Research* (New York: American Geographical Society, 1928), 411–17; and a fuller account, "At the North Pole," *Yale Review* 16 (July 1927), 739–49. Then came Amundsen and Lincoln Ellsworth, *First Crossing of the Polar Sea* (New York: George H. Doran Co., 1927). In 1928 Lincoln Ellsworth accompanied Roald Amundsen on his second effort to fly over the North Pole in the airship Norge. In 1928 Lincoln Ellsworth received a Congressional Gold Medal in honor of his 1925 and 1928 flights. He continued to publish. See Lincoln Ellsworth, *Search* (New York: Brewer, Warren & Putnam, 1932), and Lincoln Ellsworth, *Exploring Today* (New York, Dodd, Mead & Co., 1941).

8. Winton U. Solberg, *The University of Illinois, 1867–1894: An Intellectual and Cultural History* (Urbana: University of Illinois Press, 1968), idem, *The University of Illinois, 1894–1904: The Shaping of the University* (Urbana: University of Illinois Press, 2000), and idem, "President James and the University of Illinois, 1904–1920: Redeeming the Promise of the Morrill Land-Grant Act," in Roger L. Geiger and Nathan M. Sorber, eds., *The Land-Grant Colleges and the Reshaping of American Higher Education* (New Brunswick Transaction Publishers, 2013), 225–46.

9. Hovey to MacMillan, 21 December 1912, Crocker Land Expedition Papers, Mss. C76, American Museum of Natural History Library.

10. Surgeon General to the Secretary of War, 6 January 1913; E.O. Hovey to Walter B. James, 11 January 1913; Brainard of War Department to MacMillan, 17 January 1913, Crocker Land Expedition Papers, Mss. C76, American Museum of Natural History Library.

11. On 18 December Hovey invited various people to the meeting. On 20 December Osborn sent invitations to MacMillan, Ekblaw, Green, and the members of the museum committees. See also Hovey to Borup, 7 January 1913, Borup to Osborn, 12 January 1913, and Osborn to Frederic R. Lucas, 6 January 1913. Crocker Land Expedition Papers, Mss. C76, American Museum of Natural History, New York, New York.

12. Hovey to James, 13 December 1912, RS 2/5/3, B:43, F:Crocker Land Expedition, University of Illinois Archives.

13. Ekblaw to James, 30 January 1913, RS 2/5/3,B:31, F:Crocker Land Expedition, University of Illinois Archives.

14. Bayley to James, 17 January 1913, RS 2/5/3, B:43, F:Crocker Land Expedition, University of Illinois Archives.

15. Bayley to Hovey, 24 January 1913, Crocker Land Expedition Papers, Mss. C76, American Museum of Natural History Library.

16. A secretary to President Osborn, 30 January 1913, Crocker Land Expedition Papers, Mss. C76, American Museum of Natural History Library.

17. Hovey to Kinley, 27 February 1913; David Kinley to President E.J. James, 28 February 1913, RS 2/5/3, B:43, F:Crocker Land Expedition, University of Illinois Archives.

18. University of Illinois, Board of Trustees, *27th Report* (1914), 193.

19. *Ibid.*, 199.

20. James to Hovey, 22 March 1913, RS 2/5/3, B:43, F:Crocker Land Expedition, University of Illinois Archives; also, University of Illinois, Board of Trustees, *27th Report*, 209.

21. Osborn to James, 22 March 1913, RS 2/5/3, B:43, F:Crocker Land Expedition, University of Illinois Archives; also in University of Illinois, Board of Trustees, *27th Report*, 209–10.

22. Hovey to James, 2 April 1913, Osborn to James, 8 April 1913, RS 2/5/3, B:43, F: Crocker Land Expedition, University of Illinois Archives.

23. Fitzhugh Green, "Some of the Scientific Results Expected of the Crocker Land Expedition," Fitzhugh Green, Sr., Papers, B:11, F:1, Booth Family Center for Special Collections, Georgetown University Library, Washington, D.C.

24. Harrison J. Hunt and Ruth Hunt Thompson, *North to the Horizon: Searching for Peary's Crocker Land* (Camden, ME: Down East Books, 1980), 5, 6–7.

25. W.E. Ekblaw, "The Crocker Land Expedition," *The Illinois Magazine* 4 (June 1913), 247–60. Ekblaw was quoting Rudyard Kipling, "When Earth's Last Picture Is Painted" (1892).

26. Hunt and Thompson, *North to the Horizon*, 9.

27. A copy of "This Agreement" is in RS 2/5/3, B:150, F:Crocker Land Expedition, University of Illinois Archives.

28. *Crocker Land Expedition to the North Pole: (George Borup Memorial): Statement to Contributors*, a ten-page pamphlet (copy in the Maurice C. Tanquary Morgue File, University of Illinois Archives). Edmund O. Hovey was probably the author of the pamphlet. See also Edmund O. Hovey, " The Reorganized Crocker Land Expedition," *American Museum Journal* 12 (December 1912), 309.

29. W. Elmer Ekblaw, "Correlation of the Devonian System of the Rock Island Region," *Transactions of the Illinois Academy of Science*, Bloomington, IL, 23–24 February 1912.

30. Edmund O. Hovey, "The Personnel of the Crocker Land Expedition," *American Museum Journal* 13 (April 1913), 179–82; Hunt and Thompson, *North to the Horizon*, 5.

31. These salary figures are derived from documents in the Crocker Land Expedition Papers, Mss. C76, American Museum of Natural History Library.

Chapter 2

1. Fitzhugh Green left two major descriptions of the Crocker Land Expedition. His handwritten account of 143 pages, covering 29 June 1913 to 17 September 1914, I identify as a Diary. It is in the Crocker Land Expedition Papers, Mss. C76, American Museum of Natural History Library. Green also left a typewritten account of the Crocker Land Expedition of 107 typewritten pages that covers the period 29 June 1913 to August 1915. I identify it as a Journal. It is in the Fitzhugh Green, Sr., Papers, B:2, F:3, Booth Family Center for Special Collections, Georgetown University Library. In composition, the Diary was apparently the earlier of the two. Its entries are usually brief and daily, but for multiple days they are run together. The long entries in the Journal resemble essays. I have not provided reference notes that identify the location of the entries in either the Diary or the Journal since it is easy to locate a topic by reference to the date it was recorded. Green kept other diaries. They are fragmentary and are not cited in this study.

2. "The Crocker Land Expedition," *Bulletin of the American Geographical Society*, 45, No. 10 (1913), 753. A copy of the program for the Godspeed Dinner, with a photograph of the expedition members (except for Jot Small) is in RS 2/5/3, B:43, F:Crocker Land Expedition, University of Illinois Archives. Jot Small was illiterate and not at the dinner.

3. Ekblaw to President James, RS 2/5/3, B:32, F: W.E. Ekblaw, Crocker Land Expedition; Hovey to Bayley, undated, B:31, F:Crocker Land Expedition, 1913, University of Illinois Archives. The museum paid $7,600 to charter the *Diana* for two months and $327 for port charges, pilotage, etc. Other expenses in connection with the wreck of the *Diana* were $2,755. The museum paid $8,500 to charter the *Erik* for one month. *New York Tribune*, 15 September 1913.

4. Green, Diary, 15 August 1913, Crocker Land Expedition Papers, Mss. 76, American Museum of Natural History Library.

5. Donald B. MacMillan, "Geographical Report of the Crocker Land Expedition, 1913–1917," American Museum of Natural History, *Bulletin* 56, 1926–1929 (1930), 379–81; MacMillan, *Four Years*, 22–23; MacMillan to Hovey, 25 August 1913, RS 2/5/3, B:31, Crocker Land Expedition, University of Illinois Archives.

6. V.C. Frederiksen, a resident missionary at Holstenborg, Greenland, had studied Inuit migrations in Greenland. Based on the evidence of linguistics, geography, and archaeology, he concluded that the Inuit tribes reached Greenland from an original nucleus in the extreme west, traveled southward along the coast to the east, and decreased in number toward the north owing to the scarcity of game and building material. "Eskimo Migrations in Greenland," *Geographical Review* 2 (November 1916), 379. See also Peter Freuchen, *Vagrant Viking: My Life and Adventures*, trans. Johan Hambro (New York: Julian Messner, 1953), 83–86; Donald B. MacMilllan, *Beyond Etah: Or, Life Within Twelve Degrees of the Pole* (Boston: Houghton Mifflin Co., 1927), 51–53, 55–56; Peter Freuchen, *Book of the Eskimos*, ed. with a preface by Dagmar Freuchen (Cleveland: World Publishing Co., 1961), 430–33; Peter Freuchen, *Men of the Frozen North*, ed. with a preface by Dagmar Freuchen (Cleveland: World Publishing Co., 1962), 209–11. Thule Air Base, located near Thule, Greenland, is now the United States Air Force's northernmost base. It is 947 miles from the North Pole and approximately 551 miles from the North Magnetic Pole.

7. Ekblaw drew a diagram of the house and identified the use to which each room or space was put. Ekblaw to Dear Sidney and Mother, 29 December 1913, B:269, F:16, Crocker Land Expedition Papers, MSS C76, American Museum of Natural History, New York, New York.

8. Fitzhugh Green, "The Crocker Land Expedition," *Natural History* 28 (Sept.-Oct. 1928), 468-69.

9. Fitzhugh Green, "Arctic Duty with the Crocker Land Expedition: Northwards," *United States Naval Institute Proceedings* 43 (September 1917), 1973-74.

10. Green, Diary, 8, Crocker Land Expedition Papers, Mss. C76, American Museum of Natural History.

11. Hunt and Thompson, *North to the Horizon*, 32-33.

12. *Ibid.*, 35.

13. Lyle Dick, "'Pibloktoq' (Arctic Hysteria): A Construction of European-Inuit Relations?" *Arctic Anthropology* 32 (1995), 1-8; Lyle Dick, *Muskox Land: Ellesmere Island in the Age of Contact* (Calgary: University of Calgary Press, 2001), 55, quoting from the 25 October 1913 diary entry of Donald B. MacMillan.

14. John W. Goodsell, *On Polar Trails The Peary Expedition to the North Pole, 1908-09* (Austin, TX: Eakin Press, 1983), 138.

15. Dick, "'Pibloktoq' (Arctic Hysteria)," 1-42. Dick argues that "pibloktoq" was a catch-all rubric under which explorers lumped various Inuit anxiety reactions, symptoms of physical illness and perhaps feigned illness, expressions of resistance to patriarchy or sexual coercion, and shamanistic practice. According to Dick, many of these behaviors were apparently induced by the stresses of early contact between Euro-Americans and Inuit between 1890 and 1920. On "pibloktoq" see also Everett S. Allen, *Arctic Odyssey: The Life of Rear Admiral Donald B. MacMillan* (New York: Dodd, Mead & Co.,1962), 70-71, and Goodsell, *On Polar Trails*, 77.

16. Allen, *Arctic Odyssey*, 71.

17. Daniel Merkur, *Becoming Half Hidden: Shamanism and Initiation among the Inuit* (Stockholm: Almqvist & Wikselll International, 1985), passim. See also Frederic B. Laugrand and Jarich G. Oosten, *Inuit Shamanism and Christianity: Transitions and Transformations in the Twentieth Century* (Montreal and Kingston: McGill-Queen's University Press, 2000).

18. A.L. Kroeber, "The Eskimo of Smith Sound," *Bulletin of the American Museum of Natural History* 12 (1900), 265-327, reports the results of the investigations carried on under the direction of Dr. Franz Boas among the six Inuit from Smith Sound brought to New York by Peary in the winter of 1897-98.

19. Kenn Harper, *Give Me My Father's Body: The Life of Minik, the New York Eskimo* (South Royalton, VT: Steerforth Press, 2000), 20-22. This book was originally published in Canada by Blacklead Books in 1986. In Greenland Minik was known as Mene.

20. *Ibid.*, 26.

21. Geoffrey Hellman, *Bankers, Bones, & Beetles: The First Century of the American Museum of Natural History* (Garden City, NY: Natural History Press, 1968), 86-89.

22. Harper, *Give Me My Father's Body*, 85.

23. *Ibid.*, 87-88.

24. *Ibid.*, 100-04, 110-13, 129-36.

25. *Ibid.*, 114, 116.

26. "Mene Gone to Balk Peary?" *New York Times*, 14 April 1909, 5.

27. "Peary Relief Ship To Set Out Today," *New York Times*, 3 August 1909, 5, reports Mene's decision to return to the Arctic with an entirely favorable view of the Eskimo; Harper, *Give Me My Father's Body*, 147-52.

28. Freuchen, *Vagrant Viking*, 89.

29. Ekblaw to My dear Mother James (the wife of President James), 30 December 1913, RS 2/5/3, B:31, F:Crockerland Expedition 1913, University of Illinois Archives.

30. R.E. Peary, "The Cape York Ironstone," *Bulletin of the American Geographical Society*, 26 (1894), 447-88. This account is full of detail about the weather and travel but weak in its ostensible purpose—describing Peary's search for the meteorite.

31. Robert E. Peary, *Northward Over the Great Ice*, 2 vols. (New York: Frederick A. Stokes Co., 1898), 2:127-55, 553-618; R.E. Peary, "The Cape York Ironstone," *Bulletin of the American Geographical Society*, 26 (1894), 447-88. See also Richard Vaughan, *Northwest Greenland: A History* (Orono: University of Maine Press, 1991), 96-106; Douglas J. Preston, *Dinosaurs in the Attic: An Excursion into the American Museum of Natural History* (New York: St. Martin's

Press, 1986), 35–41; John R. Saunders, *The World of Natural History as Revealed in the American Museum of Natural History* (New York: Sheridan House, 1952), 29–31, and Joseph Wallace, *A Gathering of Wonders: Behind the Scenes at the American Museum of Natural History* (New York: St. Martin's Press, 2000), 12–23.

32. W. Elmer Ekblaw, "The Visit to the Meteorite," in MacMillan, *Four Years*, Appendix IV, 388–89. For contemporaneous, briefer accounts, see Ekblaw to Percival B. Coffin, 22 January 1914, and Ekblaw to Dear Mother, 23 January 1914, B:269, F16, Crocker Land Expedition Papers, Mss. C76, American Museum of Natural History, New York, New York.

33. *Ibid.*, 390.

34. *Ibid.*, 390–91.

35. Peter Freuchen, *I Sailed with Rasmussen* (New York: Julian Messner, 1958), 149–51, tells this story at length.

36. Ekblaw to Dear Mother, 388–89.

37. *Ibid.*, 395–96.

38. D.B. Böggild to Henry Fairfield Osborn, Copenhagen, 24 June 1914, RS 2/5/3, B:43, F:Crocker Land Expedition, University of Illinois Archives. On 8 July 1914, Hovey sent President James a copy of the letter.

39. Green, "Diary" 24 January 1914, Crocker Land Expedition Papers, Mss. C76, American Museum of Natural History Library.

Chapter 3

1. Donald B. MacMillan, "In Search of a New Land," *Harper's Magazine*, 131 (October 1915), 651–52; Donald B. MacMillan, *Four Years in the White North* (New York: Harper & Brothers, 1918), 38–39.

2. Fitzhugh Green, "Arctic Duty with the Crocker Land Expedition: The Polar Sea," *United States Naval Institute Proceedings*, 43 (October 1917), 2194–95, quotation at 2195.

3. MacMillan, *Beyond Etah*, 56, 75, 218; Peter Freuchen, *Book of the Eskimos*, ed. Dagmar Freuchen (Greenwich, Conn., Fawcett Publications, 1961), 162–63, 167, 169–71.

4. MacMillan, "In Search of a New Land," 654.

5. Green, "Arctic Duty with the Crocker Land Expedition: The Polar Sea," 196–97.

6. *Ibid.*, 2198–2207; MacMillan, "Geographical Report of the Crocker Land Expedition, 1913–1917," *Bulletin of the American Museum of Natural History*, 56: 1926–1929 (New York, 1930), 382–83.

7. Green, "Arctic Duty with the Crocker Land Expedition: The Polar Sea," 2207–08.

8. *Ibid.*, 2208–09.

9. MacMillan, *Four Years*, 41–42; Harrison J. Hunt and Ruth Hunt Thompson, *North to the Horizon: Searching For Peary's Crockerland* (Camden, ME: Down East Books, 1980), 43.

10. Green, "Diary," 28 December 1913, Crocker Land Expedition Papers, Mss. C76, American Museum of Natural History Library.

11. Hunt and Thompson, *North to the Horizon*, 44.

12. Green, "Arctic Duty with the Crocker Land Expedition: Northwards," 1971–73, quotation at 1973.

13. Freuchen, *Vagrant Viking*, 50–51; "MacMillan Expects Success," *New York Times*, 29 May 1914, 9. The *Times* was quoting from MacMillan's letter of 22 January to Levi H. Greenwood, Gardner, Massachusetts, which went out by dogsled.

14. Hunt and Thompson, *North to the Horizon*, 46.

15. MacMillan, "In Search of a New Land," 653–55; Freuchen, *Vagrant Viking*, 51–54; Green, "Arctic Duty with the Crocker Land Expedition: The Polar Sea," 2210–11.

16. MacMillan, "Geographical Report," 385.

17. Fitzhugh Green, "Arctic Duty with the Crocker Land Expedition: The Polar Sea," *United States Naval Institute Proceedings*, 43 (October 1917), 2212; Donald B. MacMillan, *Four Years*, 55.

18. Green, "Arctic Duty: The Polar Sea," 2212–14; MacMillan, *Four Years*, 56–57.

19. Green, Journal, 37b; Hunt and Thompson, *North to the Horizon*, 52.

20. Donald B. MacMillan, "In Search of a New Land," 654–58; MacMillan, *Four Years*, 58–59; Green, "Arctic Duty: The Polar Sea," 2215.

21. Donald B. MacMillan, "Geographical Report of the Crocker Land Expedition," 387; Green, "Arctic Duty: The Polar Sea," 2216; Hunt and Thompson, *North to the Horizon*, 52.

22. MacMillan, "In Search of a New Land," 659–60; MacMillan, *Four Years*, 62–63.

23. MacMillan, "In Search of a New Land," 660; MacMillan, *Four Years*, 64–65.
24. MacMillan, "In Search of a New Land," 661–62; MacMillan, *Four Years*, 65–68.
25. MacMillan, "In Search of a New Land," 663–65.
26. Green, "Arctic Duty: The Polar Sea," 217.
27. *Ibid.*, 73–74.
28. MacMillan, *Four Years*, 79–80.
29. *Ibid.*, 82–83, 84.
30. Macmillan, "In Search of a New Land," 922; MacMillan, *Four Years*, 75–77.

Chapter 4

1. Fitzhugh Green, Journal, 30 April to 2 May 1914, B:2, F:8, Fitzhugh Green, Sr., Papers, Booth Family Center for Special Collections, Georgetown University Library, Washington, D.C.
2. Fitzhugh Green, Diary, 2 May 1914, Crocker Land Expedition Papers, Mss. C76, American Museum of Natural History Library, New York, New York.
3. Fitzhugh Green to Donald B. MacMillan, 4 May 1914, in MacMillan's Journal, B:2, F:7, Fitzhugh Green, Sr., Papers, Booth Family Center for Special Collections, Georgetown University Library, Washington, D.C.
4. Fitzhugh Green, "Arctic Duty with the Crocker Land Expedition: The Polar Sea," *United States Naval Institute Proceedings* 43 (October 1917), 2224.
5. Fitzhugh Green, Journal, 4 May 1914, B:2, F:7, Fitzhugh Green, Sr., Papers, Booth Family Center for Special Collections, Georgetown University Library, Washington, D.C. MacMillan published two articles on the search for Crocker Land while he was still in the Arctic: "In Search of a New Land," *Harper's Magazine*, 31 (October 1915), 651–65; (November 1915), 921–30. In concluding the November article, MacMillan describes how he learned of Peeawhahto's death when Green rejoined him. He says no more on the subject.
6. Harrison J. Hunt and Ruth Hunt Thompson, *North to the Horizon: Searching for Peary's Crocker Land* (Camden, ME: Down East Books, 1980), 57. Hunt took the material in this paragraph from MacMillan's field notes, which are in the American Museum of Natural History.
7. Fitzhugh Green, "Arctic Duty with the Crocker Land Expedition: Drift Ice and Kayak," *United States Naval Institute Proceedings*, 43 (November 1917), 2456–57.
8. *Ibid.*, 2458–59.
9. *Ibid.*, 2460–61.
10. *Ibid.*, 2461.
11. *Ibid.*, 2463.
12. Fitzhugh Green, Journal, 5 May to 21 May 1914, B:2, F:7, Fitzhugh Green, Sr., Papers, Booth Family Center for Special Collections, Georgetown University Library, Washington, D.C.
13. Green, "Arctic Duty with the Crocker Land Expedition: Drift Ice and Kayak," 84–101.
14. Hunt and Thompson, *North to the Horizon*, 54–55.
15. MacMillan, "In Search of a New Land," 31 (October 1915), 651–65 (November 1915), 921–30.
16. Donald B. MacMillan, "Geographical Report of the Crocker and Expedition, 1913–1917," *Bulletin of the American Museum of Natural History*, 56:1916–1929 (New York, 1930), 400.
17. Donald B. MacMillan, *Four Years in the White North* (New York: Harper & Brothers, 1918), 92.
18. Hunt and Thompson, *North to the Horizon*, 56–57.
19. Peter Freuchen, *Arctic Adventure: My Life in the North* (New York: Farrar & Rinehart, 1935), 296.
20. Peter Freuchen, *Vagrant Viking: My Life and Adventures*, trans. Johan Hambro (New York: Julian Messner, 1953), 137–38.
21. *Ibid.*, 138.
22. Hunt and Thompson, *North to the Horizon*, 57.
23. C. Brun to Charles Evans Hughes, 22 March 1921, AGSNY, B:263, F:21, American Geographical Society Archives.
24. Kinley to Harker, 19 April 1921, RS 2/6/1, B:38, F:Harker, Judge 1920–21; C.M. McConn to Harker, 20 April 1921; Harker to McConn, 20 April 1921, RS 2/5/3, B:43, F: Crocker Land Expedition, University of Illinois Archives. The files are now in President James' papers.
25. Sherwood to Green, 12 May 1921, B:1, F: George Sherwood, Fitzhugh Green, Sr., Papers, Booth Family Center for Special Collections, Georgetown University Library, Washington, D.C.
26. Henry Fairfield Osborn to the Secretary of State, 27 June 1921, AGSNY AC1,

B:263, F:21, American Geographic Society Archives. On 29 June, Osborn sent a copy of this letter to President John Greenough of the American Geographical Society.

27. Joseph R. Baker [Department of State] to Josiah [Isaiah] Bowman, 5 November 1921, 5 November 1921, AGSNY, B:263, F:21, American Geographical Society Archives.

28. Peter Freuchen, *Ice Floes and Flaming Water: A True Adventure in Melville Bay*, trans. from the Norwegian by Johan Hambro (New York: Julian Messner, 1954), 129. Freuchen had an excellent knowledge of the Arctic and was well acquainted with the members of the Crocker Land Expedition. He often embroidered his stories. His account of the murder was written after the events described. Nevertheless, his description of the murder of Peeahwahto deserves consideration. I have silently corrected Freuchen's use of Inuit names.

29. Freuchen, *Ice Floes and Flaming Water*, 129–32.

30. *Ibid.*, 131.

31. *Ibid.*, 131–32.

Chapter 5

1. Hovey to MacMillan, 8 June 1914, Crocker Land Expedition Papers, Mss. C76, American Museum of Natural History Library.

2. *Ibid.*

3. Osborn to MacMillan, 8 June 1914, Crocker Land Expedition Papers, Mss. C76, American Museum of Natural History Library.

4. Osborn to MacMillan, 16 July 1914, Crocker Land Expedition Papers, Mss. C76, American Museum of Natural History Library.

5. Osborn to Green, 16 July 1914, Crocker Land Expedition Papers, Mss. C76, American Museum of Natural History Library.

6. Fitzhugh Green to Dr. William Ray Dobyns, 3 August 1914, B:2, F:3, Fitzhugh Green, Sr., Papers, Special Collections Library, Georgetown University.

7. Green to Hovey, 1 August 1914, Crocker Land Expedition Papers, Mss. C76, American Museum of Natural History Library.

8. Ekblaw to Eva M. Shepard, 13 April 1914, in W. Elmer Ekblaw Papers, 1914, RS 26/20/153, B:1, F:Eva Shepard, University of Illinois Archives. In his letter Ekblaw implies that he had known Shepard in the Pension Agency. I find no evidence of his working there.

9. Borup Lodge had a library, as did Rasmussen's trading station. Both followed the practice of ships that went to the Arctic. See Harry R. Skallerup, *Books Afloat and Ashore: A History of Books, Libraries, and Reading among Seamen During the Age of Sail* (Archon Books, Hamden, CT, 1974.)

10. Ekblaw to Eva Shepard, 13 April 1914.

11. Ekblaw to My dear Mrs. Coffin, 10 April 1914, B:269, F:14, American Museum of Natural History.

12. *Ibid.*

13. *Ibid.*

14. *Ibid.*

15. *Ibid.*

16. *Ibid.*

17. *Ibid.*

18. *Ibid.*

19. MacMillan to Hovey, 8 August 1914, Crocker Land Expedition Papers, Mss. C76, American Museum of Natural History Library.

20. *Ibid.*

21. Donald B. MacMillan, *Four Years in the White North* (New York: Harper & Brothers, 1918), 120; Fitzhugh Green, "Arctic Duty with the Crocker Land Expedition: Northwards," *United States Naval Institute Proceedings*, 43 (September 1917), 1942.

22. MacMillan to Green, 18 April 1915, B:1, F:14, Fitzhugh Green, Sr., Papers, Booth Family Center for Special Collections, Georgetown University Library, Washington, D.C.

23. W. Elmer Ekblaw, "The Summer at North Star Bay," Appendix I, in MacMillan, *Four Years*, 323–32.

24. *Ibid.*, 292, 294–96; MacMillan, *Four Years*, 102.

25. Ekblaw to dear Mr. Coffin, 30 July 1914, B:269, F:14, American Museum of Natural History.

26. Ekblaw's reference is to Herman G. Simmons, botanist of the Second Norwegian Expedition in the *Fram*, which spent the years 1898 to 1902 in scientific exploration of central and southern Ellesmere Island and northwest Greenland, and to Morton P. Porsild, a Danish botanist who lived and worked most of his life in Greenland. His book, *Illustrated Flora of the Canadian Arctic Archipelago* (1957) was the authority

for vascular plants of the Arctic islands of the North for years.

27. Justus W. Folsom, "Collembola from the Crocker Land Expedition, 1913–1917," *Bulletin of the American Museum of Natural History* 41 (1919), 271–303.
28. *Ibid.*
29. *Ibid.*, 326.
30. *Ibid.*, 328.
31. *Ibid.*, 328.
32. *Ibid.*, 331.
33. MacMillan, *Four Years*, 114–15.
34. *Ibid.*, 332.
35. *Ibid.*, 296–97.
36. Ekblaw to My dear Mrs. Coffin, 30 October 1914, B:269, F:16, American Museum of Natural History.
37. *Ibid.*
38. *Ibid.*, 163–67
39. *Ibid.*, Appendix VI, 403–11, examples at 406 and 408.
40. W. Elmer Ekblaw, "The Plant Life of Northwest Greenland," *Natural History: The Journal of the American Museum*, 19 (March 1919), 272–91; W. Elmer Ekblaw, "The Vegetation about Borup Lodge," Appendix V in MacMillan, *Four Years*, 397–402. Ekblaw's account in *Natural History* is accompanied by excellent black and white photographs.
41. Ekblaw, "Plant Life," 276.
42. *Ibid.*, 277.
43. *Ibid.*, 277; Ekblaw, "The Vegetation," 398.
44. Ekblaw, "Plant Life," 277.
45. *Ibid.*, 282–83.
46. *Ibid.*
47. Green, Diary, 1–2 October 1914, AGSNY, AG-1, 148–49.
48. 31 October 1914, p. 178
49. 7 December 1914, p. 215.
50. Ms. 27 Jan. 1915, p. 251–52.
51. 27 Jan. 1915, 251–52.
52. Green to Hovey, 20 November 1914, Fitzhugh Green, Sr., Papers, B:2, F:3, Booth Family Center for Special Collections, Georgetown University Library, Washington, D.C.
53. MacMillan, *Four Years*, 107–09, 111.
54. *Ibid.*,111–12.
55. *Ibid.*,116–17.
56. *Ibid.*,119.
57. *Ibid.*,124.
58. *Ibid.*,135.
59. *Ibid.*,135–36.
60. *Ibid.*,137–38.
61. *Ibid.*, 138–42.

Chapter 6

1. Donald B. MacMillan, *Four Years in the White North* (New York: Harper & Brothers, 1918), 136; W. Elmer Ekblaw, "On Unknown Shores: The Traverse of Grant and Ellesmere Islands," Appendix II, in MacMillan, *Four Years*, 333–70.
2. W. Elmer Ekblaw, "On Unknown Shores: The Traverse of Grant and Ellesmere Islands," Appendix II, in MacMillan, *Four Years*, 342.
3. *Ibid.*, 344.
4. *Ibid.*, 349.
5. *Ibid.*, 350, 351.
6. *Ibid.*, 353.
7. *Ibid.*, 355.
8. *Ibid.*, 363. Again, Ekblaw quotes faithfully but not entirely accurately.
9. *Ibid.*, 370.
10. MacMillan to Green, 22 May 1915, Green, "Report of Trip to Cape Constitution," B:2, F:5, Fitzhugh Green, Sr., Papers, Booth Family Center for Special Collections, Georgetown University Library, Washington, D.C.
11. Green, "Report of Trip to Cape Constitution," B:2, F:5, Fitzhugh Green, Sr., Papers, Booth Family Center for Special Collections, Georgetown University, Washington, D.C. Green left an account of this trip in a diary that he kept, but the diary is much less revealing than the report. The diary is also in the Fitzhugh Green, Sr., Papers.
12. W. Elmer Ekblaw, "The Ecological Relations of the Polar Eskimo," *Ecology* 2 (April 1921), 132.
13. *Ibid.*,132–34.
14. *Ibid.*,134–35.
15. Actually, Hollands Glacier, Docker Smiths Glacier, Rinks Glacier, and Pearys Glacier all debouched on Melville Bay.
16. W. Elmer Ekblaw, "The Ecological Relations of the Polar Eskimo," *Ecology* 2 (April 1921), 135–37.
17. *Ibid.*,137–38.
18. *Ibid.*,138–40.
19. *Ibid.*,140–43.
20. *Ibid.*,144.
21. W. Elmer Ekblaw, "Eskimo Dogs—Forgotten Heroes," *Natural History* 37 (1936), 173–74.
22. *Ibid.*, 174.
23. *Ibid.*, 174–75.
24. *Ibid.*, 175.
25. *Ibid.*, 175–76.

26. *Ibid.*, 176.
27. *Ibid.*, 176-78.
28. *Ibid.*, 178. Sheila Nickerson, *Harnessed to the Pole: Sledge Dogs in Service to American Explorers of the Arctic, 1853-1909* (Fairbanks: University of Alaska Press, 2014) describes sledge dogs in an earlier period than that in this book.
29. Shari Fox Gearheard and others, eds., *The Meaning of Ice: People and Sea Ice in Three Arctic Communities* (International Polar Institute, 2013), describes the influence of sea ice in three Arctic communities, one of which is northwest Greenland.
30. W. Elmer Ekblaw, "Thin Ice," in Frederick A. Blossom, ed., *Told at the Explorers Club: True Tales of Modern Exploration* (New York: Albert & Charles Boni, 1931), 83-89.

Chapter 7

1. Donald B. MacMillan, "Geographical Report of the Crocker Land Expedition, 1913-1917," American Museum of Natural History, *Bulletin* 56 (1926-1929), 406-17. The American Museum received MacMillan's report in 1919, but publication was delayed, reportedly due to lack of funds. MacMillan's report of his 1917 journey had reached America earlier. See "New Arctic Islands Found By MacMillan," *New York Times*, 6 June 1917, 6.
2. MacMillan, "Geographical Report of the Crocker Land Expedition, 1913-1917," 406-17; "The Latest News of the Crocker Land Expedition," *Geographical Review*, 4 (July 1917), 62-63.
3. "Crocker Land Party Safe," *American Museum Journal* 17 (May 1917), 346.
4. "The Latest News of the Crocker Land Expedition," *Geographical Review* 4 (July 1917), 62-63.
5. *Ibid.*, 62.
6. "Polar Regions: Safe Return of the Members of the Crocker Land Expedition, and Resurvey of the Southeastern Coast of Ellesmere Island," *Geographical Review* 4 (October 1917), 320-21; "Notes on MacMillan's Ellesmere Island Trip," *Geographical Review* 5 (February 1918), 183-94 (accompanied with photographs).
7. "Polar Regions," *Geographical Review* 5 (March 1918), 238-41.
8. W.L.G.J[oerg], "Comment on MacMillan's Manuscript on His Ellesmere Island Trip," 14 February 1918, AGSNY, AC 1, B:263, F:10.
9. "Notes on MacMillan's Ellesmere Island Trip," *Geographical Review* 5 (March 1918), 183-94.
10. George Comer, "A Geographical Description of Southampton Island and Notes upon the Eskimos," *Bulletin of the American Geographical* Society 42, No. 2 (1910), 84-90.
11. W. Gillies Ross, "George Comer (1858-1937)," *Arctic* 36 (September 1983), 294-95.
12. *An Arctic Whaling Diary: The Journal of Captain George Comer in Hudson Bay, 1903-1905*, ed. W. Gillies Ross (Toronto: University of Toronto Press, 1984).
13. F. Lester Jones to Hovey, 25 February 1918; Hovey to Comer, 26 February 1918; Hovey to Sherwood, 27 February 1918, AGSNY, AC 1, B:263, F:11. A table of reductions of high and low waters is attached to each of the first two letters cited.
14. Clark Wissler, "Archaeology of the Polar Eskimo," *Anthropological Papers of the American Museum of Natural History* 22, pt. 3 (New York, 1918), 105-66.
15. *Ibid.*, 112.
16. *Ibid.*
17. Peter Freuchen, *Arctic Adventure: My Life in the Frozen North* (New York: Halcyon House, 1935), 313.
18. Wissler, "Archaeology of the Polar Eskimo," 164-66.
19. MacMillan to Bowman, 15 April 1918, AGS NY, AC 1, B:263, F:10, American Geographical Society Archives.
20. Joerg to MacMillan, 19 April 1918, MacMillan to Joerg, 20 April 1918, AGSNY, AC 1, B:263, F:10, American Geographical Society Archives.

Chapter 8

1. American Museum of Natural History, *Forty-Seventh Annual Report: For the Year 1915* (New York, 1915), 55-56; "Arctic Relief Ship Sails," *New York Times*, 10 June 1915, 5; "Cluett At Sydney," *New York Times*, 17 July 1915, 9; American Museum of Natural History, *Forty-Eighth Annual Report: For the Year 1916* (New York, 1917), 57.
2. "Fate of the Crocker Land Expedition," *Geographical Review* 1 (February 1916), 145; Peter Freuchen, *Arctic Adventure: My*

Life on the Frozen North (New York: Farrar & Rinehart, 1935), 299–301; Peter Freuchen, *Vagrant Viking: My Life and Adventures*, trans. from the Danish by Johan Hambo (New York: Julian Messner, 1953), 138–39.

3. Freuchen, *Arctic Adventure*, 299–301; Freuchen, *Vagrant Viking*, 139.

4. Freuchen, *Arctic Adventure*, 301–02; Freuchen, *Vagrant Viking*, 139.

5. American Museum of Natural History, *Forty-Eighth Annual Report: For the Year 1916*, 57; Freuchen, *Arctic Adventure*, 302; Freuchen, *Vagrant Viking*, 139–40; "MacMillan Crew Back from Arctic," *New York Times*, 88 September 1916, xx.

6. Freuchen, *Arctic Adventure*, 303.

7. American Museum of Natural History, *Forty-Eighth Annual Report: For the Year 1916*, 57.

8. "Await Word of MacMillan," *New York Times*, 1 October 1915, 11.

9. "Present Condition of the Crocker Land Expedition," *Geographical Review* 2 (December 1916), 471.

10. Ibid.

11. Freuchen, *Arctic Adventure*, 304–05.

12. Ibid.

13. Hovey to American Museum of Natural History, 17 May [1916], AGSNY, AC 1, B:263, F:24.

14. Osborn to President James, 23 May 1916, Osborn to President John Greenough, 23 May 1916; Virgil W. Phelps to Osborn, 23 May 1916, AGS-NY Archives, AGSNY, AC1, B:263, F:24.

15. Osborn to Dr. Hugh M. Smith, 23 May 1916; Smith to Osborn, 23 May 1916; Osborn to Smith, 26 May 1916, AGS-NY Archives, AGSNY, AC1, B:263, F:24.

16. H.M. Smith to Osborn, 27 May 1916, AGS-NY Archives, AGSNY, AC1, B:263, F:24.

17. "Crocker Land Expedition," American Museum of Natural History, *Forty-Eighth Annual Report: For The Year 1916*, 57–58.

18. Frank L. Polk to American Museum of Natural History, 29 May 1916; Osborn to the Right Honorable Robert Laird Borden, Premier of Canada, 30 May 1916, AGSNY, AC 1, B:263, F:24. Polk, the acting secretary of state, transmitted Tanquary's message.

19. "Plans for Relief of Crocker Land Expedition of the American Museum of Natural History, 6 June 1916," AGSNY, AC1, B:263, F:24; "Charter Steamship to Find MacMillan," *New York Times*, 8 June 1916, 10.

20. "Charter Steamship to Find MacMillan," *New York Times*, 8 June 1916, 10.

21. "Arctic Explorers Report," *New York Times*, 19 July 1917, 10.

22. W. Elmer Ekblaw, "Across the Ice-Fields of Melville Bay," Appendix III, in Donald B. MacMillan, *Four Years in the White North* (New York: Harper & Brothers, 1918), 371–87.

23. Ibid., 375.

24. Ibid., 378.

25. Ekblaw to President Henry Fairfield Osborn, 14 February 1917, AGSNY, AC 1, B:263, F:24. Rasmussen sent the museum the expense account for his services as far as he went.

26. "Macmillan's Botanist Here," *New York Times*, 31 August 1917, 7.

27. MacMillan, *Four Years in the White North*, 381–86.

28. Ibid., 386–87.

29. Freuchen, *Arctic Adventure*, 314–17.

30. Freuchen, *Arctic Adventure*, 305–06.

31. Ibid., 306–08.

32. Ibid., 310–12.

33. "Third Relief Ship To Seek MacMillan," *New York Times*, 23 May 1917, 13.

34. George H. Sherwood to the Executive Committee of the American Museum, 21 March 1917, B:2, F:2, Crocker Land Expedition Correspondence, Fitzhugh Green, Sr., Papers, Booth Family Center for Special Collections, Georgetown University, Washington, D.C.

35. Sherwood to Messrs. W. & S. Job & Co., 4 April 1917, AGSNY, AC1, B:263, F:24.

36. W.O. Job to Sherwood, 9 April 1917; Sherwood to Captain Bartlett, 10 April 1917, AGSNY, AC 1, B:263, F:24.

37. Ibid.

38. Sherwood to Walter B. James, William B. Bayley, Isaiah Bowman, and Herbert L. Bridgman, 25 May 1917, AGSNY, AC 1, B:263, F:24.

39. News Bureau, Public Information Committee American Museum of Natural History, "Doctor Harrison J. Hunt of Crocker Land Expedition, Returns," n.d. (presumably September 1917), AGSNY, AC 1, B:264, F:24.

40. Fitzhugh Green, "Arctic Duty with the Crocker Land Expedition: Upernivik to Copenhagen," *United States Naval Institute Proceedings* 44 (January 1918), 75–77. Captain Bob Bartlett laconically wrote, "Fitzhugh Green led a party by sledge down the Green-

land coast late in 1916 bringing news that the last relief ship had failed to escape from the ice." Captain Robert A. Bartlett, *The Log of Bob Bartlett: The True Story of Forty Years of Seafaring and Exploration* (New York: G.P. Putnam's Sons, 1928), 289.
41. "A Narrative of the Crocker Land Expedition," *Geographical Review* 5 (March 1918), 242–43.
42. Bartlett *Ibid.*, 77–78.
43. *Ibid.*, 78–79.
44. *Ibid.*, 79–81.
45. *Ibid.*, 81–82.
46. *Ibid.*, 81–84.
47. *Ibid.*, 84–85.
48. *Ibid.*, 85–88.
49. *Ibid.*, 89–92.
50. *Ibid.*, 92–93.
51. *Ibid.*, 93–98.
52. *Ibid.*, 98–100.
53. *Ibid.*, 100–01.
54. *Ibid.*, 102–03.
55. *Ibid.*, 103–04
56. *Ibid.*, 104–05.
57. American Consul General, Copenhagen, to the American Museum of Natural History, 19 August, 1916, B:1, F:1 Correspondence, 1915–1916, Fitzhugh Green, Sr., Papers, Booth Family Center for Special Collections, Georgetown University Library, Washington, D.C.; "Green Reports Arctic Duty Is Done," *New York Times*, 24 August 1916, 11.
58. "Green Reports Arctic Duty Is Done," *New York Times*, 24 August 1916, 11.
59. Green to Admiral Peary, 19 September 1916, B:2, F:3, Fitzhugh Green, Sr., Papers, Booth Family Center for Special Collections, Georgetown University Library, Washington, D.C.
60. Henry Fairfield Osborn to Lieutenant Green, 7 September 1916, B:1, F:15, Fitzhugh Green, Sr., Papers, Booth Family Center for Special Collections, Georgetown University Library.
61. Green, "Arctic Duty with the Crocker Land Expedition: Upernivik to Copenhagen," 1048.
62. *Ibid.*, 1048–50.
63. "Dr. Hovey Returns from Arctic Exile," *New York Times*," 27 August 1917, American Museum of Natural History, Forty-Fifth Annual Report for the Year 1917 (New York, 1918), 59–60.
64. "Dr. Hovey's Life in Arctic," *New York Times*, 2 September 1917, 37.
65. [Isaiah Bowman], No Addressee, 1 May 1917, AGSNY, AC 1, B:263, F:24.
66. *Ibid.*
67. *Ibid.*
68. *Ibid.*
69. *Ibid.*

Chapter 9

1. Henry Fairfield Osborn to Isaiah Bowen, 7 February 1917, AGSNY AC 1, B:263, F:10.
2. Most members of the expedition had returned earlier. Now "The Crocker Land Expedition Home" was reported in the *American Museum Journal* 17 (October 1917), 365.
3. "Memorandum of Mr. Greenough of the essential points in the conversation held with Mr. Osborn at Mr. Greenough's house." AGSNY, AC 1, B:263, F:10. This brief, undated document, signed by J. Greenough, is incomplete.
4. Greenough to Osborn, 28 August 1917, AGSNY, AC 1, B:263, F:10.
5. Osborn to Greenough, 2 September 1917, AGSNY, AC 1, B:263, F:10.
6. Bowman to Greenough, 12 September 1917, AGSNY, AC 1, B:263, F:10. On 11 September both MacMillan and Bowman had initialed before a witness a memo that stated the terms described by Bowman in his letter the next day.
7. Greenough to Osborn, 17 September 1917, AGSNY, AC 1, B:263, F:10.
8. *Ibid.*
9. *Ibid.*
10. *Ibid.*
11. Osborn to Greenough, 19 September 1917, AGSNY, AC 1, B:263, F:10.
12. *Ibid.*
13. *Ibid.*
14. *Ibid.*
15. Bowman to Greenough, 20 September 1917, AGSNY, AC 1, B:263, F:10.
16. *Ibid.*
17. Greenough to Bowman, 21 September 1917, AGSNY, AC 1, B:263, F:10.
18. Greenough to Osborn, 22 September 1917, AGSNY, AC 1, B:263, F:10.
19. *Ibid.*
20. *Ibid.*
21. Greenough to Bowman, 24 September 1917, AGSNY, AC 1, B:263, F:10.
22. Osborn to Greenough, 25 September 1917, AGSNY, AC 1, B:263, F:10.

23. Osborn to Greenough, 25 September 1917, AGSNY, AC 1, B:263, F:10.
24. Greenough to Osborn, n.d. (internal evidence suggests 10 October 1917), AGSNY, AC 1, B:263, F:10.
25. Ibid.
26. Ibid.
27. Ibid.
28. MacMillan to Osborn, 24 October 1917, AGSNY, AC 1, B:263, F:29. MacMillan wrote this narrative while in Provincetown, Massachusetts.
29. J[ohn] G[reenough] to Bowman, 2 November 1917, AGSNY, AC 1, B:263, F:29. One of Aesop's fables, "The Mountain in Labor," often cited in Classical times, was applied to various situations. The fable appears in Horace's epistle, "The Art of Poetry," l. 139, which in translation reads, "Mountains will labor: what's born? A ridiculous mouse." I thank Dr. Valerie Hotchkiss, head of the Rare Book and Manuscript Library at the University of Illinois, for help on this quotation.
30. Osborn to Greenough, 29 October 1917, AGSNY, AC 1, B:263, F:10.
31. Osborn to MacMillan, 29 October 1917, AGSNY, AC 1, B:263, F:10.
32. Hovey to George H. Sherwood, 30 October 1917, AGSNY, AC 1, B:263, F:10.
33. Sherwood to Greenough, 11 December 1917, AGSNY, AC 1, B:263, F:10.
34. Greenough to Sherwood, 12 December 1917, AGSNY, AC 1, B:263, F:10.
35. MacMillan to Osborn, 24 December 1917; MacMillan to Bowman, 24 December 1917, AGSNY, AC 1, B:263, F:10.
36. Osborn to Bowman, 28 December 1917, AGSNY, AC 1, B:263, F:10.
37. Osborn to Greenough, 11 January 1918, AGSNY, AC 1, B:263, F:11.
38. Greenough to Osborn, 18 January 1918, AGSNY, AC 1, B:263, F:11.
39. Bowman to Osborn, 14 January 1918; Sherwood to Bowman, 18 January 1918, AGSNY, AC 1, B:263, F:11.
40. Osborn to Greenough, 22 January 1918; Osborn to Bowman, 22 January 1918, AGSNY, AC 1, B:263, F:11.
41. Osborn to Greenough, 20 March 1918, AGSNY, AC 1, B:263, F:26.
42. Osborn to Greenough, 15 April 1918, AGSNY, AC 1, B:263, F:26.
43. This document is located between documents dated 21 June and 23 July 1918 in AGSNY, AC 1, B:263, F:26.
44. Hovey to Osborn, 23 July 1918, AGSNY, AC 1, B:263, F:11.
45. Hovey to Osborn, 23 July 1918, AGSNY, AC 1, B:263, F:26.
46. Osborn to Greenough, 6 November 1918, AGSNY, AC 1, B:263, F:26.
47. Hovey to Greenough, 6 November 1918; Greenough to Osborn, 9 November 1918, AGSNY, AC 1, B:263, F:11.
48. Osborn to Greenough, 4 June 1919, AGSNY, AC 1, B:263, F:11.
49. Sherwood to Osborn, 26 June 1919, AGSNY, AC 1, B:263, F:11.
50. Osborn to Greenough, 3 July 1919, AGSNY, AC 1, B:263, F:11.
51. MacMillan to the American Geographical Society, the American Museum of Natural History, the University of Illinois, 2 April 1919, AGSNY, AC 1, B:263, F:26, 1–32.
52. Ibid.
53. MacMillan, Unsigned and undated, AGSNY, AC 1, B:263, F:11.
54. "Memorandum regarding the Society's relation to the American Museum of Natural History re the Crocker Land Expedition," 25 September 1919, AGSNY, AC 1, B:263, F:26.
55. Ibid.
56. "The Special Committee appointed November 20, 1919, to consider the report of the geographical results of the Crocker Land Expedition begs to submit the following," AGSNY, AC 1, B:264, F:12.
57. Ibid.
58. Ibid.
59. Osborn to Madison Grant, 6 January 1920, AGSNY, AC 1, B:263, F:26.
60. Ibid.
61. Osborn to Greenough, 8 January 1920, AGSNY, AC 1, B:263, F:26.
62. Unidentified author to MacMillan, 11 January 1920, AGSNY, AC 1, B:263, F:26. I have silently corrected three typographical errors. I find no 7 January letter in the archives. The matter is complicated; both the museum and the society had councils.
63. Greenough to Osborn, 13 January 1920, AGSNY, AC 1, B:263, F:26.
64. Osborn to Greenough, 19 January 1920, AGSNY, AC 1, B:263, F:26.
65. Ibid.
66. Greenough to Osborn, 24 February 1920, AGSNY, AC 1, B:263, F:26.
67. Osborn to Grant, 6 January 1920, AGSNY, AC 1, B:263, F:11.

68. Osborn to Greenough, 8 January 1920, AGSNY, AC 1, B:263, F:11.
69. Greenough to Osborn, 13 January 1920, AGSNY, AC 1, B:263, F:11.
70. The report was published in the *Bulletin of the American Museum of Natural History* 56 (1930), 379-435.

Chapter 10

1. *Ibid.*, 22-23.
2. "Arctic and Antarctic Collections," American Museum of Natural History, *Fifty-Third Annual Report: For the Year 1921* (1922), 22.
3. Herbert L. Bridgman, "'Four Years in the White North'—A Review," *Natural History*, 19 (January 1919), 73-75.
4. *Ibid.*, 75-76.
5. Herbert L. Bridgman, "Peary: An Appreciation," *Geographical Review*, 9 (March 1920), 161-69.
6. Donald B. MacMillan, *Four Years in the White North* (New York: Harper & Brothers, 1918), 321-22.
7. Although MacMillan submitted his "Geographical Report" to the American Museum in 1919, it was not published until 1930.
8. On 7 January 1921, MacMillan reported that Gilbert Grosvenor of the National Geographic Society had agreed to appropriate $10,000 for biological investigations on his forthcoming trip to Baffin Land and he asked Isaiah Bowman if the American Geographical Society would make an appropriation and detail a man for some branch of work in which it might be interested. MacMillan to Bowman, 3 January 1921, AGSNY, AC 1, B:263, F:12.
9. "MacMillan Sails on Arctic Voyage," *New York Times*, 17 July 1921, Section 2, p.1; "New Polar Geography," *Outlook*, 132 (27 September 1922), 136.
10. George S. Hudson, "Exploring Arctic Wastes in the 'Bowdoin,'" *Motor Boat*, 18 (25 July 1921), 15-17.
11. "MacMillan to Seek Signs of New Ice Age," *New York Times*, 28 May 1923, 17; "Menace of a New Ice Age To Be Tested by Scientists," *New York Times*, 10 June 1923, 3; "Back from the Arctic," *Outlook*, 138 (1 October 1924), 151; "The Master of the North Sails Home," *Literary Digest*, 83 (11 October 1924), 40, 42, 51; Donald B. MacMillan, "The 'Bowdoin' in North Greenland," *National Geographic Magazine*, 47 (June 1925), 677-722.
12. Richard E. Byrd, *Skyward* (New York: G.P. Putnams Sons, 1928), 135-36; Raimund E. Goerler, ed., *To the Pole: The Diary and Notebook of Richard E. Byrd, 1925-1927* (Columbus: Ohio State Press, 1998), 21-22.
13. Goerler, ed., *To the Pole*, 22-23.
14. Byrd, *Skyward*, 137.
15. Goerler, ed., *To the Pole*, 37.
16. Byrd, *Skyward*, 142-55; "The MacMillan Arctic Venture Sails," *Natural Geographic Magazine*, 48 (August 1925), 224-26; "Scientific Aspects of the MacMillan Arctic Expedition," *National Geographic Magazine*, 48 (September 1925), 348-54; "MacMillan in the Field," *National Geographic Magazine*, 48 (October 1925), 473-76; "The MacMillan Arctic Expedition Returns," *National Geographic Magazine*, 48 (November 1925), 477-518; "Planes for Arctic Flights Held Impractical," *Popular Mechanics*, 44 (November 1925), 761; "MacMillan and Arctic Exploration," *New York Times*, 15 June to 29 October 1925.
17. Byrd, *Skyward*, 157; Richard E. Byrd, "Flying over the Arctic," *National Geographic Magazine*, 48 (November, 1925), 519-32. Charles J.V. Murphy, *Struggle: The Life and Exploits of Commander Richard E. Byrd* (New York: Frederick A. Stokes Co., 1928), 121-154, on Byrd at Etah and his preparing to fly to the Pole. This popular account is not documented.
18. Roald Amundsen, *My Life As An Explorer* (Garden City, NY: Doubleday, Page & Co., 1927), 119-129. Lincoln Ellsworth had joined with Amundsen and provided funds for their flight across the Arctic Ocean. In 1913 Ellsworth had unsuccessfully applied for a position on the Crocker Land Expedition.
19. Byrd, *Skyward*, 159-97; Richard E. Byrd, *Exploring with Byrd* (New York: G.P. Putnam's Sons, 1937), 15-28; Archibald D. Turnbull and Clifford L. Lord, *History of United States Naval Aviation* (New Haven: Yale University Press, 1949), 222-23.
20. David H. Grover, "Practicing for the Pole: Richard E. Byrd and the 1925 MacMillan Arctic Expedition," *Aviation History* (March 2001), 40.
21. "MacMillan to Lead Exploration Party in Subarctic Area," *Washington Post*, 21 April 1926, 3; "Loading Schooner Sachem for Far

North Trip," *Boston Daily Globe*, 9 June 1926, 24; "3 Women and Boys on MacMillan Trip to Subarctic," *Washington Post*, June 1926, M3; "MacMillan Back Ahead of Welcome," *New York Times*, 10 September 1926, 7.

22. "Field Museum Men Make New Finds in Arctic," *Chicago Tribune*, 5 September 1928, 17.; "Borealis Fails To Cause Static, Says MacMillan," *New York Herald Tribune*, 17 September 1928, 18.

23. "Dr Cook Finds New Champion," *Boston Globe*, 24 January 1926, A5; "Aim of Dr. Cook Sound as Peary's, Amundsen Insists," *Washington Post*, 24 January 1926, M5.

24. Roald Amundsen, *My Life as an Explorer* (Garden City, NY: Doubleday, Page and Co., 1927), 225–27.

25. "MacMillan Certain Peary Got to Pole," *New York Times*, 26 January 1926, 25. For an overview of the conflict, see Clive Holland, ed., *Farthest North: The Quest for the North Pole* (New York: Carroll and Graf Publishers, 1994), 197–221.

26. W. Henry Lewin, *Did Peary Reach the Pole?* London: Simpkin, Marshall, Hamilton, Kent & Co., 1911.

27. Donald B. MacMillan, *How Peary Reached the Pole: The Personal Story of His Assistant* (Boston: Houghton Miffllin, 1934). A new edition of this book, with an Introduction by Genevieve M. LeMoine, Susan A. Kaplan, and Anne Witty, was published by McGill-Queen's University Press, Montreal, 2008. This edition has many fine photographs.

28. W. Henry Lewin, *The Great North Pole Fraud* (London: C.W. Daniel Co., 1935), 124–37 (quotations at 125, 137).

29. Donald B. MacMillan, "Why Go North?" *American Mercury*, 34 (February 1935), 202–08.

30. Hovey to Osborn, 9 January 1918, AGSNY, AC 1, B:263, F:11.

31. *Ibid.*
32. *Ibid.*
33. *Ibid.*
34. *Ibid.*
35. *Ibid.*
36. *Ibid.*
37. *Ibid.*

38. Osborn to Hovey, 16 January 1918, AGSNY, AC 1, B:263, F:11.

39. "Geographical News," *Geographical Review*, 4 (December 1917), 492.

40. Edmund O. Hovey, "Child-life Among the Smith Sound Eskimos," *American Museum Journal* 18 (May 1918), 360–71.

41. Harrison J. Hunt and Ruth Hunt Thompson, *North to the Horizon: Searching for Peary's Crocker Land* (Camden ME: Down East Books, 1980), 107.

42. *Ibid.*, 108.

43. *Ibid.*, 108–09; Osborn to Hovey, 9 May 1918; Hovey to Honorary Committee, 17 May 1918; Osborn to Hovey, 14 May 1918; Hovey to Osborn, 16 May 1918, AGSNY, AC 1, B:263, F:11.

44. Hunt and Thompson, *North to the Horizon*, 109.

45. *Ibid.*, 110.

46. John Treadwell Nichols, "Some Marine Fishes from Northwest Greenland," *Bulletin of the American Museum of Natural History*, 38 (New York, 1918), 677–83.

47. Paul S. Welch, "Oligochaeta Collected in Greenland by the Crocker Land Expedition," *Bulletin of the American Museum of Natural History,*, 44 (New York, 1921), 269–82.

48. Raymond C. Osburn, "Bryozoa of the Crocker Land Expedition," *Bulletin of the American Museum of Natural History*, 41 (1919), 603–24.

49. American Museum of Natural History, *Forty-Ninth Annual Report: For the Year 1917* (New York, 1918), 16.

50. University of Illinois, *Transactions of the Board of Trustees, 1916–1918*, 606, 619, 635; *Transactions, 1918–1920*, 198.

51. Theodore H. Frison, "Report on the Bremidae Collected by the Crocker Land Expedition, 1913–1917," *Bulletin of the American Museum of Natural History*, 41 (1919), 451–59.

52. Ekblaw wrote an introduction, "The Places of Collection of Mollusca Brought Back by the Crocker Land Expedition," to a report on the subject. Frank C. Baker of the Natural History Museum, University of Illinois, was the author of "Mollusca of the Crocker Land Expedition to Northwest Greenland and Grinnell Land," published in the *Bulletin of the American Museum of Natural History* 41 (1919), 479–517.

53. Justus W. Folsom, "Collembola from the Crocker Land Expedition 1913–1917," *Bulletin of the American Museum of Natural History*, 41 (New York, 1919), 271–303.

54. W. Elmer Ekblaw, *Geographical Review*, 12 (April 1922), 324, 324–25, 326–27, 327.

55. Ekblaw, *Geographical Review*, 12 (October 1922), 668–69.
56. "The Origin of the Eskimo," *Scottish Geographical Magazine* 33 (October 1917), 458–65.
57. Her publications included "The Operation of 'Geographic Factors in History,'" *Bulletin of the American Geographical Society*, 41, No. 7 (1909), 422–39; "The Anglo-Saxons of the Kentucky Mountains: A Study in Anthropogeography," *Bulletin of the American Geographical Society* 42, No. 8 (1910), 561–94; and "Japanese Colonial Methods," *Bulletin of the American Geographical Society* 45, No.4 (1913), 255–75.
58. W. Elmer Ekblaw, "The Material Response of the Polar Eskimo to Their Far Arctic Environment," *Annals of the Association of American Geographers* 17 (December 1927), 147–98; 18 (March 1918), 1–24.
59. Ibid.
60. Ibid.
61. Ibid.
62. Mene.
63. "Says He Has Secret of Pole's Discovery," *New York Times*, 22 September 1916, 7.

Chapter 11

1. Vergil, *Aeneid*, Book 6, line 126.
2. George Palmer Putnam, "Eskimo Killed Prof. Marvin, Perry Aide; Confesses Arctic Crime of 17 Years Ago; Victim, Reported Drowned, Was Shot," *New York Times*, 25 September 1926, 1–2. Putnam relates this story in essentially the same way in George Palmer Putnam, *Wide Margins: A Publisher's Autobiography* (New York: Harcourt, Brace and Company, 1942), 272–81.
3. "Doubts Marvin 'Cracked' in Arctic," *New York Times*, 25 September 1926, 2.
4. "Kellogg to Order Legation Inquiry on Marvin's Murder," *New York Times*, 26 September 1926, 1.
5. Thomas F. Hall to Fitzhugh Green, 20 April 1928, B:1, F:27, Fitzhugh Green, Sr., Papers, Booth Family Center for Special Collections, Georgetown University Library, Washington, D.C. Green had written to Hall on 16 and 20 April. I have been unable to locate those letters.
6. Ibid.
7. Ibid.
8. Ibid.
9. Ibid.
10. Fitzhugh Green, "Amusing Fifty Thousand Men: Another Opportunity for Government Control," *United States Naval Institute Proceedings* 3 (November 1917), 2527–40.
11. Years later Fitzhugh Green published an account of the life of Adams with the catchy title, "There's Not Much Use to Grind Unless You Advertise Your Grist," *American Magazine*, March 1927, 27, 218. On Adams, see Elmo S. Watson, *A History of Newspaper Syndicates in the United States, 1865-1935* (Chicago: n.p., 1936), 58–59.
12. On the promotion package, see the Fitzhugh Green, Sr., Papers, B:12, F:4, 5; Josephus Daniels to President, George Matthew Adams Service, 18 August 1917, Fitzhugh Green, Sr., Papers, B:4, F:4, Booth Family Center for Special Collections, Georgetown University Library, Washington, D.C.
13. Fitzhugh Green to the Bureau of Navigation, 10 October 1917, Fitzhugh Green, Sr., Papers, B:4, F:4, Booth Family Center for Special Collections, Georgetown University Library, Washington, D.C.
14. Fitzhugh Green, "Arctic Duty with the Crocker Land Expedition," *United States Naval Institute Proceedings* 43 (September 1917), 1942–76; (November 1917), 2455–94; (December 1917), 2799–2832; 44 (January 1918), 75–105.
15. Fitzhugh Green, "Types of Merchant Skippers," *United States Naval Institute Proceedings* 44 (December 1918), 2779–96.
16. Fitzhugh Green, "Rear Admiral Peary, U.S.N., Scientist and Arctic Explorer," *United States Naval Institute Proceedings* 48 (August 1922), 1315–24.
17. Fitzhugh Green, "Earth Features and the Navy Pilot," *United States Naval Institute Proceedings* 49 (November 1923), 1771–1804.
18. Fitzhugh Green, "Across the Pole by Plane," *United States Naval Institute Proceedings* 49 (June 1923), 937–48.
19. Fitzhugh Green, "The Navy and the North Pole," *United States Naval Institute Proceedings* 50 (March 1924), 373–85.
20. Fitzhugh Green, "Fixing the Decimal Point," *United States Naval Institute Proceedings* 50 (August 1924), 1292–95.
21. On this ghost writing, see the Fitzhugh Green, Sr., Papers, B;13, F:1, Booth Family Center for Special Collections, Georgetown University Library, Washington, D.C.
22. Fitzhugh Green, "The Crocker Land

Expedition. The Story of the Last Extensive Dog-Sledge Expedition in the Arctic," *Natural History* 28 (1928), 463–75.

23. Fitzhugh Green to Bureau of Navigation, 13 May 1917, Fitzhugh Green, Sr., Papers, B:4, F:4, Booth Family Center for Special Collections, Georgetown University Library, Washington, D.C.

24. Josephus Daniels to Fitzhugh Green, 27 February 1918, Fitzhugh Green, Sr., Papers, B:4, F:5, Booth Family Center for Special Collections, Georgetown University Library, Washington, D.C.

25. D.B. Beary to Fitzhugh Green, 23 November 1920, Fitzhugh Green, Sr., Papers, B:4, F:6, Booth Family Center for Special Collections, Georgetown University Library, Washington, D.C.

26. Fitzhugh Green to The Chief of the Bureau of Ordinance, 18 April 1921, Fitzhugh Green, Sr., Papers, B:4, F:6, Booth Family Center for Special Collections, Georgetown University Library, Washington, D.C.

27. Green to Captain Leigh, 12 May 1924, Fitzhugh Green, Sr., Papers, B:4, F:8, Booth Family Center for Special Collections, Georgetown University Library, Washington, D.C.

28. Halsey Powell to Green, 13 May 1924, Fitzhugh Green, Sr., Papers, B:4, F:8, Booth Family Center for Special Collections, Georgetown University Library, Washington, D.C.

29. R.H. Leigh to Fitzhugh Green, 14 May 1924, Fitzhugh Green, Sr., Papers, B:4, F:8, Booth Family Center for Special Collections, Georgetown University Library, Washington, D.C.

30. Green to Powell, 17 May 1924, Fitzhugh Green, Sr., Papers, B:4, F:8, Booth Family Center for Special Collections, Georgetown University Library, Washington, D.C.

31. Fitzhugh Green, "The Worst Menace of Another War," *New York Times*, 23 November 1924, p. SM3.

32. Halsey Powell to Fitzhugh Green, 10 December 1924, Fitzhugh Green, Sr., Papers, B:4, F:8, Booth Family Center for Special Collections, Georgetown University Library, Washington, D.C.

33. Green to the Secretary of the Navy, 9 December 1924, Fitzhugh Green, Sr., Papers, B:4, F:8, Booth Family Center for Special Collections, Georgetown University Library, Washington, D.C.

34. [Fitzhugh Green], Memo:, 9 December 1924, Fitzhugh Green, Sr., Papers, B:4, F:8, Booth Family Center for Special Collections, Georgetown University Library, Washington, D.C.

35. Green to John Stapler, 9 April 1925, Fitzhugh Green, Sr., Papers, B:4, F:9, Booth Family Center for Special Collections, Georgetown University Library, Washington, D.C.

36. Green to John Stapler, 3 July 1925, Fitzhugh Green, Sr., Papers, B:4, F:9, Booth Family Center for Special Collections, Georgetown University Library, Washington, D.C.

37. Fitzhugh Green, "Foreword," *Our Naval Heritage* (New York: The Century Co., 1925), v.

38. Fitzhugh Green, *Our Naval Heritage* (New York: The Century Co., 1925). The appraisal is penciled in on the title page of the book in the University of Illinois Library.

39. Green to John Stapler, 10 March 1926, Fitzhugh Green, Sr., Papers, B:4, F:9, Booth Family Center for Special Collections, Georgetown University Library, Washington, D.C.

40. Fitzhugh Green, "The Big Crisis," Fitzhugh Green, Sr., Papers, B:7, F:2, Booth Family Center for Special Collections, Georgetown University Library, Washington, D.C. Internal evidence (p. 9) indicates that this document of thirteen typewritten pages was written in 1945.

41. On resigning from active duty he became a commander in the Navy Reserve, from which he retired in July 1945.

42. "Green Leaves Navy for Exploring Plan," *New York Times*, 29 May 1927, 3; "Navy Man Heads New Firm to Aid U.S. Explorers," *New York Herald Tribune*, 29 May, 1927, 5.

43. The dates of publication were as follows: 23 May 1926; 15 and 26 August 1928; 19 January, 21 April (two items), 8 December 1929; 9 February, 27 April, 18 May, 29 June 1930; and 17 May 1931.

44. Sally Putnam Chapman, *Whistled Like a Bird: The Untold Story of Dorothy Putnam, George Putnam, and Amelia Earhart* (New York: Warner Books, 1997), 58–61. See also Joyce Milton, *Loss of Eden: A Biography of Charles and Anne Morrow Lindbergh* (New York: HarperCollins, 1993), 138–40.

45. *The National Union Catalog: Pre 1956 Imprints* (216:444) includes the following entry under Fitzhugh Green as the author:

Lindbergh, Charles Augustus, New York–Parigi senza scalo. Traduzione di P. Gerard Jansen. Milano: A. Mondadori, 1928.

46. George P. Putnam, *Wide Margins: A Publisher's Autobiography* (New York: Harcourt Brace and Co., 1942), 232–36.

47. Leonard Mosley, *Lindbergh: A Biography* (New York: Doubleday & Co. 1976), 120, 121–22, 406; Joyce Milton, *Loss of Eden: A Biography of Charles and Anne Morrow Lindbergh* (New York: HarperCollins, 1993), 128.

48. Green to Bowman, 11 August 1926; Green to Bowman, 18 August 1926, AGSNY, AC 1, B:187, F:22.

49. Green to Bowman, 19 August 1926, AGSNY, AC 1, B:187, F:22.

50. Green to Bowman, 25 August 1926, Bowman to Green, 27 August 1926, Green to Bowman, 30 August 1916, AGSNY, AC 1, B:187, F:22.

51. Green to Bowman, 8 September 1926, AGSNY, AC 1, B:187, F:22.

52. Green to Bowman, 13 September 1926, AGSNY, AC 1, B:187, F:22.

53. Green to Bowman, 16 September 1926, AGSNY, AC 1, B:187, F:22.

54. Putnam to Bowman, 26 September 1926, AGSNY, AC 1, B:187, F:22.

55. Green to Bowman, 18 April 1928; Bowman to Green, 24 April 1928, AGSNY, AC 1, B:187, F:22.

56. Green to Bowman, 8 May 1928, AGSNY, AC 21, B:187, F:22.

57. Green to Ellsworth, 17 December 1928, AGSNY, AC 1, B:187, F:22.

58. Amelia Earhart, *20 HRS. 40 MIN.* (New York: G.P. Putnam's, 1928), 95–105; Amelia Earhart, *The Fun of It: Random Records of My Own Flying and of Women in Aviation* (New York: Brewer, Warren & Putnam, 1932), 58–88. As agreed, Mrs. Guest paid the pilot, Wilmer Stutz, $20,000, and the mechanic, Lou Gordon, $5,000. She was to pay Amelia Earhart nothing, which she did. George P. Putnam, *Soaring Wings: A Biography of Amelia Earhart* (New York: Harcourt, Brace and Co.,1939), 190.

59. Putnam, *Soaring Wings*, 76.

60. On Margery's birth, see the U.S. Census, 1900, Michigan, Genesee County, Flint: see also Michigan Marriages, 1868–1925, accessed on www.familysearch.org

61. Bernard A. Weisberger, *The Dream Maker: William C. Durant, Founder of General Motors* (Boston, Little, Brown and Co., 1979), 314; "Robert W. Daniel, Ex-Banker Here, 56," *New York Times*, 21 December 1940.

62. Matthew J. Bruccoli, *The Fortunes of Mitchell Kennerley, Bookman* (New York: Harcourt Brace Jovanovich, 1986), 191–92, 198–99, 219–20.

63. "William Crapo Durant: The Most Spectacular Figure in Wall Street," *Current Opinion*, 77 (November 1924), 576–77.

64. Ibid., 217–18.

65. Margery Durant, *My Father* (New York: G.P Putnam, 1929), vii–viii.

66. "Margery Durant Married Quietly," *New York Times*, 21 November 1933, 24; "Durant's Daughter Marries F. Green, Lindbergh Author," *New York Herald Tribune*, 21 November 1933, 1; "Ocean Travelers," *New York Times*, 17 July 1934, 23; No headline, *New York Times*, 21 November 1933, 24.

67. "Back from the Treasure Hunt," *New York Times*, 6 April 1934, 21.

68. Fitzhugh Green, "The Passionate Eskimo," *Liberty Magazine*, 8 June 1935.

69. "Green Put on Probation," *New York Times*, 25 October 1947, 3.

70. Dick Byrd to Fitzhugh Green, 18 November 1927, Fitzhugh Green, Sr., Papers, B:1, F:5, Booth Family Center for Special Collections, Georgetown University Library, Washington, D.C.

71. "Commander Green Dies in Hospital," *New York Times*, 3 December 1947, 25.

72. "Green Died of Natural Causes," *New York Times*, 4 December 1947, 31.

73. "Mrs. Fitzhugh Green Gets Probation in Drug Case," *New York Herald Tribune*, 10 February 1948, 24.

74. "Obituary," *New York Times*, 16 February 1969, 77.

Bibliography

Primary Sources

Air Pioneering in the Arctic: The Two Polar Flights of Roald Amundsen and Lincoln Ellsworth. Part I: The 1925 Flight from Spitzbergen to 88° North. Part II: The First Crossing of the Polar Sea, 1926, ed. Howard E. Kershner. New York: National American Society, 1929.

Amedeo of Savoy, Luigi, Duke of the Abruzzi. *On the "Polar Star" in the Arctic Sea.* William Le Queux, trans. London: Hutchinson & Co., 1903.

Amundsen, Roald. *My Life as an Explorer.* Garden City, NY: Doubleday, Page & Co., 1927.

Amundsen, Roald, and Lincoln Ellsworth. *First Crossing of the Polar Sea.* New York: George H. Doran Co., 1927.

Bartlett, Robert A. "Bringing the Crippled *Roosevelt* Home," in Frederick A. Blossom, ed., *Told at the Explorers Club: True Tales of Modern Exploration.* New York: Albert & Charles Boni, 1931, 29–52.

Bartlett, Robert A. *The Log of Bob Bartlett: The True Story of Forty Years of Seafaring and Exploration.* New York: G.P. Putnam's Sons, 1928.

Borup, George. *A Tenderfoot with Peary.* New York: Frederick A. Stokes Co., 1911.

Brainard, David L. *The Outpost of the Lost: An Arctic Adventure.* Indianapolis: Bobbs-Merrill, 1929.

Bridgman, Herbert L. "Peary: An Appreciation." *Geographical Review* 9 (March 1920), 161–69.

Byrd, Richard E. *Exploring with Byrd.* New York: G.P. Putnam's Sons, 1937.

Byrd, Richard E. *Skyward.* New York: G.P. Putnam's Sons, 1928. Also *Skyward,* ed. William R. Anderson. Chicago: R.R. Donnelley & Sons Co., 1981.

Cagni, Umberto. *On the Polar Star in the Arctic Sea.* New York: Dodd, Mead, 1903.

Cook, Frederick A. "Dr. Cook's Own Story," *Hampton's Magazine* 26 (January 1911), 51–66; "Dr. Cook's Own Story: Arrival at Annoatok—Meeting with Harry Whitney—Journey to Copenhagen and Reception There," *Hampton's Magazine* 26 (February 1911), 162–76; "Dr. Cook's Own Story: Reception at New York—Receipts from Writings and Lectures—The Mt. McKinley Matter—Dunkle and Loose—Leaving New York," *Hampton's Magazine* 26 (March 1911), 295–308; "Dr. Cook's Own Story: A Year of Wandering—Pursued by Reporters—The Decision to Reappear and Tell Everything," *Hampton's Magazine* 26 (April 1911), 493–502.

Cook, Frederick A. "First Report," in "The Discovery of the Pole," *National Geographic Magazine* 20 (October 1909), 892–96.

Cook, Frederick A. *My Attainment of the Pole: Being the Record of the Expedition That First Reached the Boreal Center, 19078–1908, with the Final Summary of the Polar Controversy.* New York: Polar Publishing Co., 1911. The book was published again in New York by Mitchell Kennerley in 1911 and 1913; in New York and London by Mitchell Kennerley in 1912; in Pittsburgh by Polar Publishing Co. in 2001; and in New York by Cooper Square Press in 2001, with an Introduction by Robert M. Bryce.

Bibliography

Cook, Frederick A., *Return from the Pole*, ed. with an Introduction by Frederick J. Pohl. New York: Pellegrini & Cudahy, 1951.
Earhart, Amelia. *The Fun of It: Random Records of My Own Flying and of Women in Aviation.* New York: Brewer, Warren & Putnam. 1932.
Earhart, Amelia, *20 Hrs. 40 Min.: Our Flight in the Friendship.* New York: G.P. Putnam's Sons, 1928.
Ekblaw, W. Elmer. "Across the Ice-Fields on Melville Bay," Appendix III, in Donald B. MacMillan, *Four Years in the White North.* New York: Harper and Brothers, 1918, 371-87.
Ekblaw, W. Elmer. *Along Unknown Shores: Narratives of Exploration in the Far North.* New York: Harper and Bros. 1918. Also published as appendices in Donald B. MacMillan, *Four Years in the White North.* New York: Harper and Brothers, 1918.
Ekblaw, W. Elmer. "The Danish Arctic Station at Godhavn." *American Museum Journal* 18 (1918), 581-99.
Ekblaw, W. Elmer. "Eskimo Dogs—Forgotten Heroes." *Natural History* 37 (1936), 173-84.
Ekblaw, W. Elmer. "The Food Birds of the Smith Sound Eskimos." *Wilson Bulletin No. 106* (March 1919) 1-5.
Ekblaw, W. Elmer. "On Unknown Shores: The Traverse of Grant and Ellesmere Lands," Appendix II, in Donald B. MacMillan, *Four Years in the White North.* New York: Harper and Brothers, 1918, 333-70.
Ekblaw, W. Elmer. "The Origin of the Eskimo." *Scottish Geographical Magazine* 33 (October 1917), 458-65.
Ekblaw, W. Elmer. "The Plant Life of Northwest Greenland." *Natural History* 19 (March 1919), 273-91.
Ekblaw, W. Elmer. "The Polar Eskimo: Their Land and Life." Doctoral dissertation, Clark University, 1926.
Ekblaw, W. Elmer. "The Summer at North Star Bay," Appendix I, in Donald B. MacMillan, *Four Years in the White North.* New York: Harper and Brothers, 1918, 323-32.
Ekblaw, W. Elmer. "Thin Ice," in Frederick Blossom, ed., *Told at the Explorers Club: True Tales of Modern Exploration.* New York: Albert & Charles Boni, 1931, 81-89.
Ekblaw, W. Elmer. "The Visit to the Meteorite," Appendix IV, in Donald B. MacMillan, *Four Years in the White North.* New York: Harper and Brothers, 1918, 388-96.
Freuchen, Peter. *Arctic Adventure: My Life in the Frozen North.* New York: Farrar & Rinehart, 1935.
Freuchen, Peter. *Book of the Eskimos,* ed. with preface by Dagmar Freuchen. Cleveland: World Publishing Co., 1961.
Freuchen, Peter. *I Sailed with Rasmussen.* New York: Julian Messner, 1958.
Freuchen, Peter. *Ice Floes and Flaming Water: A True Adventure in Melville Bay,* trans. from the Norwegian by Johan Hambro. New York: Julian Messner, 1954.
Freuchen, Peter. *Men of the Frozen North,* ed. and with a Preface by Dagmar Freuchen. Cleveland: World Publishing Co., 1962.
Freuchen, Peter. *Vagrant Viking: My Life and Adventures,* trans. by John Hambro. New York: Julian Messner, 1953.
Garos, Fait [Fitzhugh Green]. "A First Lieutenant." *Sea Power* 4 (July 1918), 18-22, 64.
Garos, Fait [Fitzhugh Green]. "Eskimo Costume for our Navy." *Sea Power* 4 (January 1918), 50-52.
Garos, Fait [Fitzhugh Green]. "Getting in the First Shot." *Sea Power* 3 (October 1917), 22-26.
Goodsell, John W. *On Polar Trails: The Peary Expedition to the North Pole, 1908-09.* Revised and edited by Donald W. Whisenhunt. Austin, TX: Eakin Press, 1983.
Greely, Adolphus W. *Three Years of Arctic Service: An Account of the Lady Franklin Bay Expedition of 1881-84 and the Attainment of the Farthest North,* 2 vols. London, Richard Bentley and Sons, 1886.
Green, Fitzhugh. "Arctic Duty with the Crocker Land Expedition." *United States Naval Institute Proceedings* 43 (October 1917), 2193-2224; (November 1917), 2455-94; (December 1917), 2793-2832; 44 (January 1918), 75-105.

Green, Fitzhugh. "The Bomb that Blew the Movies Upside Down." *American Magazine* 107 (April 1929), 48–49, 118, 120, 122–23.
Green, Fitzhugh. "The Crocker Land Expedition." *Natural History* 28 (Sept.–Oct.) 1928, 463–75.
Green, Fitzhugh. "The Crocker Land Expedition. The Story of the Last Extensive Dog-Sledge Expedition in the Arctic. The Final Effort in Three Hundred Years of Dependence on Brawn and Sinew Among the Ice Floes of the Frozen North." *Natural History* 28 (1928), 463–75.
Green, Fitzhugh. "Diary," 29 June 1913 to August 1915, Booth Family Center for Special Collections, Georgetown University Library, Washington, D.C.
Green, Fitzhugh. "Diary," 29 June 1913 to 1 September 1915, Crocker Land Expedition Papers, Mss. C76, American Museum of Natural History Library, New York, New York.
Green, Fitzhugh. *Dick Byrd: Air Explorer.* New York: G.P. Putnam's Sons, 1928.
Green, Fitzhugh. "Journal," American Geographical Society.
Green, Fitzhugh. "A New Method of Teaching Swimming, with a Few Hints on Rescuing the Drowning." *United States Naval Institute Proceedings* 37 (September 1911), 865–70.
Green, Fitzhugh. "Running the British Blockade." *Sea Power* 3 (September 1917), 50–55, 66.
Hayes, Isaac I. *The Land of Desolation: Being a Personal Narrative of Observations and Adventure in Greenland.* New York: Harper and Brothers, 1872.
Hayes, Isaac I. *The Open Polar Sea: A Narrative of a Voyage of Discovery Towards the North Pole in the Schooner "United States."* New York: Hurd and Houghton, 1869.
Henson, Matthew A. "The Negro at the North Pole." *World's Work* 19 (April, 1910), 12825–37.
Henson, Matthew A. *A Negro Explorer at the North Pole.* New York: Frederick Stokes Co., 1912. Also New York: Arno Press and the New York Times, 1969.
Hovey, Edmund O. "Child-Life Among the Smith Sound Eskimos." *American Museum Journal* 18 (May 1918), 360–71.
Hovey, Edmund O. "In Search of Crocker Land." *American Museum Journal* 12 (March 1912), 83–88.
Hovey, Edmund O. "The Personnel of the Crocker Land Expedition." *American Museum Journal* 13 (April 1913), 179–82.
Hunt, Harrison J., and Ruth Hunt Thompson. *North to the Horizon: Searching for Peary's Crocker Land.* Camden, ME: Down East Books, 1980.
Kane, Elisha Kent. *Arctic Explorations: The Second Grinnell Expedition in Search of Sir John Franklin, 1853, '54, '55,* 2 vols. Philadelphia: Childs & Peterson, 1860. Also London: T. Nelson and Sons, 1861.
Klutschak, Heinrich. *Overland to Starvation Cove: With the Inuit in Search of Franklin, 1878–1880,* trans. and ed., William Barr. Toronto: University of Toronto Press, 1987.
Low, A.P. *Report on the Dominion Government Expedition to Hudson Bay on Board the D.G.S. Neptune, 1903–1904.* Ottawa: Government Printing Bureau, 1906.
MacMillan, Donald B. "The 'Bowdoin' in North Greenland." *National Geographic Magazine* 47 (June 1925), 677–721.
MacMillan, Donald B. *Eskimo Place Names and Aid to Conversation.* Hydrographic Office, U.S. Navy, H.O. Miscel. No. 10,578. N.d.
MacMillan, Donald B. *Etah and Beyond: Or, Life Within Twelve Degrees of the Pole.* Boston: Houghton Mifflin Co, 1927.
MacMillan, Donald B. Field note book[s], Crocker Land Expedition, 1913–1915, CG-1, nos. 1–6, Research Library, American Museum of Natural History, New York, New York.
MacMillan, Donald B. "Food Supply of the Smith Sound Eskimos." *American Museum Journal* 18 (March 1918), 161–76.
MacMillan, Donald B. *Four Years in the White North.* New York: Harper and Bros., 1918. Also *Four Years in the White North,* Foreword by Adolphus W. Greely, rev. ed. Boston and New York: The Medici Society of America, 1925.
MacMillan, Donald B. "Geographical Report of the Crocker Land Expedition, 1913–1917." *Bulletin of the American Museum of Natural History* 56: 1926–1929 (1930), 379–435.

MacMillan, Donald B. *How Peary Reached the Pole: The Personal Account of His Assistant*. Montreal: McGill-Queen's University Press, 2008. Originally published Boston and New York: Houghton Mifflin, 1934.

MacMillan, Donald B. "The Humorous Side of Arctic Exploration." *World's Work* 46 (August 1923), 389-96.

MacMillan, Donald B. "In Search of a New Land." *Harper's Magazine* 131 (October 1915), 651-65; (November 1915), 921-99.

MacMillan, Donald B. "The MacMillan Arctic Expedition Returns." *National Geographic Magazine* 48 (November 1925), 477-518.

MacMillan, Donald B. "New Evidence that Cook Did Not Reach the Pole." *Geographical Review* 5 (February 1918), 140-41.

MacMillan, Donald B. "Notes on MacMillan's Ellesmere Island Trip." *Geographical Review* 5 (February 1918), 183-94.

MacMillan, Donald B. "Peary as a Leader." *National Geographic Magazine* 37 (April 1920), 293-317.

MacMillan, Donald. "Record-Hunting in the Arctic." *Harper's Magazine* 137 (September 1918), 549-62.

MacMillan, Donald B. "Scenes from the Eastern Arctic." *American Museum Journal* 18 (March 1918), 177-92.

MacMillan, Donald B. "Why Go North?" *American Mercury* 34 (February 1935), 202-08.

MacMillan, Miriam. *Green Seas and White Ice*. New York: Dodd, Mead and Co., 1948.

MacMillan, Miriam. *I Married an Explorer*. London: Hurst & Blackett, 1951. This book is actually the same as *Green Seas and White Ice* with the photographs arranged differently.

McClintock, F.L. *A Narrative of the Discovery of the Fate of Sir John Franklin and His Companions*. London: John Murray, 1859. Also Boston: Ticknor and Fields, 1890.

Melville, George W. *In the Lena Delta: A Narrative of the Search for Lieut.-Commander DeLong and His Companions. Followed by An Account of the Greely Relief Expedition and A Proposed Method of Reaching the North Pole*, ed. Melville Philips. Boston: Houghton, Mifflin and Co., 1885.

Nansen, Fridtjov. *Farthest North*, ed. Denys Thompson. London: Chatto and Windus, 1955. First published New York: Macmillan, 1897.

Nansen, Fridtjov. *The First Crossing of Greenland*, trans. from the Norwegian by Hubert Majendie Gepp. London: Longmans, Green, and Co., 1892.

Nares, G.S. *A Narrative of A Voyage to the Polar Sea during 1875-6 in H.M. Ships "Alert" and "Discovery"* 2 vols. London: Sampson Low, Marston, Searle and Rivington, 1878.

Peary, R.E. "The Cape York Ironstone." *Bulletin of the American Geographical Society* 26 (1894), 447-88.

Peary, Robert E. "The Crocker Land Expedition," *American Museum Journal* 12 (May 1912), 159-63.

Peary, Robert E. "The Discovery of the North Pole," *Hampton's Magazine* 24 (January 1910), 3-24; "The Discovery of the North Pole: Recruiting the Eskimos, Hunting for Food Supplies for the Perilous Voyage North from Etah," *Hampton's Magazine* 24 (February 1910), 159-70; "The Discovery of the North Pole: The Battle with the Ice from Etah to Cape Sheridan," *Hampton's Magazine* 24 (March 1910), 329-46; "The Discovery of the North Pole: The Fall Hunting: Preparing for the Long Night," *Hampton's Magazine* 24 (April 1910), 500-16; "The Discovery of the North Pole: The Long Arctic Night," *Hampton's Magazine* 24 (May 1910), 653-68; "The Discovery of the North Pole: The Sledge Journey Across the Polar Sea," *Hampton's Magazine* 24 (June 1910), 773-88; "The Discovery of the North Pole: Over the Polar Sea to My 'Farthest North,'" *Hampton's Magazine* 25 (July 1910), 3-18; "The Discovery of the North Pole: The Pole at Last," *Hampton's Magazine* 25 (August 1910), 165-80; "The Discovery of the North Pole: Back to Civilization from the Pole," *Hampton's Magazine* 25 (September 1910), 283-95.

Peary, Robert E. "First Report," in "The Discovery of the Pole," *National Geographic Magazine* 20 (October 1909), 896-915.

Peary, Robert E. *How Peary Reached the North Pole: An Expedition Over the Ice That Went to Its Mark with the Precision of a Military Campaign and Reached the Goal Sought for Centuries*. Washington: Judd & Detweiler, 1910(?).

Peary, Robert E. "Journeys in North Greenland." *Geographical Journal* 11 (March 1898), 213-39.

Peary, Robert E. "Nearest the Pole." *Harper's Monthly Magazine* 114 (February 1907), 335-50 (March 1907), 497-510.

Peary, Robert E. *Nearest the Pole: A Narrative of the Polar Expedition of the Peary Arctic Club in the S.S. Roosevelt, 1905-1906*. New York: Doubleday, Page & Co., 1907.

Peary, Robert E. *The North Pole*. New Introduction by Robert M. Bryce. New York: Cooper Square Press, 2001.

Peary, Robert E. *The North Pole: Its Discovery in 1909 Under the Auspices of the Peary Arctic Club*. New York: Frederick A. Stokes Co., 1910.

Peary, Robert E. *Northward Over the "Great Ice." A Narrative of Life and Work Along the Shores and Upon the Interior Ice-Cap of Northern Greenland in the Years 1886 and 1891-1897*, 2 vols. New York: Frederick A. Stokes Co., 1898.

Schley, W.S., and J.R. Schley. *The Rescue of Greely*. London: Sampson Low, Marston, Searle, and Rivington, 1885(?).

Sverdrup, Otto. *New Land: Four Years in the Arctic Regions*, 2 vols., translated from the Norwegian by Ethel Harriet Hearn. London: Longmans, Green, and Co., 1904.

Sverdrup, Otto. "The Second Norwegian Polar Expedition in the 'Fram,' 1898-1902." *Scottish Geographical Magazine* 19 (1903), 337-53.

Secondary Sources

Abrahamson, Howard S. *Hero in Disgrace: The Life of Arctic Explorer Frederick A. Cook*. New York: Paragon House, 1991.

Abrahamson, Howard S. *National Geographic: Behind America's Lens on the World*. New York: Crown Publishers, 1982.

Adams, Cyrus C. *What Peary Has Discovered: The Polar Problems of Vast Import Solved by His Story—His Perfect Exploration Machine*. N.p., n.d.

Allen, Everett S. *Arctic Odyssey: The Life of Rear Admiral Donald B. MacMillan*. New York: Dodd, Mead & Co., 1962.

American Museum of Natural History, *Annual Report* 44: for 1912 (1913), 45: for 1913 (1914), 46: for 1914 (1915), 47: for 1915 (1916), 48: for 1916 (1917).

Anon. "W. Elmer Ekblaw," in W. Elmer Ekblaw Memorial Index to Economic Geography, Vols. 1-25, 1925-1949. Worcester, MA: Clark University, 1950, vii-xv.

Avery, Tom. *To the End of the Earth: One Epic Journey to the North Pole and the Legend of Peary and Henson*. New York: St. Martin's Press, 2009.

Balch, Edwin S. *The North Pole and Bradley Land*. Philadelphia: Campion and Co., 1913.

Berton, Pierre. *The Quest for the North West Passage and the North Pole, 1818-1900*. New York: Viking, 1988.

Brown, William A. *Morris Ketchum Jesup: A Character Sketch*. New York: Charles Scribner's Sons, 1910.

Bryan, C.D.B., ed. *The National Geographic Society: 100 Years of Adventure and Discovery*. New York: Harry N. Abrams, 1994.

Bryce, Robert M. *Cook & Peary: The Polar Controversy Resolved*. Mechanicsburg, PA: Stackpole Books, 1997.

Chapman, Sally Putnam, with Stephanie Mansfield., *Whistled Like a Bird: The Untold Story of Dorothy Putnam, George Putnam, and Amelia Earhart*. New York: Warner Books, 1997.

Cook, Frederick A. *My Attainment of the Pole* [1911]. New Introduction by Robert M. Bryce. New York: Cooper Square Press, 2001.

Counter, S. Allen. "The Henson Family," *National Geographic Magazine* 174 (September 1988), 422-29.
Counter, S. Allen. *North Pole Legacy: Black, White & Eskimo.* Amherst: University of Massachusetts Press, 1991.
Cowan, Mary Morton. *Captain Mac: The Life of Donald Baxter MacMillan, Arctic Explorer.* Honesdale, PA: Calkins Creek, 2010.
Davies, Eloise E., ed. *Robert E. Peary at the North Pole: A Report by the Foundation for the Promotion of the Art of Navigation.* N.p., 1989.
Davies, Thomas D. "New Evidence Places Peary at the Pole." *National Geographic* 177 (January 1990), 44-61.
Dick, Lyle. *Muskox Land: Ellesmere Island in the Age of Contact.* Calgary, Alberta: University of Calgary Press, 2001.
Dick, Lyle. "'Pibloktoq' (Arctic Hysteria): A Construction of European-Inuit Relations?" *Arctic Anthropology* 32 (1995), 1-42.
Durant, Margery. *My Father.* New York: G.P. Putnam, 1929.
Eames, Hugh. *Winner Lose All: Dr. Cook & the Theft of the North Pole.* Boston: Little, Brown and Co., 1973.
Euller, John. "The Great North Pole Lie." *Bluebook* (September 1953), 6-15.
Fisher, David E. *Across the Top of the World: To the North Pole by Sled, Balloon, Airplane, and Nuclear Icebreaker.* New York: Random House, 1992.
Freed, Stanley A. "Fate of the Crocker Land Expedition." *Natural History* 120 (June 2012), 10-19.
Freeman Andrew A. *The Case for Doctor Cook.* New York: Coward-McCann, 1961.
Gibbons, Russell W. *Frederick Albert Cook: Pioneer American Polar Explorer.* N.p.: Frederick Cook Society, 1965 (2nd ed., 1979).
Gibbons, Russell W. "An Historical Evaluation of the Cook-Peary Controversy: A Critique of the Acceptance by History and Reference Works of the Claims of Robert Edwin Peary Against Those of Frederick Albert Cook as to the Discovery of the North Pole, 1908-09." Department of History, Ohio Northern University, 1954.
Greely, A.W. "The Conquest of the Pole," *Collier's* 44 (16 October 1909), 16-17.
Greely, A.W. *Handbook of Polar Discoveries.* Boston: Little, Brown, 1910.
Greely, A.W. *The Polar Regions in the Twentieth Century: Their Discovery and Industrial Evolution.* Boston: Little, Brown, 1928.
Green, Fitzhugh. *Our Naval Heritage.* New York: Century Co., 1925.
Green, Fitzhugh. *Peary: The Man Who Refused to Fail.* New York: G.P. Putnam's Sons, 1926.
Grosvenor, Gilbert. *The National Geographic Society and Its Magazine.* 3rd ed. Washington, D.C.: National Geographic Society, 1948.
Grosvenor, Gilbert. "Peary's Explorations in the Far North." *National Geographic Magazine* 37 (April 1920), 319-22.
Grover, David H. "Richard E. Byrd and the 1925 MacMillan Arctic Expedition." *Aviation History* (March 2001), xx.
Guttridge, Leonard F. *Ghosts of Cape Sabine: The Harrowing True Story of the Greely Expedition.* New York: G.P. Putnams Sons, 2000.
Guttridge, Leonard F. *Icebound: The Jeannette Expedition's Quest for the North Pole.* Annapolis, MD: Naval Institute Press, 1986.
Hall, Thomas F. *Has the North Pole Been Discovered?* Vol. 2 (Omaha: n.p, 1920).
Hall, Thomas F. *Has the North Pole Been Discovered? An Analytical and Synthetical Review of the Published Narratives of the Two Arctic Explorers: Dr. Frederick A Cook and Civil Engineer Robert E. Peary, U.S.N. Also a Review of the Action of the U.S. Government.* Boston: Richard G. Badger, 1917.
Hall, Thos. F. "The Confession of the Murder of Prof. Marvin." Fitzhugh Green, Sr. Papers, Booth Family Center for Special Collections, Georgetown University Library, Washington, D.C.

Harper, Kenn. *Give Me My Father's Body: The Life of Minik, the New York Eskimo.* South Royalton, VT: Steerforth Press, 2000 (first published in 1986).
Hayes, J. Gordon. *The Conquest of the North Pole: Recent Arctic Explorations.* New York: Macmillan, 1934.
Hayes, J. Gordon. *Robert Edwin Peary: A Record of His Explorations, 1886–1909.* London: Grant Richards & Humphrey Toulmin, [1929].
Hellman, Geoffrey. *Bankers, Bones & Beetles: The First Century of the American Museum of Natural History.* Garden City, NY: Natural History Press, 1968.
Henderson, Bruce. *True North: Peary, Cook, and the Race to the Pole.* New York: W.W. Norton & Co., 2005.
Henighan, Tom. *Vilhjalmur Stefansson: Arctic Explorer.* Toronto: Dundurn Press, 2009.
Herbert, Wally. "Commander Robert E. Peary: Did He Reach the Pole?" *National Geographic Magazine* 174 (September 1988), 387–413.
Herbert, Wally. *The Noose of Laurels: Robert E. Peary and the Race to the North Pole.* New York: Atheneum, 1989.
Hobbs, William H. *Peary.* New York: Macmilllan, 1937.
Hobbs, William H. "Peary: The Ace Among Dog Sledgers," in *Explorer's Club Tales: True Stories of Exploration, Research and Adventure, as Told at the Explorers Club by Men of Daring and Achievement.* New York: Dodd, Mead & Co., 1936, 154–61.
Holland, Clive. *Arctic Exploration and Development c. 500 B.C. to 1915.* New York: Garland Publishing, 1994.
Holland, Clive, ed. *Farthest North: The Quest for the North Pole.* New York: Carroll & Graf, 1994.
Hoyt, Edwin P. *The Last Explorer: The Adventures of Admiral Byrd.* New York: John Day, 1968.
Hudson, George Story. "Exploring Arctic Wastes in the 'Bowdoin.'" *Motor Boat* 18 (25 July 1921), 15–17.
Hunt, William R. *To Stand at the Pole: The Dr. Cook-Admiral Peary North Pole Controversy.* New York: Stein and Day, 1981.
Joerg, W.L.G., ed. *The Geography of the Polar Regions.* New York: American Geographical Society, 1928.
Jones, W.L.G., ed. *The Geography of the Polar Regions: Consisting of A General Characterization of Polar Nature* by Otto Nordenskkold and *A Regional Geography of the Arctic and the Antarctic* by Ludwig Mecking. New York: American Geographical Society, 1928.
Keskitalo, E.C.H. *Negotiating the Arctic: The Construction of an International Region.* New York: Routledge, 2004.
Krabbe, Thomas N. *Greenland: Its Nature, Inhabitants, and History,* trans. from the Danish by Annie I. Fausbøll. London: Oxford University Press, 1930.
Kroeber, A.L. "The Eskimo of Smith Sound." *American Museum of Natural History Bulletin* 12 (1900), 265–.
Lagerbom, Charles H. "Dirigo in the Arctic: Donald B. MacMillan, Harrison J. Hunt, and the Crocker Land Expedition, 1913–1917." *Maine History* 46 (2 June 2012), 169–194.
Laugrand, Frederic B., and Jarich G. Oosten. *Inuit Shamanism and Christianity: Transitions and Transformations in the Twentieth Century.* Montreal and Kingston: McGill-Queen's University Press, 2010.
Lewin, W. Henry. *Did Peary Reach the Pole?* London: Simpkin, Marshall, Hamilton, Kent & Co., 1911.
Lewin, W. Henry. *The Great North Pole Fraud.* London: C.W. Daniel Co., 1935.
Lopez, Barry. *Arctic Dreams: Imagination and Desire in a Northern Landscape.* New York: Charles Scribner's Sons, 1986. Also Bantam Books, 1987.
MacMillan, Miriam, *I Married an Explorer.* London: Hurst & Blackett, 1951.
Marcus, G.J. *The Conquest of the North Pole.* New York: Oxford University Press, 1981.
Markham, Sir Clements R. *The Lands of Silence: A History of Arctic and Antarctic Exploration.* Cambridge: University Press, 1921.

Mary-Rousseliere, Guy. *Qitdlarssuaq: L'Histoire d'Une Migration Polaire.* Paris: Paulsen, 2008. Previously published Montreal University Press, 1980.
Maxtone-Graham, John. *Safe Return Doubtful: The Heroic Age of Polar Exploration.* New York: Charles Scribner's Sons, 1988.
McCannon, John. *A History of the Arctic: Nature, Exploration and Exploitation.* London: Reaktion Books, 2012.
McGoogan, Ken. *Race to the Polar Sea: The Heroic Adventure of Elisha Kent Kane.* Berkeley, CA: Counterpoint, 2008.
Merkur, Daniel. *Becoming Half Hidden: Shamanism and Initiation Among the Inuit.* Stockholm: Almqvist & Wiksell International, 1985.
Mirsky, Jeannette. *To the North: The Story of Arctic Exploration from Earliest Times to the Present.* New York: Viking Press, 1934.
Molett, William E. *Robert Peary and Matthew Henson at the North Pole.* Southaven, MS: William E. Molett, 1996.
Morrissey, Muriel E., and Carol L. Osborne. *Amelia, My Courageous Sister: Biography of Amelia Earhart.* Santa Clara, CA: Osborne Publisher, 1987.
Mosley, Leonard. *Lindberg: A Biography.* New York: Doubleday & Co., 1976.
Murphy, Charles J.V. *Struggle: The Life and Exploits of Commander Richard E. Byrd.* New York: Frederick A. Stokes Co., 1928.
Neatby, L.H. *Conquest of the Last Frontier.* Athens: Ohio University Press, 1966.
Neatby, Leslie H. *The Search for Franklin.* New York: Walker and Co., 1970.
Pohl, Frederick J. "Introduction" to Frederick A. Cook, *Return from the Pole.* New York: Pellegrini & Cudahy, 1951.
Preston, Douglas J. *Dinosaurs in the Attic: An Excursion into the American Museum of Natural History.* New York: St. Martin's Press, 1986.
Putnam, George P. *Mariner of the North: The Life of Captain Bob Bartlett.* New York: Duell, Sloan and Pearce, 1947.
Putnam, George P. *Soaring Wings: A Biography of Amelia Earhart.* New York: Harcourt, Brace and Co., 1939.
Putnam, George P. *Wide Margins: A Publisher's Autobiography.* New York: Harcourt Brace and Co., 1942.
Rawlins, Dennis. *Peary at the North Pole: Fact or Fiction?* Washington: Robert B. Luce, 1973.
Rickard, T.A. "The Use of Meteoric Iron." *Journal of the Royal Anthropological Institute of Great Britain and Ireland* 71 (1941), 55–66.
Robinson, Bradley. *Dark Companion.* New York: Robert M. McBride & Co., 1947.
Robinson, Michael F. *The Coldest Crucible: Arctic Exploration and American Culture.* Chicago: University of Chicago Press, 2006.
Rood, Henry E. "The Coming of Cook: A New Chapter of Polar History." *Saturday Evening Post* 182 (16 April 1910), 17–19.
Ross, M. J. *Polar Pioneers: John Ross and James Clark Ross.* Montreal: McGill-Queen's University Press, 1994.
Ross, W. Gillies. "George Comer (1858–1937)." *Arctic* 36 (September 1983), 294–95.
Sanger, Alexander. *Margery Durant Goes to Africa 1931-2.* N.p.: Blurb Inc., 2009.
Savours, Ann. *The Search for the Northwest Passage.* New York: St. Martin's Press, 1999.
Sides, Hampton. *In the Kingdom of Ice: The Grand and Terrible Polar Voyage of the USS Jeannette.* New York: Doubleday, 2014.
Stafford, Edward P. "Descendants of the Expedition." *National Geographic Magazine* 174 (September 1988), 414–21.
Stam, David H., and Deirdre C. Stam. *Books on Ice: British and American Literature of Polar Explorations.* New York: Times Books, 1987.
Stefansson, Vilhjalmur. *Unsolved Mysteries of the Arctic.* New York: Macmillan Company, 1939.
Steger, Will, with Paul Schurke. *North to the Pole.* New York: Times Books, 1987.
Stuhl, Andrew. *Unfreezing the Arctic: Science, Colonialism, and the Transformation of Inuit Lands.* Chicago: University of Chicago Press, 2016.

Todd, Alden. *Abandoned: The Story of the Greely Arctic Expedition 1881–1884*, 2d ed., Fairbanks: University of Alaska Press, 2001. Originally published New York: McGraw-Hill, 1961.
Turnbull, Archibald D., and Clifford L. Lord. *History of United States Naval Aviation.* New Haven: Yale University Press, 1949.
Vaughan, Richard. *Northwest Greenland: A History.* Orono: University of Maine Press, 1991.
Weems, John E. *Peary: The Explorer and the Man.* Boston, Houghton Mifflin Co., 1967.
Weems, John E. *Race for the Pole.* Preface by Vilhjalmur Stefansson. New York: Henry Holt, 1960.
Weisberger, Bernard A. *The Dream Maker: William C. Durant, Founder of General Motors.* Boston: Little, Brown and Co., 1979.
Welky, David. *A Wretched and Perilous Situation: In Search of the Last Arctic Frontier.* New York: W.W. Norton, 2017.
Wissler, Clark. "Archaeology of the Polar Eskimo." *Anthropological Papers of the American Museum of Natural History,* 22 (1918) 103–66.
Wright, Theon. *The Big Nail: The Story of the Cook-Peary Feud.* New York: John Day Co., 1970.

Index

Access to an Open Polar Sea in Connection with the Search After Sir John Franklin and His Companions, 1853, '54, '55 1
accident 7, 96
account 61, 74, 160, 188-189
achievement 209-210
Adams Newspaper Service 187
Advance 2-3, 82, 94
advance party 43, 45
adventure 147
Africa 207
Agassiz, Luis 6
agreement 21, 23, 149, 152-153, 156, 158, 162-166
Ahdukahingwah 92
Ahlningwah 106
Ahnahdoo 95-96
Ahngodablaho 97
Ahnokiah 93
Ahnowka 32, 94
Ahpellah 32, 43
air 188-189; travel 188
aircraft 170
Akpan 38
Akpoodashah 94
Alakrasina 66-67
Alaska 170, 202
alcohol 208
Alcoholics Anonymous 108
ale 137
Alert 3, 124
Alexander 1
Alexandra Fiord 61
Algonquian language 9
alkalinity 109
Alle alle 84
Allegro 173
Allen, Jerome L. 14, 20, 22-23, 26, 31, 41, 71, 76, 91, 105, 130-133, 137, 139, 141, 146, 148, 160, 176

Allen, Sir Young 124-125
Alopecurus 87
Alopecurus alpinus 89, 111
Alpine chickweed 86
altitude 119, 159-160
Amedeo, Luigi 5
American Art Association Gallery 206
American Consul General in Copenhagen 146
American Geographical Society 7, 13, 18, 20, 23, 27, 40, 65, 123, 125, 127, 147-158, 160-168, 204; committee 166; council 166
American Geological Society 161; members 165
American Government 63
American Library Association 192
American Magazine 188
American Merchant Marine 188, 191
American Mercury 188-189
American Minister in Copenhagen 123
American Museum Glacier 124
American Museum Journal 123, 152-153, 157
American Museum of Natural History 6-7, 13-14, 18, 20-23, 27, 34, 36, 38, 40, 48, 61, 65-66, 83, 92, 95, 97, 101, 119, 123, 126, 129, 132-133, 139, 141, 147, 150-151, 155, 157-162, 164, 167-168, 179-180, 188
American Museum's Honorary Committee on the Crocker Land Expedition 16, 129, 146
American Secretary of State 63, 185
American State Department 134
ammunition 50
Amund Ringnes 5, 76; Island 121, 123
Amundsen, Roald 5, 171, 173-174, 188
anarchy 112
Anchors Aweigh 192
Anderson Gallery 206

240 Index

Andrews, Roy Chapman 189, 192
Androsace septentrionalis 86
Anetalak 173
angakuts 40
Annapolis 192, 195, 198
Anoritok 43–44, 105–106, 108
Antennaria alpine 87
anthology 174
An Anthropological Study of the Origin of the Eskimo Culture 180
Apsidium fragrans 90
Arbuthnot, Charles R. Lieut. 125
archaeology 126, 155
archipelago 109, 210
Arctic Archipelago 125
An Arctic Boat Journey in the Autumn of 1854 2
Arctic Duty with the Crocker Land Expedition 159
Arctic Explorations: The Second Grinnell Expedition in Search of Sir John Franklin 2
Arctic heather 86
Arctic poppy 86
Arctic Researches, and Life Among the Esquimaux: Being the Narrative of an Expedition in Search of Sir John Franklin 3
Arcturus 75
Arkansas 180
Arklio 45, 49, 98, 100, 106
Armour, Allison 163–166
Army and Navy Register 16
Army Medical Corps 16
Army-Navy Club 199
Arnica Alpine 87–88
arrangement 134, 154
article 126–127, 152–153, 157–159, 179–180, 186–189, 195, 210
ascent 119
astronomical observations 161
astronomy 22; astronomical records 160
Atchison, KS 204
Atlantic 207
Atlantic Monthly 74
Augpalartok 135
Austin College 24
Austin, Nichols and Company 141
authority 22, 148
Author's Club 74
autobiography 174
autogiro 205
autumn 43
avalanche 64, 67
Aviation Service 160
Axel Heiberg 5, 50; Island 21, 210; Land 6, 17, 54, 55, 57, 60, 92, 161, 171; Shore 48
azimuth 106, 124

Bache Peninsula 98–99, 119
Baffin Bay 5
Baffin Island 3, 34, 173
Baffin Land 109, 169, 172, 202
Baine, Johnston and Company 141
Baird Inlet 124
Baker, Frank C. 180
Balchen, Bert 172
Balle, Mr. 143, 145
Bangor, ME 26, 178
barometric records 160
Barrell, Joseph 14
barrier 109
Bartlett, Robert (Bob) 36, 133, 137, 140–141, 148, 170, 201–202
base 171
Batrachium Paucistamineum 88
Battle Harbor 28, 131
Bay Fiord 47, 83, 99–100, 122
Bayley, W.S. 14, 17–18, 27, 101, 179
bear 41, 43, 45, 97, 100–101, 106–107, 116, 119; hunt 81, 99, 141; meat 96, 122, 135
bearskin 75, 113
Beechey Island 2
Beechwood Point 117
Beecroft, Chester 35
beekeeping 179
Beitstadt Fiord 45, 60, 98–99
Belcher, Sir Edward 121
Belcher Channel 121
Belcher Island 122
Belgian Antarctic Expedition 173–174
Bellevue Hospital 35
Bend, OR 201
Bend Bulletin 201
benefactor 27
Bennett, Floyd 171–172, 192
Bennett, James Gordon 3
Bennett Island 4
Bergson, Henri 74; *Creative Evolution* 74
Bering Strait 4
Berlin 202
Betula nana 87
Bickmore, Albert S. 6
Binney, Dorothy 201–202, 205
Binney, Edwin 201
biology 78
biota 80
bird 76, 80, 84–85, 90, 94, 96; life 111
biscuit 41, 93, 95, 97, 107, 121, 176; damaged 134
Bjornesundet 120, 122
black brant 111
Black Cape 144
blizzard 55, 58–59, 78, 98, 101, 118, 161
blood 58, 135

Bloodhound 141
blubber 38, 43, 79, 113, 137, 144
board of trustees 14, 65; National Geographic Society 170
Boas, Franz 34, 125
boat 28, 82, 130, 132, 138–140; power boat 132
Bob Bartlett: Master Mariner 192
body 58–59, 67
bog 86
Böggild, D.B. 39
Boothia Felix 5
Borup, George 7, 13–14, 101, 168; *A Tenderfoot with Peary* 13
Borup, Henry D. 16, 24
Borup Fiord 101
Borup Lodge 30, 43, 61, 74, 86–87, 89, 92, 120
Boston 27, 158, 172, 193, 204–206
botany 22, 155, 179, 210
Bowdoin 169–170, 172–173
Bowdoin College 24, 26–27
Bowdoin Medical College 26
Bowman, Isaiah 127, 147–148, 151–154, 157–159, 161–163, 165–166, 180, 185–186, 202–204
Bowring and Company 141
Boy's Life 188
brachiopod 101
Brainard, Sgt. David 4
Branta bernicia 84
bread 41
Bremidae 179
bridge 50
Bridgman, Herbert L. 16, 72, 168
British Arctic Expedition 124
Bronx 35
Bronxville 207
Brooklyn Navy Yard 27, 34
Brooklyn Standard Union 72
Brother John's Glacier 29, 41, 159
Brown City 151
Brun, C. 63–64
Brunswick 24
Brunton Compass 122
Brussels 202
Bryder, Doctor 136
bryozoan fauna 179
Buchanan Bay 41, 44, 124
budget 133
bug 41, 86
Bulletin of the American Museum 167
bumblebee 179
Bureau of Aeronautics 199
Bureau of Fisheries 133
Bureau of Navigation 188, 191, 193; Silver Star award 191

Bureau of Ordnance 26
burgomaster 84
burial 35
Burry Port 205
Bustin's Island 24
Byrd, Richard E. 170–172, 189, 192, 199–201, 203–204, 208

cablegram 123, 131, 133, 139, 141
Cabot quilting 29
cache 44–45, 47–48, 60, 101, 104–107, 119, 122, 135
Cadogan Inlet 124
Cagni, Umberto 5
cairn 49–50, 53, 55, 92, 99–100, 102, 106, 121–122; dilapidated 107
Cairn Point 41, 105
Cairo 207
Calamagrostis 87
California 73
Cammowitz 45
camp 47, 50, 52, 61, 80, 99, 101–103, 105, 121–122, 135
Camp Archer 104
Camp Ekblaw 99
Camp Etookashoo 100
Camp Green 99
Camp MacMillan 99
Camp Marvin 103–104
Camp Remington 102
Camp Tanquary 99
Campanula uniflora 88
Campbell, Edwin R. 206
Campbell, William C. 207
Canada 151; government 23, 71, 134
cancer 143
cannibalism 5, 60
Canon Fiord 83, 171
canyon 102–103, 110
Cap York 146
Cape Abernathy 118
Cape Alexander 37–38, 78, 84, 130
Cape Atholl 138
Cape Axel Heiberg 52
Cape Baird 104
Cape Calhoun 105–106
Cape Camperdown 119
Cape Columbia 3
Cape Constitution 104–107
Cape Faraday 124
Cape Herschel 124
Cape Holm 142
Cape Independence 107
Cape Ingersoll 106
Cape Isabella 124–125
Cape James Ross 1

Cape Kent 105
Cape Leiper 105, 107
Cape Ludvig 121
Cape Madison 107
Cape Melville 36–37, 135
Cape Nathorst 121
Cape Parry 78, 82, 117
Cape Russell 105
Cape Rutherford 41, 44
Cape Sabine 5, 40, 43–44, 103, 119, 123–124, 132, 161, 170
Cape Scott 105
Cape Sedon 81, 96, 135
Cape Sheridan 4, 85, 186
Cape South West 120, 122
Cape Thomas Hubbard 13, 16, 21, 40, 47–48, 50, 52–53, 55, 58, 60–61, 72, 77, 152, 161, 171
Cape William Wood 106
Cape Wolstenholme 71
Cape York 21, 28–30, 34, 36, 38, 96, 127, 131–135, 138, 147, 176
Carex 87, 89
cargo 28, 132
caribou 32–33, 49, 60, 83, 90, 94–95, 99, 112, 116, 137; tallow 103
Carnegie Institution 23, 170
cartography 22
Casco Bay 24
Cash Contributions Not Designated as to Guarantee 23
Cassiope tetragona 86–87
caterpillar 122
Central Africa 189, 207
Central Asia 189
The Central Eskimo 126
Century Collier's 188
Cepphus manditi 84
Cerastium alpinum 86
Champaign 180
Chandler Fiord 103
Channel Ports 207
chant 34, 40
Chantier 172
U.S.S. *Chaumont* 192
Chicago 24, 172, 187, 205
Chicago Field Museum 172, 173
Chicago World Fair 208
children 65, 112, 136, 144–145, 209
chocolate 60
Christianity 184
Christianshab 136
Christmas 42, 95
Christmas Eve 135
Clarence Head 123–125, 161
Clark University 180

Clear the Decks 192
climate 85, 108, 142, 181
clothing 112
Cluett 125, 129–134, 138–140, 148, 175, 177–178; *see also* George B. Cluett
coal 30, 72, 83, 99, 122, 133; bituminous 119; shortage 171
coast 106, 110, 123–124, 137–138; Greenland 109; uncharted 121
coastline 173
cocaine 81
Cochlearia officinalis 86, 88
coffee 97, 130, 137, 144
cold 44, 95
Colgate University 6, 23
Collembola 80, 180
colony 29, 142–143, 145
Columbia University 7, 34
Comer, George 125–126, 129–132, 139, 155, 161, 176–177; *The Central Eskimo* 126
Comers Kitchen Midden 126
Comer's Midden 126–127
Committee in Charge of the Crocker Land Expedition 14, 17, 23, 92, 131, 134, 140–141, 148–149, 165–167
communication 71, 73; wireless 92–93
compensation 64, 66–67, 152, 178
Comptroller of Central Park 6
confession 56, 63, 186
"The Confession of the Murder of Prof. Marvin" 185
Conger Mountains 5, 102
Congress 5, 205
Connecticut 205, 208–209
contact 114
contract 26, 129, 133, 153–156, 158, 162–165, 177
contretemps 153
contribution 123, 152, 157, 165
Contributors of Books to the Expedition 23
controversy 153–154; Cook-Peary 174
cook 22
Cook, Frederick, Dr. 6, 32, 173, 182, 204; *My Attainment of the Pole* 32
Coolidge, Pres. Calvin 172
Cooper, John Hampton 206–207
Copenhagen 72, 76, 94, 123, 131–133, 139–140, 146–147, 183, 187
Copenhagen University 29, 172
coral 101
Cornwall Island 122
corpse 35
correspondence 164
Cosmopolitan 205
cost 134, 138

Index 243

Creative Evolution 74
Crescent Beach 14
crime 185
Crocker, George 6
Crocker Land 6–7, 21, 39, 49–50, 52, 56, 58, 61–62, 72–74, 92, 95, 134, 147, 153–154, 161, 177; Expedition 119, 128–129, 140–141, 149, 159, 164–165, 168, 175, 187, 209–210
cub 107, 121
Culmore 205
Czar Alexander III 4

damage 21
Danbury Hospital 208
Danes 138–139, 142
Daniel, Robert W. 206
Daniels, Josephus 27, 187, 191
Danish Administration 64
Danish Arctic Station in Disko 136–137
Danish Government 142, 172
Danish Legation in Washington, D.C. 63, 66, 185
Danish Minister of Foreign Affairs 63–65; see also Brun, C.
Danish Mission 64
Danish Museum 38
Danmark 126, 131, 134, 138–140, 146, 148, 177–178
Danmarks Natur 180
darkness 45
data 21–22, 78, 127, 159–160, 163, 172
Davis, Noel 199–200
death 22, 58, 60–63, 95, 168, 184, 208
debt 163, 165–166
deficiency 157
Deisler, Clemens 208
Delineator 188
DeLong, Lt. George Washington 3–4; *The Voyage of the Jeannette: The Ship and Ice Journals of George W. DeLong* 4
Denison House 204
Denmark 28–29, 63, 129, 133, 136, 139, 142, 145, 185, 203
Department of Commerce 133
Department of Terrestrial Magnetism 170
departure 27, 46, 50, 106
deposit 126, 156
depot 41
description 126
Detroit 170
SS. *Diana* 20, 23, 27–28
diarrhea 77
diary 73, 92, 147, 157, 165
Dick Byrd: Air Explorer 192
Dickerson, Mary Cynthia 152

Did Peary Reach the Pole? 174
dinner 27, 32–33, 42, 72, 144
dirigible 171
Disco Bay 133, 145
Disco Island 72, 140
dispatch 125
dispute 151, 173
discovery 108, 123, 126, 147, 152, 156, 159, 169
Discovery 3, 124
Discovery Harbor 4
disease 107
dog 30, 43–46, 48–50, 52–53, 55–58, 60–61, 67, 75–77, 81–84, 93, 97, 100, 102–103, 107–108, 112–116, 117–120, 136–137, 141, 161, 181, 188; team 41, 59, 73, 92, 98, 103, 116, 121–124, 135, 145
dog driver 28, 115–116, 118
dovekie 84, 111, 113
Drabae 86, 88
drown 7
drug 81; narcotic 208
Dryas integrifolia 86–87
Dryopteris fragrans 86
Durant, Margery 206–209; *My Father* 207
Durant, William Crapo 206–207
dynamite 29
dysentery 45

E. Scheuchzeri 89
Earhart, Amelia 204–207; *The Fun of It* 205; *20 HRS. 40 MIN.: Our Flight in the Friendship* 205
earthquake 188
East Africa 189
East Chester 207
East Haddam 129
Easter Island 180
Eastern Maine General Hospital 178
Easy Acres 208
ecology 108–117
Economic Geography 180
Effingham, IL 24
Egede, Hans 28, 143
Egedesminde 64, 133–134, 136, 139, 143, 145
egg 76, 83–85, 94, 112–113, 144; eider eggs 81
eider duck 84, 93, 111, 113, 117
Ekblaw, W. Elmer 14, 16–18, 20, 22–23, 27, 31, 36–39, 41, 44, 47, 60, 73–76, 78, 80, 83, 92, 98, 100–108, 117–118, 130, 132, 134–140, 147, 153, 155, 158, 161, 163, 176, 178–181, 210; botany 85–86, 88–89; "Correlation of the Devonian System of the Rock Island Region" 24; Inuit 74, 108–

114; Inuit dogs 114; near-drowning 82; "The Origin of the Eskimo" 180; origins and education 24; Smith Sound Inuit 91, 119, 177; snow-blindness 80-81; Stratigraphy and Paleontology of the Devonian System in Rock Island, Illinois" 24
electricity 22, 30
Ellef Ringnes 5, 76, 119; Island 121
Ellesmere Island 2-6, 32, 40, 43-44, 74, 78, 83, 98-99, 119, 123-125, 161, 170-171, 210
Ellesmere Land 45-47, 80, 98, 161, 189; Ellesmereland 83; Glacier 122
Elliott, Natalie Wheeler 183, 207
Ellsworth, Lincoln 14-15, 204
Empetrum nigrum 87
Emuckkotailya 84
Encyclopaedia Britannica 204
England 200, 207
English Government 134
entomology 25, 80, 180, 210
entourage 172
environment 108, 112, 181
equipment 21, 45-46, 76, 83, 102, 126, 130, 133-134, 136, 176
Equisetum arvense 89
Equisetum variegatum 89
Erebus 1
Eric the Red 28
Ericson, Leif 28
Erik 28-29
Eriophorum polystachium 87, 89
ermine 100, 112
Esayoo 98-100, 102-105
Eskimo 9, 38, 58, 61-62, 81, 91, 130; *see also* Esquimau
Eskimo Place Names and Aid to Conversation 175
Esquimau 64-65
Etah 28-29, 36, 39-41, 43-45, 47, 49, 54, 60-62, 71-72, 76, 78-79, 81, 83, 85, 88, 90, 94-95, 97, 99, 107-108, 119-121, 123-124, 126, 129, 131-134, 139-140, 143, 147, 159-161, 170-171, 179-180, 210
ether 42
ethnology 22
Etookashoo 32, 45, 48, 50, 53-54, 55, 60-61, 97-98, 100, 102-105
Eureka Sound 43, 45-47, 60, 67, 83, 92, 100, 119-120, 122
Europe 188, 200, 207
evidence 174
excavation 126-127
excursion 41
executive committee 14, 71, 140

existence 44-45
Exmouth Island 122
expedition 42-44, 64-65, 72, 80, 100, 107, 109, 125, 130-131, 133-134, 139-141, 148, 151, 156, 158-159, 169, 173-174, 178, 189
expenditures 157
expense 130, 147, 179, 194
exploration 44, 80, 123; Arctic 166; Viking 172
explorer 109, 121-124, 132, 140-141, 145, 152, 173, 188-189; Arctic 147
expulsion 22

failure 44, 175
Fait Garros 187
Falco islandius 84
family 112
famine 90, 107
Far North 210
Fargo, ND 179
Faroe Islands 133, 139
fat 145
Fechteler, Rear Adm. Augustus 190
Federal Departments 23
feet 43-44, 47, 50, 55
fieldwork 107
Fifth Avenue 193; parade 205
The Film Finds Its Tongue 192
Finlay Island 119, 123
Finlay Land 123, 127
fiord 41
firms 23
flag 53, 82, 94, 105
Flagler Bay 17, 21, 45, 119, 122
Flagler Fiord 119, 123, 171
Fleischer, Mr. 145
flight 170-172, 205; nonstop 200; solo 204; transatlantic 199, 202, 205
Flint 206
flock 80
floeberg 104
Florida 207, 209
flower 83, 87-90, 94
fog 108, 122
Fogo 71
Fokker, Anthony 200
Fokker aircraft 171-172, 204
Folsom, Justus W. 80
Folson, Justin 180
Fonck, Rene 199
food 46, 53, 55, 57-59, 71, 78, 105, 107, 112-113, 122, 132, 134-135, 147, 176, 181, 185, 187; shortage 81; supply 90, 98, 111, 115, 132
foot 76, 78, 95
Ford, Edsel 170-172

Ford, James B. 149, 164
Fort Conger 4, 5, 98, 103-104
Fosheim Peninsula 48, 60, 100
Fought for Annapolis 192
Foulke Fiord 28, 109, 159
foxes 44, 48, 82, 100-101, 112, 178
Fram 5
France 200
Franklin, Sir John 1-3, 121, 147; expedition 119
Franklin Island 104
Franz Joseph Land 5
fraternity 24
Freeport 24, 147, 161
Freuchen, Peter 29, 36-37, 62-63, 76, 78-79, 81, 83, 92, 94-97, 126, 129-130, 132, 138-139, 178, 204; on death of Peeahwahto 66; on socialism 96
friendship 30, 43
Friendship 204-205
From the Greeks to Darwin 7
Frost, Holloway 192
fruit 42
fuel 58, 107, 113
fulmar 117
The Fun of It 205
funds 16-17, 160, 164-165, 167, 180, 199
funeral 35
fur 113

General Motors Corporation 206
generator 41
Geographical Report of the Crocker Land Expedition, 1913-1917 167
Geographical Review 123-125, 159, 165, 180
geology 22, 24, 46, 78, 80, 83, 98, 127, 147, 155, 179-180, 210
George B. Cluett 129, 131, 138, 140-141, 182; see also Cluett
George Borup 82-83
George Borup Guarantee 23
George Matthew Adams newspaper syndicate 187
George Washington University 14, 26
Georgetown University 23
Germany 189
ghostwriter 189
Gjoa Haven 5
glacier 41, 44-46, 77, 99, 101-102, 107, 109-110, 119, 122, 124, 147, 188; ice 123
glaciology 123
glaucus gull 84
Gletscher Fiord 120, 122
Godhavn 67, 136-137, 139-140, 142, 147
Godthaab 29, 172-173, 189
Golden Twenties 209

Goodsell, Dr. J.W. 16, 33, 40
Gordon, Lou 205
Gould, Albert 173
G.P Putnam's Sons 201-202, 205, 207
Grant, Madison 27, 163-166
Grant Land 17, 53, 80, 85, 98, 100-101, 103
graphite 177
grass 87, 89, 100; blue 89, 111-112
Gravesend Bay 200
The Great North Pole Fraud 174
Greeley Fiord 5, 83, 92, 98, 100-101
Greely, Adolphus W. 4, 102, 124; starvation party 124
Greely Expedition 170
Green, Fitzhugh 14, 16, 19-20, 22-23, 30, 42-45, 47-48, 50-54, 55-58, 60-61, 63, 65, 67, 73-74, 76, 78, 83, 91, 105-106, 108, 130-134, 137-139, 141, 143-148, 159-161, 163, 176, 182, 187, 206-207; address to the navy 191; *Anchors Aweigh* 192; *Arctic Duty* 192; *Arctic Duty with the Crocker Land Expedition* 159; "Big Crisis" 201; bird hunting 84; *Bob Bartlett: Master Mariner* 192; *Clear the Decks* 192; diary 32; *Dick Byrd: Air Explorer* 192; on the difficulties of the modern explorer 201; on Ellesmere Land 46; "Facts About Our Navy" 187; *The Film Finds Its Tongue* 192, 205; financial crisis 197-198; *Fought for Annapolis* 192; "Getting in the First Shot" 187; heart condition 196, 208; history of the navy 193-195; *Hold 'Em Navy* 192; *I'll Never Move Again* 192; on the Inuit 28, 33, 41, 49, 92-93, 184-185, 210; *Martin Johnson: Lion Hunter* 192, 205; *Midshipmen All* 192; *The Mystery of the Erik* 192; *Our Naval Heritage* 192, 195; "Our New Navy" 187; *Peary: The Man Who Refused to Fail* 192; resignation from naval service 199-201; return from Crocker Land 183-186; *The Romance of Modern Exploration* 192; *Roy Chapman Andrews: Dragon Hunter* 192, 205; "Running the British Blockade" 187; "seclusion of the soul" 200; *Shipmates* 195; *Shore Leave* 195; *Some Famous Sea Fights* 192; *Uncle Sam's Sailors* 192; *Won for the Fleet: A Story of Annapolis* 192; on working for Putnam 202-204; "The Worst Menace of Another War" 194; on writing 208; writings 187-192; *Z R Wins* 192
Greenland 28-29, 32, 35, 39, 61, 64, 78, 85-86, 88, 108, 123, 133, 136, 139, 141, 145, 147, 161, 170-172, 177, 179-180, 183, 189, 195, 201-202, 210; fauna 80; flora

89–90; North Greenland 129, 140, 203; South Greenland 36, 95, 138, 141–142
Greenland by the Polar Sea: The Story of the Thule Expedition from Melville Bay to Cape Morris Jesup 180
Greenland Ice Cap 21
Greenland Mining Company 134
Greenough, John 149, 151–157, 159–160, 162–167
Grenfell Association 129
Grenville Bay 38, 80
Grinnell, Henry 2–5
Grinnell Land 2, 83
Grinnell Peninsula 122
guano 89
Guest, Frederick E. 204
guillemot 84, 93, 111, 113, 117; Mandt's guillemot 84
gyrfalcon 84

habit 43
habitat 108
habitation 109, 112
Hadley, Arthur T. 27
Hall, Charles Francis 3, 83, 106; *Arctic Researches, and Life Among the Esquimaux: Being the Narrative of an Expedition in Search of Sir John Franklin* 3
Hall, Thomas F. 185–186, 203; "The Confession of the Murder of Prof. Marvin" 185; *Has the North Pole Been Discovered?* 204
Hall Basin 107
Hamble 207
U.S.S. *Hancock* 27
Hans 96
Hans Egede 132–133, 136, 139–140
Hans Island 104
harbor 29, 82
Harbor Grace 205
hardship 82
hare 111–112; Arctic hare 120
Harker, O.A. 65
Harper, Kenn 34
Harper & Brothers 156, 159
Harper's Magazine 72, 152–153, 158, 162–163
harpoon 43, 49, 117, 127; line 113
Hartford 208
Harvard Club, Boston 194
Harvard Division of Anthropology 23
Harvard University 151, 162, 201
Has the North Pole Been Discovered? 204
hash 60
Hassel Sound 121
hatchet 46, 51–52

Hayes, Isaac Israel 2–3, 123; expedition 95–96
Hayes, Isaac Israel: *An Arctic Boat Journey in the Autumn of 1854* 2; *The Land of Desolation: Being a Personal Narrative of Adventure in Greenland* 3; *Narrative of the Second Arctic Expedition Made by Charles F. Hall ... and Residence Among the Eskimos During the Years 1864–'69* 3; *The Open Polar Sea: A Narrative of a Voyage of Discovery Towards the North Pole, in the Schooner United States* 3, 96
Hayes Sound 44, 47
Hecla 1
Hendriksen Sound 121
herd 48, 100, 102, 104
Hesperis pallasii 88
High Priest 143, 145
Hill Cate 83
Hold 'Em Navy 192
Holstenborg 132–133, 136, 140
home 107, 119, 130, 136–138, 173
Home Geographic Monthly 180, 188
homecoming 128
Honorary Committee of the Crocker Land Expedition 17, 19, 39, 178
Hope 34, 37
Hotel Astor 35
Hovey, Edmund O. 14, 16–20, 23, 27, 39, 71–72, 76–77, 92, 126–127, 129–134, 137–140, 147–148, 151, 157, 159, 162–163, 166, 175–178
How Peary Reached the Pole: The Personal Story of His Assistant 174
Hubbard, Thomas H. 16
Hudson Bay 78, 109, 115, 125
Hughes, Charles Evans 63, 178
Humboldt Glacier 85, 94, 105, 107, 109, 124
Hunt, Harrison J. (Hal) 20, 22–23, 26, 36, 41–45, 61–63, 74, 82, 90, 93–95, 105, 123, 130, 132, 134–141, 143, 176–178; on Allen 43; diary 32; on Eskimo 32; on MacMillan 44
Huntington, Archer M. 27
Huntington, Collis P. 27
Huronian sandstones 110
Hut 29
Hyde, William DeWitt 27
Hyde Park High School 204
Hyperit Point 120
hysteria 33

ice 28, 37, 46, 50–52, 54, 59, 76, 80, 82, 90, 95, 101, 103–105, 109–110, 112, 115–119, 122, 124, 129, 131, 133–136, 138–141, 148, 171, 181

Index

Iceland 28
icepick 102
U.S.S. Idaho 26
Igalorawit 135
Igdlorsuit 145
igloo 29, 31–32, 38, 41, 44, 47–50, 53, 55, 57, 59, 93, 96, 112, 120, 122, 181; Inuit 134; native 145
Iglorssuit Peninsula 136
Ikerask 139
I'll Never Move Again 192
Illinois Arctic Club 20
Illinois Magazine 20
Illinois Petroleum Trust 180
illness 21, 32
impasse 161
import 29
Inaloo 93
indemnity 66
Independence Day 94
Indian Head 191–192, 198
indictment 208
influenza 44
Inglefield 123
Inglefield Gulf 17, 38, 109–110, 129, 184
ingot 38–39
Inighito 37
insect 80, 86, 90, 179–180
Institute for Living 208
instruments 23
insubordination 22
intermarriage 142
International Aeronautics 188
Inuit 13, 28, 30–31, 37, 40, 43–44, 46–48, 50–52, 59–60, 63, 65, 74, 77–79, 81–83, 94–95, 98–100, 102, 105, 119, 121–122, 132, 136, 141–143, 147, 161, 185, 208; character 112–113; companion 184, 210; contact with Euro-Americans 33; culture 108, 127, 181; dances 126; Danish Greenland Inuit 109; dress 181; dolichocephalic dimensions 42; encampment 106; funeral 35; habitations 101; helpers 72; hunting 181; legends 173; material culture 125; Polar Inuit 108, 115, 127, 181; psychology of time 114; religion 34, 91, 143; schools 173; wives 29; words and phrases 160
Inuit Pass 122
Inuit Point 124
Inuk 9i
investigation 170
investor 170
Ireland 205
iron 36; culture 127
Ironside Mountain 37

Ironstone Mountain 38
Isabella 1
Ittibloo 95
Itukusuk 65

Jacobshavn 145
jaegers 111
James, Edmund J. 7, 15–17, 19–20, 27, 39, 101
James, Henry 74
James, Walter B. 16, 27, 151
James, William 74
James River 206
Jeanette 3, 4
Jeannie 36
Jerusalem 207
Jesup, Morris K. 6, 34–35, 77
Joerg, W.L.G. 124–125, 127–128
John Ross Mountain 124
Johnson, Martin 189, 198
Jones Sound 83
Josephine Ford 171
journal 22, 73 126, 160; of Geographical Society 151
journey 45, 123, 134, 152, 157, 162, 173
Joy Forever 92–93
Juan Fernandez Group 180
Juncus 89

Kane Basin 2, 98, 109
Kane, Elisha Kent 2, 41, 82, 94, 105–107, 123, 145, 147; *Access to an Open Polar Sea in Connection with the Search After Sir John Franklin and His Companions* 2; Access to an Open Polar Sea in Connection with the Search After Sir John Franklin and His Companions, 1853, '54, '55 2
Kangerdluksuak 181
Kansas State College 19, 25
Kansas State Agricultural College 179
Kap York 140
Karnah 184
kayak 28, 90, 112, 127
Keatek 78
Keato 36
Kekerdat 145
Kellogg, Frank B. 185
Kennedy Channel 98, 104–105, 107, 141
Kennerley, Mitchell 206–207
Kentucky blue grass 86, 89
kerosene 43
King Christian Island 119, 121, 127, 132
King of Denmark 39
King Solomon 207
King William Island 2, 5

King's Bay 172
Kinley, David, Dr. 18, 65, 163, 166, 179
Kinner Canary 204
Kintrup-Jensen 137, 144–145
Kiotah 47
Kite 37
Kittiwakes 111
Knickerbocker Press 207
Knot 80
Knud Peninsula 99
Koch, Lauge 126
komatik 45, 83, 106–107
Koodlooktoo 37–38; *see also* Kudlooktoo
Kroeber, Alfred 35
Kudlooktoo 63, 184, 185–186; *see also* Koodlooktoo

laboratory 137, 143
Labrador 13, 36, 115, 123, 131, 172–173
Ladies Home Journal 188
Lady Franklin 7
Lady Franklin Bay 4, 103–105
Lady Lindy 205
Lafayette Bay 105, 107
La Jotte, Charles 207
lake 29
Lake Hazen 4, 76, 92, 98, 101–103; Lake Hazen Valley 83
lamp 30–31, 43
The Land of Desolation: Being a Personal Narrative of Adventure in Greenland 3
language 108; Inuit 169
Lapland 87, 208
Larus hyperboreus 84
latitude 106, 120, 123–125
Laurentian gneiss 110
Lawrence County, IL 24
Lawrenceville 24
lead 50, 52–53, 117–118
leather 113
Leaves of Grass 74
Lecante Island 124
lecture 153, 194
Leigh, R. H., Captain 193
Leitz glasses 100
lemming 100, 112
Lena River 4
letter 94, 104, 125, 129, 131, 152, 154, 156–157, 165, 177–178, 185, 193
Lewin, W. Henry 174–175; *Did Peary Reach the Pole?* 174, *The Great North Pole Fraud* 174
liability 158
Liberty 189
Liberty National Bank 206
library 73–74, 136, 170

lichen 111
Lifeboat Cove 105
light 45, 111, 117
limestone 110
Lindbergh, Charles 200, 202, 205, 207; *We* 202
Littleton Island 125
Lobipes lobatus 80
Lockwood, Lt. James B. 4
London 200, 202, 204–205
Long Island 7
longitude 106, 120, 124
Look, Amy 175
Look, Jerome 175
Look, Miriam Norton 175; *I Married an Explorer* 175
Lorenzen, C. Schultz 65–66
Loyd, Sam 189
Ludington Airlines 205
lumber 29
luminaria 111
Luxor 207
Luzula 89
Lycopodium Selago 89

Mabie, Hamilton Wright 74; *My Study Fire* 74
MacDonald, Carlisle 202
Mackenzie River 109
MacMillan, Donald B. 7, 13–14, 16, 20, 22–23, 26, 28–29, 36–37, 39–41, 43–44, 47–54, 55, 58, 60–65, 71–72, 76–77, 82–83, 92, 94–96, 98, 103, 105–106, 119–125, 128, 130–132, 134, 137, 147–148, 151–161, 164–167, 169–178, 185, 188, 210, 211; diary 66; *Eskimo Place Names and Aid to Conversation* 175; *Four Years in the Arctic* 63; *Four Years in the White North* 64, 84, 127, 162–162, 168–169; *Geographical Report of the Crocker Land Expedition, 1913-1917* 160, 162, 167–169; *How Peary Reached the Pole: The Personal Story of His Assistant* 174–175; letter to the museum 97; manuscript 24, 127, 165; origins and education 24; ornithology 84–85; popular work 163; *United States Naval Institute Proceedings* 163
Macy, John A. 74; *The Spirit of American Literature* 74
Magnetic North Pole 120–121
magnetism 22; terrestrial 169
Maher, Adrian W. 208
map 48, 50, 106, 122–124, 153, 155, 158–160, 165
mapping 21
Maravel 173

Index

Marconi Wireless Telegraph Company of Canada 71
Markham, Commander 125
marriage 144
Marshall Bay 108
Martin Johnson: Lion Hunter 192
Marvin, Ross 63, 183–186, 203; drowning 186
Mary Minturn River 76, 105
mass 51
material 22, 155; ethnographic 172
McAlpin Hotel 182
McCosh, James 7; *From the Greeks to Darwin* 7; *The Origin and Evolution of Life* 7
McDonald, Eugene F. 170, 173
McKinley, William B. 180
McLeod Head 122
meal 30, 103
measure 41
meat 28, 30, 38, 41–43, 47–48, 60, 75–76, 79, 81, 83, 93–94, 96, 99–100, 102, 104, 113, 121–122, 124, 137, 144; walrus 45, 78
mechanic 22, 171, 205
medicine 22
Melandrium triflorum 89
Melville, George 4
Melville Bay 29, 36–37, 39, 67, 76, 80–81, 85, 95–97, 109–110, 129, 131, 134, 138, 176
Melville Island 1
Memorial Day 103
Mene 35–36, 77, 80, 117–118
meridian 122
Mertensia martima 88
metal 207
Metcalf, Rowe B. 172
meteor 37
meteorite 38, 110
meteorological observations 170
Michigan 206
U.S.S *Michigan* 26
Middle East 207
Midnight Sun Camp 100
Midshipmen All 192
migrant 109
milk 41, 44, 48, 60, 81, 97
Mineralogical Museum of the University of Copenhagen 39
Minneapolis 179
Minnik 34, 45–46, 77, 181; *see also* Mene
mirage 50, 52, 54, 161
missionary 28–29, 109, 143
mist 51–52, 59, 121–122
Mitchell, Billy 196
mollusks 180
Mombasa 207
Montia lamprospermum 86

Morgan, J. Pierpont 7
morphine 81
Morrill Land-Grant Act 15
Morrissey 202–203
moss 43
Motor Boat 188
motorboat 130, 137
Mt. Arthur 102
Mt. Bayley 101
Mt. Biederbick 102
Mt. Connell 102
Mt. Hovey 100
mountain 86, 155
mumps 44–45, 77
mumukto 33, 40
murder 28, 57, 61–63, 66, 68, 92, 161, 175, 183, 185–186, 189, 209–210
murre 111, 113
museum 16–17, 27–28, 34–35, 71–72, 130–134, 138, 140–141, 149, 153–154, 165, 175–179
Museum of Natural History at Harvard 6
mushroom 90, 111
musk ox 47–49, 60, 74–75, 99–104, 107–108, 112, 119–120, 170
mutiny 50
My Attainment of the Pole 32
My Father 207
My Study Fire 74
Mya truncate 122
Myrtillus Uliginosa 87
The Mystery of the Erik 192
Myter og Saga fra Grönland 180

Nain, Labrador 173
Nansen Sound 53
Nares, Sir George S. 3, 103, 124, 147
Nares Expedition 125
Narrative of the Second Arctic Expedition Made by Charles F. Hall ... and Residence Among the Eskimos During the Years 1864-'69 3
narwhal 96–97, 112–113; meat 135
National Geographic Society of Washington, D.C. 170, 172, 185–186, 205
natives 29, 36, 44, 46, 48, 50–51, 67, 93, 109, 130, 132, 136, 139, 142–144, 161, 169, 173, 184–185, 210
nature 74
Naval Aircraft 170
Naval Hospital at the Brooklyn Naval Yard 26
Naval Institute Proceedings 159
Naval Proving Grounds 191, 198
Naval War College 192–194, 197–198
Navarana 132

navigation chart 172
navy 26–27, 188, 195–196, 199–200, 210
Navy Department 66, 146, 170, 187, 191, 193, 195, 197, 199
Navy Regulations 187
Nederland als Tuinbvouwland: Historisch en Economisch- Geographisch Beschreven 180
negotiation 134
Neptune 137, 141, 147
Nerkre 82
Nerky 36–37, 78, 130
Nevada 206
New Canaan 208, 209
The New Freedom 74
New Haven 208
New Jersey 206
New London 125
New Siberian Islands 4
New York 72, 77, 132, 139–140, 146, 148, 151, 172, 177–178, 182–183, 187, 192–195, 197–201, 205–206, 210
New York Academy of Sciences 177
New York City 34–35, 37, 204, 208–209
New York Daily Mirror 207
New York Herald 3
New York Newspaper Club 195
New York Times 131, 134, 147, 183, 185, 194, 201–203
New York Times Book Review 192
New York Tribune 72–73
Newark 206
Newfoundland 76, 82, 205
Newport 192, 194, 198
news 140
newspaper 23, 94, 182, 187
Newtown 208
Nichols, John Treadwell 178
night 111, 117
Nile Valley 207
Nilsen, Trader 139, 142–143, 145
1900 Polar Expedition 44
Njord 141
Noank 205
Nookapingwa 49
Nordenskjöld, Otto 180; Polarnaturen 180
Nordenskold 83
Normal School 151
Norse 28, 109, 172, 173
North America 123
North American Indian 108
North Cornwall 121–122
North Gorham 24
North Pole 1–2, 5, 63, 170, 172–173, 182–183, 186, 188, 192, 200, 211
North Sea 139

North Star Bay 36, 38, 76, 78, 80–83, 85–86, 95, 107, 109, 117, 126, 129, 131, 133–135, 139–140, 159, 181–182
North Stratford 182
North Sydney 169
Northwest Passage 5, 7
Norway 133
Norwegian Bay 122
notes 58, 105
Nova Scotia 203
Nucarpingwah 49, 60
Nugsuak Peninsula 136
Nukapingwa 98–100
Nuksuah 137
Nunatak 80
Nyboe, Mr. 140

obituary 209
Office of Naval Intelligence 192, 194
Office of the Secretary of the Navy 193
Ohio State University 179
Okpuddyshao 98–99
oligochaeta 179
Olrik's Bay 38
Olsen, Jens 184
Onychirus groenlandicus 80
Ooblooya 36–38, 96, 98–99
Ooloyah 106
Oomanoose 76
Ootah 36, 77, 135
Ootaq 44
The Open Polar Sea: A Narrative of a Voyage of Discovery towards the North Pole, in the Schooner United States 3
Open Road 188
operation 42
Orchesella cincta 80
The Origin and Evolution of Life 7
"The Origin of the Eskimo" 180
ornithology 22, 84, 210
Osborn, Henry Fairfield 7, 15–20, 23, 27, 39, 42, 65–66, 71–73, 101, 123, 132–134, 139, 141, 146, 148–149, 151–160, 162–166, 175, 177–179, 188
Osburn, Raymond C. 179
Osborn, Sherard 127
Osborn Mountains 101
Our Naval Heritage 192, 195
Outlook 188

Paget Point 124
pain 81
Palm Beach 207, 209
Pandora 3, 124
Panikpat 40
Papaver radicatum 86

Paris 189, 199–200, 202, 206
Parker Snow Bay 126, 131, 134, 138–139, 148, 159, 176, 182
Parry, William Edward 1
Parry Islands 16, 72, 78, 83, 119, 124, 128, 210
Paxton, IL 24
Payer Harbor 44–45, 60–61
payment 26, 154
Peabody Bay 105–107
Peary 170, 173
Peary, Robert 5, 7, 13, 16, 20, 24, 27, 33–34, 36–37, 40, 44, 50, 52, 54, 56, 61, 63, 72, 92, 96, 99, 101, 106, 124, 146–147, 169, 173–175, 177, 182–184, 186, 188, 195, 204; vision 210
Peary Arctic Club 23, 169
Peary Channel 76–77; verification of existence 161
Peary: The Man Who Refused to Fail 192
Pedicularis capitata 88
Pedicularis hirsuta 88
Pedicularis lanata 88
Peeahwahto 45–47, 50–54, 74, 77, 92, 161, 185; murder 55–67, 209, 189; *see also* Pewahtoq
pemmican 41, 44–45, 49, 52, 59–60, 95, 135
Pennsylvania 73
permission 23
Petowik glacier 38
Pewahtoq 185; *see also* Peeahwahto
Philadelphia 183, 200
Phipps, Amy 204
photograph 124–125, 177; aerial 173
piblokto 93, 109
pibloktoq 32–33; native 141
pick 53
Pillsbury, W.L. 27
pilot 171, 200, 205–206
Pim Island 124
pinnacle 51
Pittsburgh 204
Piuvaitsuq 66; *see also* Peeahwahto
plague 90–91
plane 171–172, 204, 207; amphibian 173
plankton 111
plant 80, 85–86, 90, 105, 111
Plectrophenax nivalis nivalis 80
Pleuropogon sabinii 89
Plunkett, Rear Adm. Charles P. 192
pneumonia 182
Poa pratensis 86–87, 111
polar bear 47, 74, 94, 96, 103, 112, 120–121, 124, 135
Polar Eskimo 29, 53, 181

Polar North 210
Polar Sea 42–44, 50, 53, 66, 92, 147, 161, 185, 189; exploration 171
Polar Star 5
Polaris 3, 83
Polarnauten 180
pootenook 135
Popular Science Monthly 188
Porsild, Morten P. 136
position 52
Potentillae 88
Powell, Halsey 193–194
Prince Patrick's Land 16
Princeton University 7, 151
Progressive Movement 72, 74
property 22
Proteus 4
Pröven 135–137, 142–143
Providence 172
Provincetown 24, 175
provision 29, 40, 45, 56, 79, 131–133, 141, 146; shortage 133
Provision Point 29; *see also* Reindeer Point
ptarmigan 80, 84, 88, 100, 111, 120
publicity 154, 193–194
purple saxifrage 86
Putnam, George P. 183–185, 192, 198–201, 203–206, 210; report 186; divorce 205
Pyrola rotundifolia 88

Qisuk 34–35

race 108
radar 175
radicalism 191–192
radio 170, 190
rain 108, 110
Randolph, John 206
Rantoul, IL 24
Rasmussen, Knud 29, 36, 62, 64–66, 72, 76–77, 94, 131–132, 134–135, 138–139, 161, 176, 178, 180, 185–186, 202–204; *Greenland by the Polar Sea: The Story of the Thule Expedition from Melville Bay to Cape Morris Jesup* 180; meteorite 36–39; *Myter og Saga fra Grönland* 180
Rasmussen, Kurt 78, 188
ration 135, 141
Rawson, Frederick H. 172
reconnaissance 76, 80
record 41, 92–94, 100, 122, 126, 129–130, 152, 161; Arctic records 157
Redfield, William C. 133
Reeds, Chester A. 23
Refuge Harbor 170

Reindeer Point 29
relief party 134; relief expedition 148–149
Reno 206
Rensselaer Harbor 82–83, 105, 126
reports 61, 64, 72–73, 80, 106, 123, 125, 131–132, 146, 152, 156–157, 163, 177–178, 180, 210; geographic 158–160, 165 167; MacMillan's 162; official 185; scientific 159, 165
reproduction 22
Republican party 73
rescue mission 177
research 20, 54, 71, 77, 80, 98, 129, 188; scientific 168
resources 23, 181; mineral 110
rest 108
results 21, 23, 123, 141, 153, 177; geographical 149, 152, 154–155, 157, 162, 164–165; popular 149, 164, 166; scientific 133, 146, 155, 179
rheumatic fever 196
rheumatism 36
Rice Straight 124
ridge 52
Riff Valley 207
rifle 47, 50, 55, 57, 58, 74, 105
risks 21
Ritenbink 136, 145
Robbins, Chandler 16, 151, 156
Robeson Channel 3
rock 108, 111
rock salt 20
Rodebay 145
Rodgers, Adm. Thomas S. 191
Roger Point 125
S.S. *Roosevelt* 96, 133
Roosevelt, Franklin D. 23
Roosevelt, Theodore 23, 178, 198
Rosbach, Sechmann 78–79, 81, 83, 117–118
Rosen, Pastor 136
Ross, Sir John 1, 36, 109
Ross, James Clark 1
Rossen, Pastor 144
route 40, 82, 98, 136, 160
Roy Chapman Andrews: Dragon Hunter 192
Royal Danish Company 136
Royal Geographical Society 174
Royal Greenland Trading Company 28–29
Royal Navy 36
Rudolf Island 5
Ruggles River 103
ruse 35
Russia 181
Rye, N.Y. 201, 206

Sabbath observance 32
Sachem 172
St. James Church 209
St. John's Newfoundland 131–132, 134, 139–141, 182
St. Michael 4
St. Petersburg 4
salary 21–22, 26, 156, 179, 197, 199
salinity 109
Salix arctica 87
Salix herbacea 87
salmon 94, 103
Salvelinus stagnalis 94
San Francisco 199
Sarkok 136
Saturday Evening Post 187, 188
Saunders Island 81–82, 117, 124
Savigsuit 38; see also Savikseevik
Savikseevik 38; see also Savigsuit
Saxifraga oppositifolia 86, 88
Schei Island 48, 60
Schley, Cmdr. Winfield Scott 5
schooner 172
Scientific American 188
Scott, A.W. "Lucky" 71–72, 147
scurvy 4, 28, 88, 103
Sea Power 187
sea-swallow 85
seal 47, 60, 78, 80, 90, 93, 94, 96, 97, 101, 103, 111, 119–120, 123–124, 137, 142, 181
seaplane 170
seaquake 188
Secretary of the Mission of the Cape York District 65
Secretary of the Navy 146
sedge 87, 111
seed 82
seismograph 93
seismology 22
self-defense 63, 66
Semple, Ellen Churchill 180–181
servant 137, 142
settlement 28–29, 133, 141
sex 144
sextant 122
Shackleton 188
shale 110
shamanism 34
Shanghai 198
shark 112, 137
shelter 44, 56, 135; snow shelter 118
Sherwood, George H. 65, 129, 139–141, 147–149, 158, 160, 178
Silene acaulis 89
ship 27–29, 37, 80–82, 94, 97, 131, 133–134, 138, 140, 148; relief 71, 95, 98, 119, 123,

129, 131–133, 135, 139–141, 169, 172, 175, 177, 188–189; multi-engine 200; passenger 182; whaling 125
Shipmates 195
shipwreck 168
shoal 173
shore 172
Shore Leave 195
Sims, Rear Adm. William S. 192
Sipsoo 30, 41, 43, 77, 143
skeleton 35
Skinner, Constance Lindsay 204
skins 32, 42–43, 47, 74, 76, 89, 94–95, 99–100, 104, 106–107, 113, 119–120, 137, 142, 144–145
Skottsberg, Carl 180; *Till Robinson—ön och Varldens Ande* 180
Skraelingodden 48
skull 106–107
sledge 41–42, 44–45, 47–50, 54, 56, 58, 61, 76, 78, 82–83, 94–96, 100–102, 104–105, 107, 112–113, 115–117, 119, 122, 127, 132, 135–138, 141, 144–145, 176, 178, 185, 188; journey 131, 133, 159, 196
sleeping bag 48–49, 135; trip 161
Small, Jonathan C. (Jot) 14, 20, 22–23, 26, 31, 33, 41, 82, 93–95, 99, 105–106, 120, 130, 132, 137, 139
Smith, Dr. Hugh M. 133
Smith Sound 2–3, 28, 40, 43–45, 84–85, 95, 108, 110, 119, 124–125, 127; Smith Sound Inuit 29, 34, 90, 91, 135
snow 30, 38, 43, 45, 47–48, 53, 55, 57–58, 73, 78, 80, 90, 93–95, 100, 102, 105–106, 108, 110–112, 117, 120, 122, 124, 135, 171, 181, 186
soil 109
Somateria mollissima borealis 84
Some Famous Sea Fights 192
song 76
Sonntag Bay 88
Sound Beach 201
Special Committee on Publication of Crocker Land Reports 158, 162–164, 166
specie 80, 86–88, 90, 111–112, 180; skin 116; supplies 116
specimen 17–18, 21, 39, 47, 78, 84, 94, 135, 143, 147, 173, 180, 200
The Sphere 188
spirit 34, 40
The Spirit of American Literature 74
Spitzbergen 172, 199
spring 43, 73, 92, 95, 101, 119, 122, 137, 170–171, 210
staff 26
Stapler, John 195

starvation 4, 79, 81, 90–91, 124, 135, 170; near-starvation 83
State of New York 7
Statice maritime 88
station 81, 137, 140; trading station 82, 94, 109, 142, 145
steamer 132, 139–140, 172; Danish 134
Steensby, H.P. 180; *An Anthropological Study of the Origin of the Eskimo Culture* 180; *Danmarks Natur* 180
Stefansson Arctic Expedition 16, 125
Steffanson 188
Sterna paradisaea 85
stevedore 27
Stolz Peninsula 119
Storaen Island 119
storm 54, 56, 58, 61, 78, 99, 111, 117–118, 130, 161; snowstorm 171
stove 43, 48, 55
stratification 126
stream 46, 110
Stultz, Wilmer 205
substation 171
sugar 44, 81, 137, 144
Sulwuddy 94
summer 76, 79, 81–83, 89–90, 92–93, 103, 108–110, 112, 113, 129, 140, 144, 169, 173, 181
summit 21, 46, 77, 119, 121–122, 144
Sun Bay 103
superpositions 126
superstition 143
Supervisory Committee for the Crocker Land Expedition 149, 151
supplies 47, 71–72, 79, 81, 97, 104–107, 130, 139–140, 169
surgery 19, 22, 26
surveys 170; scientific 173
survival 118
Sutherland Island 84
Svartenhuk 144
Sverdrup, Otto 5, 32, 45, 48, 54, 61, 120, 127; expedition 119
Sverdrup Islands 5, 83
Sverdrup Pass 99
Swarthmore 24
Sweden 181
Swift Balch, Edwin 162
Sydney, Cape Breton 131
Sydney, Nova Scotia 134, 140–141, 146, 203

Table Island 122
Talbot Inlet 124
Tanquary, Maurice C. 19–20, 22–23, 31–32, 41, 43–44, 76, 78, 80–81, 83, 92, 95, 97–98, 105, 130–134, 139, 141, 146, 148, 176–180, 210; origins and education 24

254 Index

Tanquary Fiord 101
Taraxacum Arctogenum 89
Tassiussak 139
Tauchingwa 46, 77
tea 41, 43–44, 55, 59, 81, 87, 95, 97, 102, 107, 120, 135
telegram 132
telegraphy 22, 72
temperature 44–45, 48, 53, 85, 93, 95, 110–111, 124, 135, 159
A Tenderfoot with Peary 13
tent 29, 105, 112, 117, 122, 134–135, 181, 186
Terror 1
Tetracanthella wahlgreni 80
U.S.S. *Texas* 183, 189, 192
Texas Agricultural Station 179
Texas State Entomologist 179
thermograph records 160
Thor 76
Thorshavn 133, 141
Thule 29, 36, 63, 78, 80, 95, 115, 117, 129, 132, 138–139, 181; station 203
tide 82, 110, 126, 129–130, 188
Till Robinson—ön och Varldens Ande 180
tobacco 44, 137–138, 144
toe 135, 139
Tookey 37
Tooktooliksuah 135–136
topography 110
Torngasuasq 40
trader 28, 109, 137, 142, 144
trading post 29, 138
traditions 38
trail 43, 53, 55, 60, 103–104, 112, 120, 122; North 94
trance 33–34
translation 175
transmission 23
travel 107, 141, 181
trees 87, 111
Trepassey Bay 205
tribes 43–44, 91, 142
Tringa Canutus 80, 83, 85
trips 43, 81, 105, 107, 124, 139, 141, 145, 173; hunting trip 117
Trisetum spicatum 88
trustees 16, 18–19, 27, 133, 149, 160; Geographical Society 162; museum 163, 166
tupik 82, 112, 181
20 HRS. 40 MIN.: Our Flight in the Friendship 205
typhoid fever 36

Ulvingen 120
Umanak 29, 36, 62, 67, 78, 82, 94–95, 126, 144, 178–179; Umanak Fiord 135; *see also* Umanaq
Umanaq 126
Uncle Sam's Sailors 192
U.S. Attorney 208
U.S. Coast and Geodetic Survey 126
U.S. District Court 208
U.S. Hydrographic Office 23, 175
U.S. Minister to Denmark 123, 139
U.S. Naval Academy 14, 25, 206; midshipman 189
United States Naval Institute Proceedings 188
U.S. Navy 23, 189, 193; *see also* navy
U.S. Senate 180, 195
U.S. State Department 65, 185
U.S. Supreme Court 178
U.S. Weather Bureau 78
University Club 27, 72
University of California 201
University of Illinois 7, 14–15, 17–19, 21, 24, 27, 40–41, 65, 75, 80, 100–101, 133, 161, 166, 168, 179–180
University of Michigan 179
University of Minnesota 179
Upernavik 29, 36, 67, 96–97, 131, 135–136, 141; South Upernavik 136–137, 144
Uria lomvia lomvia 96
U.S.S. *Utah* 188–190

Vaccinium Vitis-Idoea 87
Valhalla 39
valley 102, 110
Veery River 102
Vega 75, 83
vegetation 80, 85–87, 89–90, 105
venereal disease 178
Vergil 183, 209
vessel 133, 140–141, 189; chartering 158; relief vessel 168
Vickery, E.A. 26
Victory 1
Victrola 32, 42, 93
Viking 141
Vikings 173
village 112–113, 115, 137, 181
Vincennes University 24
Vinterberg, Governor 136–137
violation 159
The Voyage of the Jeannette: The Ship and Ice Journals of George W. DeLong 4

W. & S. Job & Co. 140–141
Wales 205
Wallace, William 34–35
walrus 38, 83, 93–94, 112, 116, 202; herd 117; liver 95; tusk 113

Wanamaker 200
war 108, 169, 187, 191; zone 189
War Council 191
War Department 175
Ward, Henry B. 27
Washington D.C. 133, 146, 170, 172, 183, 186, 193–194, 197–199, 202–203
water 50–51, 107, 126, 135; open water 53, 82, 108, 110, 116, 124, 136, 144–145
We 202
wealth 207, 209
weather 44, 48, 55, 59–60, 90, 94, 105–106, 116, 123, 133, 135–136, 138, 159, 171, 181, 188, 200
Weather Bureau of the U.S. Department of Agriculture 23
Welch, Paul S. 179
Western Reserve Academy 15
whale 112, 113, 127
Whalen, Grover 200
whaling 29, 109, 125
whip 46, 57, 59, 116, 118
Whitman, Walter 74; *Leaves of Grass* 74
Wiechert seismograph 23
wife 62–63, 66, 81, 112, 132, 142, 144, 197, 200, 209
Wilbur, Curtis D. 194–195
wildlife 189
Williams, Adm. C.S. 192–193
willow 111, 112
wind 45, 53, 55, 57, 60, 93, 95, 110, 111, 135
wine 42

winter 31, 73, 82, 93, 112–113, 129, 131–132, 134, 138–139, 169, 171, 176
Wire 53
Wiscasset 169, 173
Wissler, Clark 126–127
wolf 47, 60, 100, 112, 170
Wolstenholme Sound 38, 78, 80, 86, 109–110, 117, 126, 129
Woman's Home Companion 188
women 172
Won for the Fleet: A Story of Annapolis 192
Woodrow, Wilson 74, 133, 178; *The New Freedom* 74
Woodsia glabella 90
Woodsia silvensis 90
Worcester 24, 180
Worcester Telegram 180
World War II 175
World's Work 188
Wrangel Island 4
Wright Bay 107

yacht 173
Yale University 13–14, 18, 23, 27, 151
Youth's Companion 188
Ypsilanti 151

Z R Wins 192
Zenith Corporation 170
Zenith Radio Company 173
zoology 22, 25, 178

www.ingramcontent.com/pod-product-compliance
Ingram Content Group UK Ltd.
Pitfield, Milton Keynes, MK11 3LW, UK
UKHW041934140426
5217IPUK00014B/477